Democracy in the Dark

DEMOCRACY IN THE DARK

The Seduction of Government Secrecy

Frederick A.O. Schwarz Jr.

THE NEW PRESS

NEW YORK
LONDON

Requests for permission to reproduce selections from this book should be mailed to:
Permissions Department, The New Press, 120 Wall Street, 31st floor, New York, NY 10005.

Published in the United States by The New Press, New York, 2015
Distributed by Perseus Distribution

LIBRARY OF CONGRESS CATALOGING-IN-PUBLICATION DATA

Schwarz, Frederick A. O. (Frederick August Otto), 1935– author.
  Democracy in the dark : the seduction of government secrecy / Frederick
A.O. Schwarz Jr.
    pages cm
  Includes bibliographical references and index.
  ISBN 978-1-62097-051-5 (hardback) — ISBN 978-1-62097-052-2 (e-book)
1. Freedom of information—United States. 2. Official secrets—United States.
3. Intelligence service—Law and legislation—United States. I. Title.
  KF4774.S39 2015
  342.73'0662—dc23
                                                          2014035650

The New Press publishes books that promote and enrich
public discussion and understanding of the issues vital to our democracy and to a
more equitable world. These books are made possible by the enthusiasm of our readers;
the support of a committed group of donors, large and small; the collaboration of our
many partners in the independent media and the not-for-profit sector; booksellers,
who often hand-sell New Press books; librarians; and above all by our authors.

www.thenewpress.com

Composition by Westchester Book Composition
This book was set in Fairfield

Printed in the United States of America

2 4 6 8 10 9 7 5 3 1

To our grandchildren: Ronan, Orla, Kate, Lia,
Henry, Aiden, and Phillips

Contents

Democracy in the Dark

Introduction

"And ye shall know the truth and the truth shall make you free." These words, from the Gospel according to Saint John, are carved in large letters on the left-hand marble wall of the huge entrance lobby to the CIA's headquarters in Langley, Virginia.

I walked through that lobby in early 1975 on my way to a meeting with CIA Director William Colby. A young litigator, without previous ties to any senator or to the intelligence community, I had just been appointed chief counsel of the United States Senate's Select Committee created to undertake the first investigation of America's intelligence agencies—commonly known as the Church Committee after its chair, Sen. Frank Church of Idaho.

I met Colby at a formal lunch in his conference room. A careful man who revealed little, Colby was checking on me and a colleague to see if we could be trusted to handle highly secret information.

My first visit to the FBI's fortress-like headquarters had no such subtlety. No genial probing. No fancy meal. Instead, at the start, I was shown photos of severed Black heads on an American city street. The implication was clear: this was done by vicious killers; we protect America against such enemies; stay away from the secrets about how we operate.

As it turned out, the CIA, the FBI, and the rest of the Ford administration, eventually cooperated with the Church Committee as it conducted the most extensive investigation of a government's secret activities ever, in this country or elsewhere. This eighteen-month investigation began my long-term interest in government secrecy.

From the Church Committee, I learned three big lessons about government secrets. First, too much is kept secret not to *protect America* but to keep embarrassing or illegal conduct *from Americans.* Examples abound, including FBI efforts to drive Martin Luther King Jr. to commit suicide; the CIA enlisting Mafia leaders in its efforts to kill Cuba's Fidel Castro; and a thirty-year NSA program to get copies of telegrams leaving the United States. The Church Committee also discovered that every president from Franklin Roosevelt to Richard Nixon had secretly abused their powers.

The second lesson was that some government secrets are legitimate and worthy of protection. Indeed, one of the reasons the Church Committee succeeded, and the simultaneous House committee investigating intelligence agencies failed, is that we understood and respected the government's legitimate needs for secrecy for some information, while the House committee did not.

The third lesson was that the public must be informed when things go wrong—when agencies act illegally, improperly, or foolishly, and when presidents, other executives, or Congress fail in their responsibilities. Throughout the investigation, I pushed hard for disclosure, believing, as the Church Committee concluded, that "the story is sad, but this country has the strength to hear the story and to learn from it."[1]

With the committee, I saw my main job as exposing illegal and embarrassing *secrets* in order to build momentum for reform. Therefore, I did not then think deeply about the culture of *secrecy.* In recent years, there have been near-constant revelations about government secrets and secret programs. Now, with knowledge of a wide range of secrets and secret programs over the course of generations, including many that followed in the wake of 9/11, I use that knowledge to analyze and understand government secrecy and the ways in which its overuse undermines our experiment in democracy.

The subject of government secrecy is often viewed too narrowly. We focus on the classification system when we should also look at the underlying secrecy culture in which it flourishes. The American government operates within a secrecy culture that asks not how much information can be shared with citizens but instead decides to withhold from citizens information needed to exercise their role in our democracy. Far too much information is stamped secret, and then kept secret for much too long.

Crown-jewel secrets must remain secure. But secrecy has too often been used to cover over costume jewelry. Where lies the boundary between legitimate and illegitimate government secrets? And when there is disagreement, who decides where the boundary should be drawn? Too often the country has been having the wrong argument. Instead of focusing only on the dangers of disclosure, the American public and government should give greater consideration to the dangers of secrecy.

Why does the secrecy system have such pervasive influence? And why is it so hard to limit? Sometimes, the motive is to conceal illegality or avoid embarrassment. But secrecy stamps are also often applied, and maintained, for more banal reasons. Human nature and bureaucratic incentives favor secrecy over openness. Secrecy is seductive. In addition, secrecy that causes harm is sometimes secrecy that was appropriate at the outset. To give just one example: the warnings sent to the White House in the summer of 2001 about "spectacular" al-Qaeda attacks were, at the outset, appropriately classified top secret. But as they accumulated into sustained and serious warnings, the White House should have made the gist of them public and distributed them to all government officials responsible for protecting America against terror attacks. Had this been done, the 9/11 attacks likely would have been prevented. But the culture and seduction of secrecy is such that initial decisions on secrecy are rarely rethought.

It is expensive to maintain increasingly higher mountains of classified documents. The proliferation of secret documents also makes it harder to protect legitimate secrets. But the profligate use of secrecy stamps is a manifestation of a deeper problem tied to secrecy's many psychological attractions and the insulation and narrowness secrecy creates. The United States cannot have a flourishing democracy unless We the People are fully and fairly informed about our government. Yet for decades Americans have been living in a Secrecy Era in which the government limits public information about itself while simultaneously collecting more information about its citizens.

Secrecy and democracy have always been in tension. To appreciate openness, or government transparency—secrecy's rival—America must recall the aspirations of its democracy. In the Declaration of Independence, Jefferson said governments "deriv[e] their just powers from the consent of the governed." In the Federalist Papers, Madison said that, through voting, the people are the "primary control on the government."[2] For American democracy to attain its aspirations, both our consent and our vote must be informed. But when excessive secrecy conceals acts of our government and obscures the character of our leaders, our consent and our vote become little more than window dressing. In his Gettysburg Address, eighty-seven years after the Declaration, Lincoln called for a "new birth of freedom" so that "government of the people, by the people and for the people shall not perish from this earth." But if government is to be by the people, necessary information cannot be hidden from the people. If it is, we become a democracy in the dark.

It might seem strange to link Dick Cheney's name with Jefferson's, or Madison's, or Lincoln's. But in 1987, in a hitherto unnoticed piece of policy advice buried in part of his lengthy dissent from Congress's *Iran-Contra Report,* then-Congressman Cheney extolled transparency and warned against excessive secrecy. While Cheney claimed presidents had "monarchical" powers to disregard congressional legislation, he also argued that the White House, if it is to have lasting success in dealing with hard foreign policy or national security issues, must engage in "democratic persuasion." As Cheney put it, "unless the public is exposed to and persuaded by a clear, sustained and principled debate on the merits" democratic persuasion cannot succeed. To succeed, a wise White House should not, in Cheney's 1987 view, have an "excessive concern for secrecy."[3]

Later, as vice president, Cheney cast aside democratic persuasion and ignored his own caution against excessive concern for secrecy. Analyzing why Cheney abandoned his earlier views helps explain the seductive appeal of secrecy. But Cheney is hardly alone in changing his tune on secrecy. Other examples, from Woodrow Wilson to Harry Truman to Barack Obama, are chronicled throughout this book.

Secrecy is a hot topic today. It will continue to be. Former CIA employee and NSA contractor Edward Snowden's 2013 revelations about NSA operations reveal a preoccupation with secrecy in the highest levels of government and dramatize how a leak can force debate about what the government seeks to hide. Among the secrets Snowden exposed are that NSA was covertly collecting "metadata"—location data, duration, unique identifiers, and phone numbers for phone calls across America. The metadata program signaled a fundamental change in the relationship between the American government and the American people. Of course, the program raised questions about legality, about privacy, and about the balance between safety and secrecy in an increasingly connected world. But the NSA revelations raise a more fundamental point about government secrecy. Before George W. Bush veered in a new direction, and Obama continued to do so, the White House should have fostered an open democratic debate about the wisdom of the broad surveillance program.

Democracy is about more than holding elections, as we have learned throughout modern history, most recently from Egypt and Libya. America is lucky to have pillars that buttress real democracy, including free speech and a vibrant civil society. But unless our leaders are more open with the people and foster clear and public debates about major government policies—particularly those that fundamentally alter the relationship between government and citizen or drift away from our values and laws—America will continue blindly to depart from its founding ideals.

After putting secrecy in historical perspective, briefly examining secrecy and openness from the Garden of Eden through the British monarchy, and, at much greater length, in America from the Founding to today, this book elaborates on America's Secrecy Era, detailing the seductive power of our secrecy culture, the dangers it poses to democracy, and the ways in which secrets are exposed, exploring the question of whether checks on secrecy are working. Openness is the antidote to secrecy. So this book devotes substantial attention to newspapers, muckraking journalism, and organizations that push for greater government transparency.

American democracy must confront its secrecy problem. The toughest problem faced by secrecy proponents and critics is where to draw the line. This book is meant to contribute to debate on that question. The book ends with some thoughts on possible guidelines with which we can distinguish between legitimate and illegitimate secrets and offers some encouraging signs that a cure to our secrecy problem is possible.

PART ONE

History

From Genesis forward, the powerful have been tempted to limit access to information. Beyond the timeless link between secrecy and power, and beyond the psychological seduction of secrecy, history teaches that there are many other factors that either foster or undermine secrecy.

Changes in modes of communication have undermined secrecy through millennia. The invention in the West of the movable-type printing press led to an information explosion that empowered many to challenge powerful leaders' information monopolies. But the printing press is just one example. A common language, reading, writing, expanding literacy, translating information into popular (or vernacular) languages, photography, radio, television, computers, cell phones, camera phones, the Internet, the digital revolution, and now cloud storage have given ordinary people new ways to acquire, store, and spread previously secret information.

But new communication techniques also often stimulate the powerful to struggle to maintain secrecy. Sophisticated communication techniques have been used by regimes to intimidate their subjects (and thus help enshrine the regime's secrets)—a truth foretold in George Orwell's *Nineteen Eighty-Four*, which envisioned Big Brother's two-way telescreens connected from every room to government watchers, and reinforced in the movie *The Lives of Others*, detailing the pervasive surveillance used by East Germany's Stasi.

Changes in political systems also influence secrecy. Rome's shift from republic to empire led to *less* openness. The shift from British monarchy to democracy in America led to *more* openness. Within democracies, increases in executive power tend to increase secrecy. More bureaucracy often also leads to more secrecy. And certainly, as America's recent history proves, democracy itself is not protection against growing government secrecy.

Perhaps most consistently, wars and crises stoke fear, and fear spawns and shores up secrecy.

The history of secrecy and openness is filled with change—in both directions. Often long periods of minimal change have been followed by periods of relatively rapid change, usually connected to changes in the culture of the time and place. Along the way, history and journalism—the "first rough draft of history"—nibble away at secrecy. For historians and reporters, inquiry is the means, and truth the goal. Only with truth can history be useful.[1] To get at the truth, secrecy is always the first barrier to breach.

1

From the Garden of Eden to America's Founding

In the beginning . . . there was secrecy.

God expelled Adam and Eve from the Garden of Eden because, seeking to become "wise," they ate the forbidden fruit to learn the secret knowledge of good and evil. Then, after the Flood, people sought heaven's secrets by building the Tower of Babel. Using their "one language," the people united to build a tall tower "unto heaven." God said nothing "will be restrained from them" and then "confound[ed] their language, that they may not understand one another's speech." People were scattered across the Earth. Building stopped. Heaven's secrets remained untouched, unheard, and unseen.[1]

These two stories teach a timeless lesson about secrecy and the impulse, among the powerful, to limit the people's access to information

At the dawn of history, leaders controlled the spigots from which it was thought information flowed from the gods to the people. Though oceans apart and unknown to each other, Egyptian pharaohs and Mayan kings both exercised monopoly power over information. Egyptian pharaohs were "the sole intermediar[ies] who could serve the gods and hence maintain the flows of energy" into the world; and Mayan kings were the conduits "through which supernatural forces were channeled into the human realm."[2]

Early Egyptian dynasties provide another telling example of the timeless tendency of the powerful to control communications and thus limit access to information. Writing itself was "a centrally-controlled facility in a state which was focused on its chief representative, the king." This allowed "manipulation of scarcity" of the skill of writing, which enhanced both secrecy and kingly power.[3] Nonetheless, in later eras writing proliferated, and Egypt (and Babylon) pioneered preserving information. Herodotus praised the Egyptians for "their practice of keeping records of the past."[4]

Writing about the Greek defeat of Persia in the early fifth century BCE, Herodotus, generally recognized as the world's first historian, used the term *historia* (research or inquiry) to describe recounting facts about the past—what we call history.[5] Ancient Athenians believed their openness helped them win their epic battles with Persia. According to Herodotus, whose landmark history focuses on those battles, Athens became the great proponent of Greek freedom in opposition to Eastern despotism. Herodotus contrasted Athenian openness with the opaque Persian court: "Instead of the claustrophobic, sycophantic, sometimes fearful atmosphere of a despotic court, where such discussion as there is consists of advice, which can be given privately as well as in conclave, we have the overt, vigorous, fiercely factional and disputatious public life of the Greek city states, conducted characteristically in public debate and expressed through speeches designed to sway opinion."[6] According to Herodotus, when the Athenians were "ruled by tyrants," they were "no better in war than any of the peoples living around them," but once they were rid of tyrants and Athenians had "an equal voice in government," they became "by far the best of all."[7]

Archeological work on stone inscriptions in Athens has shown that Athens' transition to democracy was accompanied by a substantial leap in transparency. After the transition, inscriptions revealed government actions to the public—not only laws and decisions but also "accounts," "relations with foreign states," and "details of military affairs." More "inscriptions have been recovered in Athens than in all the other cities of Greece combined, and this is no accident; it derives from the character of Athenian democracy."[8] Moreover, during its democracy period, Athens subjected public officials to scrutiny of a kind that has seldom, if ever, been repeated. All were questioned in public before entering office and after their term. Indeed, the ten most important officials were publicly questioned ten times a year to ensure that they were doing their job properly. Transparency fostered accountability, for no such scrutiny would have been possible without transparency.

Athens' openness was tied to its being a direct participatory democracy—with America's closest analogue being New England town meetings. Assemblies of all citizens (that is, all free males) made key decisions. The Council of 500, a representative cross-section of citizens chosen by lot with one-year term limits, made routine decisions and set the agenda for the larger assemblies, placing important proposals on whitened boards for all citizens to read in Athens' central town square. Enacted laws were then inscribed on stele—literally written in stone in public places.[9]

Decades after its transition to democracy, Athens fought Sparta in the Peloponnesian War. In his famous funeral oration, Pericles asked, "What [was] the form of government under which our greatness grew?" His answer: "Our constitution . . . favors the many instead of the few; this is why it is called a democracy." And according to Thucydides, Pericles argued that openness and information were keys to the success of Athenian democracy. Thus, "ordinary citizens, though occupied with the pursuits of industry, are still fair judges of public matters . . . [I]nstead of looking on discussion as a stumbling-block in the way of action, we think it an indispensable preliminary to any wise action at all."[10]

Modern scholars share the view that openness and shared information were vital to Athens' success. For example, Josiah Ober's recent book on Athenian democracy says the success of classical Athens—as compared to all other Greek city-states—derived from its "institutional innovation and open access," leading to a superior use of "'knowledge in society.'" The Athenians created "a kind of machine for aggregating useful knowledge" that required the people to "grasp the value" of "transparency and accountability."[11]

Of course, Athens was a direct democracy with a small population. Aristotle contended citizens could not "distribute" offices "according to merit" or manage government, as they do in a direct democracy, unless they personally "know each other's characters."[12] But that opinion was expressed before the era of newspapers and other means of mass communication. At America's founding, James Madison argued that a republic would actually work better in a *large* community, although he also opined that direct (or "pure") democracies had "ever been spectacles of turbulence and contention . . . short in their lives as they have been violent in their deaths."[13]

Rome's history provides a good example of how change in a political system—in Rome's case from republic to empire—can affect secrecy. Augustus was just over thirty when, in the latter years of the first century BCE, following the assassination of his great uncle Julius Caesar, he succeeded in defeating his rivals and started the long line of Roman emperors. When Augustus became emperor, he kept much of the form of the Roman republic.[14] There still was a Senate, and there still were consuls. In reality, however, power shifted to one person, the emperor. Among the many consequences of this shift to imperial power was less openness and more secrecy. It is telling that there are more records of the first thirty years of Augustus's life, up through and including his early reign, than there are about his much longer later life as emperor. This is due not only to the lost texts but also to a "lack of governmental transparency" after the shift to the imperial system.[15]

Writing some two thousand years ago, shortly after the beginning of the imperial system, Roman historians made the same point. At the beginning of his *Histories*, Tacitus—whom Thomas Jefferson called "the world's greatest writer"—described a time when "the interests of peace demanded the concentration of power in the hands of one man [and the] great line of classical historians came to an end. Truth, too, suffered [from] an understandable ignorance of policy."[16] Cassius Dio, writing a *Roman History* in Greek around the turn of the third century CE, similarly complained that under the imperial system "most events began to be kept secret and were denied to common knowledge. . . . [M]uch that never materializes becomes common talk, while much that has undoubtedly come to pass remains unknown, and in pretty well every instance the report which is spread abroad does not correspond to what actually happened."[17]

Rome's transition to an imperial system was accompanied by a change in the location of power, as well as by an increase in bureaucracy. Both enhanced secrecy. During the Roman republic, decisions had been vociferously debated in the open Roman Forum. But in the empire decision-making moved up the hill to the Palatine, where Augustus lived and worked. The historian was "obstruct[ed]" by a "retreat of political life and the decision-making process from open places (the Senate and Forum) into privacy."[18] Moreover, under the empire, "the secrets of power, the *arcana imperii*, were to be untrammeled by rules."[19] Relying heavily on former slaves (or freedmen), Augustus also vastly increased the bureaucracy (or *familia Caesaris*) responsible for much of the empire's ongoing business. This had many advantages for emperors, chief among them that the bureaucrats did not report to anybody but the emperor. So, "what they did was easily kept secret."[20]

Jumping far ahead in time, heresy challenged the Church's power during the Middle Ages. Although the doctrinal issues are interesting, one aspect of heresy is especially relevant to secrecy—Bible translations. Using Bibles translated into vernacular (or local) languages, which opened up their information to a much wider audience, eventually became a mark of heresy. Particularly when coupled with preaching by laymen, this led to burning the books, and sometimes the bodies, of heretics who used vernacular Bibles to challenge the Church's information monopoly.[21]

The printing press was an even greater challenge to the secrets and power of kings and popes. Gutenberg's invention of the movable-type printing press in the mid-fifteenth century made the spread of information both much cheaper and much faster. Printing undermined information monopolies, shook the powerful, and threatened secrecy. Initially, however, the revolutionary implications of the printing press were overlooked. Moreover, book connoisseurs who liked their libraries filled with beautiful hand-lettered books dismissed print—saying that had even one printed book been in their library, "it would have been ashamed in such company."[22] But shame faded away, and the numbers of printed books eventually exploded. Printers also profited from printing posters, pamphlets, broadsides, and newspapers, all of which spread information and advocacy much more widely, quickly, and cheaply.

As its revolutionary potential began to appear, some saw the printing press as a "villainous Engine," and they longingly looked back to a "happy time when all Learning was in Manuscript, and some little Officer . . . did keep the Keys of the Library."[23] Across Europe, the powerful counterattacked, seeking to maintain their control over information.[24] In the sixteenth century, King Henry VIII of England prevented printers from printing *anything* unless licensed by the government. The king also banned certain books and halted importation of foreign books published in English. The French monarchy followed suit with printer licensing requirements and book banning, including restrictions on the importation of books from Protestant countries. The Church also took action. In the late fifteenth century, for example, an archbishop pressured the town council of Frankfurt, Germany, to establish a censorship office whose first edict suppressed vernacular Bible translations. Shortly thereafter, popes began to subject books to supervision and issued the *Index librorum prohibitorum* (Index of Prohibited Books), which was revised and in effect for several centuries.[25]

But as information spread and printing opened more eyes to information, including tales of lands beyond Europe, monarchs concluded that censorship was insufficient to preserve their power and resorted to proclaiming their absolute right to absolute control. The era was epitomized by France's King Louis XIV, who announced *"L'état, c'est moi,"* and by the English Stuart kings who asserted their right, or "prerogative," to ignore laws of Parliament.

Linked to the absolutist position of both the French and British monarchs, and to their efforts to control the distribution of printed information, was an extreme view of secrecy. In pre-revolutionary France, the "absolute authority of the King was bolstered by a practice of strict secrecy in public affairs." The "law of silence" prohibited public discussion of matters of state.[26] Supportive French theorists warned that with publicity, the king's plans "would be about as effective as an exploded mine."[27] Similarly, Cardinal Richelieu, Louis XIII's powerful chief minister, said that secrecy is "essential" for success of the state: "nothing can be more."[28] Louis XIV sought still more secrecy, advising his son in his two-volume "Instructions" that the key to a successful monarchy was not only being "informed of everything" but also "maintaining greater secrecy in my affairs than any of my predecessors."[29] Louis XIV also advised the ministers of his government that "the first thing I desire from you is secrecy."[30]

In Great Britain, King James I ordered the Speaker of the House of Commons "to acquaint that house with our pleasure that none therein shall presume to meddle with anything concerning our government or mysteries of State."[31] Matters of state "are not themes or subjects fit for vulgar persons or common meetings."[32] Later, the Glorious Revolution of 1688 rid Great Britain of the most extreme monarchical powers, and kings could no longer claim a prerogative right to ignore laws of Parliament.[33] However, a presumption of secrecy about government remained a basic British belief. Parliament was closed to the public, which consisted largely of "vulgar persons" below the level of gentlemen. Only the aristocracy or the "better classes" generally could be trusted with important information, or "mysteries of state."

A telling example of the view that information about affairs of state should be confined to the better classes was the British attorney general's reaction to a pamphlet by Thomas Cooper, a scientist and lawyer who later emigrated to America. In 1792, Cooper and James Watt Jr. (son of the engineer who perfected the steam engine) visited France and proclaimed their support for the French Revolution. Their activities enraged Edmund Burke, who denounced them in a secret session of Parliament. Cooper struck back with a pamphlet. When Cooper considered printing a second, cheaper and more widely distributed, edition, the British attorney general Sir John Scott stepped in. It was permissible to reveal secret Parliamentary debates in an expen-' sive tome "so as to confine it probably to that class of readers who may consider it coolly." But, the attorney general warned, as "soon as it is published cheaply for dissemination among the populace, it will be my duty to prosecute."[34]

After America revolted against Great Britain and became an independent nation, there erupted a fierce fight about the proper role of "the People" in public affairs. As with the British attorney general's message to Cooper, part of this debate played out in skirmishes about secrecy.

2

More Openness to More Secrecy: America from the Founding to the Secrecy Era

From America's beginning there was, of course, some secrecy, particularly in times of war. But for a long time America favored openness. During the Cold War and after 9/11, however, the balance between government openness and government secrecy tilted sharply toward secrecy.

Proponents of openness and proponents of secrecy can both find support in America's Founding Era, running roughly from the Declaration of Independence to the ratification of the Constitution, and on through the presidencies of George Washington and John Adams. During this period, actions consistent with openness were sometimes matched by actions moving in the opposite direction—the new nation was feeling its way. Then, accelerating with Thomas Jefferson's election as president in 1800, America's culture changed. "We the People," who had ordained and established the Constitution, were no longer seen as synonymous with the rich, the wellborn, and the educated upper classes, but rather included all Americans—that is, all who were white and male. As part of this move toward a more participatory democracy, the new nation fostered the wider and faster spread of information. These changes led to more openness, less secrecy, and a stronger democracy.

Throughout history, governments traditionally obtained information about their subjects but kept most information about themselves secret. In the new United States, however, the government strove to increase citizens' access to information about government, as well as citizens' ability to communicate among themselves. This was demonstrated, for example, by subsidization of newspaper circulation, increased federal funding to grow the postal system (coupled with a ban on government opening the mail), allowing members of Congress to send official letters to constituents without a stamp, and support for widening education.[1] The U.S. Census departed from the tradition, lasting for millennia, of censuses providing government with information about individual subjects for tax or military purposes. By contrast, in America, the government was barred from using information about individuals obtained by the Census. Rather, the Census made available to the government and to the people aggregate statistical information to be used to allocate representatives and serve other broad public purposes.[2]

After the victory for openness led by Jefferson and his followers, there were some clashes about particular instances of governmental secrecy, but there were no government programs the very existence of which was secret. The openness culture dominated until the mid-twentieth century, when an enormous growth in presidential power led to what Arthur Schlesinger Jr. called the "Imperial Presidency."[3] More presidential power was coupled with growth of bureaucracies, including a mighty military and intelligence establishment. Fear flowed from the atomic bomb, the Cold War, and the 9/11 terror attacks. All this fueled the Secrecy Era, in which a secrecy culture came to dominate government activity. America became a nation with a vast and permanent national security bureaucracy, growing mountains of classified information, and continuing efforts to conceal the existence of entire government programs.

Americans are now again engaged in a vigorous debate about the benefits and harms of secrecy and openness. Today's debate is also influenced by progress in information technology, which, of course, makes it far easier to store and distribute information. This debate, as in America's early years, speaks to the question of what it means to be a democracy.

The Founding Era

As in any nation, including all democracies, some secrecy was imperative from the start, particularly for military operations. As George Washington wrote to Patrick Henry during the Revolutionary War, "there are some Secrets, on the keeping of which so, depends, oftentimes, the salvation of an Army." Washington used secrecy to help beat the British by, for example, hiding his shortages and fooling the British in Boston that his army had more men and more

gunpowder than it actually did. Later, Henry opposed Virginia's ratification
of the Constitution, in part because the Constitutional Convention had de-
liberated in secret and the Constitution allowed Congress to keep parts of
its work secret. Henry conceded, however, he would not wish material related "to military operations or affairs of great consequence, the immediate
promulgation of which might defeat the interests of the community" to be
published. But, Henry added, secrecy should last only "till the end which required their secrecy should have been effected."[4]

Such general agreements aside, the Founders differed sharply about the
extent of openness that would best fit the new nation. Consideration of this
question was part of the debate about whether America should be a republic
or also a democracy. Should educated gentlemen control and have favored
access to information? Or should "the People" (or, more precisely, the portion of the public that was white and male) control and be privy to the information necessary to control? While this debate has been well covered in
American history,[5] its tie to openness and secrecy has not been emphasized.

The seed of openness had been planted by the Declaration of Independence. Although the Declaration's long litany of complaints against King
George III does not mention secrecy, support for openness is implicit in one
of the most eloquent parts of the Declaration's creed: Governments "deriv[e]
their just powers from the consent of the governed."[6] Beneath this simple statement lies recognition that consent is not meaningful unless the governed are
informed about their government and its leaders.

Jefferson, the Declaration's principal author, later made this explicit when
he explained in a letter to a colleague that "[t]he basis of our governments being the opinion of the people," the people must have "full information."[7] Jefferson's conviction applied not only to government's operation but also to its
formation. While serving as American ambassador in Paris, Jefferson learned
the Constitutional Convention was deliberating in secret and colorfully expressed his sorrow for the "abominable . . . tying up the tongues of [the] members." Secret debates, Jefferson said, could be explained only by "the innocence
of their intentions, and ignorance of the value of public discussions."[8]

Nonetheless, the Constitutional Convention did deliberate in secret for four
months in Philadelphia during the spring and summer of 1787. At the start,
the delegates passed a "Secrecy Rule" that prohibited disclosure of their work.[9]
As James Madison told Jefferson, the Secrecy Rule was "thought expedient"
to "secure unbiassed [sic] discussion within doors, and to prevent miscon-

ceptions and misconstructions without, to establish some rules of caution which will for no short time restrain even a confidential communication of our proceedings."[10] Of course, secrecy also hid the fact that by drafting a wholly new Constitution, the Convention was exceeding its mandate to amend the Articles of Confederation.

George Washington chaired the Convention. As the young nation's most revered, respected, and feared leader, he cautioned the members about possible leaks. After a delegate left on the floor a copy of propositions being considered by the Convention, Washington reprimanded the unknown delegate for carelessness.

"I must entreat Gentlemen to be more careful, lest our transactions get into the News Papers, and disturb the public repose by premature speculations. I know not whose Paper it is, but there it is [throwing it down on the table], let him who owns it take it." At the same time he bowed, picked up his Hat, and quitted the room with a dignity so severe that every Person seemed alarmed. . . . It is something remarkable that no Person ever owned the Paper.[11]

Even in his own private diary, Washington kept the Convention's secrets, limiting his daily notations only to "Attended convention as usual."[12]

Secrecy proponents point to the Secrecy Rule at the hallowed Constitutional Convention. But the tale of the 1787 Constitutional Convention does not make a broad case for secrecy. It was well known, of course, that the Convention was meeting. As for its deliberating in secret, many of the harmful handmaidens of secret decision-making were absent.

The participants in the Convention were not a narrow coterie of like-minded thinkers but a group of representatives with different interests. They engaged in energetic debates and formed shifting coalitions. The Convention's decisions were publicly released as soon as the document was finished; the Constitution was set in type the day the Convention adjourned and was printed in newspapers in all thirteen states as rapidly as possible in 1787.[13] Most important, before the proposed new Constitution could go into effect, it was vigorously—and publicly—debated in state ratification campaigns and conventions. The people themselves needed to approve. Indeed, as Madison said, the Constitution "is to be of no more consequence than the paper on which it is written, unless it be stamped with the approbation of those to whom it is addressed."[14]

Subsequent constitutional amendments have been formulated and extensively debated in public. These include the Bill of Rights, which in 1789 was publicly debated in the House, although passed by the Senate behind closed doors. The Civil War Amendments, which, as Abraham Lincoln prophesied in the Gettysburg Address, gave rise to "a new birth of freedom," were all debated in public.[15] So was the Nineteenth Amendment, which granted women the right to vote. At most, the secrecy surrounding the Constitutional Convention supports an argument that some meetings considering public policy issues ought not be held in the open.

As for the Constitution itself, the first three words of its Preamble—"We the People"—made the people, not the states, the ultimate sovereign that ordained and established the Constitution. To be truly sovereign, the people require information. The body of the Constitution also expanded congressional openness as compared to British and colonial precedents. And the power the Constitution granted to Congress to "establish Post Offices and post Roads" turned out soon to lead to significant action subsidizing newspapers and encouraging openness.[16]

The Constitution itself makes no explicit reference to secrecy except for the "Journal Clause," which requires each house of Congress to "keep a Journal of its Proceedings and from time to time publish the same, excepting such Parts as may in their Judgment require Secrecy." (However, at the "Desire of one fifth of those Present," the "Yeas and Nays" of the members on any question must be entered in the Journal.)[17]

These provisions and early practices under the Constitution turned historical norms on their head. In the British Parliament, in America's colonial legislatures, and in the Continental Congress during the Revolution, secret proceedings were the practice.[18] Under America's new Constitution, however, the norm would be openness, secrecy the exception. From its start, the House of Representatives opened its debates to the public, including reporters. This was a significant break with the past, and caused some controversy. Vice President John Adams warned his wife, Abigail, that opening the House to what he considered to be a divisive press was risky. It could even "break the Confederation."[19]

In contrast, the Senate continued for a while to deliberate secretly, and even barred House members from its sessions.[20] Closing the Senate's doors prompted the first serious national debate about secrecy. Various state legislatures urged the Senate to meet openly, as was required by the constitutions of some. But the most impassioned case for openness was made by a journalist—Philip Freneau, Madison's Princeton classmate. In 1791, Secretary of State Jefferson appointed Freneau as a translator. But even though Freneau was working for the government, Jefferson and Madison persuaded him to work simultaneously as editor of the *National Gazette*, a new newspaper created to attack the Federalists.[21] (The Federalist "faction," or party, was led by John Adams and Alexander Hamilton, and was generally supported by George Washington.)

With dramatic flair, Freneau advocated ending the Senate's secrecy, which, he said, adopted "the secret privileges of the [British] House of Lords," saying, "[S]ecrecy in your representatives is a worm which will prey and fatten upon the vitals of your liberty" and "Secrecy is necessary to design and a masque to treachery; honesty shrinks not from the public eye." At the core of Freneau's stance was an impassioned plea for an informed citizenry:

Are you freemen who ought to know the individual conduct of your legislators, or are you an inferior order of beings incapable of comprehending the sublimity of Senatorial functions, and unworthy to be entrusted with their opinions? How are you to know the just from the unjust steward when they are covered with the mantle of concealment? Can there be any question of legislative import which freemen should not be acquainted with? What are you to expect when stewards of your household refuse to give account of their stewardship?[22]

After six years of criticism, the Senate voted in 1794 to open its doors in its next session. Although the *National Gazette* was by then closed, Freneau's broadsides had stoked the debate. A free press fueled discussion that increased government openness. In addition, some Federalist Senators from New England switched sides to support opening the Senate's doors because they concluded "the old, elitist style in politics was obsolescent," and, possibly more important, they saw their rivals in the House were benefiting politically from greater public awareness of their work.[23] Power in the new America was increasingly based on publicity and openness, not the closed culture of aristocratic England.

Another early skirmish over secrecy involved the Jay Treaty, which stemmed from the 1794 meetings in London of John Jay and Lord William Grenville, the British foreign secretary, to negotiate on issues left open after the Revolution. At the time, Jay was serving as the Supreme Court's first chief justice. Earlier, Jay had written five of the Federalist Papers that urged New York to ratify the Constitution. One of these claimed that an advantage of the Constitution giving presidents the power to negotiate treaties was that it permitted the secrecy necessary to diplomatic negotiation.[24] But later, in 1793, Chief Justice Jay expressed a slant toward secrecy in less lofty terms, urging that problems with the federal courts "should be corrected quietly" because if "those Defects were all exposed to public View in striking Colors, more Enemies would arise, and the Difficulty of mending them encreased [sic]."[25]

The Jay-Grenville negotiations were highly secret. The two usually met alone; there were no written records. As Jay's chief aide later commented, he and his British counterpart "had a real holiday for a month."[26] Then, after the two negotiators agreed on a proposed treaty, President Washington and Secretary of State Edmund Randolph kept its terms secret until the Senate decided whether to approve it.[27]

The treaty involved matters of great emotional and commercial significance, including trade rights with the West Indies, British conscription of American seamen, and the fate of British frontier posts.[28] There were rumors about the treaty's substance, but "[s]ecrecy itself, as much or more than the possible contents of the treaty, became the dominant issue." Anti-Federalist editor Benjamin Franklin Bache—Benjamin Franklin's grandson, derided as "Lightning-Rod Junior" by the Federalists—"pounded away at Federalists for refusing to publicly reveal the document's contents and implied that secrecy was used as a cover to hide dark dealings."[29]

Although Jay agreed to the treaty in London in November 1794, it did not reach George Washington for several months. Its arrival was initially delayed when copies were thrown overboard to avoid capture by a French privateer; a second ship was held up by strong winds. The Senate did not meet on the treaty until June 1795. Meeting in secret, it ratified the treaty by 20 to 10—just enough to meet the constitutionally required two-thirds vote for ratification. The Senate majority then voted to ban any member from copying the document.[30] Defying the ban, Virginia senator Stevens Thomson Mason smuggled a copy to Bache, who promptly published it.

Violent protests followed. Jay was burned in effigy in Philadelphia, New York, and Boston, and former secretary of the treasury Alexander Hamilton was stoned in New York City as he tried to defend the treaty. Nonetheless, seven weeks after the Senate's approval, President Washington signed the treaty, believing that while flawed and less favorable to America than he had hoped, it served the nation's interests.

Secrecy probably backfired on treaty supporters by fueling suspicions about the treaty and fanning the flames of opposition. The Jay Treaty dispute also highlighted the intense emotions underlying the controversy about ordinary people's participation in public affairs. One Federalist reacted to Hamilton's stoning by saying opponents of the treaty (or, as he put it—evoking the violence of the French Revolution—"the Jacobins") must have believed that by "knock[ing] out Hamilton's brains," they would "reduce him to an equality with themselves."[31]

In the nation's early years, the Jay Treaty was one of many examples of Congress, in this case the House, pressing presidents for information. No clear pattern emerged; each controversy "called forth a very particularistic discussion" without "public articulation of a consistent set of guidelines that could be referred to in subsequent cases."[32]

Washington's first response to a congressional demand for information was to turn over materials on an Indian massacre of an army division.[33] Later, Washington provided some information to congressional investigations of an American ambassador to France, Gouverneur Morris, and the first treasury secretary, Alexander Hamilton.[34] Washington's last response was to refuse the House any information on the Jay Treaty, claiming the House (unlike the Senate) had no right to it.[35] After Washington's refusal to give the House any Jay Treaty information, John Adams's first response as president was an immediate and nearly total delivery of papers Congress had demanded about the XYZ affair—an attempt by Talleyrand, the French foreign minister, to coerce and seek bribes from American envoys who were in Paris to negotiate a new treaty with France. ("XYZ" stands for the names of three French diplomats whose names were redacted from the disclosure.)[36]

For its part, Congress was careful not to push too hard. The early House automatically granted presidential requests for confidentiality. This practice came under substantial criticism in Benjamin Franklin Bache's *General Advertiser*.[37] However, even after the House repealed its Rule, it continued to be deferential.[38] For example, when it sought information concerning the president's instructions to Hamilton about foreign loans, the House asked only for such information as Washington "may think proper."[39]

The final skirmish over secrecy in the 1790s involved the Sedition Act.

Passed in 1798 by the Federalists in Congress and signed into law by President John Adams, the act authorized federal prosecutions of citizens for criticizing President Adams and his administration.[40] The prosecutions were mostly against newspaper editors and publishers of handbills or pamphlets.[41] Government lawyers argued that it was a crime for ordinary citizens to "raise surmises and suspicions of the wisdom" of the president's "measures," for to do so "was to excite the hatred of the good people of this country against their President."[42]

Neither the Sedition Act nor the prosecutions under it were secret. But the purpose and effect of the act was to suppress information and dissent. The connection between the act and secrecy was made clear in Rep. Albert Gallatin's speech opposing its passage when he argued that, throughout history, tyrants had used laws against political criticism to "prevent the diffusion of knowledge" and to "throw a veil on their folly or their crimes."[43] Similarly, Rep. John Nicholas opposed the act because it would deprive the people of "information on public measures, which they have a right to receive, and which is the life and support of a free Government."[44] Moreover, in his report supporting Virginia's attack on the act, Madison wrote that elected governments needed a "greater freedom of animadversion" than monarchies. This implied more "freedom in the use of the press" because newspapers were necessary for "canvassing the merits and measures of public men."[45]

One of the first targets for prosecution was Benjamin Franklin Bache, whom the president's wife, Abigail Adams, called a "lying wretch" and whom the Federalist *Porcupine Gazette* dubbed a "dull-edged, dull-eyed, haggard-looking hireling of France." Bache was indicted for common-law seditious libel but died of smallpox before he could be tried.[46] Among the ten people convicted under the Sedition Act was Thomas Cooper—the man earlier threatened with prosecution by the British attorney general if he published cheaply his critique of a British politician. In his unsuccessful jury argument, Cooper made an explicit comparison to England: "I know that in England the king can do no wrong, but I did not know till now that the President of the United States had the same attribute."[47]

Revealingly, the Sedition Act of 1798 expired on March 3, 1801, the date of the next presidential inauguration. That date was chosen to prevent Jefferson from using the act if he won the next election, which he did. In addition, the act specifically protected the incumbent president (John Adams) against sedition charges, but tellingly did not protect the vice president, who just happened to be Jefferson. Once he became president, Jefferson pardoned everyone convicted under the Sedition Act. Moreover, in his Inaugural Address, Jefferson said any "abuses" of the diffusion of information should be "arraign[ed] . . . at the bar of the public reason," not in a courtroom, reiterating his belief that diffusion of information was a cornerstone of good government.[48]

All these skirmishes took place in the context of a broader battle over the nature of the new American nation: What slice of America should participate in governance and politics? Was America to ape British hierarchical habits where members of the public were merely bystanders between elections? Or would America chart a new course where the public would be regularly informed about government affairs? The Federalists yearned for a version of the British hierarchical and aristocratic system in which the rich, the well-born, and the most educated were expected to rule. The wider public would have little voice between elections. The other faction—first generally known as Republicans and then as Democrats—wanted a country in which all citizens (as long as they were white males) would participate in elections and express their views between elections. They described the new nation as a democracy, as well as a republic.

For much of the Federalist gentry, democracy was a dirty word. One of those who raised his voice against democracy was Gouverneur Morris, who at the Constitutional Convention had "revise[d] the stile" of the Constitution.[49] At the convention, Morris had unsuccessfully urged a federal property qualification for voting, warning "the people never act from reason alone" and "[t]he rich will take advantage of their passions." Moreover, "[g]ive the votes to people who have no property, and they will sell them to the rich." Twenty-five years later, Morris contended that "in the degenerate state to which democracy never fails to reduce a nation, it is almost impossible for a good man to govern, even could he get into power, or for a bad man to govern well."[50]

The Jeffersonian vision of openness and democracy prevailed. Citizens became engaged between elections. Information was emphasized. Change began before Jefferson's election as president in 1800 and continued after he left office, but Jefferson was a rhetorical force, and his election was an important turning point. Becoming a democracy was a victory for Jefferson's earlier argument that "the basis of our governments being the opinion of the people," they must have "full information." As John Taylor of Caroline—a fellow slaveholder, whom Arthur Schlesinger Jr. called the "philosopher of

Jeffersonian democracy"—later wrote in a critique of "executive secrecy," "How can national self-government exist without knowledge of national affairs? [O]r how can legislatures be wise or independent, who legislate in the dark upon the recommendation of one man?"[51] In a letter favoring expansion of public education, Madison eloquently captured the connection between information and effective democracy, for "[a] popular Government, without popular information, or the means of acquiring it, is but a Prologue to a Farce or a Tragedy; or, perhaps both. Knowledge will forever govern ignorance: And a people who mean to be their own Governors, must arm themselves with the power which knowledge gives."[52]

The development of political parties was another reason for America's need for broadly disseminated information. In the Federalist Papers, Madison's concept of what we now call checks and balances had been that each "part" or "department" of the government—Congress, the Executive, and the Courts—would be "the means of keeping each other in their proper places." Madison concluded that "security against a gradual concentration" of power lay in "giving to those who administer each department the necessary constitutional means and personal motives to resist encroachments of the others." Put more pithily, "[a]mbition must be made to counteract ambition."[53] But with the rise of political parties, loyalty to a public official's own branch was often diluted by party relationships between members of Congress and presidents. Therefore, checks and balances—which Madison in *Federalist No. 51* had referred to as only "*auxiliary*" precautions—became less of a bulwark against encroachments. The people's vote remained "the *primary* control on the government."[54] Thus the rise of political parties made public access to information even more necessary to support our constitutional system and our democracy. Indeed, as Jefferson commented, "perhaps this party division is necessary to induce each [party] to watch and delate to the people the proceedings of the other."[55]

A Second Revolution: More Democracy, More Education, More Information, and More Openness

As powerfully articulated by Dr. Benjamin Rush, a Founder who was a scientist and a doctor by trade, while Americans had "changed our forms of government" after winning the Revolution, doing so was only "the first act of the great drama." The new nation still needed "a revolution in our principles, opinions, and manners so as to accommodate them to the forms of government we have adopted."[56] As the nation developed, there was, in fact, such a second revolution—a cultural transformation and *information* revolution. In the late eighteenth century and early nineteenth century, post offices, newspapers, schooling, and voluntary associations all proliferated, creating new avenues for exchanging and understanding information. Information diffusion, which Jefferson saw as an essential principle, breathed life into American democracy and helped hold secrecy at bay.

Initially, the federal government was tiny. When Washington became president, there were more workers at his Mount Vernon plantation than in the federal government.[57] At the start, the postal system was the biggest part of government, and it grew rapidly. In 1790, there were 75 post offices. Congress created a national postal system in 1792, leading to twelve times as many post offices by 1800. By 1820, there were 4,500 post offices; by 1840, more than 13,000.[58] Expansion of the postal service coincided with, and indeed helped drive, newspaper circulation. Madison had argued the "real sovereign" in government is public opinion and that in large countries such as the United States, "a free press, and particularly a circulation of newspapers through the entire body of the people" is favorable to liberty.[59] The next year, Congress subsidized newspaper circulation in the Post Office Act of 1792.[60] Its discounted delivery costs coupled with Americans' hunger for information fostered huge increases in the number of papers and their circulation. In the 1790s, the number of papers doubled to about 200. It shot up to 1,200 by 1833. By the early 1830s, more than 90 percent of the mail (by weight) consisted of newspapers. But because of subsidies, newspapers accounted for less than 15 percent of postal revenue.[61]

Jefferson viewed newspapers as vital to democracy, once proclaiming that "were it left to me to decide whether we should have a government without newspapers, or newspapers without a government, I should not hesitate a moment to prefer the latter."[62] Still, Jefferson—as is no doubt true for all political figures—occasionally lamented and lambasted some of what was written about him. An overwrought President Jefferson criticized many papers for "present[ing] only the caricatures of disaffected minds." He even told Pennsylvania's governor that a few state prosecutions would have "a wholesome effect in restoring the integrity of the presses."[63]

Outside observers also noted newspapers' importance in America. When the young French aristocrat Alexis de Tocqueville wrote *Democracy in America* in the mid-1830s, he expressed wonder at the vitality of American democracy, finding the most powerful explanation lay in customs and non-government institutions that facilitated or promoted access to information. Of these, Tocqueville placed the most weight on newspapers and voluntary associations, with a nod to education as well.

In Tocqueville's view, newspapers were particularly necessary in nations like America, where the old bonds of aristocracy had been loosed. In aristocracies, men are "strongly held together" by loyalty to their lords; but in democracies, "men are no longer united among themselves by firm and lasting ties." Therefore, in a democracy, you must "persuade every man whose help you require that his private interest obliges him voluntarily to unite" with others. Only newspapers do this "habitually and conveniently," for "nothing but a newspaper can drop the same thought into a thousand minds at the same moment." And in America, there was "scarcely a hamlet" without a newspaper. These caused "political life to circulate through all the parts of that vast territory," "detect[ed] the secret springs of political designs," and "summon[ed] the leaders of all parties in turn to the bar of public opinion."[64]

Tocqueville also emphasized voluntary associations, observing that "[w]herever at the head of some new undertaking you see the government in France, or a man of rank in England, in the United States you will be sure to find an association." Moreover, "newspapers make associations, and associations make newspapers." Both supported democracy by allowing Americans to share information and promote their views.[65]

Tocqueville's book is widely known. Largely unnoticed now is an equally sweeping book, written in 1837 by Francis J. Grund, an Austrian immigrant who became an influential diplomat, writer, and political maneuverer in the United States. Grund reached similar conclusions about the importance of access to information for American democracy. According to Grund, Americans read more than other people. And the number of newspapers "baffle[d] all attempts at computation"; there was "hardly a village or a settlement of a dozen houses in any part of the country, without a printing establishment and a paper."[66]

From the Information Revolution to the Secrecy Era

America generally continued to opt for openness during the long period from the Information Revolution to the Secrecy Era. Nonetheless, there were skirmishes over secrecy, mostly with respect to making treaties or war.[67]

Abraham Lincoln and Woodrow Wilson provide useful historical landmarks. In 1848, Lincoln, then in his only term as a congressman, criticized President James Polk's description of the origins of the Mexican War. He questioned whether Mexicans sparked the conflict by firing the first shots on American soil, as Polk had claimed. Lincoln said that in pushing for war, Polk had withheld the fact that the Mexican Army had killed Americans in a disputed sliver of land. "Let him [Polk] remember he sits where Washington sat; and, so remembering, let him answer as Washington would answer." "As a nation should not, and the Almighty will not, be evaded, so let him attempt no evasion, no equivocation." Polk had made, Lincoln added, an "open attempt to prove by telling the *truth*, what he could not prove by telling the *whole truth*."[68] Deception, as often, was secrecy's friend.[69]

After becoming president, Lincoln himself used deception in his struggle to persuade Congress to pass a constitutional amendment abolishing slavery. On the morning of an excruciatingly close vote in the House of Representatives, rumors about Confederate peace envoys threatened to scuttle the proposed amendment. "The report is in circulation in the House that Peace Commissioners are on their way or in the city," Congressman James Ashley wrote to Lincoln. If the commissioners appeared in Washington, opponents of the constitutional amendment could argue passage would cause the Confederates to end peace talks. "If it is true I fear we shall lose the bill. Please authorize me to contradict it if it is not true." Lincoln knew the envoys were in fact on their way to Fort Monroe in Virginia, en route to Washington, but, using the kind of lawyerly logic popularized in the movie *Lincoln*, the president wrote back, "So far as I know, there are no Peace Commissioners in the city or likely to be in it." Later that day, January 31, 1865, the House narrowly voted to abolish slavery.[70]

Lincoln, like any wartime president, sought to keep battle plans secret. However, during the Civil War much more was known than usual, perhaps because a civil war necessarily makes secrecy harder, perhaps because newspaper reporters were in the battle zones, and perhaps because of Congress's unusually close supervision and investigations of generals and battles. Lincoln also made available a trove of current diplomatic communications after Congress called on him to release all correspondence with the English, French, Spanish, and other governments referring to recognition of the Confederacy. The White House initially balked at the request, but its eventual compliance signaled the significant role of the legislative branch in foreign affairs, and began the release of what later became known as the *Foreign Relations of the United States* (or *FRUS*) series by the State Department.[71] Publication was roughly contemporaneous until the turn of the twentieth century, when it was delayed significantly by the close of Theodore Roosevelt's presidency. Today, parts of the FRUS record, particularly documents relating to the CIA, are delayed by decades.[72]

Lincoln's rhetoric is as important as were his actions. "Four score and seven years" after Jefferson's Declaration of Independence, Lincoln's Gettysburg Address became another pillar of support for openness. As eloquent as the Declaration are the closing words of the Gettysburg Address.

> We here highly resolve that these dead shall not have died in vain—that this nation, under God, shall have a new birth of freedom—and that government of the people, by the people, for the people shall not perish from the earth.

But if necessary information is hidden *from* the people, government *by* the people will perish.

A half century after Lincoln, Woodrow Wilson became an example of a president smothering earlier promises of transparency with the heavy hand of secrecy. In 1912, during his successful presidential campaign, Wilson preached an absolutist, unrealistically broad version of openness for American government, proclaiming that "secrecy means impropriety" and "[i]f there is nothing to conceal, then why conceal it?" Therefore, "government ought to be all outside and no inside." Indeed, "there ought to be no place where anything can be done that everybody does not know about."[73] Wilson's statements were remarkably categorical, even for campaign speeches. However, as president when faced with World War I, Wilson pushed for passage of the Espionage Act, designed to suppress dissent and control information, and a new Sedition Act, which resulted, for example, in a fifteen-year prison sentence for a Vermont minister who cited Jesus as a proponent of pacifism. It also led to a lengthy prison sentence for Eugene V. Debs for criticizing military conscription. While in prison in 1920, Debs received more than 900,000 votes as the Socialist Party's candidate for president.[74]

President Wilson nonetheless reiterated his campaign talking points about openness in the context of international relations. In his "Fourteen Points" speech to a joint session of Congress in anticipation of peace negotiations at the end of World War I, Wilson presented America's goals, declaring that the "processes of peace, when they are begun, shall be absolutely open, and that they shall involve and permit henceforth no secret understandings of any kind." Indeed, the first of his fourteen points promised "[o]pen covenants of peace, openly arrived at."[75] But then, in formulating the Treaty of Versailles, Wilson opted to join closed-door negotiations at the Paris Peace Conference in early 1919 that established the peace terms for Germany and other defeated nations. Wilson sided with Prime Ministers Georges Clemenceau of France and David Lloyd George of the United Kingdom, who worried that public knowledge of day-to-day discussions would stir up controversy and delay the conference. After Wilson balked at press requests either to hold open negotiations or provide daily summaries, American journalists and senators cried hypocrisy.[76]

Still, openness continued to be the dominant practice throughout the long period leading up to the Secrecy Era. There was no secrecy culture, no classification regime, and no government programs whose very existence was hidden. Of course, before the Cold War, crisis and fear episodically had led presidents to ignore the Constitution's wise restraints that keep us free. But none of these earlier episodes lasted long, and, more critically, prior to the Cold War, presidents did not paper over such episodes with layers of secrecy. Generally, they acted openly: Adams with the Sedition Act; Lincoln with unilateral suppression of habeas corpus and taking possession of the nation's telegraph lines; Wilson with prosecuting war critics; Wilson's attorney general, assisted by J. Edgar Hoover, with dragnet raids against thousands of immigrants without warrants or access to counsel; Franklin Roosevelt with the internment of Japanese American citizens without evidence of a single act of espionage or treasonable activity.[77] All these actions—however wrongheaded—were taken in the open. So voters had the ability to judge the actions, and Congress and the courts had the power to stop them, if they had the will.

During the decades before the Secrecy Era, newspapers also continued to flourish. In 1870, America had nearly 580 daily papers. By the end of the century, there were more than 2,200. Circulation of daily papers alone increased from 2.6 million to more than 15 million.[78] Papers became less dependent on political parties, and the availability of advertising allowed the price of papers to drop substantially. In addition, magazines specializing in muckraking, with stories exposing the secrets of American corporations, labor, and governments, thrived.

The development of the electric telegraph in the 1830s and 1840s and the telephone in the 1870s were examples of changes in technology that undermined secrecy, with information reaching the public much faster. The information available to the public also became more graphic, more revealing, and more emotionally powerful. Photography undermined the secrecy shielding details of war and poverty by exposing to millions the gore of the former and the human face of the latter.

By the early twentieth century, new concerns about secrecy arose as Americans became aware of the vast increase in corporate power. A congressional investigating committee shocked Americans when it revealed in 1913 that a small network of interests headed by J.P. Morgan controlled more than three times the value of all real and personal property in New England.[79] Corporate secrecy accompanied expanding corporate power and created a new challenge to American government and American society.

Movements by government to rein in corporate power began to gain traction. In 1910, former president Theodore Roosevelt—back from his flamboyant hunting exploits in Africa and beginning to think about running for president again—made a powerful speech advocating more public control of "mighty commercial forces." Roosevelt called for "complete and effective publicity of corporate affairs." He also stressed the need for corporations to disclose their campaign contributions.[80]

Three years later, future Supreme Court Justice Louis Brandeis condemned the power of the "Money Trust" and famously argued for more openness because "publicity is justly commended as a remedy for social and industrial diseases. Sunlight is said to be the best of disinfectants; electric light the most efficient policeman."[81] Later, in the 1930s, Ferdinand Pecora, counsel to a landmark Senate investigation into Wall Street improprieties, stressed secrecy's role in the financial calamities of the Great Depression. "Legal chicanery and beneficent darkness were the [banks'] stoutest allies." Wall Street abuses stemmed from the "secrecy with which the management was allowed to operate." Had there been full disclosure, the "schemers . . . could not long have survived the fierce light of publicity and criticism."[82]

Progressive reformers helped pass government laws and regulations to require disclosure of hidden business information on food safety, securities offerings, and, later, the environment. In America, more than in most other industrial democracies, disclosure came to be seen as a vital cure for corporate abuse and a key check on corporate power. The progressive movement in the early twentieth century also witnessed the birth of U.S. laws requiring disclosure of government information. Long before Congress passed the Freedom of Information Act in 1966, some states had similar laws. The somewhat surprising first "sunshine state" was Florida, which in 1909 passed a public-records law.[83]

FDR: A Bridge Between the Openness and the Secrecy Eras

For more than twelve years starting in 1933, when he faced the Great Depression, and through most of World War II, Franklin Roosevelt led America. Roosevelt's fireside chats innovatively used the new medium of radio to reach unprecedentedly wide audiences with information relating to public policy choices. During the war, the government necessarily kept many military plans and activities secret; in this respect, Roosevelt was no different from, say, Washington or Lincoln. The repressive wartime act for which Roosevelt is most criticized—the internment of more than 100,000 law-abiding Japanese American citizens—was done openly, although we now know that the Army and the Justice Department were deceptive in defending detention in the Supreme Court. Nonetheless, Roosevelt did play a role in edging America toward a secrecy culture. But the Roosevelt years lacked the all-consuming fear—first of the nuclear-armed and potentially expansionist Soviet Union, and then of terrorism after 9/11—that has driven the Secrecy Era. Franklin Roosevelt's administration thus served as a bridge between the Openness and the Secrecy Eras.

Before America's entry into World War II, Congress gave Roosevelt discretion to protect information about military and naval installations.[84] FDR followed with an executive order that created a multilayered classification system covering secret, confidential, and restricted information.[85] Roosevelt later also established a largely voluntary system of press self-censorship related to national defense information.[86] These orders, while broad and vague, were public. However, two momentous acts of Roosevelt's were kept secret—one inappropriately, the other appropriately.

Roosevelt issued orders to the FBI that opened the door to secret investigations of law-abiding Americans' beliefs and noncriminal activities. In 1938,

Roosevelt joined with Attorney General Homer Cummings and with FBI Director J. Edgar Hoover to conceal these orders from Congress and the American public. A few years later, again secretly, Roosevelt ordered Attorney General Robert Jackson to let the FBI continue warrantless wiretapping of Americans. These orders were inappropriately secret.

An appropriate military secret was the Manhattan Project, code name for the massive secret effort to produce the atomic bomb.[87] The project's budget was enormous: some $25 billion in today's money was spent at laboratories and manufacturing plants in Oak Ridge, Tennessee; Hanford, Washington; Los Alamos, New Mexico; Chicago, Illinois; and several other locations.[88] These huge costs were concealed in congressional budgets. According to House Minority Leader Joseph Martin's memoir, Secretary of War Henry Stimson and Gen. George Marshall came to the Capitol in 1944 for a secret meeting with Martin, Speaker Sam Rayburn, and Majority Leader John McCormack. Marshall described the bomb's technical details. Stimson then said that "if the Germans got this weapon first, they might win the war overnight." The visitors asked for an additional $1.6 billion—some $21 billion in today's money—to build the bomb. And "[b]ecause of the overriding necessity for secrecy, they made the unique request that the money be provided without a trace of evidence as to how it would be spent."[89] And so it was. Several months later, the same briefing, with the same outcome, was provided to three senior members of the Senate.[90]

It is often said that even Vice President Harry Truman knew nothing about the atomic bomb until he became president. But in fact, Truman had gleaned hints when he ran a Senate committee focusing on military spending. During his investigations, Truman's staff picked up "puzzling hints" of huge military expenditures for something identified only as the Manhattan Project. Truman asked Secretary Stimson about it, and Stimson told him that "[i]t's part of a very important secret development" for a "unique purpose." In response, Truman agreed to forgo any investigation.[91] About a month later, however, Truman told a colleague he knew that the government's vast land acquisitions in Hanford, Washington, were for "the construction of a plant to make a terrific explosion for a secret weapon that will be a wonder."[92] Later, in November 1943, Truman sent an investigator to look into complaints of waste at Hanford, but after being sharply reminded of his agreement with Stimson, Truman called off the inquiry.

The conventional wisdom, articulated by *New York Times* science writer

William Laurence, was that from 1940 to the Hiroshima bombing in August 1945, the subject of atomic energy "vanished" from the American media. This is entirely wrong.[93] Commentators also erroneously reported that "hardly a word leaked out" about the bomb during the war, and that any leaks were "of a minor nature."[94] In fact, as the records of the government's Office of Censorship show, there were "numerous" leaks and "some of them were extremely serious."[95]

Some articles contained general statements about atomic research.[96] One labeled uranium as the "most potent stuff on earth."[97] Others mentioned the huge Manhattan Project research centers, such as an article in *Business Week* that the Oak Ridge, Tennessee, facility housed "the Army's most secret project."[98] In June 1945, *Newsweek* revealed that there had been "rigid censorship restrictions" on scientific experiments with nuclear physics.[99]

Stories that cut closer to the bone included:

- In 1943, one *Washington Post* columnist wrote that "a practical means of releasing atomic energy, might suddenly outmode and overwhelm all the weapons of warfare in existence." A few months later, another *Post* columnist wrote of rumors about a huge Army research project described as "one of the largest single projects that's to be built from scratch in the Nation's history."[100]
- A few Tennessee papers quoted an Army general saying the Oak Ridge facility housed "'production of a weapon that possibly might be the one to end this war.'"[101]
- Then, a year before the bomb was dropped on Hiroshima, the *Minneapolis Tribune* wrote, "All known explosives are popgun affairs compared to the dreadful power sub-atomic energy might loose," adding the fact that the government was restricting uranium sales.[102]
- Around the same time, a radio host told his 2 million listeners that "the Army would soon create a new weapon based upon the splitting of the atom."[103]

Fortunately, neither the Nazis—whose scientists were trying to develop an atomic bomb—nor the Japanese picked up on these bomb hints.[104] In today's Internet age, such blindness would be impossible. Enemies can now search by key words and gain instant access to such information. Now they also could determine the importance of America's work on the bomb by being able to note the deletion of revealing references from later editions of papers or from editions sent outside the United States.[105]

Thus, during the presidency of Franklin Roosevelt, World War II and the push to build the atomic bomb made secrecy more important and more widespread than ever before. Still, it was a few more years before the Cold War gave birth to America's pervasive secrecy culture.

The Birth of the Secrecy Era

The Secrecy Era did not suddenly spring forth fully formed like Athena from the brow of Zeus. Like water in a pot on a stove, it steadily got warmer rather than jumping from cool to boiling.

Shortly after World War II, newspaper editors began to notice more restrictions on access to information. James S. Pope, chair of the Freedom of Information Committee of the American Society of Newspaper Editors and managing editor of the Louisville Courier-Journal, expressed concern about information suppression in the United States, mostly in cities and states, but also in Washington, D.C., where a "legend that agency and department heads enjoyed a sort of personal ownership of news about their units [was] blossoming."[106] Government reluctance to release facts that might make the "governor or the mayor or the county judge, or the major general, squirm with embarrassment" had frequently led to conflict with reporters. But, said Pope, only recently had editors seen that "these familiar little guerrilla skirmishes now are part of a broad-scale offensive against freedom of information"[107]—a phrase that did not become prominent until the early 1950s.[108]

A lot more had to happen, however, before secrecy became pervasive enough to say that America had entered the Secrecy Era. The evolution from openness to secrecy was part of larger changes in America: the development of a permanent and huge national security state, and the growth of what President Dwight Eisenhower called the "military industrial complex." Fear accelerated the evolution. Russia's possession of the atomic bomb and America's greater perceived peril bred fear that spawned secrecy. Government leaders felt embattled, needing to intervene all over the world, with secrecy seeming more natural when facing a secretive enemy. The "born secret" Atomic Energy Act of 1946 was a harbinger. The government vastly increased the size of the federal bureaucracy and created whole new agencies, including the

CIA in 1947 and the NSA in 1952, whose missions suggested, and whose prestige demanded, fortresses of secrecy.

Fear of Communists at home also fueled secrecy. In August 1950, Julius and Ethel Rosenberg were indicted for providing atomic bomb secrets to the Russians. Within eight months, they were convicted and sentenced to death. This and other thefts of secrets led to calls for more and more secure secrecy. Federal employees were required to take loyalty oaths, which implied the need to protect information.

Technological advances in America and around the world, aided by increased global access to scientific and technical information, eventually lessened the protection of the vast ocean barriers surrounding America. Thus, a great irony: along with America's growth in power, which had been fostered by access to more information, came an increased sense of vulnerability, and with it the fear that fueled a culture that sought to curtail access to information.

Certainly by September 1951, when President Truman directed all federal agencies to classify records in the interest of "national security"—which, unlike "national defense," was a relatively new and more amorphous term that gave all executive agencies classification authority that FDR had earlier granted only to the Army, Navy, State Department, and the Department of War—America had entered the Secrecy Era.[109] But Truman's order did not get off to an auspicious start. Newspaper editors immediately voiced fears that the authority would be abused because of officials' tendency to "resolve any doubts about security by just reaching for the rubber stamp marked 'secret.'"[110] Truman defended his order as aimed at "prevent[ing] us from being wiped out," claiming it was narrowly concerned with military secrets, "designed to keep security information from potential enemies," and not to be used to "withhold non-security information or to cover up mistakes made by any official or employee of the Government." Truman even argued that by clearly segregating security from non-security information, the order would provide Americans with "more, rather than less, information about their government."[111] Just two days later, this dubious assertion was undermined when Truman had to rescind a directive issued by an assistant director of the Office of Price Stabilization that employees were not to disclose any information that "might prove embarrassing to the O.P.S."[112]

After the inauspicious start of Truman's classification regime, secrecy's seduction bloomed, the secrecy culture blossomed, and the levels and amount of secrecy grew and grew.

PART TWO

Legitimate Secrets, and Secrecy's Dangers, Harms, Culture, and Seduction

Secrecy is most dangerous when government officials use it to shield broad programs that are illegal or clash with American values. J. Edgar Hoover's tenure as FBI Director during the Cold War and Dick Cheney's tenure as vice president after 9/11 provide vivid examples. But even when government officials lack malign motives, the secrecy culture can cause great harm. The failure of White House officials even to consider making public the sustained and serious series of warnings they received in the summer of 2001 about al-Qaeda attacks is one example. Specific harms aside, the more general problem is that the secrecy culture suppresses thought about whether there should be secrecy in the first place, or whether it should last so long.

Government secrecy involves more than just classified stamps on documents. It includes anything people in power do to keep information from reaching the public or its representatives. The U.S. government's prolonged ban on media photography of soldiers' coffins returning to Delaware's Dover Air Force Base is a good example. So is the 180-year-long tradition, lasting from George Washington to Richard Nixon, that presidents owned "their" documents and could destroy or limit access to them or bequeath them to heirs who could do the same. Also vital White House decisions are often made by a small coterie of like-minded officials who rely on shared assumptions without debate or benefit of differing views. But presidents who isolate themselves with like-minded advisors are more likely to make unwise decisions. Insular and opaque presidential circles stifle healthy White House debate in the same way that excessive classification squelches healthy public debate.

Secrecy is seductive. Beyond the timeless link between secrecy and power, secrecy is safer. It seems easier and faster. It limits challenges and pesky questions. It fosters illusions of grandeur. Fear, awe, jealousy, and lethargy all help cement a culture of secrecy. Secrecy's seduction and prestige and all the powerful forces of human nature supporting secrecy show why real change is hard.

This has been true throughout America's Secrecy Era. During the Cold War and the post-9/11 period, Americans have lived in two long periods of crisis coupled with fear—a "life of perpetual fear and tension," as President Eisenhower characterized it in 1953.[1] While the secrecy culture and the level of secrecy generally grew during the Secrecy Era, there have been chinks in secrecy's wall opened by journalists, starting in the late 1960s, and by government investigations, starting with the Church Committee. The latter part of the twentieth century also saw strengthening of secrecy watchdogs, including the establishment of Senate and House Intelligence Committees, the growth of independent agency inspectors general, and President Jimmy Carter's creation of the Information Security Oversight Office, designed to increase openness in government, limit classification, and accelerate declassification.[2] After the end of the Cold War, President Bill Clinton issued executive orders that ultimately led to declassification of about a billion pages of historical records. Clinton also created a commission on government secrecy, named for its chair, Sen. Daniel Patrick Moynihan, which produced a history of secrecy and many recommendations for reform.[3]

Despite these efforts to chip away at secrecy's walls, the walls stood strong throughout the Cold War and were buttressed after 9/11. There are differences and there are similarities between the Cold War period and the period after 9/11. The basics are identical: fear is the driving motive; secrecy is the key implementing tool. In the following chapters, most points are illustrated by examples from both periods. However, because there has not yet been a comprehensive investigation of the post-9/11 period, there are fewer post-9/11 examples for some points; it would be surprising if there were not many more waiting to be unearthed.

The technology available to the government is one difference between the two periods. Senator Church warned in 1975 that NSA's capability was so great that if turned on the American people "there would be no place to hide"—indeed that the technology would enable a malign future government to "impose total tyranny."[4] But the technology Church feared was from the Stone Age compared to today, as Edward Snowden's revelations of the breadth of NSA's post-9/11 data gathering confirm. Paradoxically, however, while today's technology is more intrusive, it also makes it harder to keep government actions secret. Digital creation, storage, retrieval, and transmission make much more information available more widely and quickly—and therefore harder to protect.

Another reason why the shelf life of secrets in the post-9/11 period is shorter than it was in the Cold War period is that there is a much larger oversight infrastructure. While all are imperfect, there are permanent congressional committees and courts with supervisory power, as well as inspectors-general and lawyers who are informed about government secret programs.

Secret government programs continue to challenge American values, and secrecy remains hard to tame. The Church Committee warned that "the United States must not adopt the tactics of the enemy." But after 9/11, when it used torture, the United States actually did adopt the tactics of the enemy. The Bush administration used waterboarding, for which we had prosecuted Japanese officials as war criminals after World War II. More generally, the administration's secret torture techniques were derived from techniques used by North Korea during the Korean War to extract false confessions from captured U.S. soldiers. The military used these techniques to prepare American soldiers to resist torture. But after 9/11, these enemy tactics were adopted and used by the United States. The Obama administration banned torture, but it has aggressively used the "state secrets" doctrine to prevent innocent victims from suing to recover for torture used against them.

Compared to the Cold War era, much more information is now classified as secret or top secret, or covered by even more stringent "code word" protections. Moreover, secrecy begets higher levels of secrecy as government memo writers struggle to get attention for their individual missives by escalating levels of secrecy. For generations, expert bipartisan reports have found that there is too much secrecy. The reports have had little or no impact because it is far easier and less personally risky to classify than declassify. Secrecy is seductive; it has many powerful psychological lures. Too often the secrecy culture turns America into a democracy in the dark.

Nonetheless, curtailing excessive secrecy is made harder because, despite all its excesses, secrecy can also serve to defend safety and privacy, and thus liberty and freedom. Making change that requires drawing lines between legitimate and illegitimate secrets is obviously harder than just condemning excessive secrecy.

3

Appropriate Secrecy and Its Limits: 9/11, the Cuban Missile Crisis, and Where to Drop the First Atomic Bomb

9/11
Secrecy Without Thought

It is easy to forget that the 9/11 attacks did not come out of nowhere. In the summer of 2001, before the terrorist bombings, the CIA notified the White House of many warnings about a "spectacular" al-Qaeda attack. The best-known warning—the CIA's August 6, 2001, *President's Daily Brief*, or PDB, headlined "Bin Ladin [*sic*] Determined to Strike in US"—was actually more historical than current.[1] Indeed, its heading aside, it was not particularly menacing. But it should be viewed in the context of many other top-secret reports warning of al-Qaeda's current plans for "spectacular" and "calamitous" attacks. As CIA Director George Tenet later said, the "system was blinking red" with warnings about bin Laden's plans for attack in the months leading up to September 2001. According to the *9/11 Commission Report*, there were more than forty intelligence articles in the PDBs that related to bin Laden during the nine months between January and September 10, 2001.[2]

Before 9/11, the Bush administration circulated PDBs to just six people (down from fourteen during the Clinton administration).[3] Those who did *not* receive them included Attorney General John Ashcroft; FBI Director Louis Freeh; his successor, Robert Mueller; and White House counterterrorism chief Richard Clarke. While these officials and a few others did get somewhat less detailed Senior Executive Intelligence Briefs (SEIBs), which also had a drumbeat of reports on the bin Laden threat during the summer of 2001, many government officials with responsibilities for detecting and defending against terrorism received neither PDBs nor SEIBs.[4]

As the 9/11 Commission revealed, the PDBs, SEIBs, and other secret, limited-distribution documents, contained a series of dire predictions made by al-Qaeda. Something "very, very, very, very big was about to happen." "Al Qaeda members believed the upcoming attack would be 'spectacular,' qualitatively different from anything they had done to date." The attacks would result in "numerous casualties." Indeed, according to the commission, "the intelligence reporting consistently described the upcoming attacks as occurring on a calamitous level, indicating that they would cause the world to be in turmoil."[5] The Bush administration considered the threat information crucial and credible enough to share with foreign governments.[6]

The CIA's secret warnings were bolstered by Osama bin Laden's violently anti-American, and public, fatwas. In 1996, to protest American soldiers in Saudi Arabia, bin Laden publicly called for action against the "occupying U.S. enemy," assured youths they would "enter paradise" by killing Americans, and urged Muslims to fight jihad "with everything that would drive them out of the Islamic holy places." His second fatwa, in 1998, was shorter, broader, and bloodier. "To kill the Americans and their allies—civilians and military," he wrote, "is an individual duty for every Muslim who can do it in any country."[7] Moreover, al-Qaeda allies had already tried to destroy New York City's World Trade Center in 1993 by detonating a truck bomb in the North Tower garage. In 1998, a few months after bin Laden's second fatwa, al-Qaeda exploded massive truck bombs in simultaneous attacks on the U.S. embassies in Dar es Salaam, Tanzania, and Nairobi, Kenya, killing more than two hundred people. And in October 2000, al-Qaeda detonated an explosives-laden skiff alongside the USS *Cole*, killing seventeen American sailors in the port of Aden in Yemen.[8] Then came the chorus of top-secret CIA warnings in the summer of 2001.

The pre-9/11 warnings received by the White House were stamped top secret and shared only with the tiny group of high-level administration officials. The exclusivity of these high-level reports added to the CIA's prestige. And the recipients were proud to be part of an elite group of trusted high-level insiders. There is no evidence, or even a suggestion, that there was any deliberation about keeping the warnings hidden. Perhaps the White House thought the threats a distraction from its major foreign policy concerns. In any event, the White House did not inform rank-and-file government officials responsible for preventing terrorist attacks. And the American public remained in the dark. Might 9/11 have been prevented if the White House had circulated the gist of these warnings?

The increasingly dire threat information about al-Qaeda was kept secret from on-the-ground agents doing counterterrorism work. One was an FBI agent in Phoenix who warned in summer 2001 about the "possibility" of "a coordinated effort" by bin Laden to send students to aviation schools, noting the "inordinate number of individuals of investigative interest" in Arizona flight schools.[9] Another uninformed FBI agent, this one in Minneapolis, noted that Zacarias Moussaoui wanted to start his training by learning how to fly a Boeing 747, and concluded Moussaoui was an "Islamic extremist preparing for some future act in furtherance of fundamentalist goals."[10]

If the White House had been concerned enough to take the unusual step of disclosing top-secret threat warnings, the Phoenix and Minneapolis agents would have been taken more seriously, and the FBI presumably would have done more to avert 9/11. A San Diego flying-school instructor had a similar snippet of information when he observed two men—later identified as among the 9/11 hijackers—asking to start their flying lessons with sophisticated jet planes and taking no interest in takeoffs or landings.[11] Had all this flight-school information been put together, it should have led to action against 9/11 participants, particularly if the information was assessed against the background of a White House warning about serious threats. Indeed, according to the 9/11 Commission, "a maximum effort to investigate Moussaoui" alone might have "brought investigators to the core of the 9/11 plot."[12]

Many government officials had pieces of relevant information. Had they known the White House took the al-Qaeda threats seriously—seriously enough to release the essentials of top-secret warnings previously shown only to an elite few—it is reasonable to assume government officials would have thought harder and reacted more quickly. They might have—more likely would have—uncovered or prevented the plot. Moreover, as they had done to combat other threats, government officials could also have created a mock terrorist team to brainstorm possible "spectacular" attacks causing "numerous casualties."[13]

What about the public? What might citizens and expert analysts have done if they had been given the gist of the warnings? Even if no one within the government envisaged using huge airplanes loaded with over 11,000 gallons of fuel as suicide bombs—hardly a leap of genius requiring a once-in-a-century

Newton or Einstein—some smart citizen might have. After all, worldwide news had covered a 1994 Air France hijacking thwarted in Marseilles, in which a terrorist group demanded the jet be refueled with a suspicious amount of fuel and allowed to fly to Paris. An Associated Press report, reprinted nationwide at the time, opened with, "The plane would have been a flying bomb."[14] A CIA cable to British intelligence on August 24, 2001, described "suspicious 747 flight training" and characterized Moussaoui as a possible "suicide hijacker."[15] The data from the flying schools would have strongly suggested the possible use of passenger airplanes as huge suicide bombs.

The possibility of using airplanes as massive suicide bombs was not buried within bits of secret intelligence reports. In 1999, a U.S. customs official arrested a likely bin Laden supporter crossing into the United States with bomb-making material in the trunk of his car. (This followed—but apparently was not triggered by—the Clinton administration's decision to release warnings of threats of terrorist attacks in connection with the forthcoming millennium celebrations.) A newspaper story about the arrest reminded the country of the Air France hijacking and observed that the hijackers had "envisaged crashing an Air France jet into the Eiffel Tower."[16] It also was well known that in World War II, Japanese pilots had used (much smaller) planes loaded with explosives in "kamikaze" suicide dive-bombing attacks on U.S. naval vessels.

A thoughtful citizen or government employee could also have raised an alarm about the practice of keeping airplane cockpit doors unlocked. This would have seemed particularly sensible to anyone focused on using airplanes as huge suicide bombs, as opposed to hijacking planes to fly to some foreign destination or to hold passengers hostage to exchange for an al-Qaeda prisoner.[17]

To be fair, threats to the government come all the time and government cannot—and should not—publicly disclose every one. Promiscuous publicity about threats can be counterproductive: the repetitive use of color-coded levels of terror alerts in the run-up to the 2004 election is a good example. Repeated alerts could leave the public panicked, numbed, or cynical about political motivation. Publicizing threats could add to the prestige of the body behind the threats. Extended public discussion about threats conceivably could give terrorists new ideas. Also, sources should be protected: friendly foreign intelligence services, or spies and informers, or electronic surveillance. But as was the case with the August 2001 PDB when it was released, such references can be redacted.

Fairness, however, also requires recognition that in 2001 the repeated high-level warnings about the threat of a serious attack were neither transitory nor trivial, particularly in light of al-Qaeda's previous violent acts and bloody threats. Bin Laden's threats were sustained and serious.

All that was missing from the top-secret threat warnings circulating within top levels of government was the possible use of hijacked airplanes as weapons—as a hugely powerful suicide bomb—and even that actually had been mused about in bits of intelligence reports.[18] There was plenty of intelligence information about al-Qaeda's aims, but the big picture was known only by the White House and a handful of high-ranking government officials. The most important failure regarding the 9/11 attacks was not that intelligence agencies failed to share data with one another. Rather it was that the White House failed to share the big picture with *anyone*.

The issue is not simply whether the release of the secret threat predictions could have prevented 9/11. The concern is that without any real thought, and consistent with the secrecy culture, the predictions were kept in a tight cocoon of elite officials. Seduced by the prestige secrecy confers, these inner-circle officials did not consider disclosing the al-Qaeda threats to the public or sharing them with all relevant government officials. As is too often the case, after the threat information was stamped top secret and shown only to elite leaders, the elite leaders reflexively kept it secret.

We judge the White House's failure here with the benefit of hindsight. We now know the "chatter" was about an attack upon the United States itself. Before 9/11, no one *knew* this. But recognizing the possible distortion of hindsight does not immunize individuals such as President Bush and Vice President Cheney from criticism for their failure to share the threat information more widely.

The 9/11 Commission's report was an admirable piece of work; it was thorough, incisive, and well written. The commission correctly noted "the institutions charged with protecting our borders, civil aviation, and national security did not understand how grave [the] threat could be."[19] Similarly, as the commission said, "no one working on these late leads in the summer of 2001"—leads such as Phoenix and Moussaoui—"connected the case in his or her in-box to the threat reports agitating senior officials and being briefed to the President.

Thus, these individual cases did not become national priorities."[20] The commission also persuasively called attention to the harm done by one aspect of secrecy: the creation of "silos" or "stovepipes" where government agencies keep important information to themselves because they feel "they own the information they gathered at taxpayer expense." The commission called for fundamental change. Agencies should end their "'need-to-know' culture of information protection" and instead promote a "'need-to-share' culture of integration."[21]

All this was correct. But the commission failed to take aim at the more significant failure of the White House to disclose the serious and sustained threats. That was one reason for what the commission described as the failure of the institutions charged with protecting the nation to understand how grave the threat could be. Moreover, the agents working on the "late leads" had no possible way to connect the cases in their in-boxes to the "threat reports agitating senior officials" because those threat reports had been kept secret from the agents.

The commission's agency "stovepipe" metaphor was too narrow. In fact, the White House was responsible for keeping information secret that would have helped responsible agents and agencies understand "how grave the threat was." That information never made it out of the White House oven into the agency stovepipes—or more generally into public awareness.

The 9/11 Commission had waged a ferocious battle to get access to the August 6 PDB, and then to make it public. The commission had to struggle to get a glimpse at, or even a summary of, the many more pointed warnings that were available to the White House. The commission's battles over disclosure had been long and hard.[22] The commission focused on keeping its members unified without partisan fissures. Perhaps after waging its long battles, the commission felt it could not also take on the question of whether the serious and sustained pre-9/11 threat information should have been kept secret by the White House. But however understandable, the *9/11 Commission Report* would have been more complete, and more admirable, had it addressed that question.

The Cuban Missile Crisis: Endless Secrecy[23]

Nearly four decades before 9/11, President John F. Kennedy and his closest advisors wrestled with a crisis that brought the world as close as it has ever come to nuclear Armageddon. In October 1962, secret satellite photos revealed that the Soviet Union had snuck missiles and atomic warheads into Fidel Castro's Cuba, ninety miles south of Florida. After thirteen tense days, the Soviets backed down and removed the missiles and atomic warheads.

When the crisis was resolved, administration officials and the press highlighted JFK's toughness. But Kennedy administration insiders hid a secret deal with the Soviets: in exchange for removal of the Soviet missiles from Cuba, U.S. insiders agreed that after a few months it would remove its aging Jupiter nuclear missiles from Turkey, a few miles south of the Soviet Union. For decades, only the president, his brother Robert, and seven other advisors knew about this agreement. Even Vice President Lyndon Johnson and several other members of the executive committee who consulted with the Kennedys during the missile crisis were not told.

Did keeping the Turkish missile deal secret limit the American public's sophistication in considering how relations are managed with adversaries? Did the secrecy make it harder for President Johnson to compromise to end the Vietnam War after his martyred predecessor had been lionized for toughness? And did the secrecy contribute to Soviet leadership changes that led to a tougher line with the United States? This chapter presents reasons why the answer to all these questions is likely yes. But whatever the answers, the record shows that Kennedy insiders gave no thought to whether keeping the deal with the Soviets secret for years, indeed decades, *could* cause harm.

After the United States' discovery of the missiles in Cuba, President Kennedy created a small group of advisors known as EXCOMM (an ad-hoc Executive Committee of the National Security Council) to consult with him on how to respond. In its first days, EXCOMM kept secret the missiles' existence. This was sensible, because it let EXCOMM devise a plan without outside speculation and pressure, and before the Soviets realized the United States knew about the missiles. Kennedy kept his public schedule, including a previously scheduled meeting and black-tie ball for Soviet foreign minister Andrei Gromyko. During his conversation with Gromyko, Kennedy never mentioned the missiles; while guests attended the State Department ball, EXCOMM was meeting one floor below. So as not to risk breaching secrecy by having a fleet of limousines arrive at the White House to meet with the president, nine EXCOMM members crammed into Robert Kennedy's limo for the short ride over from the State Department. That night most of the group recommended Kennedy impose a blockade on future shipments to

Cuba. If necessary, the Navy would intercept, board, and inspect Soviet ships bound for Cuba.

But JFK did not immediately decide on a blockade. The Joint Chiefs of Staff, who were members of EXCOMM, were recommending air strikes to destroy the missiles. And before leaving for a campaign trip to the Midwest, Kennedy did not foreclose a military option, telling speechwriters to draft different versions of an address to the nation.[24] He would deliver the speech Monday, October 22.

Claiming an "upper respiratory infection," Kennedy cut short his campaign trip and returned to Washington on Saturday. The next day he settled on a blockade, which he described with a less bellicose term: "quarantine." The missiles' existence and the interim step of a quarantine became public when Kennedy made his seventeen-minute speech on Monday evening.

After the speech, for the remaining six days it took to resolve the crisis, EXCOMM (and sometimes smaller groups within it) continued to deliberate in secret. This was appropriate; secrecy allowed time for vigorous debate, thoughtful reflection, and consideration of a wide range of options. Short-term secrecy facilitated a prompt and peaceful resolution of a world-threatening crisis.

Exchanges with Nikita Khrushchev, the Soviet leader, and with his ambassador in Washington helped settle the crisis; these exchanges were made public, except for the last-minute deal to remove U.S. missiles from Turkey. On Friday, October 26, Khrushchev told Kennedy in a private letter that the Soviets would remove their missiles if the United States agreed not to attack Cuba. The crisis seemed on its way to resolution. However, the next day, Khrushchev broadcast on Radio Moscow another letter with a much tougher tone, including a demand that the United States pull *its* missiles out of Turkey. It was publicly understood at the time that Kennedy cleverly chose to ignore the tougher letter and to reply to and largely accept Khrushchev's first letter, that Khrushchev then agreed to remove the missiles (and Soviet airplanes) from Cuba, and that the missile crisis was resolved on Sunday, October 28.

What was not then known was that on the evening before the crisis ended, the president had his brother Robert make a secret visit to the Soviet ambassador in Washington, Anatoly Dobrynin. RFK told Dobrynin that without a resolution the United States would escalate its response. He also made clear that if the Soviets withdrew their nuclear missiles from Cuba, the United

States would shortly thereafter withdraw its land-based Jupiter nuclear missiles from Turkey—as it did some six months later. But the Soviets had to agree to keep that understanding secret.[25]

This swap was known to only nine people: the Kennedy brothers, Secretary of State Dean Rusk, Secretary of Defense Robert McNamara, National Security Advisor McGeorge Bundy, Ted Sorensen, and three others. After meeting in the Oval Office to hammer out the message for Dobrynin, the group "agreed without hesitation that no one not in the room was to be informed of this additional message [about the missiles in Turkey]."[26] The vice president, the Joint Chiefs of Staff, and several other members of EXCOMM were not informed. The men who did know kept silent for twenty years, until the surviving Oval Office participants jointly penned a letter in *Time* magazine describing lessons from the Cuban Missile Crisis. Even then, however, the participants stuck with the inaccurate assertion that the "private assurance" "could not be a 'deal.'"[27]

After the missile crisis was successfully resolved, President Kennedy was hailed as a hero in America and around the world. Virtually all contemporary accounts lionized Kennedy for his toughness in standing up to the Soviets, as have most later accounts. And toughness produced the most enduring metaphor of the crisis: Secretary of State Dean Rusk's boast at the time of the blockade that "we were eyeball to eyeball, and the other fellow just blinked."[28] *Time* praised JFK's "resolve" as "one of the decisive moments of the 20th century."[29] The *Chicago Tribune* (generally a strident opponent) praised JFK for having "thrust his jaw in a fighting attitude."[30] The *New Yorker*'s Richard Rovere stressed JFK's "steady nerves."[31] President Kennedy himself bragged to close friends that "I cut his balls off," referring to Soviet premier Khrushchev.[32]

The Saturday Evening Post ran a lengthy "exclusive, behind the scenes report" providing an "authoritative account of [EXCOMM's] top-secret sessions."[33] From start to finish, the article stressed JFK's toughness. "The other fellow just blinked" was on the magazine's cover. Those were also the first words of the article; and its ending was "a President's nerve is the essential factor when the two great nuclear powers are 'eyeball to eyeball.'" The article quoted an anonymous administration official who ridiculed UN ambassador Adlai Stevenson for proposing to "trade American missiles in Turkey, Italy and Great Britain" for Soviet missiles in Cuba.[34] Stevenson was said to have suggested a "Munich"—a reference to British prime minister Neville Chamberlain's 1938 Munich deal with Adolf Hitler to allow Germany to take over the German part of Czechoslovakia in the futile hope it would assure "peace in our time."

JFK was in fact tough, and for good reason. He made clear to the Soviets that the missiles must go. He stood up to American generals who wanted to bomb Cuba and its Russian facilities. But JFK was also flexible, and there was a serious problem with how JFK's resolve and toughness were described: accounts left out the secret deal with the Soviets. Administration officials also never revealed that the president had mused about a Turkey deal in EXCOMM meetings and was, according to Max Frankel's subsequent historical account (which uses the later release of transcripts of EXCOMM meetings), "the leading dove in the room."[35]

High-ranking Kennedy administration officials did more than conceal the deal with the Soviets. They lied about it. In testimony before an executive session of the Senate Foreign Relations Committee concerning the planned removal of U.S. missiles from Turkey, Rusk affirmed this was in no "way, shape or form, directly or indirectly connected with the settlement" of the missile crisis.[36] McNamara, also in executive session, said "absolutely not" to a question about a deal, adding that the Soviets raised the issue, but the "President absolutely refused to even discuss it."[37] National Security Advisor McGeorge Bundy announced on *Meet the Press* that there was no secret deal, arrangement, or promise.[38] As for President Kennedy, he told a reporter in 1963 that "I can tell you very flatly there were no commitments made that have not been discussed and revealed."[39]

Thus far, this amounts to a classic—but unusually important—case of high-level administration officials leaking information about secret negotiations that cast themselves in a favorable light, then dissembling about details they fear would cast them less favorably. The story is more complicated, however. There were both foreign policy and domestic political reasons for *initially* keeping the deal secret. From the foreign policy perspective, even though the land-based Jupiter missiles in Turkey were obsolete and soon to be replaced by more powerful, more accurate, and less exposed Polaris (submarine) missiles, there was concern that Turkey—and other allies—might doubt U.S. resolve to protect their interests when U.S. interests were threatened.

The emphasis on JFK's toughness also strengthened him politically—particularly after the Bay of Pigs invasion of Cuba had failed to overthrow Castro eighteen months earlier and the president had appeared weak in his subsequent meeting with Khrushchev in Vienna. Moreover, if the understanding with the Soviets was disclosed, hardline Republicans, including Barry Goldwater, a likely opponent of JFK's in the 1964 election, could attack. There is no record of these political points being discussed; they were obvious to the Kennedy insiders. In addition, "very privately," according to Dobrynin's later memoir, Robert Kennedy told Dobrynin that "some day—who knows?—he might run for president, and his prospects could be damaged if this secret deal about the missiles in Turkey were to come out."[40]

The political reasons for keeping the Turkey deal secret did not, however, justify secrecy after the resolution of the crisis. Perhaps the diplomatic reasons justified a short period of secrecy—particularly because, given the rapidity of the endgame, it would have been impossible to consult with the Turkish government to make explanations and arrangements before announcing the resolution. This, however, did not justify secrecy for any significant time. Which motive—political or diplomatic—was more important can be debated. The diplomatic risk was important at the moment of resolution. But as time passed and the surviving holders of the secret kept their Oval Office agreement that no one "not in the room" was to be informed, the political motive—protecting the Kennedy brothers' political plans, and their reputations after they were assassinated—became more important.

In addition to the covert deal that prompted repeated lies by senior administration officials, continued secrecy undermined the credibility of insider historians who were less than candid about the missile crisis's resolution. Ted Sorensen "confess[ed]" at a 1989 gathering in Moscow of missile crisis veterans from the United States, Russia, and Cuba that when he had used Robert Kennedy's diary to produce *Thirteen Days*—Kennedy's posthumous book about the Cuban Missile Crisis—the "diary was very explicit that [removing the Turkish missiles] was part of the deal." But when *Thirteen Days* was published in 1969 after RFK's assassination, the secret was known on the American side only to those who had met in the Oval Office before Robert Kennedy spoke with Soviet ambassador Dobrynin. "So," said Sorensen, "I took it upon myself to edit [the deal] out of his diaries."[41]

Far more important than less-than-independent journalism and sanitized histories was harm done to Americans' understanding of foreign policy. Continued secrecy about the Turkish deal with the Soviets deprived American citizens of information that would help the public better understand the subtleties of foreign policy. Resolving crises often depends on reaching understandings and compromises that avoid humiliating your adversary; diplomacy is usually not a simple eyeball-to-eyeball staring contest. The "triumphant myth" of no missile-crisis compromise is thought by some foreign policy experts to continue to harm U.S. foreign policy today.[42]

Secrecy about the Turkish deal also led many in Russia to conclude that Khrushchev and the Soviets had indeed been humiliated. Despite his bluster, Khrushchev was, for the time, a Kremlin moderate. Almost two years to the day after the missile crisis began, Khrushchev was ousted in a coup led by hardliner Leonid Brezhnev, who proceeded to escalate the arms race. Even McGeorge Bundy opined in a book written a quarter century later that keeping the Turkish understanding secret "may have had a role in his [Khrushchev's] forced retirement two years later."[43]

Some believe that keeping the deal secret tied Lyndon Johnson's hands in Vietnam, claiming that praise for the assassinated president's toughness limited LBJ's options.[44] This is unprovable and somewhat undermined by the fact that it *was* publicly known that JFK had made a deal not to invade Cuba. The psychology underlying Johnson's Vietnam decisions is also far too complex to permit any simple or singular explanation. Yet we do know that Johnson was haunted by the memory of his predecessor. While JFK's legacy may not have been the primary reason Johnson escalated the war, it is likely that the public impression of Kennedy's toughness with the Soviet Union was one factor in Johnson's desire to appear equally resolute.[45]

There is, moreover, substantial doubt as to whether Johnson himself was told about the Turkish deal even after becoming president. It is clear he had not been told when the deal was made.[46] But after JFK was assassinated, was Johnson told by those who did know and who later served in his administration, particularly Rusk, McNamara, and Bundy? There is no statement that any of the Oval Office group did tell him; their comments about knowledge continuing to be limited to those who met in the Oval Office were categorical at the time and were confirmed afterward.[47] Moreover, had they told Johnson, he could have exploited their lies. And it might have opened RFK, whom Johnson despised, to attacks from Johnson for being soft.

If Johnson was *not* told by his high-level advisors after he became president, that certainly was an extraordinary misuse of secrecy. Furthermore, it would prove that the long-lasting secrecy had not been for diplomatic reasons, but rather was for political reasons relating to the Kennedys.

Failing to weigh potential future harms resulting from keeping decisions secret is both easy and common. But wherever the balance would come out in any given case, the question of future harms resulting from lasting secrecy should at least be addressed. Usually it is not; and it was not here. Keeping the Turkey deal secret for so long is a classic example of just letting secrecy roll on when no justifiable reason for continued secrecy exists. In any event, the truth usually comes out, as it did many years after the missile crisis. Each time a government lie is exposed, each time the public learns it was misled so secrets could be preserved, public trust in government erodes and cynicism about government leaders grows. Again, this reinforces the larger lesson that secrecy itself makes it too easy to avoid considering the long-term problems that secrecy can cause.

Where to Drop the First Atomic Bomb: The Insularity of Necessary Secrecy

When a tiny group of officials secretly decided to drop the first atomic bomb on a densely populated Japanese city, the decision was appropriately kept secret, as are many other military decisions. But secrecy allowed the officials to avoid outside pressure to revisit their decision, challenge their preconceptions, or take account of changing facts after the initial plan was put in place. While whether to unleash the awesome power of the bomb at all is beyond the scope of this book, secrecy thus reinforced the limitations of the secret internal decision-making process.

Around the time of Germany's surrender on May 8, 1945, American officials concluded that an atomic bomb might be ready to use against Japan in the foreseeable future. They then began to consider where to drop the bomb. On May 31, 1945, Secretary of War Henry Stimson convened a secret meeting of an "Interim Committee" of high-level presidential advisors aided by four leading scientists working on the Manhattan Project—the code name for the massive project to build a bomb.[48] Their task was to consider a wide range of momentous subjects: a review of likely future scientific developments; the power of bombs then being worked on, as well as future bombs; transparency in future fundamental research; how to deal with Russia; and the future "International Program" for the bomb.[49] After the subject arose at lunch, the committee briefly turned to the anticipated "effect of the bombing on the Japanese" and discussion of targeting. According to the then-top-secret notes from the meeting, the committee concluded that while "we could not concentrate on a civilian area . . . we should seek to make a profound psychological impression on as many of the inhabitants as possible." Finally, "at the suggestion of Dr. [James] Conant, [chairman of the National Defense Research Committee and president of Harvard University], the Secretary [Stimson] agreed that the most desirable target would be a vital war plant employing a large number of workers and closely surrounded by workers' houses." The Japanese, the officials agreed, should not be given "any warning."[50]

On the next day, the committee reconvened.[51] Again, according to its top-secret notes, most of its discussion was on other topics. When the committee reached the question of where to use the first bomb, James Byrnes (the personal representative of President Truman and later his first secretary of state) recommended, and the committee agreed, that while "the final selection of the target was essentially a military decision, the present view of the Committee was that the bomb should be used against Japan as soon as possible; that it be used on a war plant surrounded by workers' homes; and that it be used without prior warning."[52]

A few months after the end of the war, Secretary Stimson, aided by McGeorge Bundy, wrote an article in *Harper's* titled "The Decision to Use the Atomic Bomb," in which Stimson said "the conclusions of the committee were similar to my own," although noting that he had "ultimate responsibility." Stimson added that his belief was, in order to induce surrender, the Japanese "must be administered a tremendous shock."[53] Stimson's article left out the fact that just before the Interim Committee met and briefly discussed targeting, Gen. George Marshall, Army Chief of Staff, had recommended to Stimson that the first target should be a "straight military" target "such as a large naval installation."[54]

Shortly after the committee's meetings, in a letter requested by the committee from the group of four scientists who comprised the committee's Scientific Panel, J. Robert Oppenheimer and his three colleagues commented on the "initial use of the new weapon."[55] The scientists noted that the opinions of other scientists knowledgeable about the Manhattan Project were "not unanimous." Some urged a "purely technical demonstration," stressing that use in the war would "prejudic[e]" America's position in future talks to "outlaw the use of atomic weapons." Others emphasized "the opportunity of saving American lives by immediate military use." Oppenheimer and his three colleagues were "closer to these latter views" because "we can propose no technical demonstration likely to bring an end to the war; we see no acceptable alternative to direct military use."[56] Secretary Stimson's *Harper's* article quoted the relevant paragraphs of this letter in full. Oppenheimer did not explain, nor was he apparently ever asked, what he and his colleagues meant by "direct military use."

After the Interim Committee's June 1 meeting, its "present view" was never revisited. All the many unsettled issues underlying the committee's vague principles were left unexamined. Indeed, all that survived were the "no warning" and "profound psychological impression" parts. Instead, attention turned to a secret military Target Committee controlled by Gen. Leslie Groves, the director of the Manhattan Project. Being in charge of the largest and most secret weapons program in history, producing the bomb that fulfilled the hope to end the war, Groves was not prone to second thoughts or self-doubt. He was delegated substantial authority to pick the specific targets to hit with the bomb.[57] In fact, before the Interim Committee met, Groves's group had already started its work and was focusing on targeting densely populated cities.[58] With the exception of Secretary Stimson ruling out an attack on Kyoto, Groves made the specific targeting decisions.[59] Revealingly, General Groves's autobiography does not contain even a single reference to the Interim Committee's views on targeting.[60]

As a fig leaf, the chosen target cities had to have *some* military importance. But clearly the main aim, as Stimson's Interim Committee and Stimson himself said, was to produce a "profound psychological impression" and a "tremendous shock."[61] Similarly, in his 1962 book describing how he approached target selection, General Groves said, "I had set as the governing factor" that the targets should be places "the bombing of which would most adversely affect the will of the Japanese people to continue the war."[62] This supported the use of the bomb to cause the vast killing of civilians in densely packed population centers. Indeed, early work by Groves's target committee had put Kyoto first on the target list because "from the psychological point of view, there is the advantage that Kyoto is an intellectual center for Japan and the people there are more apt to appreciate the significance" of the bomb. There was no mention of any military significance in this first proposal to bomb Kyoto.[63]

After the decision was made to start by dropping the bomb on crowded cities, but before the bomb was actually dropped on two crowded cities, the facts changed. The bomb was found to be far more powerful than expected, and there would be more bombs available. In the early morning of July 16,

1945, an atomic bomb was successfully tested in the New Mexico desert. Groves told Stimson that the power of the test explosion, code-named Trinity, "far exceeded the most optimistic expectations and wildest hopes of the scientists." Its flash was visible for some 250 miles, and the sound carried for some 50 miles.[64] A half mile away, the blast tore a forty-ton, six-story tower "from its foundations, twisted it, [and] ripped it apart." At that distance, "permanent steel and masonry buildings would have been destroyed. . . . None of us had expected [the tower] to be damaged."[65] As Stimson recorded in his diary, the test "revealed far greater destructive power than we expected."[66] Then another change occurred: production sped up. By the time the bombs were dropped on Japan in early August, more bombs were on schedule to be available.[67] This addressed Stimson's concern—expressed in his *Harper's* article—that "we had no bombs to waste."[68]

Yet despite the test bomb's surprising destructive power and the accelerated schedule of bomb availability, the secret early decision to start the nuclear attack by bombing crowded Japanese cities was never revisited. Knowing that the power of the bomb "far exceeded the most optimistic expectations" and that there were more bombs, might Truman's advisors have changed their minds and started with a predominantly military target in Japan if they had continued to focus after their June 1 decision—which had, after all, only been characterized as their "present view"? In a group of some of the nation's most astute policy minds and some of the nation's top scientists, not one person seems to have thought to reexamine earlier conclusions in light of new evidence.

On August 6, 1945, the first bomb exploded over Hiroshima. The second bomb hit Nagasaki three days later. Both cities had *some* military importance.[69] But the primary effect—and the clear aim—was to incinerate civilians and their homes in order to cause the maximum "shock," make a "profound psychological impression," and "affect the will of the Japanese people." Indeed, while Hiroshima had generally been approved as a target by Secretary Stimson, General Groves's specific decision was to drop the bomb on the middle of Hiroshima's population center. This, he concluded, was the best way to get data on how widespread the destructive power of the new weapon would be. This secret decision by Groves was not shared with even the tiny group of civilian government officials who were ultimately responsible for the bomb's use. One consequence of Groves's targeting decision was that most of the military/industrial facilities located on Hiroshima's outskirts were *not* destroyed, while more than 100,000 people were killed—more than 60,000 immediately, and the rest from radiation and other aftereffects.[70]

Use of the atomic bomb was earth-shattering. The Japanese effectively surrendered the day after Nagasaki, with the formal surrender on August 15, 1945. While World War II would have been won without the bomb, using the bomb did, according to most historians, accelerate the war's end.[71] It is clear, however, that even though those making the decision on where first to drop the bomb were all smart and sophisticated, their secret decision-making process was neither thoughtful nor extensive. None of the civilian decision-makers continued to focus on where to drop the first bomb even after the facts changed. Secrecy, while appropriate, shielded them from advice and criticism, and foreclosed possible changes in response.

Perhaps our greater knowledge of just how devastating the bomb turned out to be makes unfair the suggestion that the decision-makers should have considered a first attack on a predominately military target. Moreover, the earlier firebombing of Tokyo (and Dresden, Germany) had caused huge civilian casualties. Indeed, Gen. Curtis LeMay boasted that "we scorched and boiled and baked to death more people in Tokyo" than, he claimed, were killed at Hiroshima and Nagasaki combined.[72] Perhaps this had desensitized some officials to the massive killing of civilians.[73] Furthermore, the Japanese did not immediately surrender after the bomb was dropped on Hiroshima. Still, the United States would have been on higher moral ground if it had started with a predominantly military target, coupled with a demand for prompt surrender, and only escalated if the demand were not accepted.

While President Truman was not involved in choosing the targets, he did approve them. He had been told by the time of the July 1945 Potsdam Conference with Joseph Stalin and Winston Churchill that the bomb "might be so powerful as to be potentially capable of wiping out entire cities and killing people on an unprecedented scale."[74] Truman's July 25 diary says he told Stimson "to use [the bomb] so that military objectives and soldiers and sailors are the target and not women and children."[75] In the diary, Truman also described the bomb as "the most terrible bomb in the history of the world," adding that as "the leader of the world for the common welfare," America could not go beyond a "purely military" target, even though "the Japs are savages, ruthless, merciless and fanatic."[76] In *Danger and Survival*, McGeorge Bundy referred to the diary as a bit of "self-deception." David McCullough's largely adoring biography of Truman is milder in the words but consistent in the thought—saying Truman wrote the diary "as if to convince himself" the bomb would be used on military targets only, "which he knew to be only partly true."[77]

In fact, Truman knew the bomb would kill many civilians, including women and children. But a broader point should be made than an aside about Truman's self-deception. Assuming Truman did say something about military objectives—even if not precisely what he wrote in his diary—it is revealing that his concerns did not trigger further analysis about whether it was necessary and proper to start by dropping the bomb on a densely populated city.

As with so many secrets and secretive decision-making, no one revisited the question about where to drop the first bomb even after the facts changed. Thus the initial targets remained unaltered despite the surprisingly awesome power of the bomb and the availability of more bombs. Indeed, it is remarkable how little analysis, give and take, discussion or debate there was. Ideas were put forward but not explored. What had Marshall meant by starting with a "straight military" target? What had Conant and then the Interim Committee intended by proposing "use on a war plant surrounded by workers' houses"? What had Oppenheimer meant by "direct military use"?

And how could the detailed targeting of the selected cities be delegated to Groves? To be sure, Stimson and Truman had more to think about than the targets. Stimson may also have been exhausted. So Groves became the real decision-maker. Looking back, Groves characterized Truman's role as "one of noninterference—basically, a decision not to upset the existing plans."[78] And as Groves saw it, Stimson's only role in targeting was to veto Kyoto. Groves was a hero for getting the bomb built. But it was a huge mistake to let him choose where to drop the first bomb. He was a bomb builder, not a policy person. One of his criteria for the first target was that the city should be big: "of such size that the damage would be confined within it, so that we could more definitely determine the power of the bomb."[79] Determining the "power of the bomb" is an aim for a bomb maker or a scientist. It is not a criterion for a policy maker secretly deciding how the nation should act in wartime or, more important, how to use a weapon of unprecedented force that would fundamentally change the world.

Rigid compartmentalization had proved effective in protecting the secrecy of building the bomb. As Groves's biographer says, it also was the "method by which [Groves] consolidated his own substantial power and control."[80] But the propriety of secrecy in one sphere does not automatically translate to propriety in other spheres. Assuming it was, on balance, appropriate to use compartmentalization to give one person such great power and control in bomb-*building*, the justifications do not apply to giving one person— particularly the same person—so much secret power and control in making policy decisions on bomb-*dropping*.

Unfortunately all the key figures had become accustomed to the secret process used for building the bomb. They failed to think about whether a similar process should be used to decide where to drop it, a question that deserved a much more thoughtful and continuing process of debate and discussion.

Groves and Stimson continued to evade the issues after the war was over. Speaking fifteen months after the bomb was dropped, Groves said he had "been asked if a demonstration of the power of the bomb on some barren island would not have been enough to cause Japan to capitulate and thus avoid the bombing of her cities." His answer was "[e]mphatically no." The Japanese reaction "would have been to discount our determination to force them into submission as quickly as possible. They would have interpreted our failure to use the bomb [in the field of battle] as a sign of weakness."[81] But Groves's speech attacked a straw man. Surely, there was middle ground between a "barren island" and the center of a densely populated city. Dropping the bomb on a predominantly military target in Japan, followed by use against her cities if the Japanese did not quickly surrender, would hardly have been a "failure to use the bomb." Two months later, in his *Harper's* article, Secretary Stimson also derided the idea of a "demonstration in some uninhabited area." This, he said, was "not regarded as likely to be effective in compelling a surrender of Japan" and was thought to be "damaging to our effort to obtain surrender" if the demonstration turned out to be "a dud."[82] Both points seem correct. But Stimson's article again assaulted a straw man, referring to an "uninhabited area" but ignoring the possibility of starting by bombing a predominantly military target in Japan.

Groves's and Stimson's straw-man arguments were misdirected and defensive. But the main point here is that when a decision has been made secretly about a momentous future action, it is particularly important for the few knowledgeable insiders to continue to revisit their thinking and to consider whether changed circumstances should alter an earlier decision. In contrast, when a plan for important future actions has been made public, incisive and informative comments from outsiders can cause insiders to reevaluate their initial views. Not so when the initial decision is kept secret, known only to a handful. And when—as with the decision on where to drop the first atomic bomb—the decision itself is too sensitive to be made public, it is essential that holders of the secret remember to continue to review, to analyze, to weigh competing alternatives and new facts, and continue to ask hard questions. Nobody did any of this before the fateful dropping of the first atomic bomb in the middle of a crowded city.

4

Building Power Through Secrecy:
J. Edgar Hoover and Dick Cheney

For nine decades, from 1919 until 2009, J. Edgar Hoover and Dick Cheney were central to America's secrecy culture. Hoover and Cheney's combined careers spanned the "Red Scare" after World War I, World War II, the atomic bomb, the Cold War, loyalty programs, proliferation and escalation of classification, the civil-rights movement, the Vietnam War, Watergate, Iran-Contra, the Gulf War, 9/11, and the Iraq and Afghanistan Wars, coupled with secret snooping, suppression of dissent, warrantless wiretapping, and torture. Hoover and Cheney reshaped American government and American life. Their stories illustrate secrecy's ties to power, its lures, and its capacity to harm the nation.

Hoover was named director of the FBI in 1924, when he was only twenty-nine. For nearly half a century until his death in 1972, Hoover ruled the Bureau, serving with eight presidents and seventeen attorneys general. Three years after Hoover's death, Cheney became President Gerald Ford's chief of staff, at thirty-four the youngest in history. Cheney went on to serve for ten years as Wyoming's lone member of the House of Representatives before becoming secretary of defense in George H.W. Bush's administration. Then, after an eight-year hiatus in the oil industry, Cheney joined George W. Bush and became the most powerful vice president in American history.

Hoover sought to enhance the power of the FBI, Cheney the power of the presidency. Both initially recognized, or said they recognized, the value of restraints. Then, at the height of their power, each became an apostle of unchecked authority and excessive secrecy.

Hoover used the FBI's secret power to break the law, suppress dissent, cow lawmakers, and manipulate presidents. As vice president, Cheney favored a decision-making process where he and President Bush talked alone, or where the president heard only from a tiny coterie of like-minded colleagues. Vice President Cheney fought to keep key decisions secret from most of the executive branch, Congress, and the public.

Hoover and Cheney were master manipulators of information. They spoon-fed to the press secret information supporting their positions. They concealed contrary information, denying the public the opportunity to fulfill its role as "the primary control on the government."[1] To win their way, they selectively leaked information, including classified information, sometimes simply to embarrass opponents. Both defended secrecy as necessary to protect sources and methods, which is a legitimate claim but which also can be abused, as when Hoover manipulated the Kennedy brothers into letting him wiretap Martin Luther King Jr.

Hoover and Cheney both yearned for a time without meaningful checks and balances. Hoover also pined for the insular, homogenous America in which he grew up. No uppity blacks. No student dissent. No women's liberation movement. No sexual revolution. And no congressional or media prying into FBI snooping or law-breaking. Cheney's nostalgic gaze wandered back even further, all the way to seventeenth-century England. Consider this nugget buried in Cheney's dissent from the 1987 congressional report on Iran-Contra: America's "Chief Executive will on occasion feel duty bound to assert *monarchical* notions of prerogative that will permit him to exceed the law."[2] As vice president, Cheney relied on this "monarchical" theory of our Constitution, to justify, for example, secret illegal torture and warrantless wiretapping.[3]

J. Edgar Hoover[4]

In 1924, J. Edgar Hoover sought the job of FBI director from Calvin Coolidge's new attorney general, Harlan Fiske Stone, former dean of Columbia Law School and a future Supreme Court Justice. Though later described as "untouchable" in David Halberstam's book *The Fifties*,[5] the younger Hoover had to plead his case by groveling before Roger Baldwin, the founder and head of the American Civil Liberties Union. Hoover assured Baldwin that as chief of the Justice Department's General Intelligence Division (known as the Radical Division), he had played only an "unwilling part" in the aggressive tactics used in the Palmer Raids. Named for A. Mitchell Palmer, Woodrow Wilson's second attorney general, these dragnet raids led to the deportation of many "radical" immigrants after "[i]ndiscriminate arrests of the innocent with the guilty" and "unlawful searches and seizures by federal detectives."[6]

Based on Hoover's assurances, Baldwin wrote Stone, "I think we were wrong in our estimate of his attitude."[7] But as secret government files later revealed, Hoover was hardly an unwilling participant in the raids. In fact, he prepared them. Moreover, Hoover claimed detainees should not have lawyers because it "defeats the ends of justice." He further argued that no evidence of guilt was required to hold detainees, because evidence might turn up later "in other sections of the country."[8]

So, to leap over an early hurdle to his promotion, Hoover was able to lie by hiding behind secret government files. Stone appointed Hoover to direct the FBI, but instructed him that the Bureau ought not be "concerned with political or other opinions of individuals [but only] with their conduct and then only with such conduct as is forbidden by the laws of the United States" because "a secret police may become a menace to free government and free institutions."[9] For many years, despite continuing secret investigations of law-abiding institutions like the ACLU, Hoover parroted Stone by saying—to his superiors—that the FBI should be restrained and show respect for civil liberties. Indeed, almost a decade after his appointment, Hoover told a new attorney general that because the Bureau was subject to "the closest scrutiny," it should not investigate matters that "from a federal standpoint, have not been declared illegal." To open the door to broader investigations would subject the Bureau to charges of "secret and undesirable methods."[10]

But then, in 1938, Franklin Roosevelt covertly opened the door to the expansion of secret and undesirable methods by expanding the Bureau's investigative authority to include the amorphous term "subversion." From this buried seed, Hoover's power grew and grew. Hoover's power was fueled by the fear stemming from the Cold War and concerns about Communist infiltration. By the mid-1950s, the FBI had become more an intelligence operation than a law-enforcement agency. This had enormous advantages: more secrets, more secrecy, more power, and less accountability. Heading an intelligence agency also gave Hoover more opportunities to shape national policy. And Hoover's bin of intelligence secrets—including the peccadilloes of the powerful— helped make him untouchable.

The public gave Hoover a free ride. So did Congress, the White House, and the Justice Department. This came partly out of love, partly out of fear, and partly from the secret enabling of Hoover by his bosses. The love part did not lie in a secret nest. It was hatched by a carefully orchestrated publicity campaign that touted the Bureau's mastery of crime, with Hoover always portrayed as the relentless, fearless, and pugnacious pursuer of individual criminals—even though he did not make a single arrest in his first decade on the job, and later staged his personal role in apprehending criminals.[11]

The fear and the enabling of Hoover's FBI *did* depend upon secrets and secrecy. The FBI's massive covert intelligence-gathering reached public figures, all of whom knew Hoover had a trove of secrets. Many, perhaps most, feared he had tucked away pieces of their own dirty linen. Hoover built this fear by feeding gossip to friendly reporters, such as Walter Winchell, the most powerful gossip columnist of the day, whose daily newspaper column and Sunday radio broadcast reached millions.[12] Aiming at American activists, Hoover similarly instructed FBI agents to "enhance the paranoia . . . and get the point across that there is an FBI agent behind every mailbox."[13]

The movie *The Lives of Others*, which portrays the East German secret police (the Stasi), dramatizes how the Stasi's motto—"To Know Everything"— led to tyranny. Supreme Court Justice Robert Jackson forecast a similarly tyrannical outcome when he warned that a national police with "enough on enough people, even if it does not elect to prosecute them . . . will find no opposition to its policies. Even those who are supposed to supervise it are likely to fear it."[14] And so it was with the FBI.

After Franklin Roosevelt, who opened the door to FBI investigations into "subversives," became Hoover's first enabler, Herbert Brownell, Eisenhower's attorney general, added to Hoover's power by secretly permitting Hoover to use bugs on his own authority. Moreover, for decades, during the administrations of many presidents, the White House accepted, and sometimes requested, political information and gossip—often salacious gossip—that Hoover happily shoveled over.[15] Naughty nuggets helped empower Hoover.

Hoover frequently used secret information to influence public figures. It took two scholars thirteen years and two lawsuits to obtain FBI materials they characterized as "J. Edgar Hoover's Secret Supreme Court Sex Files." These included a file on Supreme Court Justice Abe Fortas, an occasional FBI informant who had revealed internal discussions among the Justices about "an electronic surveillance case of special importance to FBI Director Hoover."[16]

Another informant alleged "possible homosexual activities on the part of Justice Abe Fortas."[17] Hoover's deputies urged sending the report to Attorney General Ramsey Clark. But Hoover (who "despised" Clark) told his close aide Cartha ("Deke") DeLoach to "see Fortas." When he did, Fortas denied the accusation, and asked that "his thanks be extended to the Director for having handled the matter in this manner."[18]

Scholars generally assume the Fortas accusation was false. Hoover's manner in handling the matter nonetheless gave him sway over the Justice. Hoover often told public figures like Fortas that he had highly embarrassing material about them; don't worry, Hoover assured the officials, the director could be trusted to handle delicate material with discretion. Yet Hoover's making points with a Supreme Court Justice by revealing he had embarrassing but probably untrue information pales in significance to his pressuring the president of the United States by revealing he had devastatingly harmful, and true, information about the president himself.

To pressure President Kennedy and his brother, in February 1962 Hoover wrote Attorney General Robert Kennedy and Kenneth O'Donnell, the president's special assistant, noting the White House had had numerous telephone conversations with Judith Campbell, a mistress of Sam "Momo" Giancana, the Chicago Mafia boss.[19] Campbell, who was herself being wiretapped, even called the White House once from Giancana's tapped phone.[20] After his letter, Hoover had lunch with the president; a few hours later, Kennedy placed a call to Campbell's number—the last of seventy calls between the White House and Campbell's number.[21]

Judith Campbell (later known as Judith Exner) was not just any woman. She was one of President Kennedy's mistresses, having been introduced to JFK by Frank Sinatra. Given Hoover's knowledge of this particularly explosive presidential relationship—one of many dangerous JFK liaisons of which Hoover had knowledge, at least one known to Hoover based on bugs in rooms of assignations—the Kennedy brothers, Hoover's only superiors, had little leverage to control, let alone replace him.[22]

Under these circumstances, Hoover at the same time pressured Robert Kennedy to approve wiretaps of one of Martin Luther King Jr.'s closest advisors.[23] In the years after Dr. King vaulted into national importance during the 1955–56 Montgomery bus boycott, the FBI had shown only desultory interest in the civil rights leader. However, after King criticized the FBI for lax civil-rights enforcement in November 1961, Hoover became obsessed with King, and sought approval for wiretaps, beginning when he wrote Attorney General Kennedy a letter characterizing Stanley Levison, a close advisor to King, as "a member of the Communist Party, USA."[24] Three months after his first letter, Hoover sent Robert Kennedy another memo. This time Levison was said to be "a *secret* member of the Communist Party."[25]

Kennedy administration officials, including the president himself, told King about Hoover's allegations. President Kennedy warned King in the White House Rose Garden that Levison was a Communist, adding King could "lose [his] cause" because of loyalty to a friend. The president also told King he was under tight surveillance. When King questioned the Levison accusation and demanded proof, the president said he would arrange for that.[26]

No proof was forthcoming. Instead, the FBI accusations escalated. Burke Marshall, assistant attorney general for civil rights, told King's colleague Andrew Young that the Bureau claimed Levison was a "Rudolf Abel"—a Soviet spy smuggled into the United States who had spent twenty years providing U.S. secrets to the Soviets.[27] But Hoover did not supply the Kennedys with support for the claim that Levison was a Communist, much less a secret member of the party, or a Russian spy. Hoover insisted there be no disclosure that could jeopardize a secret source. Neither Hoover's nominal boss, Robert Kennedy, nor the president, nor any other administration official demanded details or challenged the implicit notion that neither the president nor the attorney general could be trusted with details.

Reporting later revealed that the Bureau's Levison information dated from the 1950s, long before Levison became a major advisor—indeed the closest white advisor—to King. The Bureau had no proof Levison was a current member of the Party—secret or otherwise—but told the Kennedys he was. The FBI's information was drawn from a source called "Solo"—actually a fraternal duo of Party officials turned informants, Jack and Morris Childs. Through them, the FBI was told that, starting in the mid-1940s, Levison had been a financial benefactor of the Party and from 1953 to 1955 had assisted Party chiefs in managing the Party's secret funds. But at some point in 1955, "Levison's central role in secret CP financial dealings declined greatly."[28]

When Levison terminated his "direct dealings" with the Party, "the CP hierarchy was very unhappy about Levison's loss of interest," according to Jack Childs. The FBI removed Levison from its "key figure" list of Communists, and then unsuccessfully attempted to recruit him as an informant.[29] From that time forward, Hoover was uninterested in Levison until he discovered he was King's close advisor.

As for the claim that providing details would expose their source, there would have been no risk if the FBI had simply provided an honest chronology. To do so would not require using the informants' names. Conceivably, if the nature of the dated information provided by Solo had become public, it might have led a knowledgeable member of the Communist Party's inner circle to guess a Childs brother had been talking. But the precise information could have been masked. To be fair with its use of secrets, moreover, the Bureau should also have said that, at the very time Hoover was pushing for wiretaps, Hoover had "scrambled" to find more current evidence against Levison. But his agents found the opposite. The FBI's New York office told headquarters they had "interviewed their best fourteen informants, only to find that not a single one recognized Levison's name or photograph." The agents told Hoover it was useless.[30] The Kennedy team was told not a word of this more contemporary information.

Eventually, Robert Kennedy approved taps, starting with Levison in March 1962, and later adding King, the Southern Christian Leadership Conference, and others.[31] Along with its wiretapping, the Bureau also began bugging King in 1963, including bugging hotel rooms used by King in his travels.[32] Seeming to forget about Levison's influence on King, the Bureau instead used the product of those hotel bugs to try to covertly undermine King's moral authority.[33] But operating in a very different media culture from today, the Bureau failed in its efforts to get publicity for the salacious secret information it peddled to the media.

Notwithstanding all the transcripts of thousands of hours of electronic surveillance of King, Levison, Clarence Jones (Dr. King's lawyer and speechwriter)[34] and the SCLC, the Bureau never came forward with anything on its miles of tapes to show Levison was serving any interest other than the civil rights movement and Dr. King.[35]

What led the Kennedy brothers to approve the wiretaps? Neither was known for passivity, nor were they easily intimidated. How could these activist leaders, known for quizzing their subordinates, choose not to push for details? The usual explanation is they were concerned about the fate of pending civil rights legislation if King were exposed as tied to a Communist. According to King, the president, in a Rose Garden talk, referred to the administration's pending civil rights bill and said if "they shoot *you* down, they'll shoot us down too."[36] But this concern, if anything, should have led the Kennedys to insist on more details about the accusations.

A better explanation for the Kennedys' passivity lies in Hoover's knowledge of JFK's numerous liaisons, especially the one with the Mafia boss's mistress.

As the Church Committee later learned from the FBI's secret files, the FBI went beyond taps and bugs to undertake sustained and malignant efforts to destroy Dr. King.[37] According to the Bureau, King was the nation's "most dangerous and effective Negro leader," as shown by his "powerful demagogic speech"—a speech we today treasure as the "I Have a Dream" speech delivered at the August 1963 March on Washington. Dr. King had to be destroyed because he was a potential "messiah" who could "unify and electrify" the "black nationalist movement."[38] King was dangerous because he might "abandon his supposed 'obedience' to white liberal doctrines (non-violence)."[39] So, in Hoover's topsy-turvy secret world, a fervent apostle of nonviolence had to be secretly attacked and destroyed as insurance against the possibility he might abandon his core philosophy of nonviolence.

As part of its effort to destroy Dr. King, the Bureau sent him a composite tape recording from bugs placed in his hotel rooms. The tape contained intimate encounters and came with an anonymous letter to King that said, "You know you are a complete fraud . . . an evil, vicious one at that . . . your end is approaching." It concluded:

> King, there is only one thing left for you to do. You know what it is . . .
> You are done. There is but one way out for you. You better take it before
> your filthy, fraudulent self is bared to the nation.

Dr. King and his associates interpreted the letter as an attempt to induce him to commit suicide.[40]

Hoover's effort to shape public life extended beyond vendettas directed at King and many less prominent Americans. Hoover also selectively supplied politicians with inaccurate secret intelligence information designed to influence debate on important national issues, such as civil rights and the Vietnam War. On civil rights, the Bureau never found any evidence to rebut its initial conclusion, based on secret infiltration of the NAACP, that Communists had *not* subverted or even influenced civil-rights groups.[41] Nonetheless, Hoover hinted to the White House in 1956 that Communist organizations were to blame for "a marked deterioration in relationships between the races." According to one historian, Hoover's briefing of Eisenhower's cabinet on alleged Communist influence on civil-rights groups "reinforced Eisenhower's inclination to passivity" on civil-rights legislation.[42] Later, in 1963, when Hoover received a memo from his Intelligence Division on failed Communist efforts to exploit black discontent, he made clear "we had to change our ways or we would all be out on the street." The division generated a new memo: "The Director is correct." King was the "most dangerous Negro" from the "standpoint of communism . . . and national security." It was "unrealistic" to limit FBI analysis to "legalistic proofs or definitely conclusive evidence." Communist influence over Negroes "one day *could* become decisive." Yet even this was not Hoover's message in subsequent testimony to Congress, where he represented that Communist influence among Negroes and civil-rights organizations *was* "vitally important."[43]

Hoover made equally misleading comments about the Vietnam War. When President Johnson told Hoover in 1965 he had "no doubt" Communists were behind anti–Vietnam War demonstrations, Hoover said he agreed. Then, back at the FBI, Hoover told his associates that while the Bureau might not be able to "technically state" what the president wanted, the director demanded— and got—a "good, strong memorandum" that made Communist "efforts" read like Communist successes.[44]

Hoover disliked Clark Kerr, the chancellor of the University of California system, for his opposition to FBI surveillance of students. When Johnson was considering Kerr for secretary of health, education and welfare, Hoover's background report included allegations that Kerr was "pro-communist" and had employed two women who were dismissed for security reasons. However, Hoover failed to note that FBI agents had learned that the supposed source of the pro-Communist remark denied it, and the agents had also found the dismissal charges were untrue.[45] Similarly, the FBI gave an anti-Kerr university regent a memo about faculty involved in the Berkeley Free Speech Movement (FSM), that featured immunology professor Leon Wofsy saying Wofsy had been a Communist. The memo left out that there was no evidence Wofsy had been involved with the Party since 1956 or influenced the FSM.[46] Based upon such evidence, federal courts later ruled FBI files relating to Kerr and the FSM had no immunity under FOIA because the FBI's aim was to "harass political opponents of the FBI's allies among the regents, not to investigate subversion and civil disorder."[47]

As the Church Committee revealed, the Supreme Court's interpretation of the First Amendment's guarantees of freedom of speech and assembly frustrated the FBI by making, according to the Bureau, criminal prosecution of Communist Party members "ineffective" or "impossible." Hoover's response was to take the law into his own hands. In 1956, the Bureau launched a secret program called COINTELPRO (or Counter Intelligence Program) that relied on tactics better suited to a police state than to the United States. With COINTELPRO, the Bureau went beyond excessive intelligence gathering to launch covert actions designed to "harass and destroy" organizations and individuals. A few members of Congress and executive-branch officials were given obscure hints of its existence—but not a whisper of its tactics or its breadth. The public had no knowledge.[48]

In fact, COINTELPRO had nothing to do with "counterintelligence." Rather, the Bureau disrupted groups and secretly meted out punishments to law-abiding citizens. COINTELPRO lasted from 1956 until April 1971 when Hoover suspended it because he feared public exposure.[49]

COINTELPRO began by seeking to harass and destroy the Communist Party, and then incrementally added the Socialist Workers Party, "White Hate Groups" (particularly the Ku Klux Klan), "Black Nationalist Hate Groups," and finally the "New Left." The FBI defined all these targets extremely broadly. The "Communist Party" program swept up not only Party members but also, for example, members of the Committee to Abolish the House Un-American Activities Committee and civil-rights leaders tagged as insufficiently "anti-Communist." The "Black Nationalist Hate Groups" label covered groups as varied as Dr. King's Southern Christian Leadership Conference, which preached nonviolence; most black student groups at universities; and the Black Panthers.[50] Disruption of the "New Left" also lacked boundaries, allowing FBI agents to target emerging protest groups, consisting mostly of young people, including Students for a Democratic Society, all students at Antioch College, publishers of underground newspapers, and students protesting university censorship of student publications.[51]

Members of the Unitarian Society of Cleveland were among the hundreds of law-abiding citizens secretly targeted by COINTELPRO. The members became targets because some, including the society's minister, had circulated a petition calling for the dissolution of the House Un-American Activities Committee. Nonviolent citizens opposed to the Vietnam War were targeted because they gave "aid and comfort" to violent demonstrators by "lending respectability to their cause."[52]

The harm COINTELPRO did to law-abiding citizens cannot be overestimated. COINTELPRO destroyed reputations, got teachers fired, broke up marriages, sabotaged political campaigns, falsely labeled intended victims as government informers to encourage violent reprisals against them, and provoked "numerous beatings and shootings."[53] All of this was done secretly, without any authorization either by statute or by anybody outside the Bureau in the executive branch.

In one extreme case, the Bureau sought to provoke violence by forging a letter from the Chicago Black Panthers to the leader of the Blackstone Rangers, a "black extremist organization in Chicago." The letter falsely said the Panthers had "a hit out" on the Rangers' leader. Predicting the letter would lead to "reprisals" against the Panthers' leadership, the internal Bureau request for headquarters' approval to send the letter explained that agents believed the Rangers were prone to "violent type activity, shooting and the like." Headquarters approved.[54] In the same vein, the San Diego FBI office *boasted* to headquarters that COINTELPRO fomented violence in the "ghetto":

> Shootings, beatings and a high degree of unrest continues to prevail in the ghetto area of Southeast San Diego. Although no specific counter-intelligence action can be credited with contributing to this overall situation, it is felt that a substantial amount of the unrest is directly attributable to this program.[55]

Hoover, who specialized in smearing the reputations of others, always counseled his colleagues not to "embarrass the Bureau." Individual COINTELPRO actions, for example, were approved as long as they would not do so.[56] But to Hoover, embarrassment only meant public disclosure. Hoover's cautions were not intended to, and did not, stop secret illegal and improper actions. They were just a warning not to get caught. Toward the end of his life, however, Hoover started to order halts to illegal actions, including break-ins (or "black bag jobs") to plant bugs or to steal documents that were suspended after Solicitor General Thurgood Marshall revealed an illegal break-in to the Supreme Court.[57] COINTELPRO was suspended after documents stolen in a break-in at the FBI office in Media, Pennsylvania, revealed the name COINTELPRO. Hoover clearly became more risk-averse in his later years. In 1970, he stopped the so-called Huston Plan, where President Nixon had authorized, among other things, secret mail opening and break-ins. But neither Hoover nor any of the other intelligence officials working on the plan mentioned that these activities had been going on before the president's authorization, or that they continued after authorization was withdrawn.[58]

Why did Hoover step back? Some FBI officials testified it was because, with Hoover having exceeded the retirement age of seventy, presidents could review his tenure each year. Others said Hoover was concerned because Presidents Johnson and Nixon, while welcoming the results of illegal operations, would not clearly authorize them. Some intelligence officials at other agencies speculated that Hoover's top aide and close companion Clyde Tolson advised Hoover that "if these techniques ever [emerge], your image and the reputation of the Bureau, will be badly damaged."[59]

In his later years, Hoover was no longer confident the FBI's dark history would remain concealed. But most of Hoover's secrets did outlive him. Then, after Hoover's death, the secrets began to be exposed, mostly by the Church Committee, grievously injuring Hoover's reputation and the important institution he had built.

Hoover's secrecy hid actions that undermined democracy in America. Without secrecy, Hoover could not have ordered illegal mail-opening, break-ins and burglaries, fomenting of violence among dissident groups, or the breakup of marriages of civil-rights workers. Without secrecy, Hoover could not have placed informants inside the NAACP for over twenty-five years without a single shred of evidence of illegality. Nor ordered agents to infiltrate the "Women's Liberation Movement." Nor vacuumed up information on countless law-abiding Americans by collecting too much from too many for too long. Without secrecy, Hoover could not have used COINTELPRO. Without secrecy, Hoover could not have misled presidents or fooled the public. Secrets and secrecy allowed Hoover to act with impunity.

Had there been no Dick Cheney and no Bush administration, Hoover could serve as the poster boy for secrecy's dangers. But Cheney joins Hoover as a vivid reminder of how secrecy fosters actions that counter American values, harm our reputation in the world, and, in Cheney's case, even lead to war.

Dick Cheney[60]

During his varied government career, Cheney voiced three approaches to secrecy. The first, when he was White House chief of staff, stressed openness inside the White House and secrecy outside it. When it was announced on November 3, 1975, that Deputy Chief of Staff Dick Cheney would succeed his mentor, Donald Rumsfeld, as the White House chief of staff, almost no one outside of Washington had heard of Cheney. A *New York Times* profile after his appointment was announced noted that Cheney was not listed in *Who's Who*, and that "few men have risen so high with so much anonymity."[61] The *Washington Post* profile quoted Cheney as saying, "I really do believe a staff man should be anonymous."[62]

Openness was Cheney's mantra within the White House. Presidents should make decisions only after hearing all sides. An idea that reaches a president must first "get shot at by its enemies and its opponents." If not, unwise decisions are more likely.[63] Four years after the end of the Ford presidency, Cheney was still preaching that it is vital for a president to hear diverse opinions. James Baker, Ronald Reagan's incoming chief of staff, called on Cheney for advice. Baker took four pages of notes. To "'protect the Pres[ident],'" you must ensure that any proposal has been tested against other views. "'Be an honest broker. Don't use the process to impose your policy views on [the] Pres[ident].'"[64] Then, shortly before becoming Bush's vice-presidential candidate, Cheney made the same point at a presidential historians' conference: What is "absolutely critical" is "who gets involved in the meetings, who does the president listen to, who gets a chance to talk to him before he makes a decision." "It has to be managed in such a way that it has integrity."[65]

Whatever openness Cheney encouraged *inside* the Ford White House, he had a very different approach to those outside it. He urged Ford to veto expansion of the Freedom of Information Act; and opposed what ultimately became the Foreign Intelligence Surveillance Act (or FISA), which restrained executive power to use warrantless wiretaps. One of the continuing headaches for Cheney and the Ford administration was the Church Committee's wide-ranging investigation. In fact, one of the reasons for ousting William Colby, George H.W. Bush's predecessor at the CIA, was "the feeling in the White House and the State Department that he was not doing a good job containing the Congressional investigations." With Bush, "a new face," the White House hoped it could delay or forestall the investigations.[66]

Cheney's resistance to the congressional investigations went beyond who led the CIA. Cheney actively worked to undermine the Church Committee. Six months before he became chief of staff, Cheney, still Rumsfeld's deputy, read a front-page *New York Times* story, detailing a secret Navy submarine program to tap into undersea Soviet communications cables and eavesdrop from within Soviet waters.[67] Three days later, Cheney suggested considering, among other things, search warrants for the papers of legendary investigative reporter Seymour Hersh, and even indictment of Hersh and the *Times*.[68] But Hersh was not Cheney's true target. The goal of prosecuting Hersh would be to "create an environment" to "bolster our position [to curb] the Church Committee investigations."[69] Attorney General Edward Levi ultimately blocked any government action against Hersh.

Cheney learned another lesson from congressional investigations. If you write nothing down, there is no paper trail to uncover later. Indeed, in 2005, Cheney said that because of "the investigations that have occurred over the years," he did not keep a diary, write letters, or use e-mail.[70] Reams of written information and proposals would "flow into" Vice President Cheney's office, but "almost nothing flow[ed] out," according to Bush administration officials. Cheney's aides described this as a "one-way valve."[71]

Not only did Vice President Cheney write little, he said little too. In meetings with President Bush and other officials, Cheney "made calculated silence his calling card." A White House colleague reported Cheney "just sits there and listens with that crooked grin on his face. He almost never speaks."[72] Given Cheney's nearly unfettered individual access to the president during Bush's first term, Cheney's circumspection kept secrets and consolidated power—making it less likely that historians will learn what he said to the president.

Cheney's second approach to secrecy came as a congressman, when he gave surprising recommendations for more presidential openness. When Cheney was sworn in as the lone congressman from Wyoming in 1979, he was hardly a typical House freshman. Cheney had spent years working for Rumsfeld at various government agencies and the White House. He had been White House chief of staff—a position many consider the second most powerful in Washington. Moreover, congressional leaders could not dismiss him as a bureaucratic policy wonk. Cheney had worked on Ford's unsuccessful 1976 reelection campaign, which included a brutal fight with Ronald Reagan at the Republican National Convention. Rarely has someone in the modern era accumulated such a formidable résumé before serving in Congress.

It was no surprise that Cheney rose rapidly in the House leadership. By 1985, he was chair of the Republican Policy Committee, an idea incubator for GOP legislative proposals. Two years later he would be elected House minority whip—the second most powerful position in GOP House leadership.

At about the same time as Cheney was busy with intramural House struggles, the White House was launching a covert intelligence operation that would ultimately rock the Reagan administration. In 1985, President Reagan secretly decided to sell TOW antitank and HAWK antiaircraft missiles to Iran. Governed by a hardline Shia Muslim regime, Iran was embroiled in a bloody war with Iraq, and with few Western nations willing to supply it with weapons. Many, including the United States, had imposed an arms embargo. Reagan himself had labeled Iran a "terrorist" state. Nonetheless, Reagan hoped the covert arms sales to Iran would lead to the release of American hostages being held in Lebanon, and might also open relations with Iran to America's strategic benefit.

Initially, the missiles were sent to Iran circuitously, giving the administration "deniability" if the operation was exposed. Israel sent the weapons to Iran, and the United States resupplied Israel with new missiles. A secret offshore entity known as the Enterprise, secretly created by the White House's national security staff, led by Lt. Col. Oliver North, handled these transactions, with its own pilots, airfields, and Swiss bank accounts. Later, "Iran" merged with "Contra" when the Enterprise funneled the money Iran paid for the missiles to the Nicaraguan Contras, who were rebelling against Nicaragua's left-leaning Sandinista government. For several years, with Reagan's fervent support, the CIA had covertly supported the Contras; in one covert operation it mined Nicaraguan harbors without informing Congress as required.

Congress tried to put a stop to this, passing two budget amendments that banned payments to the Contras. These were called the Boland Amendments, named after their sponsor, Massachusetts congressman Edward Boland, who chaired the House Intelligence Committee. But Congress was not informed about either the sale of missiles to Iran or the diversion of the Iranian money to the Contras. Indeed, according to Reagan's national security advisor, Adm. John Poindexter, even Reagan was not informed of the money transfer to the Contras. Poindexter's explanation was that he was sure Reagan would approve, and he "did not want him to be associated with the decision."[73]

A Lebanese weekly was the first to report the United States was selling arms to Iran, apparently as an "arms-for-hostages" deal: the weapons would be sent in exchange for release of six American hostages held in Lebanon by an Iranian-backed group. The Iranian government confirmed the story. President Reagan then asked Attorney General Edwin Meese to gather more facts and prepare a quick public report. The *Meese Report* revealed the Enterprise and the payments to the Contras.[74]

Back on Capitol Hill, Representative Cheney assumed the funding of the Contras was kept secret from the president. He said that "a full scale congressional investigation was inevitable, and that he will support it," adding the administration's foreign policy was "in pretty bad disarray."[75] Three weeks later, Cheney said: "I tried to defend him [Reagan] initially, but it's hard." "You have to say it's a pretty fundamental flaw that would allow a lieutenant colonel on the White House staff to operate in defiance of the law."[76]

Both the House and Senate appointed committees that held joint hearings and issued a joint report.[77] The House committee consisted of nine Democrats and six Republicans, with Cheney chosen as the ranking Republican. Cheney was later described by a progressive columnist as "by far the brightest of the Republicans chosen for the committee."[78]

Ten months later, the Iran-Contra Committee issued its joint report. Cheney, joined by all the House Republicans and two of the five Senate Republicans, wrote a lengthy dissent. To summarize the merits of the differences, Cheney's minority report described as mistakes what the majority believed in many cases was illegal. And while critical of Reagan, North, Poindexter, and other key figures, Cheney expressed empathy for, and understanding of, their "mistakes," including the National Security Council's decision to deceive Congress before the plan was discovered. The harsher majority report said "secrecy was used to justify lies to Congress."[79]

Along with these substantive differences, the media featured the minority's attack on the majority report as a "hysterical" "weapon in the ongoing guerrilla warfare" between the White House and Congress.[80] The media also paid some attention to the minority's legalistic defense of robust presidential power, although Cheney's view that presidents possess "monarchical" powers was not mentioned.

But several parts of Cheney's 202-page dissent also made suggestions about how a *wise* White House should address difficult foreign policy and national security issues. He stressed openness and criticized excessive secrecy. Although this advice stands as an indictment of how the Bush White House was later run, in all the many critiques of Cheney's role in the Bush administration not one has used Cheney's own words from the 1987 dissent to contrast with his conduct as vice president. Reading his 1987 report, it is hard to believe that it came from the man who became Vice President Dick Cheney. Direct quotes from Cheney's dissent make the point:

Inform the President and Congress

- "At a minimum, [Iran-Contra] should generate a fuller awareness in the executive branch of the serious negative ramifications of risky and short-range decisions that have not had a full airing in the Presidential office, let alone in the halls of Congress."[81]
- Disagreements within the intelligence community should be "highlight[ed]" to the president. The problem was that "the views of U.S. intelligence were not properly passed up the line and highlighted to the President."[82]
- Similarly, "one of the best guarantees against an intelligence bias is the widespread circulation of CIA analyses on Capitol Hill, allowing particularly the intelligence committees' scrutiny of virtually everything the CIA and intelligence community produces."[83]
- High-ranking executive branch officers (particularly those who disagree with a ruling) should "insist that the President periodically review important policy decisions so all power is not left in the hands of the people most committed to pushing forward."[84]

Make Your Case to the Public

- To be "sustained," "substantial successes" require presidents and their supporters to engage in "democratic persuasion."[85]
- "The requirement for building long-term political support means that the Administration would have been better off if it had conducted its activities in the open."[86]
- "Democratic persuasion" will not succeed "unless the public is exposed to and persuaded by a clear, sustained, and principled debate on the merits."[87]

Excessive Secrecy Is Counterproductive.

- "[T]he lack of regular procedures, fostered by an excessive concern for secrecy, short-circuited the process of periodic review and evaluation—both of the substantive desirability of continuing the initiative, and of the decision not to notify Congress."[88]
- It was a "fundamental mistake for the NSC staff to have been secretive and deceptive about its actions."[89]
- "[I]t was self-defeating to think a program this important could be sustained by deceiving Congress. Whether technically illegal or not, it was politically foolish and counterproductive to mislead Congress, even if misleading took the form of artful evasion or silence instead of overt misstatements."[90]

Later, as vice president, Cheney ignored his own advice that openness should be the hallmark of a wise White House. But he did not forget Iran-Contra, at one point trivializing it as merely an attempt to "criminalize a policy difference."[91] On another occasion, however, Cheney stressed the dissent's importance, focusing on its legalistic parts that emphasized presidential power. On his way to Muscat, Oman, in December 2005, Cheney told reporters that the minority report was an "obscure text" that was "very good in laying out a robust view of the President's prerogatives with respect to the conduct of especially foreign policy and national security matters."[92] Not surprisingly, however, Cheney has never called attention to other parts of his dissent, which stand in sharp contrast to the conduct of the Bush-Cheney administration.

Cheney's third approach came when he was vice president, where in waging war on terrorism and in forging other Bush administration policies, Cheney rode roughshod over his earlier principles concerning openness and secrecy.

Inside the White House, Cheney ignored his own insight that "any proposal has [to be] tested against other views." What he had predicted decades earlier came true: failure to force a "full airing in the Presidential office" will have "serious negative ramifications." The Cheney-inspired, overly narrow process of presidential decision-making on national security issues in the Bush-Cheney White House is quite well known: for example, warrantless wiretapping, torture, and moving away from the Geneva Conventions. But the same occurred with domestic issues, including environmental policy. For example, in 2000, during the presidential campaign, in a speech designed to counter Al Gore's environmental appeal, George Bush promised to "require all power plants" to reduce emissions of four pollutants, including carbon dioxide. In early March 2001 (after clearing her remarks with Bush's chief of staff), Christine Todd Whitman, Bush's EPA administrator, confirmed that promise at a European conference. Then, hearing rumors that Bush might be reconsidering the policy, Whitman arranged a White House meeting with Bush on March 9. But earlier that morning, with no discussion or debate, Cheney got Bush to sign a letter rejecting government-imposed limits on power-plant emissions, adding that carbon dioxide was "not a pollutant" under the Clean Air Act. Whitman arrived at the White House too late, as did Secretary of State Colin Powell, who wanted to contend that backing off on global warming would be harmful with allies.[93]

Cheney even kept key facts secret from the president. In 2004, Bush did know the Justice Department was refusing to continue to sign off on the administration's secret surveillance program. Urged by Cheney, Bush signed an order continuing the program on his own authority. But what Cheney did not tell the president was that if the program went ahead against the Justice Department's advice, the attorney general, his deputy, the director of the FBI, and many other high officials planned to resign in protest. When Bush learned this, he canceled his order and required the administration to negotiate changes to satisfy the concerns of Justice Department officials, avoiding what would have been administration-rocking resignations akin to the Saturday Night Massacre that turned the public against the flailing Nixon administration.[94]

Outside the White House, rather than using "democratic persuasion," the Bush-Cheney administration had an "excessive concern" for secrecy. When making crucial decisions, the administration withheld important information and even misled Congress and the public. Whether Cheney *knowingly* made "overt misstatements" in beating the drum for the Iraq War has not been shown. But at the very least Cheney's "artful evasion" was misleading, particularly in implying a connection between al-Qaeda and Saddam Hussein. Moreover, on post-9/11 detention and interrogation tactics and on the return to warrantless wiretapping, the Bush-Cheney administration never permitted the public to "be exposed to" a "clear, sustained and principled debate on the merits," without "excessive secrecy."

What explains Cheney's abandonment of many of his earlier principles? Brent Scowcroft worked with Cheney in the Ford White House. (A few months before Ford died in 2006, he paired Cheney and Scowcroft as his two "best subordinates.")[95] When Scowcroft was national security advisor for George H.W. Bush, he also worked closely with then Secretary of Defense Cheney. But later during the George W. Bush administration, Scowcroft became a Cheney critic, saying: "The real anomaly in the Administration is Cheney. I consider Cheney a good friend—I've known him for thirty years. But Dick Cheney I don't know any more."[96] Even Ford, who described Cheney as "an excellent chief of staff. First Class" came to a dimmer view of Cheney as vice president, telling a reporter that Cheney had become "much more pugnacious."[97]

As for presidential decision-making within the White House, there is no way to square Vice President Cheney's White House with the Cheney who earlier had insisted that any proposal to a president should be tested against other views and have a full airing in the presidential office. What happened? Scowcroft and Ford sort of threw up their hands. Cheney was just a different person. Some say that Cheney's heart attacks and his open-heart surgery changed his personality. But there is no proof of this affecting his decisions. While there is not now a clear answer, and Cheney's reticence about explaining himself and his secretive and spare way with documents will make the job of future historians harder, there are some other ideas to test.

President George W. Bush's style and personality are relevant. As Cheney had observed in his Iran-Contra dissent, the "best organization" for a particular White House "is the one that works best for the elected official who bears final responsibility." In other words, the best organization may be different for each president. George W. Bush was well known for his distaste for details and debate. He was never strong in formulating or changing his views based upon a complex give and take. Bush was "the decider"—but not an engaged listener, particularly in his first term and the early years of his second. Therefore, to be kind, in avoiding wider meetings and broader discussions in the Oval Office, Cheney perhaps meant to spare Bush frustration, or even embarrassment. But kindness is not called for. Cheney's experience over decades was that decisions arrived at without a "full airing" are more likely to be unwise. And at a minimum, before privately pushing a position with the president, Cheney himself should have listened to all views. He didn't.

Cheney might have felt a full airing was necessary before 9/11, but not afterward because of ongoing threats. This explanation is possible, but not persuasive. For, as the Christine Whitman pre-9/11 clean-air story reveals, Cheney also choked off discussion in areas utterly unrelated to terrorism. Moreover, while responding to terror may, at times, mandate an accelerated process, it hardly suggests elimination of *all* process. Indeed, concern with a long-term terrorist threat should have suggested more care in reaching decisions that affect America's long-term interests and values.

Conceivably, Cheney might have feared leaks if he allowed others, even high-ranking colleagues such as Secretary of State Colin Powell or National Security Advisor Condoleezza Rice, to participate in discussing questions such as whether to observe the Geneva Conventions. But this explanation is not plausible. First, if they couldn't be trusted, why were they still part of the administration? Second, once the decision to ignore the Geneva Conventions was made, it was public. So why act in a way that increases the likelihood of a harmful media story headlining how key experts were not even consulted?

Finally, perhaps Cheney thought *he* was the real "decider." Perhaps he felt he already knew all and understood all, and therefore there was no need for meetings to discuss objections because he had no need to hear more. This was pretty arrogant and pretty risky, but nonetheless plausible as a matter of human nature, for short-term power is greater if no critics are heard.

Turning to secrecy outside the White House, a possible cynical explanation is that Cheney only voiced, but did not believe, the lofty principles set forth in the Iran-Contra dissent about the open and candid ways in which a wise White House should deal with the public. But cynicism would not be fair, for—agree with him or not—throughout his career Cheney has consistently seemed to express his true beliefs, more so than many public figures. Moreover, months before the written dissent, Cheney personally voiced similar sentiments in his oral remarks at the close of the Iran-Contra hearings: "I fervently hope that future Presidents will take away from these hearings one important lesson: that no foreign policy can be effective for long without the wholehearted support of the Congress and the American people."[98]

If one rejects the view that Cheney merely voiced but did not believe his Iran-Contra advice on openness and candor, the most likely explanation for his changed view of the way to operate *outside* the White House seems clearer than why he departed from his years of insistence on a full airing of issues *within* the White House. Based on what is now known, temporary power is key.

Vice President Cheney certainly did abandon his Iran-Contra advice on "democratic persuasion," openness with Congress and the public, the dangers of an "excessive concern for secrecy," and the foolishness of misleading through "artful evasion or silence." But Vice President Cheney's secretive pattern with Congress and the public was nevertheless quite consistent with his aim, ever since the Ford White House, to restore and expand presidential power—at least in the short term.

In his Iran-Contra dissent, Cheney had observed that long-term public support is fostered by openness. But in the Bush-Cheney administration, Cheney opted for short-term victories cloaked by secrecy. In his Iran-Contra dissent, Cheney had mused both about the need for "democratic persuasion" *and* about presidents' occasionally exercising "monarchical" powers. In the Bush-Cheney administration, monarchical powers bested democratic persuasion.

The jury is still out on whether Cheney's secret actions actually undermined his vision of a much more powerful, indeed at times monarchical, presidency. Certainly, those actions did cause a decline in respect for America abroad, and reduced support for the administration at home. Nonetheless, as Zhou Enlai, Mao Tse-tung's premier, is supposed to have said, when asked for his assessment of the French Revolution some two centuries after it happened, "It's too soon to say."[99]

Particularly since so much is still smothered by secrecy, debate over the lawfulness, propriety, wisdom, and impact of the Bush-Cheney actions since 9/11 is ongoing. Cheney remains a forceful defender of his administration's secret actions, by lobbing, for example, vituperative accusations of laxity and weakness at the Obama administration for ruling out torture and revealing some secrets about it. But Cheney has not deigned to address the critique that his secret path to protect America made us less safe and eroded America's values.

5

Six Secrecy Stories:
From Slavery to Science

Dick Cheney and J. Edgar Hoover dramatize the way individuals can use and misuse secrecy to enhance their own power and harm the nation. But, as the following six stories illustrate, secrecy is often institutionally ingrained and longer lasting. The stories also illustrate how secrecy evolves and provide examples where long-lasting secrecy has been limited or even eliminated.

Slavery

Slavery in America was not itself a secret. Yet it was veiled in secrecy and obfuscation. Many Founders dealt with it evasively. So did the Constitution. Government leaders routinely kept embarrassing actions concerning their slaves under wraps. The House of Representatives and Southern post offices suppressed information about slavery. Finally, Harriet Beecher Stowe's *Uncle Tom's Cabin* exposed the secret hidden in plain sight, revealing human horrors to millions and providing a spark to end slavery.

For a long time, establishment historians ignored or downplayed the role of free Blacks and slaves who supported the American cause during the Revolution.[1] Few history students before the 1930s learned that Lafayette used a slave to spy on the British by infiltrating its army under the guise of being an escaped slave.[2] Still, many more slaves joined the British side as offers of freedom lured them away from plantations of men such as Washington, Jefferson, Madison, and Patrick Henry. This "massive black defection from slavery" has been described as the Revolution's "dirty little secret."[3]

A few years later, slavery became the Constitution's dirty little secret. The Framers never used the S word. Instead, the Constitution resorted to convoluted circumlocutions to characterize slaves as "Persons" or "other Persons." This was done in apportioning Congressional seats among the states by indicating that "other Persons" (that is, slaves) would be counted as three-fifths of a person; in banning laws limiting importation of "such Persons" until 1808; and in requiring the return of any "Person held to Service or Labor" who had escaped to a free state.[4] Sixty-seven years after the Constitution, Abraham Lincoln incisively captured its evasion in his famed speech in Peoria, Illinois: "[T]he thing is hid away, in the Constitution, just as an afflicted man hides away a wen or a cancer, which he dares not cut out at once, lest he bleed to death."[5]

Evasiveness about slavery continued in the First Congress. In early 1790, in his last public act, Benjamin Franklin presented a petition on behalf of the Pennsylvania Abolition Society urging Congress to "devise means for removing this inconsistency from the character of the American people," since equal liberty was "the birth-right of all men."[6] The Senate took no action. A House committee erroneously concluded Congress could not act at all, because the Constitution banned laws on slave importation until 1808, and the House passed a resolution that "Congress have no authority to interfere in the emancipation of slaves."[7] As historian Joseph Ellis put it, all this reflected a decision that the American Revolution's "ultimate legacy" for slavery was that it "not be talked about at all." Slavery was "the unmentionable family secret, or the proverbial elephant in the middle of the room."[8]

Many Founders were slaveholders, including Washington, Jefferson, and Madison. This created the irony voiced by Samuel Johnson: "[H]ow is it that we hear the loudest yelps for liberty among the drivers of negroes."[9] Aware of slavery's inconsistency with the values they championed, the Founders seldom spoke about it, usually not forcefully, and often in private. Madison, for example, mused in his diary on a trip to upstate New York that Northern states were more democratic than Southern ones, because "[i]n proportion as slavery prevails in a State, the Government, however democratic in name, must be aristocratic in fact."[10]

George Washington freed his slaves in his will and—for decades—had a close bond with one: Billy Lee.[11] But as president, Washington secretly engaged in duplicitousness to keep slaves in bondage. When the national capital was in Philadelphia for a few years in the 1790s, Washington faced a

Pennsylvania law he believed freed slaves residing in the state for six consecutive months.[12] The president (and his wife, Martha) evaded the law by sending slaves out of Pennsylvania for short periods of time. Pretexts included fulfilling a promise that a slave could periodically visit his wife in Virginia; sending another slave home to help cook when Martha was visiting Mount Vernon; and taking slaves for brief visits across the New Jersey border.[13]

Washington asked his personal secretary and close aide, Tobias Lear, to keep these actions hidden from all except himself and Mrs. Washington. "Pretext," he said, should be used to "deceive" both the slaves and the public.[14] Similarly, when Ona Judge, a favored female slave assisting Martha, escaped, the president confidentially instructed Oliver Wolcott, then his treasury secretary, to have a customs collector kidnap her and send her back to Virginia.[15]

Some four decades after Washington left office, suppression of discussion of slavery increased in response to abolitionists mailing antislavery tracts to the South. Southern states passed laws banning such "incendiary literature." Then, despite the protection mail had from being read by government, and despite Congress confirming that promise in 1836, Southern postmasters (abetted by one in New York City) removed abolitionist tracts from the mail. Starting with the Andrew Jackson regime, federal postmasters general allowed the removals to go on.[16]

At around the same time, in 1835, the House passed a "gag rule" that suppressed discussion of slavery in the House itself. All petitions about slavery should be "laid on the table" without being printed or referred to committee.[17] The gag rule was passed despite the First Amendment, which prohibits Congress from "abridging . . . the right of the people . . . to petition the government for a redress of grievances." The aging, crusty, and resourceful John Quincy Adams—who served in the House for seventeen years after being defeated in his 1828 reelection campaign for president—found creative ways to ridicule the gag rule and discuss antislavery petitions.[18] Nonetheless, antislavery petitions were regularly and routinely "tabled"—and thus simply ignored—until the gag rule's repeal in 1844.

Later, after the Civil War began, Lincoln was said to have greeted Harriet Beecher Stowe as "the little woman who wrote the book that made this big war."[19] Whether or not that was said, Stowe's *Uncle Tom's Cabin* did expose many to the hidden human horrors of slavery. Stowe's book became "one of the most astonishing phenomena in the history of the printing press and of advocacy."[20] In its first year, it sold more than 300,000 copies in the United States.[21]

Stowe's writing *Uncle Tom's Cabin* is an example of secrecy backfiring. In response to the gag rule, the American Anti-Slavery Society, the main outside generator of protests against the rule, produced a graphic book exposing gruesome examples of slavery's horrors: *American Slavery As It Is: Testimony of a Thousand Witnesses*.[22] Stowe read the book, and was said to have kept it "in her work basket by day, and slept with it under her pillow by night, till its facts crystallized into Uncle Tom."[23] So the House's attempt to suppress information about slavery had the unintended effect of helping to widen knowledge about slavery.

Photography

Just as *Uncle Tom's Cabin* brought home to millions a secret hiding in plain sight, photography changed the course of history by peeling away veils obscuring shameful facts. Photos undermined power and, as with the advent of the printing press centuries earlier, power responded by seeking to shutter information. Presidents across the political spectrum from Ronald Reagan to Barack Obama have, on occasion, used their power to control what pictures the public could see.

A single photograph can expose broad truths the powerful hoped would stay hidden. A picture can indeed be worth a thousand words.[24] Photography often challenges power by providing a clearer, sharper perspective, and by making a much larger portion of the public care about wrongs previously known only by a limited elite. Pictures on television, the Internet, and social networks have the same effect.

At the turn of the twentieth century, Jacob Riis and Lewis Hine used their cameras to expose human degradation in urban slums;[25] and in the 1960s, Charles Moore's photo essays for *LIFE* brought Americans face-to-face with the hidden, vicious side of segregation. Riis used the newly invented magnesium flash to illuminate New York City's downtown slums, so "the half that was on top" could see how the poor lived, piled into dirty tenements, sleeping on the floor for "five cents a spot." Hine's photos in the first two decades of the twentieth century forced America to look into the eyes of preteen children whose cheap labor in dangerous factories, mills, and mines was fueling the industrial revolution.[26] Half a century later, in May 1963, Moore's camera captured Birmingham, Alabama, police chief Bull Connor attacking peaceful black civil-rights demonstrators with snarling, biting dogs and fire hoses that shot demonstrators with water at a force of 100 pounds per square inch. As *LIFE*'s picture essay noted, "If the Negroes themselves had written the script, they could hardly have asked for greater help for their cause than . . . 'Bull' Connor freely gave."[27] The photos illuminated the power images have to reveal hidden truth and change the course of public opinion. Several years later, Arthur Schlesinger Jr. opined that "[t]he shocking photographs of Bull Connor's dogs, teeth bared, lunging viciously at the marchers, transformed the national mood. Legislation [for civil rights] now was not only necessary: it was possible."[28]

Some forty years later, photos taken at Abu Ghraib unmasked physical and sexual abuse of Iraqi prisoners. The photos compelled America to face the war's underbelly—that American soldiers had put human beings on leashes and dragged them around like dogs, forced prisoners to masturbate with one another while being jeered at by a female soldier, and hooded one prisoner, then strapped him to wires in order to simulate execution. Uproar followed, thrusting America into a debate about the treatment of post-9/11 detainees. Abu Ghraib became shorthand for torture even though the conduct was much milder than the subsequently revealed "enhanced interrogation" the CIA was using to question "high-value" detainees. But for Abu Ghraib there were photos. Aware of the power of pictures, the CIA later destroyed the videotapes of its far more brutal treatment of high-value detainees.[29]

Grisly photos had also eroded public support for the Vietnam War.[30] The facts had not been stamped secret, but they were largely unknown until graphically revealed by photographers. Photos and television "spilled the blood on the rug" in American living rooms, transforming the Vietnam War from an abstraction about combat in a distant land.[31] (Today the blood has moved from the TVs in living rooms to the cell phones in people's pockets.) Three iconic Vietnam photographs were particularly important.[32] In June 1963, as protests convulsed the South Vietnamese government, newspapers ran Malcolm Browne's photo of an elderly Buddhist monk sitting serenely on a Saigon street as flames from the gasoline he had lit engulfed his body. Five years later, Americans saw the grimace on a handcuffed captive's face as the American-supported Vietnamese national police chief executed him on the street at point-blank range with a gunshot to the temple. And in 1972, when support for the war was waning, the front page of the *New York Times*—the same paper that nine years earlier refused to run the photo of the self-immolating monk—gave America its most harrowing image of the Vietnam War: a group of children running away from a napalm blast in an incinerated village with their faces contorted as they screamed in pain. No one who saw that photo will ever forget the young girl in the center running toward the camera stark naked, her clothes burned off, napalm melting away parts of her skin, her arms spread and her mouth agape in a scream.

These images flew in the face of American values. They shook Americans' faith by recording the war's human toll. Images can sear the mind. Just think, for example, how history might have changed if the beastly, horrifying photos of the secret Nazi concentration camps that appeared when they were liberated in 1945 had appeared earlier.[33]

The U.S. government thought a lesson from the Vietnam War was to be careful of the secrecy-eroding power of pictures. The Reagan administration barred journalists and photographers from covering the invasion of Grenada in 1983. Only Defense Department photographers could document the invasion, and even their photos were censored by the Pentagon.[34] In 1991, Secretary of Defense Dick Cheney prohibited photographs of caskets arriving back in the United States.[35] The ban lasted until 2009, when President Barack Obama and Defense Secretary Robert Gates gave families of dead soldiers the right to permit such photos.[36]

But President Obama has also twice moved to keep photos secret, first by fighting a court order requiring production of photos showing abuse of detainees in Iraq and Afghanistan.[37] When the administration's request for Supreme Court review was pending, Congress, at the urging of the president, passed a law prohibiting their release.[38] Supported by the military, Obama said release would "further inflame anti-American opinion and put our troops in greater danger."[39] In addition, because the facts were known and the individuals involved had been punished, the president maintained that "publication of these photos would not add any additional benefit to our understanding of what was carried out in the past."[40] Even assuming his decision was correct, Obama's denial of "any additional benefit to our understanding" flew in the face of history. Clearly, photos often enlarge and deepen public understanding.

President Obama also banned distribution of photos showing Osama bin Laden's corpse. Again, as Obama said on CBS's 60 Minutes, the basic facts were known: bin Laden had been killed; he was "shot in the head."[41] Again, the president expressed concern about photos "floating around as an incitement to additional violence. As a propaganda tool."[42] Moreover, he said "we don't trot out this stuff as trophies." People are glad bin Laden is gone, "but we don't need to spike the football."[43]

Of course, in earlier centuries, the decapitated heads of defeated enemy leaders were used as trophies and often displayed—indeed "spiked"—on city walls in order to prove death and humiliate the vanquished. But customs do change.

Health (and Sex)

Changes in customs and culture have eroded secrecy about the health of American leaders, which has increasingly been seen as a matter of legitimate public interest—as is the health of business leaders such as Apple's Steve Jobs. Nonetheless, leaders often push to keep health problems from public knowledge, doing so for both power and privacy reasons. Serious health problems of American public officials have often been concealed and lied about.

Today it is impossible to imagine the press withholding photographs of President Franklin Roosevelt in a wheelchair. Our culture has changed, and technology now allows cell-phone holders to snap and immediately share a picture. Similarly, while the contrast between Lyndon Johnson's public display of his gallbladder operation scar[44] and George Washington's concealment of his dental problems[45] reflect differences in the two men's demeanor, it also reflects changes in our culture. America has become less reserved and less private—indeed, in some cases, exhibitionist. It has become customary for presidents to reveal current health problems in great, perhaps excessive, detail, and for most presidential candidates to reveal much of their health history and current status. This too reflects cultural changes. But it also is one of many consequences of the powers of the presidency having multiplied, making secrecy about a president's health of greater concern.[46]

Part of the Constitution's Twenty-Fifth Amendment underscores this shift. The 1967 amendment concerns presidential succession, with one section covering serious impairment of a president's physical or mental health: if the vice president plus a majority of cabinet secretaries declare a president is "unable to discharge" his duties, the vice president immediately becomes acting president.[47] This amendment responded to several instances when severe presidential impairments had been concealed.

When an assassin shot President James A. Garfield in 1881, the public believed Garfield was convalescing at the White House and at his vacation home in New Jersey before he died eighty days later. Garfield's doctor, however, had kept secret the president's true condition and falsely described Garfield's condition and prognosis.[48] Thereafter, health crises for presidents Grover Cleveland and Woodrow Wilson were concealed, falsely described, and sheltered by secrecy, as was the health status of Franklin D. Roosevelt and John F. Kennedy.

Grover Cleveland left Washington in 1893, in the midst of a national financial crisis, to have three cancer surgeries, all secret. To help ensure secrecy, he did not even inform Vice President Adlai Stevenson. Doctors removed several portions of the president's left jaw and most of his palate, and substituted an artificial rubber jaw, doing so clandestinely on a friend's yacht in Long Island Sound and Buzzards Bay, Massachusetts, and at Cleveland's vacation home.[49] Cleveland was unseen from June 30 to August 5, when he returned to Washington appearing to be healthy and capable of normal speech.

When he was away, the Philadelphia *Press* published a story that, without using the word "cancer," reported doctors had removed a large part of Cleveland's jawbone. Government officials denied the report or refused to confirm it. Moreover, the president's close friend, the editor of the Philadelphia *Public Ledger*, falsely claimed the problem had been only a toothache. A quarter century later, however, one of Cleveland's surgeons conceded the Philadelphia *Press* had been "substantially correct."[50]

Originally kept secret because of concern about markets during a financial panic, Cleveland's operations remained secret for decades. This may have been because of morbid fear of, and disgust about, cancer. Obituaries at the time did not use the word "cancer" to describe the cause of death but relied on euphemisms like "a wasting disease." Even after 1937, when FDR signed a law that established the National Cancer Institute, cancer remained the "great unmentionable, the whispered-about disease that no one spoke about publicly."[51] As late as the 1950s, when two breast-cancer survivors tried to run a *New York Times* notice for a meeting of survivors, the society editor told them, "'the *Times* cannot publish the word *breast* or the word *cancer*,'" suggesting instead a notice for a "'meeting about diseases of the chest wall.'"[52]

In 1919, a quarter century after Cleveland's secret surgeries, President Woodrow Wilson set out on a train trip seeking support for the League of Nations, saying that "[e]ven though, in my condition, it might mean the giving up of my life, I will gladly make the sacrifice to save the Treaty."[53] Wilson's trip was scheduled for twenty-six days, averaging ten speeches per day. But after three weeks, Wilson collapsed in his train compartment, probably from a minor stroke. A few days later, his second wife, Edith, found him unconscious on the floor of a White House bathroom from another stroke. For months, the president had no contact with anyone except his wife, doctor, and a trusted advisor. Wilson's wife and doctor concealed the causes of Wilson's incapacity and the limits on his ability to function.[54] Later, Edith Wilson denied she had "made a single decision regarding the disposition of public affairs." Whether or not true, she conceded she *did* make the decisions on "what was important and what was not" and "when to present matters to my husband." Her priority was "first my beloved husband whose life I was trying to save." Only "after that," she said, was he the president.[55]

Franklin Roosevelt's health precipitously declined in his last years. In 1943, Roosevelt began to lose weight and suffer shortness of breath. FDR's family dismissed the White House physician's opinion that the president was merely recovering from the flu, and had him examined in March 1944 by a cardiologist at Bethesda Naval Hospital, who diagnosed him with hypertension, an enlarged heart, and congestive heart failure. Not even Roosevelt himself was told the grim news.[56] After FDR won an unprecedented fourth term in November 1944, the White House physician dispelled rumors about the president's condition by saying he was "perfectly O.K."[57] Less than three months after he took the oath of office, however, Roosevelt was dead.

As a presidential candidate in 1960, John F. Kennedy cultivated an image of youthful vitality, meant to contrast with Dwight Eisenhower, who was seventy when he left office. While energetic, JFK had many health problems. Some were impossible to hide—such as an eight-month recovery from back surgery and continuing back problems. But the severity of his health problems was a secret jealously guarded by Kennedy and his family for decades. Even when Joseph Kennedy's estate opened personal papers to researchers in 1995, reports to the elder Kennedy about his son's health remained closed.[58]

In 2002, administrators of JFK's papers opened years of medical records, which disclosed that when he entered the Oval Office, Kennedy had been diagnosed with colitis and Addison's disease, a disorder of the adrenal glands that inflates risks from other health issues, particularly surgeries like the three unsuccessful ones Kennedy had to relieve back pain. Historian Robert Dallek and Dr. Jeffrey Kelman, a chief medical officer at the Federal Centers for Medicare and Medicaid Services, reviewed JFK's medical records in 2002, concluding, "He was never healthy."[59]

> By the time he was president, he was on ten, 12 medications a day. He was on antispasmodics for his bowel, paregoric, lamodal transatine [ph], he was on muscle relaxants, Phenobarbital, Librium, Meprobomate, he was on pain medications, Codeine, Demerol, Methadone, he was on oral cortisone; he was on injected cortisone, he was on testosterone, he was on Nembutal for sleep. And on top of that, he was getting injected sometimes six times a day, six places on his back, by the White House physician, with Novocain, Procaine, just to enable him to face the day."[60]

Voters in 1960 did not know the facts about Kennedy's health problems—or his bravery in facing them.[61]

Customs, culture, and even the Constitution have changed to decrease privacy about leaders' health. As often, a dramatic public revelation of a secret leads to secrecy cutbacks. When George McGovern was nominated as the Democratic Party's candidate for president in 1972, he chose Missouri senator Thomas Eagleton as his running mate. Less than two weeks later, Eagleton announced that thrice he had received treatment for depression, twice receiving electroshock therapy. After first saying he stood "1,000 percent for Tom Eagleton," McGovern dropped him and selected Kennedy's brother-in-law, Sargent Shriver, as his new running mate.[62]

According to Lawrence Altman, a doctor who has covered health issues at the *Times* for more than forty years, "vetting" candidates' health started after Eagleton. And presidential candidates themselves increasingly revealed medical information.[63] While disclosure has sometimes been incomplete or inaccurate, it has become the expectation.[64] Had he won in 2008, John McCain would have been seventy-two at the time of his inauguration, the oldest person ever elected president. Rumors circulated about McCain's health because of four surgeries he had for melanoma, the deadliest form of skin cancer. In May 2008, McCain let reporters examine nearly 1,200 pages of medical records. Yet the extent of, and prognosis for, McCain's skin cancer dogged him throughout the campaign—especially after he chose Alaska governor Sarah Palin as his running mate. More than 2,700 physicians signed an ad in October 2008 calling for "full, public release" of McCain's medical records.[65]

Secrecy about a candidate's health had become the subject of spirited—and partisan—debate.

Changing attitudes about health and privacy mirror shifting ideas about sexual improprieties and about whether these are matters best publicly ignored. The culture that protected JFK from public revelation of his many liaisons has been replaced by a culture of transparency in which personal matters of public figures are subject to public view.[66] The evolution of American culture has frayed the veil that once, with few exceptions, covered public officials' sexual conduct. Changes in technology have also increased the likelihood of exposure, with camera phones, instant messaging, social networking, and the permanence of digital content making information instantaneous and freely available. Some politicians have been slow to see the dangers, with more than one officeholder turning himself into a laughingstock by using social media to boast of sexual prowess.

With sex, as with much else, secrets revealed by images have greater impact than more serious conduct unaccompanied by photos. New York congressman Anthony Weiner resigned his congressional seat because of sexually suggestive photos he sent by Twitter, Facebook, e-mail, and phone to women he had never met.[67] Only a few months earlier, Christopher Lee, Weiner's colleague in the House, had resigned, also for using his cell phone to take skin-baring photographs in mirrors, which he e-mailed to a woman he had "met" in the Craigslist personal ads.[68] In contrast, Louisiana's self-styled "family values" politician, U.S. Senator David Vitter, simply apologized for a "very serious sin" when his number was found in a prostitution ring's records.[69] Without photos, there was less life to the revelation that he paid for the prostitutes' services. Vitter comfortably won reelection.

Budgets

As medical examinations help keep individuals healthy, budgets help keep government healthy. Skipping regular checkups is risky for human health. Annual budgets are part of regular checkups for government. Budgets help weigh the relative merits of programs. Which are worthy? Which are wasteful? For a meaningful budget checkup, adequate budget information is needed. Indeed, there is no government function that should be more open to public scrutiny than how taxpayer money is spent. Taxation without representation was a rallying cry for the Revolution. Taxation with representation, but without spending disclosure, is little better. During the Cold War, however, a tradition developed of concealing the money being spent by America's intelligence agencies from the public and Congress. The spending for intelligence agencies was hidden away in vague budget categories. Intelligence spending for a given year was kept secret for generations, which is akin to a fifty-year old *never* having had a medical exam. The secrecy continued after the Cold War ended, but has gradually begun to lift.

So-called black budgets have been attacked on both Constitutional and policy grounds. In the Constitution, the Framers required openness in government accounts. Article I, Section 9, Clause 7—known as the Statement and Account Clause—reads:

> No money shall be drawn from the Treasury, but in consequence of Appropriations made by Law; and a regular Statement and Account of the Receipts of all public money shall be published from time to time.[70]

The words "made by Law" could be read to require, at the least, that Congress know the purposes for which it appropriates money. However, for a long time, all that most members of Congress knew about the intelligence agencies was that Congress was appropriating unknown but vast sums of money for unknown purposes. This early version of "don't ask, don't tell" was part of the long lapse in congressional oversight of the intelligence community. As onetime White House counsel and secretary of defense Clark Clifford put it, "Congress chose not to be involved and preferred to be uninformed."[71]

The second half of the Statement and Account Clause requires periodic statements of how government money is spent. The public cannot know what it is paying for without such statements. They help check fraud and waste and allow the electorate to see, in concrete terms, the government's priorities. Nonetheless, secrecy proponents have fastened on the phrase "from time to time" to excuse perpetual secrecy for intelligence spending. The history of the clause does not support this. "[F]rom time to time" was suggested by Madison at the Constitutional Convention as a substitute for an annual statement proposed by George Mason, Madison's fellow Virginia delegate. According to Madison, the words "from time to time" would require "the duty of frequent publications and leave enough to the discretion of the Legislature." Moreover, said Madison, the rule of "half-yearly publications" under the Articles of Confederation, had failed because it "[r]equire[d] too much and the difficulty will beget a habit of doing nothing."[72] In the Virginia Ratifying Convention—again in opposition to Mason—Madison explained that "from time to time" ensured the required published amounts would be "more full and satisfactory to the public, and would be sufficiently frequent."[73] It appears that while not rigid, the Statement and Account Clause calls for frequent disclosure of government spending. Surely "from time to time" cannot mean "for all time." It cannot possibly justify delaying publication of budget information for generations.

The Supreme Court has ducked the issue. In 1974, in a 5–4 decision written by Chief Justice Warren Burger, the Court held a taxpayer had no standing to bring a claim that the Statement and Account Clause required revealing the CIA's budget.[74] In a footnote, Burger said it was for Congress, not the courts, to decide what the Constitutional provision meant. But Burger stretched his opinion to favor secrecy, claiming "historical analysis of the genesis" of the clause "suggests that it was intended to permit some degree of secrecy in government operations."[75] "Some degree" cannot mean perpetual secrecy, and secrecy was not part of the reasoning of Madison, the author of the "from time to time" clause. Another obvious point Burger missed was the contrast with another Constitutional clause that uses "from time to time." The Journal Clause requires the House and Senate to keep journals of their proceedings and to publish them "from time to time *except the parts thereof as in their judgment require secrecy.*"[76] The Statements and Accounts Clause has no such green light for secrecy.

Assuming the courts are neutered by Burger's opinion, the issue is a policy question for Congress and the people. An open debate on policy is probably healthier for democracy. Moreover, courts are not well suited to drawing sharp lines on how much should be disclosed and how fast.

Proponents of budget secrecy also stress a 1790 act of the First Congress that appropriated $40,000 for a contingent fund for George Washington to use at his discretion for sensitive intelligence needs. The appropriation, which grew in later years, required the president to "account specifically" for all payments that "in his judgment may be made public," and then to provide the "amount of such expenditures as he may think it advisable not to specify."[77] The 1790 law, however, was quite different from the modern practice of far broader budget concealment. Both the general purpose and the amount of Washington's contingent fund were known. Just the details of some portion of how the fund was spent could be kept secret. The modern analogue would be, for example, publicly allocating $X million for CIA covert operations, but then allowing amounts spent on specific covert operations to be kept secret.

So what are the policy arguments pro and con for black budgets? And for keeping categories of spending secret for generations? The case *for* budget secrecy is that enemies *might* learn something from openness. The case *against* budget secrecy is that Americans—Congress, expert analysts, and the public—*would* learn something from openness. With openness, they could better analyze the effectiveness of various intelligence programs, assess them relative to the threats facing the nation, and weigh them against other national priorities.

Nonetheless, starting with the CIA's creation in 1947 and continuing with the growth of the modern American intelligence community, budget secrecy prevailed. Even the aggregate budget for the entire intelligence community—which became known as the "Top Line"—was hidden. This secrecy went unchallenged for decades. Virtually all members of Congress accepted nondisclosure, or subscribed to the view that the less members knew about intelligence the better, for they could not be held accountable. A few maverick members asked questions, but they were promptly slapped down. Ed Koch was one such maverick. As a congressman, Koch met with CIA Director Richard Helms at CIA headquarters in 1971 for "a great breakfast on gold service." As Koch described it, after Helms's presentation, the director opened the floor for questions: "Gentlemen, this is probably the only time you will ever have an opportunity to ask any question of the CIA." Never shy, Koch asked how many people the CIA employed and what the size of its budget was. "There are only two questions I can't answer," Helms said, "and those are the two." Koch replied, "[A]re you telling me, that I, a Member of Congress, can't learn the size of your budget? After all, I vote on that budget." "That is exactly what I am telling you," Helms concluded. "That budget item is buried . . . and you will never know what it is."[78]

Over the years, a growing chorus of voices began to ask questions like Koch's. In 1976, the Church Committee concluded "a full understanding of the budget of the intelligence community is required for effective oversight," adding that "secrecy makes it impossible for Congress as a whole to make use of this valuable oversight tool."[79] Nothing changed in response. After the Cold War ended, however, the budget issue received more attention. Secrecy advocates continued to resist public disclosure, arguing that adversaries might learn something through analysis of spending patterns. Virginia School of Law professor Robert Turner—a thoughtful advocate for budget secrecy—articulated what he referred to as the "conspicuous bump theory," suggesting that "a foreign intelligence service might be able to confirm the existence of an expensive new program or technology by spotting a change in the CIA or Intelligence Community budget."[80]

The proper question, however, is whether the claimed disadvantages of openness outweigh the advantages.

If the total-secrecy argument were valid for America's intelligence agencies, couldn't adversaries learn something by analyzing shifts in our *military* budget? Yet the Defense Department's aggregate annual number is public, as are the numbers for the Army, Navy, Air Force, and Marines. In any case, the annual intelligence budget had been, for years, "the worst kept secret in the Capital."[81] The Congressional Research Service reported that "[e]ven during the height of the Cold War, Soviet authorities . . . undoubtedly had a reasonably accurate knowledge of the extent of the U.S. intelligence budget."[82] Presumably, the same is now true for the Chinese. Terrorists like al-Qaeda would learn nothing of value from knowing the size of intelligence budgets.

The argument against disclosure of the Top Line is particularly weak when laid against the benefits from openness. Perhaps the fervid arguments against Top Line disclosure were pressed as a ruse. Drawing a sharp line at the Top Line kept the focus away from the aggregate budgets of particular agencies, such as the CIA and NSA. Here, all the same arguments for openness apply, and all the same weaknesses of secrecy exist. Not only does the military reveal its services' budgets but also, as the front-page *Washington Post* series on "Top Secret America" showed, meticulous investigative journalism can uncover details about the size and scope of intelligence agencies' spending.[83]

The fall of the Soviet regime left America the lone superpower, and increased the calls for more budget transparency. In 1997, the Clinton administration responded to a Freedom of Information Act lawsuit by the Federation of American Scientists by releasing the Top Line National Intelligence Budget: $26.6 billion. But the administration stopped there, saying, "[W]e will continue to protect from disclosure any and all subsidiary information concerning the intelligence budget: whether the information concerns particular intelligence agencies or particular intelligence programs."[84]

The budget-transparency debate was renewed in the wake of 9/11. Among the reforms suggested by the 9/11 Commission was that "the overall amounts of money being appropriated for national intelligence and to its component agencies should no longer be kept secret." The Commission did not propose going further: "The specifics of the intelligence appropriation would remain classified, as they are today."[85] In October of 2007, Congress adopted the recommendation. Since then, the aggregate National Intelligence Program (NIP) numbers have been disclosed within thirty days of the end of the fiscal year.[86] No one has shown any negative national security impact.

Moreover, starting in 2010, the Obama administration began to release the budget Top Line for the Military Intelligence Program (MIP)—the second major component of America's intelligence expenditures; it also later released the MIP total going back to 2007.[87] However, for both NIP and MIP, the Obama administration has repeated, almost by rote, the language about not going further than the Top Line.[88]

Lost in the debate on Top Line numbers is a more pointed question—why stop there? Few suggest complete, immediate disclosure of every line item in intelligence budgets. That would inevitably risk harm. But the vast chasm between full disclosure and the Top Line forecloses a meaningful budget checkup for intelligence agencies. The total intelligence budget requested for the NIP and MIP for the 2014 fiscal year was just over $70 billion, a large public expenditure that taxpayers and members of Congress cannot scrutinize based on a single aggregate number.[89]

There is a reasonable middle ground between Top Line and full budget transparency. The Defense Department budget is a fair start. Although it has lots of black holes, the defense budget lists the amounts for the four service branches. Why should the public and Congress not be able to review the amounts spent by each of the intelligence community's seventeen member agencies? How is that information any more dangerous for adversaries to learn than the amount being spent by each of the American armed forces? Moreover, without harm, but with substantial benefit, more detail beyond an agency total could be provided: for example, the CIA could provide the figures for its groups responsible for covert action and analysis.

As for Congress, the intelligence committees can now see more detailed budget figures. As a result, they can oversee the amount of spending and the quality of work on, for example, language translation or government efforts to make sense out of the vast amount of data NSA collects each day. Strengths and weaknesses in such specific areas might be kept secret from adversaries. But they are too important not to be carefully scrutinized by the congressional committees.

While more transparent, the Defense Department budget has had big "black holes." Traditionally a place to bury intelligence spending, the Defense Department budget has also historically concealed a number of its own sensitive or technologically advanced military projects, including the Stealth radar-evading bomber and a huge project for a new generation of spy satellites. Both exceeded time and cost estimates by years and billions. The new satellite system was abandoned, and the Stealth program has not lived up to its massive expenditures. In both cases, there was waste.[90] But to make such defense-budget expenditures public annually might aid adversaries. Oversight by the relevant congressional committees should, therefore, be extra-vigorous to make up for the absence of insight provided by experts and the media.

Who Owns History?[91]

When the intelligence budget is a black hole beyond the Top Line, the public cannot make fully informed decisions, and Congress cannot adequately make decisions about spending or meaningfully oversee current governmental operations. Restricted access to presidential papers and records after an administration has left office hurts history and therefore wounds democracy. Without an administration's records, future leaders cannot make sense of and learn from the past, and the public is inhibited from directing the nation's future.

Do presidents and other high-ranking government officials *own* the documents they write or receive while serving in public office? Yes seems a strange answer. After all, the officials perform the people's business paid for by the taxpayers. So it seems unfair—indeed absurd—that presidents and their heirs could claim ownership of these documents; keep them secret forever or for however long they wish; could destroy them all, or any they find embarrassing; and, to top it off, could sell them back to the government or take tax deductions for donating them.[92] Yet beginning with George Washington and for nearly two centuries until the aftermath of Watergate, individual ownership was the assumption and the practice.

The tradition began when, in order to serve both "the present age [and] posterity," George Washington began organizing his papers during the Revolutionary War.[93] After the end of his presidency, Washington planned to construct a building at Mount Vernon to store and secure his papers.[94] However, no depository was built, and Washington bequeathed the papers to his nephew Bushrod Washington, a Supreme Court Justice, who in turn bequeathed them to *his* nephew, George Corbin Washington (GCW), a Maryland congressman. In the 1830s and 1840s, GCW sold the documents to the government except those of a "private nature, or [those] which it would be obviously improper to make public." In 1835 and 1836, the government paid GCW $25,000, paying an additional $20,000 in 1849, after it was clear that papers were missing.[95] All told, GCW netted a pretty penny for papers penned on government time—more than $1.1 million in today's currency.

While the concept of continuing presidential ownership now seems bizarre and unacceptable, in the late eighteenth century it was more understandable (but nonetheless harmful). Back then, the government had no repository for delicate documents. Indeed, it was not until 1897 that the Library of Congress built its Manuscript Division for long-term document storage.[96] It is also worth recalling that the new nation's prospects for survival were uncertain.[97] Indeed, two years into the War of 1812, the British burned down the President's House, as the White House was then called.[98] Also, government was much smaller. And there were some reasons to consider documents personal. They were handwritten, often by the presidents themselves. And early presidents paid for their secretaries and other staff.[99] Congress first appropriated funds for White House staff in 1857, when it paid for a presidential secretary.[100]

Moreover, when writing in the 1830s, Tocqueville observed that in America there was little interest in the past. Indeed, according to Tocqueville, fewer records were kept in nineteenth-century America than in "France during the Middle Ages":

> [N]o one cares for what occurred before his time: no methodical system is pursued, no archives are formed, and no documents are brought together when it would be very easy to do so. Where they exist, little store is set upon them. I have among my papers several original public documents which were given to me in the public offices in answer to some of my inquiries. In America, society seems to live from hand to mouth, like an army in the field.[101]

In fact, many early leaders did care about their historical legacy, and many Americans hungered for connections to their past. Nonetheless, there was less care for preserving the past, particularly documents that were parts of creating history rather than the final product. For example, one of Washington's heirs spent hours "cutting up fragments from [Washington's] old letters and accounts . . . to supply the call for Any thing that bears the impress of his venerated hand."[102]

All these points are tied to earlier conditions that have changed. They imply a *tradition* of taking the documents, not a *right* to own them. None suggests a principled position or a legal doctrine that presidents actually owned the papers.[103] Therefore, when conditions changed, when the government had secure depositories, when documents began mostly to be typed and easy to duplicate, when there were millions of White House documents, when the White House became a huge bureaucracy, when presidents were well paid and supported by large paid staffs, when Americans began to care more about their history, there was no principled reason to keep alive any vestige of the concept that presidents *owned* their administration's documents.[104]

The tradition had harmful consequences. Chief among these was the harm in delaying—indeed, all too often preventing—access to parts of the nation's history.[105] This deprived the public of its birthright in a democracy. It kept public officials from learning lessons from the past. George Santayana's warning that "those who cannot *remember* the past are condemned to repeat it" has become a cliché.[106] But the presidential-ownership tradition was more insidious: presidents and their heirs had the power to *obscure or distort* the past by hiding, or destroying, vital evidence.

Many presidential documents were lost or destroyed in whole or in part: some by fire;[107] others by presidents, their wives, or their heirs.[108] As Chester Arthur's grandson told federal officials, the president had "caused to be burned three large garbage cans, each at least four feet high, full of papers which I am sure would have thrown much light on history."[109] Other presidents gave away documents to friends, admirers, or collectors, as did their heirs.[110] Bushrod Washington agreed to send to Lafayette all Lafayette's correspondence with George Washington because Lafayette had lost his copies "in the revolutionary storms of Europe."[111] Andrew Jackson's surviving documents were so widely dispersed that it took "some 100 distinct" purchases, gifts, or transfers to begin to reassemble them.[112]

Even presidents and their heirs who were careful about documents sometimes placed unreasonable restrictions on their disclosure. John Quincy Adams bequeathed his parents' and his own papers to his son Charles with a request that Charles build a fireproof building to store them. Charles built the Stone Library in his grandfather's home, the Old House, where the Adams family papers stayed until they were donated to the Massachusetts Historical Society in 1902. But Adams's descendants did not make the papers publicly available until 1956—130 years after John Adams's death and more than 150 years after he left office. The release of Lincoln's papers was also delayed far too long. After Lincoln's assassination, his papers were handled by his son, Robert Todd Lincoln, who probably destroyed some. He gave the rest to the Library of Congress in the 1920s but required they be kept secret from the public until 1947, twenty-one years after Robert's death and eighty-two years after his father's.[113]

Sometimes presidents used their document troves to beef up lucrative autobiographies long before others had access to their papers. Grant, Truman, Eisenhower, and Johnson are examples.[114] Sometimes heirs gave favored biographers early and exclusive access to presidential papers. Examples are Chief Justice John Marshall's and Jared Sparks's access to Washington's papers, and John Nicolay's and John Hay's to Lincoln's.[115] Of course, it was useful that these favored biographers put out information, but exclusive history from favored historians raises questions of bias. Moreover, some favored historians misfiled, lost, or damaged documents as they worked. According to Bushrod Washington, his colleague John Marshall told him the George Washington papers were "extensively mutilated by rats and otherwise injured by damp" while Marshall was writing his five-volume biography.[116]

Madison's handling of his extensive notes on the Constitutional Convention was injurious to the new nation's understanding of its history. Madison believed, as a matter of principle, that what was said at the Convention was irrelevant to the Constitution's meaning. He also felt the Convention's secrecy agreement should last for fifty years. Some other participants disagreed and made public their versions of particular events at the Convention, as George Washington did during the argument about the Jay Treaty.[117] Despite urging from Jefferson and others, Madison refused to release his notes, leaving them to his wife, Dolley, who sold them to the government in 1837, a year after Madison's death and fifty years after the Convention.[118]

Some have claimed that by keeping his notes secret for half a century, Madison distorted subsequent slavery debates.[119] Whether or not this is true, what is clear is that delaying the release of the notes for so long harmed history. Madison also disserved all the other Constitutional Convention participants who were quoted or referred to by Madison in his contemporaneous notes. They had no opportunity to disagree with or elaborate upon what Madison said. Fifty years later, they were all dead.

In addition to changes in the nature of the presidency, in the size and responsibilities of government, in how documents were written and copied, and in how many documents were produced, some government actions eroded the presidential-ownership tradition. After the Library of Congress established the Manuscript Division in 1897, most presidents donated all or most of their papers—accompanied, however, by access restrictions.[120] While the new facility reduced risk of loss or physical damage, it provided only a space, and maybe a catalogue. Then, in 1938, Franklin Roosevelt announced plans for a presidential library on his family's property in Hyde Park, New York.[121] Seven months later, Congress passed a law placing the Roosevelt library under the jurisdiction of the Archivist of the United States.[122] Although some congressmen were hostile—and blasted FDR as "an egocentric megalomaniac" for wanting a space separate from the Library of Congress—the bill passed easily.[123]

At the library's dedication in 1941, Roosevelt said, "A Nation must believe in three things. It must believe in the past. It must believe in the future. It must, above all, believe in the capacity of its own people so to learn from the past that they can gain in judgment in creating their own future."[124] Later, Congress enacted the Presidential Libraries Act, which made the Roosevelt option available to others.[125] Under the Act, a former president must raise the money for land and construction, but the federal government pays the ongoing maintenance costs. Even with this taxpayer support, for nearly three decades, former presidents were still unilaterally setting the rules for access to the documents.[126]

Then, to end the tradition, scandal was—as is often the case—required for reform. Watergate nudged Congress to catch up with changes that had already rendered the George Washington tradition anachronistic as well as harmful.

On September 8, 1974, President Gerald Ford pardoned Richard Nixon. Later that day, the White House announced an agreement between Nixon and the head of the General Services Administration.[127] The agreement allowed Nixon to destroy his White House tapes after September 1979 and required destruction of all tapes by Nixon's death or September 1984, whichever came first.[128] Regular documents were to be "deposited temporarily" in a federal "facility"—presumably to grant access to prosecutors. After three years, however, Nixon could withdraw the documents—of which there were said to be 42 million pages—although Nixon said he planned to donate the papers to the United States with "appropriate restrictions."[129]

A bill was promptly introduced in Congress to block Nixon from destroying any papers or recordings. The bill passed, and Ford signed it in December.[130]

Nixon challenged the law, but it was upheld by a unanimous three-judge district court,[131] then by a 7–2 decision in the Supreme Court.[132] The Supreme Court's opinion by Justice William Brennan characterized past practice as "a hit-or-miss approach" to preservation.[133] The Court relied heavily on the district court's conclusion that the new law served the public interest, because ability "to understand [a nation's] past enriches [citizens'] lives and helps . . . evaluate and perhaps to shape the present and future . . . promotion of such understanding could hardly be more integral to a society based on democratic principles and devoted to freedom of expression . . . ."[134] The Supreme Court added that an incumbent president seeking records relevant to current decisions "should not be dependent on happenstance or the whim of a prior President."[135] The district court was more explicit about one risk of unbridled control by a prior president:

> Any former President is virtually certain to be concerned with the light in which history will view the record of his tenure. His quite natural hope is that his conduct will be viewed with favor, and if he were to possess unbridled control over the papers of his administration—the raw materials from which historical judgments will be fashioned—there is always some risk that those items that might paint a different picture from the one he would like to portray will be subject to destruction or alteration. . . . [136]

Chief Justice Warren Burger and Justice William Rehnquist dissented, with Burger decrying "a grave repudiation of nearly 200 years of . . . historical practice" and disregard of a president's "implied prerogative" to control "his work papers."[137]

The law preventing destruction of Nixon's tapes and documents also called for a commission to study the "Records and Documents of Federal Officials." The commission—chaired by former Attorney General Herbert Brownell—

concluded the work records and documents of *all* federal officials should be public property. This included the documents of judges and members of Congress, as well as presidents and other executive-branch officials. Ironically, for a commission pushing public access, it did not print its own extensive research papers.[138]

Congress's response was mixed. Having previously prevented its Subcommittee on Government Information from holding a hearing on congressional secrecy, it was not surprising that House leadership rejected the proposal that its own papers should be public property. It also rejected any change for judges. But Congress did act on presidential records. In 1978, the tradition that George Washington began ended with the Presidential Records Act: "The United States shall reserve and retain complete ownership, possession and control of Presidential records."[139] While "Presidential records" were broadly defined,[140] the law placed a number of complex, and questionable, limits on *access*, including permitting a president to bar public availability to six categories of material for twelve years,[141] including "properly classified" materials "kept secret in the interest of national defense or foreign policy" and certain "confidential communications . . . between the President and his advisors, or between such advisors."[142] After the end of a president's bar, the documents are subject to FOIA.

Despite the Presidential Records Act, presidents continued to push back. The Reagan, Bush I, and Clinton administrations all argued the law did not require them to preserve e-mails and that White House e-mails need not be transferred to the Archivist. The challenges failed,[143] as did the effort by Reagan's Office of Legal Counsel to require the Archivist to honor an executive privilege claim by a former president.[144] Nonetheless, in a nod to monarchial tradition, Bush II subsequently issued an order giving substantial power over presidential records to former presidents and vice presidents (like his father), and to their heirs (like him). The order was widely derided by politicians from both parties, political scientists, and historians.[145] It was revoked by Barack Obama in an order issued the day after he was inaugurated.[146]

There is an enormous gulf between how the Bush and Obama orders handle claims of executive privilege by a former president. Bush gave the families of former presidents a right to claim the privilege. Obama recognized only claims by living former presidents. Bush required an incumbent president to concur in a former president's claim of privilege "absent compelling circumstances." Whatever a former president claimed, Obama required the Archivist to abide by instructions given by the incumbent president, unless otherwise directed by a final court order.

One line in Obama's order was especially significant for an audience of one: "'Presidential records' refers to those documentary materials maintained by NARA [the National Archives] pursuant to the Presidential Records Act, *including Vice Presidential records*."[147] Displaying his penchant for secrecy, Vice President Cheney had earlier claimed the Records Act did not apply to him. David Addington, then serving as Cheney's chief of staff, managed to keep a straight face as he told Congress a vice president is not really part of the executive branch. Rather, Addington argued, the vice president is "attached" to the legislative branch because the vice president occasionally presides over the Senate.[148] The new president ended this sophistry in four words.

Coming as it did in the midst of the Cold War, the Presidential Records Act was an uncommon reduction in presidential authority to keep information secret. No longer could presidents decide to destroy what they hoped to hide. Nor could they delay public access indefinitely. But presidents still retain power to delay public access. Access by the people to previously secret history is still not sufficiently prompt.

Science

Words from long ago still tell truths. "No man is an Island, entire of itself."[149] Written nearly four hundred years ago by John Donne in the context of a religious meditation, those words foreshadow America's problem with widespread scientific secrecy. In today's world, when it comes to science, no *country* is an island, entire of itself.

America is no longer the unrivaled scientific leader it was following World War II. Scientific competence has grown throughout the world, and the Internet facilitates the immediate spread of scientific ideas across continents. These developments are generally helpful to science in America, as elsewhere. But the regulations created to conceal U.S. scientific achievements from the Soviets—and then strengthened after 9/11—are now often futile.

Just as pervasive secrecy clashes with the founding creeds of our democracy, so too does it undermine the foundation of modern science. Secrecy is antithetical to good science; there is no other discipline where openness is more advantageous. Freedom to collaborate, exchange ideas, and publish enables scientists to build on the efforts of others, thereby advancing knowledge. As Isaac Newton put it at the dawn of modern science: "[I]f I have seen further, it is by standing on the sholders [*sic*] of Giants."[150] Openness enables peer review, which ensures intellectual rigor and uncovers error. Scientific secrecy, on the other hand, curbs collaboration and stifles creativity. Moreover, America's secrecy regulations for science, which were designed to serve safety, now often make us less safe. These regulations constructed a scientific Fortress America that is crumbling. We now have a *national* silo of scientific information cutting off American research from the rest of the world's work. Shoving American science into a silo has the potential to undermine our national security every bit as much as intelligence-information silos did before 9/11.

Of course, some scientific secrets should be protected. But the science secrecy regime is now backfiring.[151] As Gordon England, the George W. Bush administration's deputy defense secretary, said, "The greatest long-term threat to America" is not terrorists with weapons of mass destruction. "The greatest long-term threat to America . . . is falling behind in science and technology."[152] That slippage stems in part from the unintended consequences of America's long-standing effort to seal up scientific and technological progress on sensitive subjects.

In the course of history—before classification, limits on foreigners studying science in America, and other modern forms of secrecy—the powerful sometimes tried to *suppress* science. Pope Urban VIII sought to punish Galileo for his support for Copernicus's heliocentric cosmology. After confessing he had breached an agreement not to present his ideas provocatively, Galileo was convicted of heresy in a 1633 trial that itself was held in secret to avoid further dissemination of his dangerous ideas.[153] Nonetheless, although Galileo spent the last nine years of his life under house arrest, this attempt at suppression did not bottle up his discoveries for long. While—at least in the West—suppression of basic scientific truths is now rare, it is not dead. Just a few years ago, the George W. Bush administration sought to gag James Hansen, the top climate scientist at NASA, from discussing the science of global warming. It also sought to excise references to global warming from government publications.[154] But the central threat to American scientific advancement has not come from government efforts to suppress basic truths.

It has come from efforts to keep scientific or technological applications secret. The Manhattan Project led the way. While the project to build the bomb was properly kept secret, some contend secrecy slowed the job.

General Leslie Groves, who ran the Manhattan Project, was a career officer in the Army Corps of Engineers.[155] Understandably obsessed with keeping the project secret, Groves insisted on rigid compartmentalization of the scientists' work. The project had lots of small and large scientific silos, restricting information for individual employees to "the minimum necessary for the proper performance of his duties" and also separating the work by scientists in different Project centers. After the war, Leó Szilárd, a noted physicist who had drafted Einstein's letter to President Roosevelt urging attention to nuclear fission, told Congress, "We did not put two and two together because the two twos were in a different compartment." Indeed, said Szilárd, the rules limiting exchange of ideas may have set back the work by more than a year, consequently delaying the war's end.[156]

Compartmentalization had security benefits, and it is unclear if Szilárd (who had soured on the project for unrelated reasons) was correct about the accompanying harm. Nonetheless, some other project scientists continued to claim scientific secrecy had been carried too far. In later years, Edward Teller, the father of the hydrogen bomb, a man not known for being soft on communism, also came out against the secrecy system, arguing it had been applied so that "highly qualified scientists are barred from discussions of defense problems for lack of the required clearance."[157]

Albert Einstein made a more fundamental point: secrecy was a threat not just to science but to democracy itself. The implications of scientific discoveries were too important to be trusted to elites at the upper echelons of government. "To the village square we must carry the facts of atomic energy," he said, adding that the nuclear age "directly concerns every person in the civilized world." Choices about survival "depend ultimately on decisions made in the village square."[158] The first draft of the Atomic Energy Act moved in that direction by calling for "free dissemination of basic scientific information and for maximum liberality in dissemination of related technical information."[159] However, when the final version reached Truman's desk in 1946, the act contained the most sweeping secrecy doctrine in American history. Known as "born secret," *any* information pertaining to atomic energy was deemed classified unless it was specifically declassified.[160]

As the Cold War heated up, openness lost; scientific secrecy became the order of the day. Classification covered more technological work. Moats surrounding Fortress America to keep out foreign scientists and PhD candidates were dug deeper. Yet even during the height of the Cold War, government reports by experts recognized the danger the secrecy system posed to American science. In 1957, a Defense Department Commission warned of "dangers to national security that arise out of overclassification of information which retards scientific and technological progress." This "deprive[d] the country of the lead time that results from the free exchange of ideas and information."[161] A decade later, these concerns escalated in the 1970 *Report of the Defense Science Board's Task Force on Secrecy*, which called for "major surgery" on the secrecy system. Classified scientific information, the task force said, should be "decreased perhaps as much as 90 percent." Excessive classification was creating "barriers to rapid development," and labs doing classified work were "encountering more and more difficulty in recruiting the most brilliant and capable minds." In any event, "never in the past has it been possible to keep secret the truly important scientific discoveries."[162]

The 1957 and 1970 reports focused on the harm that excessive secrecy was doing to science in the United States. Today, excessive secrecy is weakening American science's world standing. This new concern is highlighted in two recent reports written by distinguished panels for the National Academy of Sciences.[163] Echoing the 1970 task force's call for "major surgery," the panels urged "fundamental change." But the reasoning of the recent reports springs from a very different global community, one that is "increasingly integrated and competitive."[164] Moreover, the United States is now only *"among the leaders"* and is "increasingly interdependent with the rest of the world." Indeed, the Cold War system limiting sharing of information between U.S. scientists and the rest of the world "was designed for a world that no longer exists." The outmoded secrecy rules now also weaken American business and hamper university research.[165] According to the National Academy, "export controls" on scientific ideas and increasingly stringent visa controls are choking the flow of promising foreign students and accomplished scientific professionals into the United States. Many world-class American universities refuse to do government-sponsored scientific research because of the handcuffs that come with government contracts.[166]

Concerns about excessive secrecy were expressed by the National Academy even about a topic that would seem suited for secrecy: pathogen research. Publishing pathogen research "could provide terrorists with recipes for their production, enabling an attack that could endanger our population." But "[p]olicies aimed at limiting access by malicious parties . . . can constrain the efforts of those desiring to put such information to good use."[167] Globalization of scientific research exacerbates the tension between openness and secrecy. Foreign nations perform a considerable amount of pathogen research. Therefore, even with ironclad restrictions on access to U.S. scientific discoveries, it is difficult to keep information out of the hands of sponsors of terrorism. After weighing these issues, the National Academy concluded the harm done to U.S. science by bottling up research—even on a subject as sensitive as pathogens—weighs heavier in the balance between openness and secrecy.

The difficulty of balancing secrecy in science with national security took on an international character in a 2012 skirmish involving a federal advisory committee on biosecurity, researchers in the United States and abroad, the World Health Organization, and two prominent scientific journals. The tension involved the pros and cons of publishing research on a deadly strain of flu—bird flu, or A/H5N1. Since its discovery in 1997, bird flu had infected about six hundred people who lived or worked close to infected birds; more than half died.[168] Health experts worried the virus could evolve to spread by human coughing or sneezing. If so, a new virus with no vaccinations or built-up immunities could possibly be as deadly as the 1918 "Spanish" flu, which killed more than fifty million people worldwide.[169]

Based on research funded by the National Institute of Allergy and Infectious Diseases, scientists at the University of Wisconsin and the Erasmus Medical Center in Holland introduced genetic changes in the virus that made it transmittable among ferrets, whose lungs, sneezes, and coughing closely resemble those of humans. The National Science Advisory Board for Biosecurity asked *Science* and *Nature* magazines not to publish parts of the research for fear "terrorists might use the data to weaponize influenza."[170] Later, after the World Health Organization recommended publication, the advisory board reversed itself[171] and *Nature* and *Science* published the articles.[172]

The case for publication, according to *Science,* was that it would "motivate many more policy-makers and scientists to work to reduce the likelihood that this virus will evolve to cause a pandemic."[173] Or, as Dr. Anthony Fauci, the director of the National Institute for Allergy and Infectious Diseases, said, "[B]eing in the free and open literature makes it easier to get a lot of the good guys involved than the risk of getting the rare bad guy involved."[174] Additional factors said to favor publication were that preventing publication of research would deter talented professionals from entering the field; and, given that many other nations have the capacity to do breakthrough research, U.S. censorship is likely to be ineffective. Indeed, even if research is never published but only discussed among professionals, it is likely to wind up on the Internet.

Still, in light of the harm that could be done to science as a whole if in just one situation a "bad guy" did take advantage of the overall sensible advice to strike a balance in favor of openness, a broad array of professionals and public officials should convene to further explore and explain such issues. The question is not limited to pathogens. Cryptography and computer security are two other fields in which thinkers "have been wrestling for decades" with similar problems. Over time, restrictions in these fields have been loosened because, according to an article in *Science*, "the bad guys make use of this research too, but the beneficial uses far outweigh the malicious ones."[175]

The choices for some secrecy issues are hard (as with pathogen research). Others are made to seem hard when they aren't (as with budgets). Perspectives change as the country changes (as with the handling of presidential documents and the health of government leaders). One constant is the tension between an openness culture and a secrecy culture. Another constant is the seduction of secrecy.

6

Cultures of Secrecy

During the Secrecy Era, investigative reporters, Congress, and executive-branch watchdogs have exposed many government secrets. However, the exposures—of torture at Abu Ghraib and efforts to destroy Dr. King, for example—and subsequent press coverage have emphasized the individual secrets without examining the secrecy culture in which they were bred.[1] The reasons for this are many. Specific secrets are sexy. They sell. And highlighting embarrassing or illicit secret acts helps call government and public attention to a problem. Focusing on the underlying secrecy culture is more complicated and less dramatic. But it is essential if the country is to address secrecy's dangers. Reform requires exploration of key aspects of the secrecy culture that shroud government and public life.

Don't Stop Thinking About Tomorrow

When major decisions are made secretly, there are no outside observers or critics to point out risks and call attention to changed circumstances. When their decisions are secret, leaders are more likely to stop thinking about their proposals, and fail either to look into how their actions turn out or to provide future institutional checks. In addition to atomic-bomb targeting, these consequences of secret decision-making are exemplified by early expansions of FBI and CIA powers and by the Bush administration's turn to torture.

In 1938, President Franklin Roosevelt secretly expanded the FBI's investigative authority, going beyond former Attorney General Stone's standard that the Bureau should investigate only criminal conduct forbidden by U.S. law. Some directives took the form of secret presidential orders; others were embedded within secret memos by FBI Director Hoover, which described oral conversations with the president. Roosevelt directed the Bureau to investigate espionage, sabotage, and violations of neutrality regulations—all of which were forbidden by the criminal laws of the United States. In some of his instructions, however, Roosevelt dramatically broadened the FBI's authority by tacking on mandates to investigate what Roosevelt termed "subversion."[2] Neither Roosevelt nor Hoover defined this amorphous, imprecise term.[3]

Roosevelt did not ask Congress for a law that would allow the FBI to undertake expanded domestic security investigations. It was, Hoover said, "imperative" that the expansion go forward "with the utmost degree of secrecy in order to avoid criticism or objections." Attorney General Homer Cummings counseled that plans for expanded domestic investigations "be handled in the strictest confidence."[4]

A few years later, Roosevelt's new attorney general, Robert Jackson, ordered the FBI to stop warrantless wiretaps of Americans because Jackson read a recent Supreme Court ruling as implicitly prohibiting them. Jackson also reinstated the FBI manual's description of warrantless wiretapping as "an unethical practice."[5] Soon, however, FDR disputed Jackson's legal reasoning, saying in a confidential memorandum to the attorney general that he was "convinced" the Court did not mean to apply its decision to "grave matters involving the defense of the nation." Roosevelt then secretly ordered that government agents continue intercepting communications of "persons suspected of subversive activities."[6] Once again, FDR provided no explanation as to what "subversive" meant. Neither did he say why judicial warrants could not be sought for such interceptions or point to anything in the Supreme Court ruling that supported his conviction.

Hoover used the Bureau's mandate to investigate "subversion" sparingly during FDR's administration.[7] Later, however, the vague new mandate opened the door to widespread abuse by the FBI. Because FDR's message to Hoover expanding the FBI's domestic-security mandate and his wiretap instruction to Jackson were secret, neither Congress nor the public could consider the implications of the vague subversion standard. Roosevelt failed to consider whether a broad, imprecise grant of power to an internal security police force could lead to improper or illegal actions. He imposed no checks upon Hoover's future use of power.

The FBI's secret powers were increased further during the Eisenhower administration, once again in the context of a Supreme Court ruling restricting electronic surveillance. In 1954, the Court ruled that California police had "flagrantly, deliberately, and persistently violated" the Fourth Amendment's protection against unreasonable searches by planting a bug in a suspect's home without a warrant. The Court was particularly offended that the microphone was hidden in a bedroom.[8] After the decision, Justices took the unusual step of forwarding the case file to Attorney General Herbert Brownell, asking him to determine whether the police surveillance had violated federal criminal laws. But then, in the teeth of this clear signal of judicial disapproval, Brownell sent a secret memo to Hoover authorizing continued "unrestricted use" of bugs by the FBI in the "national interest." Brownell told Hoover the Bureau could decide to use bugs without a warrant, and without the approval of its nominal boss, the attorney general, because "considerations of internal security and the national safety are paramount."[9]

Brownell's secret memo, predicated on the loose, open-ended term "national interest," manifested a clear disregard for the law and the courts. For more than two decades, until the Church Committee's revelations in 1975 and 1976, Brownell's memo also opened the door to concealed abuses, including the FBI's later bugging of Martin Luther King Jr.'s hotel rooms—for reasons that had absolutely nothing to do with the national interest, or internal security, or national safety. Ironically, Brownell, who was for the time a progressive on civil rights and instrumental in the appointment of pro-civil-rights judges in the South, is now also known for unwittingly facilitating Hoover's assault on King. This should serve as a stark reminder to government officials: history is rarely kind to leaders who fail to consider secrecy's potential harms.

A major expansion of CIA powers was also initially kept secret from the public and Congress. When the National Security Act of 1947 created the CIA, the Agency's roles were described as making "recommendations" about "coordination" of intelligence by other government departments, "correlat[ing] and evaluat[ing] intelligence relating to the national security," and "advis[ing]" on intelligence activities. The act made no mention of either covert action or espionage—which together came to dominate CIA activities. Instead, the legislation used open-ended language to mention other possible missions for the CIA, giving it authority "to perform such other functions and duties related to intelligence affecting the national security as the National Security Council may from time to time direct."[10]

Then, within a year of the law's passage, President Harry Truman's National Security Council issued a secret directive empowering the CIA to use "subversion," including "assistance to . . . guerillas," "sabotage," "economic warfare," and "propaganda" in covert action overseas.[11] This transformative shift in the character and scope of the CIA's mission was promulgated behind closed doors without debate. Neither Congress nor the people had any opportunity to debate whether the tactics were consistent with the nation's character (or "related to intelligence"). And as with FDR and the FBI, Truman failed to put checks upon the CIA's vague new mandate or establish meaningful oversight mechanisms in the executive branch.

The Bush administration's secret use of torture and other post-9/11 tactics also provide telling examples of granting authority with little thought about tomorrow. The decision-making process leading to torture involved quick judgments by a small band of like-minded officials. The deciders shut out voices that would have urged caution. Even friends and allies later criticized the administration. Most troubling, despite their own vicious terror tactics, al-Qaeda and its terrorist allies were able to turn America's descent to torture into a propaganda weapon.

Blind and Deaf to the Law

The ability to exercise unchecked power fueled intelligence agencies' culture of ignoring the law. As Sen. Walter ("Fritz") Mondale's cross-examination revealed to the Church Committee, William Sullivan, longtime leader of the FBI's Domestic Intelligence Division, admitted that for years the Bureau acted against law-abiding American citizens without anyone raising the question "Is this course of action which we have agreed upon lawful, is it legal, is it ethical or moral?" The Bureau "never gave any thought to this line of reasoning, because we were just naturally pragmatic." Similarly, the NSA's deputy director, Benson Buffham, admitted the legality of an NSA surveillance program "didn't enter into the discussion," and expressed amazement at the idea it might have.[12] This echoed the NSA's general counsel's statement to me that "the Constitution does not apply to NSA."

After 9/11, Vice President Cheney, his counsel David Addington, and Justice Department lawyer John Yoo moved beyond secretly ignoring the law to claiming (also secretly) that mere laws could not limit a president's "monarchial" powers.[13]

Secrecy's Slide: Mission Creep

Surely when President Roosevelt secretly expanded the FBI's power by authorizing the Bureau to investigate subversion, he did not contemplate anything like COINTELPRO, infiltration of the women's liberation movement, or widespread illegal mail-opening and burglaries. Nor did Attorney General Brownell imagine the FBI would bug Dr. King's hotel rooms. But the extensive record of past abuse teaches that the secrecy culture's failure to think about tomorrow—to impose restraints or checks—begets improper conduct. Programs expand in secret; mission creep sets in. Tom Charles Huston, the former Nixon aide who had coordinated the short-lived Huston Plan authorizing widespread spy-agency illegality, colorfully described mission creep to the Church Committee as a "move from [a focus on] the kid with a bomb to the kid with a picket sign, and from the kid with the picket sign to the kid with the bumper sticker of the opposing candidate. And you just keep going down the line."[14]

The FBI's warrantless wiretapping is a good example of mission creep. When Truman became president, Hoover got Truman to reauthorize Roosevelt's order. But Hoover did not reveal that FDR had requested Attorney General Jackson to limit warrantless subversive-activity taps to "a minimum" and "insofar as possible to aliens."[15] After Truman's reauthorization, the FBI used its warrantless wiretapping authority against countless law-abiding American citizens.

Mission creep is always toward the more extreme. The FBI's COINTELPRO first targeted Communist Party supporters, using a definition of "Communist" that was, to say the least, nebulous. The program then moved on to "harass or destroy" nonviolent Black religious leaders and student dissidents. Like the FBI, the CIA expanded its mission. In the early 1950s, the CIA conducted drug experiments on humans. Its first subjects were substance abusers in prison who volunteered—and were rewarded for participation with their drug of choice. Then the CIA moved to experimenting on unsuspecting or, as it euphemistically put it, "unwitting" victims.[16] The CIA's illegal mail-opening program is yet another example of mission creep. The Agency initially advocated the program as a way to catch foreign spies, but then moved to opening mail of peace-minded American citizens, including members of the American Friends Service Committee, a Quaker social reform organization.[17] Similarly, under Operation SHAMROCK, NSA (and its predecessor the Army Security Agency) for thirty years obtained telegrams that left the United States. SHAMROCK started with perusal only of encrypted telegrams from foreign embassies to their home countries. Later, however, NSA moved on to review the telegrams of American citizens who were Vietnam War protestors and civil-rights leaders.[18]

Mission creep also includes tactics used overseas secretly migrating to the United States. FBI Assistant Director Sullivan noted that COINTELPRO "brought home" to America tactics previously used only overseas in combating the Soviets.[19] Decades later, when the Bush administration chose its torture tactics, it borrowed from the SERE (Survival, Evasion, Resistance and Escape) manual the military used to prepare U.S. troops for enemy torture. The SERE manual, in turn, had been based on tactics that were used by North Koreans to obtain false confessions from Americans.[20]

Finally, mission creep occurs within the mechanics of the secrecy system itself. The three labels that govern classification—confidential, secret, and top secret—have been supplemented by many more code-word-protected secrets. Also, a particularly sensitive document may be "top secret/sensitive eyes only." At the same time, access to unclassified information may be restricted by nebulous labels such as "sensitive but unclassified."[21] The proliferation of classification labels to ever-higher levels of restriction has engendered a system in which some government officials read only documents classified at the highest level. And low-level staff seeking superiors' attention are tempted to overclassify.

Secrecy's Sinkhole: Floating Authority

Missions tend to creep when programs remain secret for long periods of time with few limitations and little, if any, oversight. A related danger is the assumption that once a secret program has been authorized by one leader, it needs no further authorization from later leaders.

CIA officials embraced the idea of floating authority, applying it even to the most risky and controversial covert operations, including assassination attempts on foreign leaders. CIA Director Allen Dulles authorized plots to assassinate Cuba's Fidel Castro, but Dulles was later replaced by John McCone. Knowledgeable CIA officials did not discuss the ongoing plots with McCone—who later said he would not have approved.[22]

The FBI was also prone to never-ending investigations facilitated by the secrecy culture. The Bureau first infiltrated the NAACP in 1941 at the Navy's request, after Black mess attendants had protested against racial discrimination. After this, the FBI kept an informer in the NAACP for at least twenty-five years, even though there was never any evidence of unlawful activity.[23] Similarly, for many years, the FBI wiretapped and lodged COINTELPRO actions against Bayard Rustin, the preeminent proponent of nonviolence who advised Dr. King and was the principal organizer of the 1963 March on Washington. After a lengthy investigation, the Bureau's New York office concluded Rustin, who had been investigated because he was a suspected Communist "sympathizer," in fact had no Communist ties. Hoover nonetheless ordered that the investigation continue because "[w]hile there may not be any evidence that [Rustin] is a Communist neither is there any substantial evidence that he is anti-Communist."[24]

In testimony before the Church Committee, Nicholas Katzenbach, the first attorney general in the Johnson administration (and Deputy AG under Kennedy), described a common element in these never-ending FBI investigations: The "custom was not to put a time limit on a tap, or any wiretap authorization." "Indeed," Katzenbach continued, "the Bureau would have felt free in 1965 [when Katzenbach was AG] to put a tap on a phone authorized by Attorney General Jackson before World War II."[25]

Unknown Unknowns: Secrecy's Most Dangerous Feature

In an oft-ridiculed 2002 press-conference statement, Secretary of Defense Donald Rumsfeld provided, perhaps unwittingly, a useful frame for analyzing America's secrecy culture:

> [T]here are known knowns; there are things we know we know. We also know there are known unknowns; that is to say we know there are some things we do not know. But there are also unknown unknowns—the ones we don't know we don't know.[26]

Rumsfeld used this convoluted wording to evade press questions about weapons of mass destruction during the lead-up to the Iraq War. In the memoir he published nine years later, Rumsfeld supplied as an example of an unknown unknown the possibility of "[n]ineteen hijackers using commercial airliners as guided missiles to incinerate three thousand men, women, and children," which Rumsfeld argued the administration could not have possibly contemplated. There is a logical fallacy here. By piling on details, such as the number of hijackers or number of deaths, almost by definition no one would have imagined the attacks. But a major attack from al-Qaeda was definitely imagined. So was the possibility of using jets as suicide bombs. Nonetheless, Rumsfeld was correct that behind the "enigmatic language" of unknown unknowns lies a "simple truth about knowledge . . . there are things of which we are so unaware, we don't even know we are unaware of them."[27]

In his original statement, Rumsfeld said "unknown unknowns" have been the "most difficult" category in U.S. history. Rumsfeld was referring to information the U.S. government did not know it did not know. When, however, it is the government itself that has kept the very existence of a broad program secret from the American public and from Congress, unknown unknowns are more than "most difficult." They are also most dangerous.

The grant of unchecked power to intelligence agencies sometimes results in agencies taking abusive or illegal action that is hidden even from presidents. In COINTELPRO, the FBI severely harmed its reputation by secretly taking the law into its own hands to harass and destroy law-abiding Americans who dissented or protested on public issues. Secret experiments with drugs and radiation by the CIA, the military, and the Atomic Energy Commission were shameful because they preyed upon ordinary citizens who were unaware that they had been drugged or radiated.[28] One experimental drug was LSD. It was known as a powerful psychiatric drug, whose hallucinogenic properties were considered of potentially great value in psychotherapy. So it was hardly a surprise that the CIA—keenly interested in all aspects of human behavior—wanted to study the drug. CIA officials wondered what might happen if LSD was given to a captured American agent and whether it would be useful for the CIA's own interrogations of captured spies. These were legitimate questions. What was not legitimate was administering LSD to "unwitting" subjects.

The unsuspecting victims of the CIA's curiosity had no medical screening or follow-up. No doctor controlled the dosages or was at the ready in case something went awry. Many subjects became ill. In one case, at a scientific retreat, a CIA scientist secretly slipped a dose of Cointreau laced with LSD into the drink of a scientist working for the Army Biological Center at Camp Detrick, Maryland. Nine days later, after being sent to New York for psychiatric treatment, the drugged Army scientist committed suicide by jumping out a hotel window. In an early example of silo secrecy, the CIA did not tell the military about the cause of death, even though it knew the military was also experimenting with LSD on unsuspecting subjects.[29]

After the suicide, Richard Helms, then a CIA deputy director, sought and obtained approval to continue the secret program. "While I share your uneasiness and distaste for any program which tends to intrude on an individual's private and legal prerogatives," he wrote to his boss, "I believe it is necessary that the Agency maintain a central role in this activity, keep current on enemy capabilities [concerning] the manipulation of human behavior, and maintain an offensive capability."[30] Decades later, after Helms became CIA director, he ordered destruction of records detailing the Agency's experiments with LSD and other "chemical, biological, and radiological materials."[31] Nonetheless—as often is the case after document destruction—a number of documents remained that laid bare why the CIA wanted to keep the experiments hidden. One was a 1957 CIA inspector general report that warned, "Precautions must be taken not only to protect operations from exposure to enemy forces but also to conceal these activities from the American public in general." The report added that "knowledge that the Agency is engaging in unethical and illicit activities would have serious repercussions in political and diplomatic circles and would be detrimental to the accomplishment of its mission."[32]

This advice eerily echoed an earlier Atomic Energy Commission memo on secret nuclear radiation experiments using humans, which said, "It is desired that no document be released which refers to experiments with humans and might have [an] adverse effect on public opinion or result in legal suits. Documents covering such work field should be classified 'secret.'"[33] And so they were for decades, until Hazel O'Leary, President Clinton's energy secretary, ordered a massive release of her department's secret files.

Euphemism: Secrecy's Lullaby

Euphemisms seed and then shelter secrets. Deftly used, language acts as an antiseptic that can make the unacceptable seem acceptable—both to the speaker or writer and to the listener or reader.[34] The failure to call dirty business by its rightful name increases the chance of dirty business being done. This failure is fuel for the secrecy culture.

Helms's memo to his boss supporting further tests of drugs on the unwitting is one example. Consider the sanitized language: "uneasiness," "distaste," "tends to intrude"—bleached, lifeless words about stark realities of death and secret lawlessness. Whom did Helms seek to fool? History? Or himself? Certainly not his boss, who understood the reality.

The Bush White House, masters of euphemistic sanitation, called its supersecret warrantless wiretapping program the "Terrorist Surveillance Program" and called torture "enhanced interrogation." This echoed the pattern from decades earlier when not one CIA operative involved in the previously secret plots to assassinate foreign leaders could bring himself to use the words "kill," "murder," or "assassinate." Instead, when they testified before the Church Committee, they used words like "dispose of," "get rid of," or "eliminate," or some such euphemistic circumlocution.[35]

The name "COINTELPRO" suggested the FBI was involved in counterintelligence, when in fact it sought to harass and destroy domestic dissidents. The internal label may have been intended to make agents more comfortable. But the FBI also used euphemism to foil its superiors. After glimmerings of COINTELPRO had been exposed by a break-in at the FBI office in Media, Pennsylvania, and a subsequent FOIA claim was made by reporter Carl Stern, Attorney General William Saxbe ordered Assistant Attorney General Henry Petersen to conduct an internal investigation. The Bureau persuaded Petersen that important security interests would be undermined if its bosses saw the raw facts. So it offered summaries instead of the actual documents describing each COINTELPRO incident. Neither Saxbe nor Petersen pushed back. As with the Bureau's successful effort to persuade the Kennedys to allow it to wiretap Martin Luther King Jr. and his close advisors, this undermine-security assertion was used as a sword by the FBI to mislead its nominal bosses and cover up damaging facts with euphemisms. In one brazen example, the FBI documents showed an effort in Chicago to induce "violent type activity, shooting, and the like" by the Blackstone Rangers against the Black Panthers, but the FBI's summary sugarcoated this violent scheme by euphemistically describing it as an effort to "hopefully drive a wedge" between the two rival black groups.[36]

The Bureau also engaged in verbal gymnastics by labeling the burglaries it conducted as "black bag jobs." Similarly, the CIA called the risk of getting caught in the criminal business of opening the mail its "flap potential."[37] Were these euphemisms meant to help agents (and their bosses) forget they were breaking the law? Later, when Oliver North devised a secret way to evade congressional laws barring aid to the Nicaraguan Contras, he created the "En-terprise," an offshore entity with its own airplanes, secure communications, and secret Swiss bank accounts.[38] Was a businesslike name designed to make improper or illegal conduct seem more respectable?

Euphemisms not only abet the creation of improper secret activities but also help minimize damage when the activities are exposed. Parts of Gen. Antonio Taguba's courageous 2004 report on abuses at the Abu Ghraib prison in Iraq graphically described "sadistic, blatant and wanton abuse of detain-ees by [American] military personnel."[39] When the secrecy stamp on Tagu-ba's report was challenged, the report was declassified. A Defense Department official acknowledged portions of the report had been overclassified but avoided conceding they had been classified to conceal illegal and embarrassing con-duct, proffering instead the euphemistic excuse of "the tempo of operations, lack of training and oversight."[40]

Sometimes exaggeration, not euphemism, is used to obscure odious con-duct. In the 1960s the FBI branded Martin Luther King's Southern Chris-tian Leadership Conference as a "Black nationalist hate group," even though the SCLC was made up of Black Baptist ministers who preached nonvio-lence.[41] Who was this meant to fool? Not the public, since the Bureau's ef-forts to destroy the SCLC were secret. Was it to make agents feel better about the dirty business they were engaged in? Perhaps.

Although not exactly euphemisms, labels like "national security" or "sub-versive activities" are so broad and vague that they allow government leaders to fool the public—and perhaps even fool themselves—by coating secret con-duct with a comforting gloss. As the Church Committee concluded, its enor-mous record showed that "imprecision and manipulation" of open-ended labels when "coupled with the absence of any outside scrutiny, has led to . . . im-proper use" of intrusive techniques against law-abiding Americans.[42] The "na-tional security" label was used to justify secret reports on telephone calls made by people like Eleanor Roosevelt, journalists, the chair of the House Agri-culture Committee, White House aides, and Supreme Court Justices William Douglas and Potter Stewart.[43] Similarly, the label justified opening the mail of organizations such as the American Friends Service Committee and the Federation of American Scientists, and writers such as John Steinbeck and Edward Albee.[44] In the post-9/11 period, the term "national security" con-tinues to be used loosely, including in the Bush and Obama administrations' assertion of a "state secrets" privilege to stop courts from reviewing claims based on warrantless wiretapping and torture.

The nebulous term "national security" has also been used after the fact to shield—and perhaps to justify in officials' own minds—obviously illegal conduct. In 1973, President Richard Nixon and White House Counsel John Dean were recorded on the secret Oval Office taping system discussing the break-in Nixon had ordered of the Los Angeles office of the psychiatrist of Daniel Ellsberg, who had leaked the Pentagon Papers to the *New York Times* and the *Washington Post*. A worried Nixon asked what might be done if the break-in were revealed, prompting Dean to suggest, "You might put it on a national security ground basis, which it really, it was." Later, the president took up Dean's suggestion as if it were his own, saying "the whole thing was national security." Dean replied, "I think we can probably get by on that."[45]

The break-in itself was born of secret conversations based on a deformed view of "national security" and an acceptance of monarchial presidential powers. Eventually, some of the true believers came to see how the "banner" of "national security" had converted their "perceived patriotism" into illegality. One reformed true believer was Egil Krogh, a young Nixon White House aide who was involved in planning the break-in. Krogh came to believe that the effort to steal information to discredit Ellsberg was a "repulsive and an inconceivable national security goal." In his view, the words "national security" blocked critical analysis because "freedom of the President to pursue his planned course was the ultimate national security objective . . . invocation of national security stopped us from asking 'Is this the right thing to do?'"[46]

As Krogh illustrates, small cliques developing policy in secret are particularly likely to be lured by the simplicity of slogans. "National security" is clearly a genuine priority. But the elastic—sometimes cynical—invocation of the phrase limits thought. The same is true for other pat phrases, as Justice Jackson said when he condemned the "loose and irresponsible use of adjectives . . . without fixed or ascertainable meanings"—such as "inherent," "war," or "emergency"—to describe presidential powers.[47] Francis Biddle, another attorney general under FDR, wrote of this danger in his autobiography, explaining that the internment of Japanese Americans during World War II, which he had opposed, demonstrated "the power of suggestion which a mystic cliché like 'military necessity' can exercise on human beings."[48]

Several decades later, when George W. Bush issued a memo announcing the "Humane Treatment of al Qaeda and Taliban Detainees," he used that same mystic cliché to proclaim that U.S. armed forces would "continue to treat detainees humanely and, to the extent appropriate and consistent with *military necessity*, in a manner consistent with the principles of [the] Geneva Convention."[49] Bush did not even mention the CIA. By using the vague exception for "military necessity," Bush hedged on having a genuine check on the military. Did he, or any of his advisors, have any idea of the unhappy history of the loose application of those words?

As William Safire, a conservative columnist and former Nixon White House speechwriter, wrote near the end of the Bush administration, some words "begin as bland bureaucratic euphemisms to conceal secret crimes," but bland terms like "the final solution" now send "a chill through our lexicon." And so, said Safire, it was with "waterboarding"—a bland word that covered over the "deliberate infliction of excruciating physical or mental pain to punish or coerce."[50]

Tucking Away Secrets

Officials keep information secret not only from enemies but also from friends, often doing so by hiding information in agency "silos" or "stovepipes." All sorts of motives exist for stovepiping, including the desire to hide embarrassment and bureaucratic rivalries and battles. Senator Moynihan, in his book on secrecy, noted that secrets are often "organizational assets, never to be shared save in exchange for another organization's assets."[51]

The 9/11 Commission stressed the danger of agencies not sharing secrets with one another. This is a long-lasting and continuing problem that goes beyond interagency rivalry. Secrets are hidden within agencies. Sometimes, they are hidden from bosses, including presidents, attorneys general, and agency heads. And often they are hidden from Congress.

Stuffing secrets into silos can harm the very national security that secrecy is meant to serve. The failure by the White House to reveal the gist of the many secret warnings it received about al-Qaeda threats in the summer of 2001 did so. Secrecy surrounding covert actions against Cuba in the early 1960s is also illustrative. When CIA Director Allen Dulles and Richard Bissell, head of the CIA's covert action wing, briefed President-elect Kennedy, they told him about the plan for the Bay of Pigs invasion but not about the plots to kill Fidel Castro.[52] CIA covert operators did not tell John McCone, the CIA director who succeeded Dulles, about their continuing plots to kill Castro. And when the CIA planned the Bay of Pigs invasion, operators in the covert-action division did not consult the experts on Cuba in the CIA's analysis division. Had they done so, they would have been told the hope of sparking a Cuban uprising was fanciful.[53]

Despite the 9/11 Commission's cautions, the enormous expansion of highly secret programs after 9/11 exacerbated the problem. Only a few senior officials in the Defense Department, known as "Super Users," have clearance to know about the existence of all the Department's intelligence programs. Moreover, "only about half of the 150 most highly classified technological programs within the Defense Department are shared with the staff charged with developing war plans for individual adversarial countries."[54] Perhaps such restrictive information sharing, even within the same agency, is necessary. But it risks damaging security by feeding the cultural tendency to jealously guard one's own secrecy fiefdom.

Turf wars have a long-standing place in the history of America's intelligence agencies. Hoover called the CIA "drunk with power" and full of security risks. Alan H. Belmont, Hoover's assistant in charge of intelligence, described the CIA as full of "waste, inefficiency, and plain boondogglery."[55] Despite Hoover's departure and the post-9/11 recognition of the importance of increased information-sharing between intelligence agencies, the silo approach persists. After the FBI opposed the CIA's use of torture in the interrogation of high-level al-Qaeda detainees, for example, the CIA began to keep information away from the FBI.[56]

The silo problem is not only within or between intelligence agencies. It also includes agencies keeping relevant secret information away from official bodies and even presidents. Allen Dulles did not tell the Warren Commission investigating President Kennedy's assassination (on which Dulles served) about the Castro assassination plots.[57] And at the start of the Cold War, the Army and the FBI did not tell President Truman of their success in breaking Soviet codes (the Venona Project). Therefore, when told about Soviet infiltration of the American government, Truman assumed the intelligence had been exaggerated, which allowed the House Un-American Activities Committee and Sen. Joseph McCarthy to exploit the issue.[58]

Haystacks and Needles

The culture of secrecy and the increasing abundance of raw information make it harder to find vital nuggets of information. This was as true in the paper age as it is in the digital age. According to testimony from local police chiefs, during the Cold War period, the FBI's "dissemination of large amounts of relatively useless or totally irrelevant information" reduced their efficiency.[59] The availability of massive amounts of digital information compounds the problem today. In March 2013 alone, NSA collected 97 billion pieces of intelligence from computer networks worldwide.[60] According to its own estimates, NSA "touches about 1.6 percent" of Internet traffic daily.[61] The Pentagon is "attempting to expand its worldwide communications network, known as the Global Information Grid, to handle yottabytes (10^{24} bytes) of data"—a unit so large that no one has yet coined a term for the next higher magnitude.[62] But at the same time as they have expanded their reach, secret agencies have been slow to develop technology that might make it possible to pan the gold nuggets from all the sand. According to Attorney General Janet Reno, before 9/11, "the FBI didn't know what it had . . . [T]he right hand didn't know what the left hand was doing." Still, four years after 9/11, only one-third of its employees were connected to the Internet.[63] Over at the Defense Department, NSA has been flummoxed by the technological difficulties of separating wheat from chaff in the mind-numbing amounts of data it collects.

Secrecy's Shield: Protecting Presidents from Responsibility

From the start of the Secrecy Era, secrecy and deception have shielded presidents from responsibility for risky and controversial secret acts. The techniques have evolved, but the aim has been constant. Some years after Truman's secret NSC directive gave the CIA power to use subversion, sabotage, and the like, it became generally known that the CIA had a secret program to destabilize or overthrow—as well as support—foreign governments. Indeed, as Clark Clifford, counsel to President Truman at the time of the 1947 National Security Act and a close advisor to several other presidents, told the Church Committee, this had become so widely believed that our "country has been accused of being responsible for practically every internal difficulty that has occurred in every country in the world."[64] Nonetheless, when the

CIA engaged in covert actions, the government used the thick fog of plausible deniability to obscure responsibility.

Originally intended to help shield from other countries U.S. responsibility for particular covert actions, plausible deniability came, in a kind of mission creep, to include efforts to shield presidents and other high officials from "knowledge, and hence responsibility" for cloak-and-dagger operations.[65] What started as a device to fool foreigners about American responsibility morphed into misleading devices to hide the truth from Americans and their elected officials. The Church Committee concluded this "permitted the most sensitive matters to be presented to the highest levels of Government with the least clarity." Plausible deniability was "[a]t times a delusion and at times a snare." It "created the risk of confusion, rashness and irresponsibility in the very areas where clarity and sober judgment were most necessary."[66] It was the "antithesis of accountability."[67] Because Congress was fenced out from knowledge of covert action programs, including assassination plots and plots to overthrow democratically elected foreign leaders, covert action also offered a "secret shortcut around the democratic process."[68]

When, in the 1980s, the Reagan administration carried out its Iran-Contra operations, it did not inform the new congressional intelligence committees about the arms deal with Iran or the money funneled to the Contra rebels in Nicaragua. Echoing the Church Committee, the congressional Iran-Contra investigation concluded that secrecy was used "not as a shield against our adversaries, but as a weapon against our own democratic institutions."[69]

More recently, there were suggestions that Vice President Dick Cheney embraced the principles of classic plausible deniability and tried to keep details of some unseemly actions away from President Bush.[70] But the Bush administration primarily relied on a new doctrine to try to shield the White House from responsibility. It sought refuge from responsibility by finding compliant lawyers to write secret opinions that, if the actions were ever exposed, enabled the president to say his lawyer said it was legal. Those were President Bush's exact words in 2010 when asked about torture. His administration used the same device for warrantless wiretapping.[71]

The legal rationales for the secret programs were themselves kept secret. This was dubious for two reasons. First, when the Justice Department's Office of Legal Counsel (OLC) issues opinions, they are binding on everyone in the executive branch (except the president). OLC opinions are, in effect, laws. But in a constitutional democracy, there is no justification for secret laws.[72] Second, when legal opinions narrowly define what constitutes torture under U.S. laws and treaties, or rule a president has some inherent power to ignore laws such as FISA in order to return to warrantless wiretapping, Congress and the public should know, whether one agrees or disagrees with the legal analysis. Secret legal opinions prevent the public from scrutinizing whether programs are wise or unwise, helpful or harmful, legal or illegal. They also prevent Congress from changing the law to conform to what *it* had wanted before executive-branch lawyers construed—or misconstrued—its aims. If OLC opinions are sound, there is no reason to fear disclosure. And withholding OLC opinions about the meaning of a law from every member of Congress, the body that wrote the law, is unjustifiable.

In its early days, the Obama administration released the Bush-era OLC opinions relating to torture, over CIA objections. But when the bell tolled for its own OLC opinions, such as on targeted killings, including those of American citizens, the actual opinions have not yet been publicly released, although summaries have been. The administration stalled, tried to get by with summaries instead of actual opinions, and then fought disclosure in court. After the Second Circuit Court of Appeals held the administration had waived protection of its legal analysis and of the role of the CIA by repeatedly referring to both in public statements, the administration abandoned Supreme Court review but only to save the nomination to another federal court of appeals of the author of the opinion. When the opinion finally appeared, the arguments for secrecy were exposed as frivolous—except for details of the intelligence about the dangerousness of Anwar al-Awlaki, the American citizen residing in Yemen who was the target of the attack. This was information that could have been kept secret by an agreement at the outset. As was all too often the case, the secrecy was eventually exposed as unnecessary.[73]

The post-9/11 tactic of seeking to evade responsibility by hiding behind secret legal opinions is unavailing. To begin with, the legal opinions only purport to *permit* certain actions such as torture or warrantless wiretapping, but the opinions *require* nothing. So it was President Bush, Vice President Cheney, and a close-knit circle of like-minded advisors who decided what to do. Second, the process of generating the opinions renders them suspect. John Yoo, a mid-level lawyer whose monarchical views of presidential power were well known, was selected to write the opinions on torture and warrantless wiretapping—presumably by his close friend David Addington, a Cheney aide who shared Yoo's views. Because of the extreme secrecy required by the White

House, Yoo produced the opinions without the usual collegial review. Had there been such a review, Yoo's faulty reasoning would not have survived. Keeping the opinions secret after they were written delayed the withering public reviews they ultimately received even from a key lawyer in the Bush administration, Jack Goldstein, the OLC chief under Bush who ultimately withdrew Yoo's opinions, characterizing them as "legally flawed, tendentious in substance and tone, and overbroad."[74]

Understanding how the legal opinions came to be written and used prevents them from shielding presidents from responsibility. Instead, it actually increases presidential responsibility. The choice to use torture raised moral and policy questions. Even if the legal opinions were sound, and not woefully weak, no lawyer can absolve a president and his close colleagues from responsibility for the secret moral and policy choices they make.[75]

Ignoring America's Fundamental Values

Fear incubates and fervor sustains the secrecy culture. While the fear may be understandable and the fervor genuine, the secrecy culture too often erodes fundamental precepts of American democracy. The secrecy establishment—from presidents to agency directors to lower-level agents—is zealous about defending the nation. Even for those whose secret actions harmed the nation, their aim was to help the nation. But how they risked harming it was apparently beyond their ken. Take just three examples. In 1953, Kermit Roosevelt, a CIA official and grandson of Theodore Roosevelt, fomented a coup that overthrew the democratically chosen prime minister of Iran, Mohammad Mosaddegh, whose efforts to wrest control of Iran's oil industry from the British angered Western officials and commercial interests. Mosaddegh was also accused of leaning toward communism. He was toppled and the pro-Western Shah Reza Pahlavi installed. But the shah's brutal regime fertilized the ground from which erupted the virulently anti-American revolution of 1979, the heirs to which control Iran to this day.[76]

Then there is the case of James Jesus Angleton, the CIA's counterintelligence chief responsible from the mid-1950s to the mid-1970s for defending against foreign intelligence incursions. He had rather extreme views, believing, for example, that both Albania's and China's splits with the Soviet Union were ruses designed to fool America to let down its guard; and that at least one CIA director had been a Soviet mole. In establishing the CIA's long-lived illegal mail-opening campaign, Angleton's aim was to try to catch foreign spies. But when the illegal operation was exposed by the Church Committee as having violated the rights of many law-abiding American citizens, it tarnished the CIA's reputation.[77]

John Yoo is a more recent example with his secret Justice Department opinions blessing torture and a return of warrantless eavesdropping. The opinions that have been revealed are extreme examples of Yoo's theory that American presidents have the monarchial, prerogative powers of English kings. But even in England, that theory had been rejected in the Glorious Revolution of 1688—a century before our Constitution. Yoo's theory also clashed with the purpose of the American Revolution and the structure of the American Constitution, as well as ignoring key Supreme Court rulings. Nonetheless, Yoo had been expounding similarly extreme theories of presidential power in his academic work before he joined the Justice Department. And in his own mind, he was, at the Justice Department, seeking to use law to help protect the nation.[78]

It was the secrecy culture that insulated Yoo's opinions from legal and other experts exposing the extremity of his views. It was the secrecy culture that prevented outsiders from telling Angleton that opening mail was illegal. And it was the secrecy culture that kept Kermit Roosevelt from hearing that America ought not be in the business of overthrowing democratically elected leaders to help the oil industry—as well as hearing that the overthrow of a democratically elected leader and the reinstallation of the shah had the potential to stoke extreme anti-Americanism.

In each case, the secrecy culture helped isolate zealots from considering long-term consequences. Neither Yoo nor Angleton nor Roosevelt—nor their supervisors—remembered Louis Brandeis's caution that "The greatest dangers to liberty lurk in insidious encroachment by men of zeal, well-meaning but without understanding."[79]

7

The Seduction of Secrecy

On a December morning in 1968, Daniel Ellsberg arrived for a private meeting with Henry Kissinger at the high-end Pierre Hotel in midtown Manhattan. Kissinger, who had been designated as President-Elect Nixon's national security advisor, wanted to discuss an options paper on Vietnam that he had asked Ellsberg to write.[1] Ellsberg was a military analyst at the RAND Corporation and had been a guest lecturer on negotiation in Kissinger's course at Harvard. At the close of their conversation, Ellsberg warned Kissinger about secrecy and its allure. "You're about to receive . . . a whole slew of special clearances, maybe fifteen or twenty of them, that are higher than top secret." At the start, "you'll be exhilarated by some of this new information," but then, "almost as fast, you will feel like a fool for having studied, written, talked about these subjects . . . without having known of the existence of all this information." But that, Ellsberg told Kissinger, will be short-lived. Later "you will forget there ever was a time when you didn't have [this information], and you'll be aware only of the fact that you have it now and most others don't . . . and that all those *other* people are fools." Indeed, even though there are limitations to the super-secret data, you will become "incapable of learning from most people in the world, no matter how much experience they may have in their particular areas that may be much greater than yours."[2]

Once ensconced as national security advisor, Kissinger continued to reach out to Ellsberg, inviting him to Washington and later to his summer White House office in San Clemente, California. There, in August 1970, Ellsberg urged Kissinger to read "the McNamara Study" about earlier administrations'

Vietnam decisions—which later became known as the Pentagon Papers. Kissinger declined, telling Ellsberg that "after all, we make decisions very differently now."[3] Also at San Clemente, Kissinger made it quite clear he had been seduced by secrecy in just the way Ellsberg had warned against. Expressing irritation with a group of Harvard consultants who had resigned as a bloc to protest the secret bombing of Cambodia, Kissinger dismissively derided the entire group: "They never had the clearances," he said.[4]

In 1997, two decades after Gerald Ford left the White House, he spoke of having been overly awed by secrecy's aura and its proponents' prestige. But unlike Kissinger, Ford admitted it. In remarks at the National Press Club about his years in Congress, Ford mentioned a CIA briefing using secret charts and figures where the CIA director and his analysts "were very prestigious . . . acknowledged to be the wisest, brightest people we had in the government." Their "scary presentation" was that the United States would soon be "behind the Soviet Union in military capability, in economic growth, in the strength of our economy." But, Ford added, "they were 180 degrees wrong."[5]

The secret, prestigious projections about the Soviet economy's inexorable growth misled Congress. The statistics were also "what presidents in the grimmest years of the Cold War knew, and what they knew was mostly wrong."[6] As Senator Moynihan observed, the CIA's estimates of Soviet economic growth turned out to be based on "absurd" reliance on "notoriously inflated statistics provided by the Soviet Union" itself.[7] Had the CIA's secret estimates about Soviet economic growth and the reports underlying them been made public, knowledgeable economists (and even ordinary travelers to the Soviet Union) could have exposed fallacies before presidents and Representative Ford and his congressional colleagues in Congress were seduced by the prestige of the CIA to support expensive budgets predicated on faulty secret presentations.

The intelligence community uses the label OSINT (Open Source Intelligence) for information culled from open sources like newspapers, magazines, books, TV, radio, and the Internet. OSINT makes up about 80 percent of the material available to intelligence analysts who study developments abroad. Much of the information is valuable. OSINT is even found in the super-secret *President's Daily Brief*.[8] Still, many recipients of intelligence have "little patience and less interest" in reading information derived from open sources. Rather they want super-secret "material from spies, intercepts, or any of the other more exotic sources."[9] Similarly, an experienced intelligence community professional put it starkly in 2011: whatever the actual merits, "policy makers in the White House and on Capitol Hill privilege the classified over the unclassified, believing that the top secret stuff must be the real juice."[10] "Secret" is, all too often, conflated with "true."

Secrets are seductive not just to recipients of classified information but to those who provide it as well. At times, intelligence-agency professionals report they are valued only for what they steal.[11] Theft, shielded by secrecy, adds prestige and credibility. Belonging to a top-secret agency is itself a source of pride, but that pride sometimes shuts out data from unclassified sources, leading to error and to bureaucratic silliness. When pressure from both the 9/11 Commission and the Commission on Intelligence Capabilities of the United States Regarding Weapons of Mass Destruction forced the creation of an Open Source Center at the CIA, the Agency "clos[ed] the lid on really imaginative change" by restricting employment at the new center to people who already had top-secret clearances.[12] Sometimes, secrecy causes those with access to what are deemed to be the most important secrets to pay little attention to other sources. A supervisor for Ultra—the super-secret World War II project for breaking Nazi codes—noted that during the war some agents made a "facile error, induced by inertia" to allow Ultra to be a "substitute for analysis and evaluation of other intelligence."[13]

Ironically, the more information proliferates and the more the number of secrets multiplies, the more intelligence-community professionals are tempted to use secrecy—and escalate its level—as a way to get noticed. Secrecy spawns more secrecy. If you want your individual snowflake report to be read, and not be lost in an avalanche of paper or buried by blizzards of bytes, you better be sure it is classified and, indeed, escalate its level of classification. A general is reported to have said he "only reads things that were marked 'Top Secret.' If it was less than that, it wasn't worth his time."[14] Even "top secret" is sometimes insufficient to warrant attention. More than two decades ago, former CIA Director Stansfield Turner observed that "an intelligence document that is Top Secret, but not further restricted by a code-word, is considered barely classified."[15] In the years following Turner's remarks, the number of code-word restrictions proliferated.

So the multiplication of secrets (and the growth of information generally) creates new pressures to use a secrecy stamp, as well as to escalate the secrecy level—from secret, to top secret, to levels beyond top secret that are code-word restricted. Escalation may well be in the parochial interest of an individual who wants to be noticed just as it is in the interest of an individual fisherman to catch as many fish as possible. But if all fishermen catch the maximum, it diminishes the fishery for everyone. The ultimate effect of many individuals and institutions adding to the rising mountains of secrets and escalating the level of classification is to harm secrecy by cheapening all secrets. Indeed, after 9/11, the multiplication of long, redundant secret reports caused many "decision makers" to "avoid the electronic pile altogether."[16]

Escalating secrecy helps an individual get noticed and adds to both individual and institutional prestige. For example, each day the CIA prepared for presidents its *President's Daily Brief,* or PDB, saying "For the President Only." While many PDBs deserve top secrecy, others might better be put in the public domain. One reason that CIA bureaucrats fiercely fought to keep PDBs super secret is that to let any become public would reduce the seductive aura surrounding PDBs—"the most prestigious document provided to senior policy officials by the nation's so-called intelligence community."[17]

Heightened secrecy adds to the prestige of agencies as well as individuals. The size of a SCIF (or sensitive compartmented information facility)—an eavesdropping-proof room where classified information is stored—became a post-9/11 status symbol within the intelligence community. SCIFs range in size from a closet to "four times the size of a football field." Protection of such facilities is appropriate. Nonetheless, human nature can, once again, cause agencies to push for too much. As a specialist in constructing SCIFs put it, in the intelligence community "they've got the penis envy thing going. You can't be a big boy unless you're a three-letter agency and you have a big SCIF."[18] There are "literally thousands" of SCIFs in the Washington, D.C. area, belonging to both government agencies and private contractors, and, according to one national security reporter, they are "a sanctuary, the ultimate members-only club for the keepers of secrets."[19]

With prestige comes power; and lust for power is among the elements of human nature that seed and fertilize secrecy. On the twenty-fifth anniversary of the publication of the Pentagon Papers, Max Frankel, the *New York Times*' former Washington bureau chief, recalled that President Nixon initially welcomed the historic leak. "The papers covered none of his [Nixon's] actions; they mostly belabored his Democratic predecessors, Kennedy and Johnson," Frankel wrote. But Nixon's attitude soon changed. "Henry Kissinger, the champion leaker of his generation, soon reminded Nixon that even harmless secrets were coins of power to be hoarded."[20]

Similarly, agencies fight for power and prestige by hoarding "their" secrets and hiding them from other agencies. Critical agencies often jealously guard secrets buried on their turf. Sometimes this is because they fear leaks, or even moles, at the other agency. But it often is also for more parochial turf protection. During World War II, believing it had exclusive power to investigate "subversion" and to spy in the United States, the FBI sought to exclude the Office of Strategic Services (or OSS), the CIA's predecessor, from operating domestically. When OSS operators tried to steal information from the Spanish embassy in Washington, D.C., by climbing up drainpipes to break into the embassy, they were foiled by FBI agents sitting in cars on the street outside who rhythmically sounded their sirens.[21]

The same kind of turf protection was evident six decades later, when the CIA failed to provide the FBI with information it garnered overseas about suspected terrorists who had entered the United States—and later became part of the 9/11 hijacking team. As the 9/11 Commission concluded, this and other pre-9/11 failures by federal agencies to share relevant information sprang from "a system that requires a demonstrated 'need to know' before sharing. . . . Such a system implicitly assumes that the risk of inadvertent disclosure outweighs the benefits of wider sharing. Those Cold War assumptions are no longer appropriate."[22] Nonetheless, after 9/11, critical agencies not only continued to withhold information from one another, but also jealously guarded access to captured suspected terrorists—even in instances in which other agencies had far more expertise on a particular subject. For detainee interrogation, CIA agents sometimes rendered important prisoners to a third country rather than allow the FBI to interrogate them.[23]

The eminent German sociologist Max Weber, writing around the time of World War I, studied bureaucrats and remarked upon their desire for secrecy and the prestige and authority it confers. With its "pure interest . . . in power," every bureaucracy "seeks to increase the superiority of the professionally informed by keeping their knowledge and intentions secret." Weber's conclusion was that "bureaucracy naturally welcomes a poorly informed and hence a powerless parliament."[24] Weber was, of course, correct that those who are "poorly informed" have less power. But sometimes "parliament"—the Congress in the United States—actually welcomes being poorly informed. Ironically, sometimes secrecy seduces those kept in the dark, because *not* having the information serves their political interests.

Secrecy in foreign affairs or national security matters is not, as Nicholas

Katzenbach observed, "a one-way street born of presidential ambition for power." There are political risks for members of Congress in being fully informed before tough decisions are made. It is tempting for some members to let a president make decisions based on secret information, wait to see what happens, and "let future events determine the length of his coattails."[25] Along the same lines, when Senate Majority Leader Mike Mansfield urged the Senate to create what became known as the Church Committee in 1975, he noted that Congress habitually had been tempted to avoid the risks of knowledge. To avoid risks, "[i]t used to be fashionable . . . for members of Congress to say that insofar as the intelligence agencies were concerned, the less they knew about such questions, the better."[26]

While the Church Committee insisted on getting classified information and the executive branch provided it, as it has sometimes since, old habits do die hard. Thus, when faced with whether to go to war with Iraq, only a handful of members of Congress opted to read the classified National Intelligence Estimate (NIE) that spoke to whether Saddam Hussein had weapons of mass destruction or was acquiring them.[27] What the Bush administration offered up to the rest of Congress (and the public) was a white paper that "provided readers with an incomplete picture of the nature and extent of the debate within the Intelligence Community regarding those issues."[28] The identities of dissenting agencies and an entire dissenting opinion disappeared into oblivion.

Secrecy is also attractive because it helps avoid pesky questions, debate, and dissent. Within the White House, presidents are often tempted to listen only to a small coterie of like-minded advisors. The Bush administration's decision to opt for torture is a telling example of harm caused by succumbing to this temptation. The decision to permit torture was made by a group who knew nothing about effective interrogation, and who consulted no experts from the State Department, the military, or the FBI. Apart from the immorality of a descent to torture,[29] and apart from the fact U.S. law banned torture,[30] those shut out from the meetings could have made the case that torture would weaken America with our allies, strengthen our enemies, and add to risks for our soldiers or CIA officers when they were captured. Those shut out could have reminded President Bush that when George Washington was fighting the Revolutionary War, he barred mistreatment of prisoners of war: "Treat them with humanity, and Let them have no reason to Complain of our Copying the brutal example of the British Army in their Treatment of our unfortunate brethren."[31] They also could have pointed to Lincoln's ban on torture during the Civil War.[32] And that, after World War II, the United States led the way in drafting the Geneva Conventions, which prohibit torture and other forms of inhumane treatment.[33]

Those who were shut out could also have protested the planned use of waterboarding by pointing out that, after World War II, the United States had prosecuted Japanese soldiers as war criminals for using this very technique on American prisoners and explained that most techniques being considered by the Bush administration were copied from torture techniques used to produce *false* confessions from American prisoners in the Korean War.[34] Actual FBI interrogators could have told the narrow group in the White House that creative, noncoercive techniques historically had been successful in obtaining useful information and productive in interrogation of al-Qaeda terrorists.[35]

Most fundamentally, letting only a tiny group of passionate yea-sayers decide upon torture shut out any debate about American values.

Decades earlier, a similar narrowness contributed to mistakes in developing our Vietnam policy. James C. Thomson Jr., a White House and State Department official from 1961 to 1966, asked, "How Could Vietnam Happen?" A "central question, at the heart of the policy process," was "[w]here were the experts, the doubters, and the dissenters?" Thomson expressed concern that "a recurrent and increasingly important factor in the decisionmaking process was *the banishment of real expertise.* Here the underlying cause was the 'closed politics' of policy-making as issues become hot: the more sensitive the issue, and the higher it rises in the bureaucracy, the more completely the experts are excluded while the harassed senior generalists take over (that is, the Secretaries, Undersecretaries, and Presidential Assistants)." Thomson continued that "the frantic skimming of briefing papers in the back seats of limousines is no substitute for the presence of specialists; furthermore, in times of crisis such papers are deemed 'too sensitive' even for review by the specialists."[36]

Sometimes those who seek to bury openness start by praising it. George W. Bush's first attorney general, John Ashcroft, sent a memorandum to all federal agencies that began by proclaiming it is "Only through a well-informed citizenry that the leaders of our nation remain accountable to the governed." But then the substance of the attorney general's memo *eased* the standards for Agency opposition to FOIA requests.[37] President Nixon also praised openness when words were cheap and easy. In March 1972, Nixon said the classification system "failed to meet the standards of an open and democratic society" and "frequently served to conceal bureaucratic mistakes or to prevent embarrassment to officials and administrations."[38] But then when faced with Watergate, Nixon quickly took refuge in a fortress of secrecy to hide criminal activity behind claims of national security.

President Lyndon Johnson also flip-flopped on public access to information. Behind the scenes, as the original FOIA bill gathered steam in 1965, Johnson told House Democratic leaders that the "goddamn bill will screw the Johnson Administration," and that its congressional sponsor should be "brought into line."[39] But when FOIA passed, Johnson signed it—on July 4, 1966—rhapsodically expressing his "deep sense of pride that the United States is an open society in which the people's right to know is cherished and guarded." Yet according to his press secretary, Bill Moyers, "LBJ had to be dragged kicking and screaming to the signing ceremony. He hated the very idea of the Freedom of Information Act, hated the thought of journalists rummaging in government closets, hated them challenging the official view of reality . . . He signed 'the f . . . thing,' as he called it, and then went out to claim credit for it."[40]

In office, President Truman had led the way in bolstering the classification system. Yet after he left office, Truman emphatically and categorically opined that "secrecy and a free, democratic government don't mix."[41]

The common thread is that public figures frequently bow publicly toward openness because of its deep roots in American democracy. But they then often bend in the direction of secrecy because its lures are so compelling.

The seduction of secrecy dovetails with human nature to help explain why it is so hard to reduce the amount of classified information. Over the six decades during which the classification system has existed, America's secrecy culture has created mountains of classified documents. The total amount of classified material today is mind-bogglingly large. Officials made 95 million decisions to classify information in 2012—a 950 percent jump since the new century began.[42] Over 1.4 million Americans hold "top secret" clearances.[43] New secrets are created every day, and despite substantial declassification activity, the pool of classified material keeps growing. (Although "original" classification decisions are trending down, "derivative" classification decisions are skyrocketing, reflecting the growth of electronic records like e-mail.)[44]

Along with the desire for prestige and recognition already described, lethargy and fear also contribute to keeping the secrecy mountains steep. Given the huge and growing mass of secrets, how can enough eyes be found, and who has the energy to do the work of reviewing for release all the mountains of material inappropriately kept hidden by secrecy? Where will such time-consuming and manpower-devouring jobs stand among the priorities of government leaders busy with current crises? And what will be the repercussions if a few legitimate secrets are missed in an effort to clear out the bloated secrecy bins? The fear of seeming soft can also deter political leaders from pushing hard to prune secrets.

There *is* a substantial amount of "declassification" work done each year. In 2012 alone, some 20 million pages were declassified.[45] But given the much larger number of new classified documents, the net result is that secrets continue to grow. In Greek mythology, the torment of Sisyphus was to push a heavy rock up to the top of a hill only to have it repeatedly roll down for him to push up again. For secrets, the torment is worse—after each climb, the hill gets higher.

Today's secrecy mountains began as hills that grew higher and higher. All the incentives favor multiplying secrets.[46] Human nature works to favor classification and disfavor openness, making a secrecy stamp the way to play safe. This shortcoming was emphasized near the dawn of the Secrecy Era by a special committee created by Charles Wilson, President Eisenhower's secretary of defense. The Committee found that "[a] subordinate may well be severely criticized by his seniors for permitting sensitive information to be released, whereas he is rarely criticized for over-protecting it. There is therefore an understandable tendency to 'play safe' and to classify information which should not be classified, or to assign too high a category to it."[47] In 1958, two years later, a report issued by Congressman John Moss—a leading congressional voice for openness who later sponsored the Freedom of Information Act—found that "the Defense Department's security classification system is still geared to a policy under which an official faces stern punishment for failure to use a secrecy stamp but faces no such punishment for abusing the privilege of secrecy, even to hide controversy, error, or dishonesty."[48]

Five decades later, little had changed. In 2004, the 9/11 Commission found that "[c]urrent security requirements nurture overclassification and excessive compartmentation of information among agencies. Each agency's incentive structure opposes sharing, with risks (criminal, civil, and internal administrative sanctions) but few rewards for sharing information. No one has to pay the long-term costs of overclassifying information. . . ."[49] This is still correct. As a 2011 Brennan Center report by Elizabeth Goitein said, "a multitude of forces pushes in the direction of classification while no force pushes meaningfully in the other direction."[50] Individuals still face no sanctions for overclassifying but are subject to criticism and punishment for underclassifying.[51] Whole agencies reflect human nature by wanting to hold on to "their" secrets, being proud of their own security systems and wary of other agencies' systems. As the 9/11 Commission found, "each agency or department needs its own intelligence apparatus to support the performance of its duties. It is hard to 'break down stovepipes' when there are so many stoves that are legally and politically entitled to have cast-iron pipes of their own."[52] The commission added that the "biggest impediment" to "connecting the dots" is "the human or systemic resistance to sharing information."[53]

The lure of secrecy and its staying power is also shown by the *lack* of impact caused by prestigious government reports that have warned since the 1950s how too much information was being classified and too much of that information was then kept classified for too long. Since the Eisenhower administration, expert reports have consistently decried overuse of classification: "overclassification has reached serious proportions" (1956); "in the course of its studies, the Commission has been furnished with information classified as 'confidential,' which could have been so classified only by the wildest stretch of the imagination" (1957); "innumerable specific instances" of unnecessary secrecy "which ranged from the amusing to the arrogant" (1958); "the volume of scientific and technical information that is classified, could profitably be decreased by perhaps as much as 90 percent . . ." (1970); at the Department of Defense, "too much information appears to be classified and much at higher levels than is warranted" (1985); "the classification system, largely unchanged since the Eisenhower administration, has grown out of control" (1994); the classification system "is used too often to deny the public an understanding of the policymaking process" (1997); "three-quarters of what I read that was classified shouldn't have been" (2004, from the chair of the 9/11 Commission).[54] Still, the proliferation of classified information continues.

Secrecy professionals and the nation as a whole have failed to heed sound observations made by Machiavelli centuries ago. Although the term "Machiavellian" conveys cynicism, and some of his counsel was indeed cynical, much of Machiavelli's advice is sensible and balanced. At the heart of his advice to "every wise prince" was to keep his "eyes trained not only on present problems, but also future ones . . . because when one sees these problems approaching, they can still be remedied, whereas, if one waits for them to arrive, it will be too late to administer medicine." Moreover, "[a]s physicians say of consumption: In the first stages it is easy to cure though hard to detect, but with the progress of time, if not detected or treated, consumption becomes easy to detect but hard to cure. This can also be said of the affairs of state."[55]

The same can also be said of secrecy's seduction in America. The problem of too much secrecy, of excessive classification, has been detected from the beginning. But it has never been treated, and with each passing year it becomes harder to cure. Indeed, generations of detecting the problem but failing to cure it prove just how hard it is to cure.

PART THREE

Exposing Secrets and Checking Secrecy

So far, this book has concentrated on secrecy's importance, its growth, its harms, its culture, and its seduction, largely focusing on the secrecy that surrounds the work of presidents and other members of the executive branch. This part focuses on the exposure of secrets, and on institutions responsible for checking secrecy, including Congress and the courts, as well as journalists and other private watchdogs.

Secrets have been exposed since the birth of the nation. The expansion of the national security state, and the growth of classification during the Secrecy Era, meant there were more secrets to expose. There is not, however, a one-to-one correlation between the quantity of secrets and the number of exposures. There was, for example, a notable increase in exposure of government and corporate information by journalists during the Progressive Era in the early twentieth century—long before the Secrecy Era. In contrast, during the first decades of the Secrecy Era, there were relatively few exposures by journalists. Similarly, while, from the Founding until today, Congress has episodically investigated and exposed executive-branch secrets, productive and responsible congressional investigations hit a low during the early Cold War period. Then, starting in the late 1960s, there was a burst of press and congressional disclosures. There have been ups and downs ever since.

In the Openness Era, newspapers played a key role in spreading information that, while not technically secret, was not widely known by the general public. *Diffusion* of information was vital. During the Secrecy Era, the engines of diffusion proliferated, and journalists instead played a vital role in *uncovering* secret information.

Documents (including photos) are often crucial in making discoveries resonate with the public. This is true both for investigative journalism and congressional investigations. And it explains why efforts to obtain historically important documents by nonprofit watchdogs such as the National Security Archive and the American Civil Liberties Union play such an important role in our democracy.

Secrets sometimes seem like Tennyson's brook: "for men may come, men may go. But I go on for ever."[1] But most secrets do, sooner or later, see the light of day. The brook eventually emerges from the shadows, and when it does, when the secrets flow into public sight, their exposure often highlights basic facts about secrecy: that it was unnecessary or inappropriate, or that the veil of secrecy concealed information for too long. Government overreactions to revelations of secrets often tarnish secrecy. Nonetheless, in some cases, exposure of secrets has caused or threatened to cause real harm.

There was no justification, for example, for the *Chicago Tribune* to publish its 1942 story headlined "Navy Had Word of Jap Plan to Strike at Sea." Written during the U.S. naval victory over the Japanese at Midway in June 1942—which turned the tide in the Pacific theater—the story made no sense unless the United States had broken the Japanese naval code, which it had done.[2] With that advantage, the commander of the U.S. Pacific fleet "knew more ab[o]ut the Midway Operation than many of the Japanese officers involved in it."[3] Fortunately, the Japanese seem not to have seen the article. A year after Midway, a Kentucky congressman irresponsibly revealed that U.S. submarine success in the Pacific was in part due to a Japanese error in depth-charge tactics. According to the commander of the U.S. Pacific submarine fleet, the subsequent Japanese recalibration caused the loss of ten submarines and eight hundred American sailors.[4]

More recently, some of Chelsea Manning's massive electronic leak to WikiLeaks created risks of harm from disclosure of names of people who had cooperated with the United States on a confidential basis. On the other hand, publications that partnered with WikiLeaks were careful *not* to print names or other information that would have risked serious harm. This practice of prudent self-restraint became more customary after the Supreme Court allowed publication of the Pentagon Papers, rejecting the government's plea for a "prior restraint"—legalese for an order preventing publication. Without fear of restraint, papers are more willing to talk to the government about its secrecy concerns before they publish. Similarly, successful congressional investigations have involved discussions with the executive branch to work out ways to avoid revealing unnecessary and harmful secret details.

Congressional committees, leakers, investigative journalists, whistleblowers, executive-branch inspectors general, and nonprofit groups all expose secrets. The Freedom of Information Act, passed by Congress to open cracks in secrecy's door, has often helped. Agency bureaucrats usually fight fervently to keep their own secrets, but a few agency leaders have concluded that exposure of past secrets was necessary to maintain the strength—or even assure the survival—of their agencies. CIA Director William Colby did this in the mid-1970s, and Energy Secretary Hazel O'Leary in the mid-1990s. Similarly, while presidents usually build upon the mountains of secrets left by their predecessors, some presidential executive orders have limited the duration of secrets or required particular kinds of secrets to be reviewed for release. And of course presidents and other high-level government officials leak secret information all the time to achieve policy goals or to spice up their memoirs.

Some leaks are developed by investigative journalists whose stories grow from leads and who skillfully coax or pry secrets out of government officials. Journalists' revelations may ignite congressional investigations that uncover more secrets. Or vice versa. Sometimes, high government officials make policy arguments by seizing upon "facts" in stories based upon leaks they arranged. When Vice President Dick Cheney and National Security Advisor Condoleezza Rice built a case for the Iraq War by warning of "mushroom clouds" on Sunday-morning TV talk shows, they relied on Judith Miller's story in that morning's *New York Times*, reporting that Iraq possessed aluminum tubes used for making uranium for atomic bombs. That claim—which turned out to be wrong—was in turn based on an administration leak.[5]

As checks on excessive secrecy, both the courts and Congress have had a mixed record, both habitually deferring to executive claims of secrecy. The courts have failed to recognize that a functioning democracy depends upon maximum openness, and have turned a blind eye to their own bad experiences with excessive secrecy. They often fail to distinguish between parts of a document that need secrecy protection and the rest of the document that does not. They regularly decide FOIA and "state secrets" cases by simply parroting broad executive-branch arguments for secrecy without any searching examination of either the secrecy claims or the underlying secret material.

Fear affects both courts and Congress. The courts are afraid they lack the expertise to weigh the risks. Members of Congress have often felt it safer not to know the facts. But after the Church Committee exposed decades of unseemly facts and inadequate oversight, Congress created the new Senate and House Intelligence Committees to oversee intelligence agencies. This has helped, but sometimes, particularly after 9/11, these committees have become more cheerleaders than overseers, and sometimes their oversight has been undermined by the executive branch's practice of providing information in ways that make meaningful oversight difficult if not impossible.

8

Leaks, Investigative Journalism, and Nonprofit Watchdogs

Leaks force discussion of what governments seek to hide and often raise fundamental public-policy questions.[1] In 2013 and 2014, the leaks by Edward Snowden—including the revelation of NSA programs to collect metadata on nearly every domestic phone call Americans make and to scoop up the content of overseas electronic communications—opened the door to widespread debate about the breadth, legality, privacy impact, and security benefits of American surveillance at home and abroad. Snowden said this was, in fact, his purpose.[2] Similarly the 2005 *New York Times* exposure of the Bush administration's secret return to warrantless wiretapping sparked derision of the claim that presidents have authority to flout the law. And Daniel Ellsberg's 1971 leak of the Pentagon Papers, which exposed White House duplicity with respect to its war aims, intensified debate about the Vietnam War and helped set in motion events that led to President Nixon's resignation.

Government leaks aren't new. Some two thousand years ago, Emperor Caesar Augustus broke the legs of a secretary for selling the contents of a letter.[3] WikiLeaks founder Julian Assange sparked similarly fiery emotions. On Facebook, Sarah Palin mused that Assange should be pursued as "we pursue al Qaeda and Taliban leaders," and in the *Weekly Standard*, William Kristol asked why the United States couldn't "neutralize" Assange and "whack" WikiLeaks.[4]

While there have always been leaks, leaking rises and falls, with technology being one factor in the ease and volume of leaks. This can be illustrated by comparing an unlikely quartet of leakers: Benjamin Franklin, Daniel Ellsberg, Chelsea Manning, and Edward Snowden. In 1773, Benjamin Franklin

helped fuel the American Revolution by leaking to the Massachusetts legislature a small packet of thirteen original handwritten letters from the royal
governor of Massachusetts, Thomas Hutchinson, to a high-ranking British
government official. The letters showed that then Lt. Gov. Hutchinson had
urged the British to *toughen* their restraints on the colonists, including by
"abridgment of what are called English liberties."[5] Two hundred years later,
Daniel Ellsberg fanned opposition to the Vietnam War by leaking most of
the seven thousand pages of the government's secret history of escalation in
Vietnam, known as the Pentagon Papers. The documents Ellsberg leaked were
typed and could be copied by a machine. But it took Ellsberg several weeks
to surreptitiously Xerox the papers.

In the twenty-first century, leakers have used digital technology to access,
copy, and transfer much more information than ever before, in smaller and
smaller packages, and from far-flung locations. While serving as a U.S. Army
private in Iraq in 2010, Chelsea (then Bradley) Manning was able to access
classified government computer networks, and with a few keystrokes, burn
to rewritable CDs more than a hundred times the volume of the Pentagon
Papers. Manning provided WikiLeaks with electronic copies of some 700,000
secret government documents.[6] Three years later, Edward Snowden, a private NSA contractor, exploited NSA's antique cybersecurity system and, from
his office in Hawaii, remotely downloaded onto thumb drives more than 1.7
million U.S. intelligence files, thousands of British spy files, and thousands
of files other countries had shared with the United States. The Snowden files
shed more light on NSA actions than had ever been done and ignited controversy and public-policy debate in the United States and around the world.

Not surprisingly, the increase in the number of people with access to secrets occasions a predictable increase in the risk of leaks. The 9/11 Commission had warned that sealing up information in silos reduced the intelligence
community's effectiveness, and urged that the need-to-know culture should
be replaced by a need-to-share culture. An overreaction to this appropriate
observation led to an Army private stationed in Iraq (Manning) gaining access to U.S. State Department diplomatic cables from all over the world. We
may well continue to have alternating scandals with inconsistent complaints
ranging from How could they not connect the dots? to How could they make
so many dots available to so many people?[7]

The prevailing culture in society also affects the level of leaking. The publicity surrounding leaks about Watergate and the executive branch's approach

to the Vietnam War created a false sense that the entire past century was an era of enterprising journalists and supportive Deep Throats who were forever working together to ferret out secrets. This was not the case. There had been much watchdog journalism throughout the early twentieth century but from shortly after 1910 into the latter 1960s, government officials and the press were largely muted. Two world wars and Cold War anti-Communist fervor made leaks and publication of secrets appear unpatriotic. Popular attitudes were also affected by Duke Ellington's hit song entitled "A Slip of the Lip (Can Sink a Ship)," which reached number one in 1942.[8] But then, in the 1970s, trust in government plummeted, leaking rose, and, except for a brief pause after 9/11, has risen ever since.

In the early twentieth century, a few investigative journalists—or "[men] with a muck-rake" as Teddy Roosevelt disapprovingly dubbed them despite his long-lasting collaboration with many of them—dug deeply to "let in the light" and expose wrongdoing by government, business and labor.[9] Like today's investigative journalists, muckrakers did time-consuming (and therefore expensive) research. In most cases, the secrets they uncovered were hidden away in hard-to-find files scattered across the land, or could only be obtained in careful and far-ranging interviews. So muckrakers largely discovered secrets hidden in plain sight—secrets that no one else had the time, energy, or imagination to discover.

Muckraking magazines were relatively cheap, and many gained huge audiences. As Richard Hofstadter said in *The Age of Reform*, the muckraking magazines were "newspapers in periodical form," whereas the "old, respectable" magazines like *The Atlantic* and *Harper's*, which were more expensive and reached many fewer people, were "book[s] in periodical form."[10] The iconic platform for muckraking in this period was *McClure's Magazine*, named for its founder and publisher/editor Samuel Sidney ("S.S.") McClure.[11] *McClure's*, a monthly, sold for ten cents (about $2.50 today). Its average circulation grew from around 27,000 in its first year to 450,000 in 1905, by which time it carried the most advertising of any American magazine.[12]

A high point of *McClure's* muckraking came in its famous January 1903 issue,[13] which included exposés by Lincoln Steffens on municipal corruption,[14] Ray Stannard Baker on abuse of power by labor unions,[15] and Ida Minerva Tarbell on illegal tactics used by John D. Rockefeller's Standard Oil Corporation.[16] Rockefeller understood "how essential it was that he keep it secret"— the "it" being the special rates he got from railroads carrying his oil, with the rebates rising when the railroads carried oil produced by competitors of Standard Oil.[17] Tarbell's articles were a major contributor to the antitrust case that led the Supreme Court to order the breakup of Rockefeller's Standard Oil behemoth into many smaller separate companies.[18] In the index to Ron Chernow's comprehensive biography of Rockefeller, Tarbell has the most entries of anybody not named Rockefeller.[19]

McClure himself supported his magazine's revelations by echoing the belief that the people need to be well informed to perform their proper role in a democracy. The powerful, McClure said, were "breaking the law, or letting it be broken." With such broad complicity—among not only "capitalists, workingmen, politicians" but also lawyers, judges and churches—"there is no one left; none but all of us."[20] In 1910, Amos Pinchot—a Theodore Roosevelt intimate—used *McClure's* to express support for openness by ridiculing the arguments "urged by the special interests and their representatives to show that there is no divergence of purpose between themselves and the people." Pinchot called out special interests for hiding behind a "paradoxical lullaby, sung in unison by the financial and political machines, to the effect that nobody is doing anything wrong, but that nevertheless it is wicked and unsafe to disturb business and politics by letting in the light." But the lullabies did not always work. Muckrakers cast light on America's surreptitious oligarchy. Pinchot contended that "the people of the United States [were] fully awake to the great issue that is staring the country in the face."[21]

Little did Pinchot or McClure know the muckraking flame would soon die down.[22] Nor could they predict that, as one recent observer has noted, "between Lincoln Steffens, Ida Tarbell, and Ray Stannard Baker . . . and Woodward and Bernstein in 1972 and 1973, [investigative journalism] had no culturally resonant, heroic exemplars."[23] Though largely true, it is an exaggeration to suggest there was *no* investigative journalism in the decades between *McClure's* and Watergate. There were some reports that exposed secrets about poverty and race. And, perhaps deterred by two world wars and the Cold War, investigative journalists generally stayed away from the national government and instead focused on unearthing municipal and state government secrets. Indeed, when newspaper editors began to worry about a new culture of governmental secrecy, they initially focused on the "broad-scale offensive against freedom of information" by state and local—rather than federal—officials.[24]

The few investigative journalists who focused on national issues during the quiet period include I.F. Stone, a thoughtful progressive—or radical—journalist for more than six decades.[25] Stone got some stories from secrets leaked by high-level officials—including Harold Ickes, FDR's interior secretary—but most of his revelations came from meticulous work spent combing through government documents. Stone generally uncovered secrets hidden in plain sight—secrets that no one else was finding.

During the Secrecy Era's early years, the establishment press was more likely to accept government requests not to publish classified information than it is today.[26] Then, in the late 1960s and early 1970s, barriers broke. What was uncommon between the muckraking of the early twentieth century and Watergate became common: more leaks and more investigative reporting uncovering secrets. With the revelation of more embarrassing and illicit secrets, secrecy also became more suspect. Vietnam, Watergate, and congressional investigations from the Church Committee to Iran-Contra made the public and the press—as well as many government officials—much more skeptical of government actions and the concealment of improper or illegal conduct.[27]

There are many high-profile examples of leaks and changing press attitudes in the late 1960s and early 1970s: *Ramparts* ran a 1967 article about CIA funding of the National Student Association; Seymour Hersh wrote an article revealing that, in March 1968, a group of U.S. Army soldiers massacred at least 350 civilians at My Lai, Vietnam; the *New York Times* reported on secret bombing in Cambodia in 1969; and the *Times* and the *Washington Post* published the Pentagon Papers in 1971.[28] These exposures reinforced the perception of a "credibility gap" between what the government was telling the American people about the Vietnam War and the secret reality on the ground and within the White House.

Despite all the attention now paid to dissidents like Ellsberg, Manning, and Snowden, much leaking comes from top-level officials who routinely leak secrets when it helps win political battles or adds to their prestige. And there is a long history of public officials spicing up their memoirs with secrets after they leave office. As John F. Kennedy supposedly said, "The ship of state is the only ship that leaks from the top."[29] High-level leaking undermines secrecy's legitimacy—and adds a whiff of hypocrisy to efforts to punish lower-level leakers.

In a lengthy affidavit in the Pentagon Papers case, Max Frankel, then Washington bureau chief of the *New York Times*, gave examples of top officials engaging in a "widespread traffic in secret information" for self-serving

reasons. "Presidents make 'secret' decisions only to reveal them for the purposes of frightening an adversary nation, wooing a friendly electorate, protecting their reputations." High-level officials "reveal secrets in the search
for support of their policies." Middle-rank officials reveal secrets "to attract
the attention of their superiors or to lobby against the orders of those superiors." The military services leak classified research to enhance their budgets
or gain "the vote of a congressman or the favor of a contractor."[30] "A small
and specialized corps of reporters and a few hundred American officials
regularly make use of so-called classified, secret, and top secret information
and documentation. It is a cooperative, competitive, antagonistic and arcane
relationship."[31] Frankel argued that "practically everything that our Government does, plans, thinks, hears and contemplates in the realms of foreign policy is stamped and treated as secret—and then unraveled by that same
Government, by the Congress and by the press in one continuing round of
professional and social contacts and cooperative and competitive exchanges
of information."[32]

One of Frankel's examples was particularly telling in the context of the
information in the Pentagon Papers. Frankel pointed out that the memoir of
George Christian, one of Lyndon Johnson's press secretaries, revealed "a great
deal of detailed information, all still highly classified, about the secret negotiations with North Vietnam in Paris."[33] But when he leaked the Pentagon
Papers, Daniel Ellsberg deleted the four volumes on diplomatic efforts to end
the war, believing that revealing those secrets might harm peace efforts. Ellsberg was more careful than the high-ranking government official.

Some of Frankel's assertions are a tad categorical—it's a stretch to say "practically everything" in the realm of foreign policy is "unraveled" by government
officials themselves. Nonetheless, Frankel's gist was, is, and always has been
correct. It was echoed by a Pentagon Papers affidavit from the *Washington
Post*, whose chief diplomatic correspondent referred to the "regular practice"
of government officials leaking classified information when an official "deems
it in his or his administration's interest to do so."[34]

The points about self-serving high-level leaking made in the Pentagon
Papers litigation are borne out by practice earlier and ever since. Near
the end of World War II, I.F. Stone made similar points after the arrest of
six people—a naval officer, two State Department employees, and three
journalists—charged with leaking classified documents relating to foreign
policy to a left-leaning journal, *Amerasia*. Stone said the arrests criminalized

"the favorite Washington pastime of letting 'confidential' information leak out," adding, "[i]f this is a crime, all but a hopelessly inefficient minority of Washington's officials and newspapermen ought to be put in jail."[35] Stone also claimed an ideological slant in government leaking. The State Department constantly leaked to "favored reporters," while a "very tiny handful" of department progressives leaked stuff to "people like yours truly." Stone observed that State Department leadership "regards leaks in the former class as legitimate discussions of facts and policy," but leaks to the other side lead to investigations and arrests.[36]

Bob Woodward's bestsellers about presidential administrations starting with Nixon's could not have been written, and would not have sold in boxcar numbers, without leaks from high-ranking officials. The steady stream of high-level leaks to Woodward and others has led to hypocrisy charges against the last two administrations. If a critic discloses classified information, the Bush administration is "going to investigate, they're going to really stop it. When it comes to people in-house, people they like, people they trust, well, the investigation hasn't even started with regard to those people."[37] Journalist Michael Isikoff leveled the same charge against the Obama administration for its marked increase in leaking prosecutions: "How can they credibly prosecute mid-level bureaucrats and junior military officers for leaking classified information to the press when so many high-level officials have dished far more sensitive secrets to Woodward?"[38]

More recently, after the killing of Osama bin Laden, there were several leaks about the highly secret White House meetings leading up to the Navy SEALs' successful raid into Pakistan. Apparently, some advisors wanted to wait to be more certain bin Laden was in Abbottabad, while others favored a bombing attack as less risky to U.S. forces than a raid. President Obama chose the riskier plan.[39]

This incident dramatizes two general points about high-level leaking: many leaks are about White House deliberations, and, not surprisingly, the leaks often shine a favorable light on presidents. While it is often important to keep deliberations secret, once a decision is reached and action taken, the value of secrecy decreases but the harm to democracy grows. For better or worse, the die has been cast. After the event, some presidential advisors (and some presidents) may seem like sages, others like fools. Yet there is no reason for the American people not to know reasonably quickly how major decisions were reached, and why.

Of course, once officials are out of office their memoirs often reveal "se-crets entrusted to them."[40] And so it is that bookstore shelves are crowded with memoirs full of revelations and carefully hoarded secrets. Presidents write revelatory memoirs, as do vice presidents, top White House officials, cabinet members, and even CIA directors. For decades, these leaks, a form of high-priced declassification, have increased cynicism about secrecy: "the classification system has been used to deprive the American people of vital information, which is then later sold to them by political leaders whom they elected or by appointees of those elected leaders."[41] The continued massive leaking from the top makes government susceptible to charges of hypocrisy when it attacks leakers it does not like. And it undermines the legitimacy of the secrecy system itself, buttressing the claim that there is far too much classification which lasts far too long.

Some of the strongest arguments against excessive secrecy have emerged from episodes where the executive branch has attacked leaks. Controversies about the Pentagon Papers and about three post-9/11 leaks concerning the super-secret National Security Agency make the point.

When Daniel Ellsberg leaked the Pentagon Papers in 1971, it quickly be-came the most notorious leak in American history at least until Snowden's leaks.[42] The Papers provided many examples of how government had sur-reptitiously misled the American people and Congress about the escalation of the Vietnam War and its prospects for success. The Nixon administra-tion's effort to suppress publication on national security grounds exposed, as never before, exaggeration of government secrecy claims.

Secretary of Defense Robert McNamara had conceived the Papers in 1967 after turning from a fervent supporter of the Vietnam War to a worried skeptic. Formally entitled a "History of U.S. Decision-Making Process on Vietnam Policy," the Papers covered the administrations of Presidents Truman, Eisenhower, Kennedy, and Johnson, with a larger focus on the two later administrations.[43] (The history stopped on March 31, 1968, when Johnson had announced he would not seek reelection in order to concen-trate on peace in Vietnam.)[44] The study had forty-seven volumes, consisting of 3,000 pages of history and 4,000 pages of documents.[45] All were classi-fied "top secret/sensitive" because of a Defense Department rule that if any portion of a document or compilation of documents was marked "top se-cret," then everything else is.[46] Only fifteen copies were made.

Ellsberg had done some minor work on the Pentagon Papers and later got a copy of the complete report while a consultant at the RAND Corporation. A onetime war supporter, Ellsberg had turned against it, believing that Nixon and Kissinger, like their predecessors, were claiming to seek peace while actually escalating the war. Ellsberg desired to reveal the past to change the future, believing policy makers should read the Papers and learn lessons from them. After Kissinger declined to read the study, and a series of senators and one congressman with whom Ellsberg dealt said they could not reveal classified material, Ellsberg decided to leak the Papers (minus the diplomatic materials). He chose Neil Sheehan at the *Times*.[47] After the *Times* was temporarily enjoined from publication, Ellsberg then leaked the Papers to the *Post* and other papers and filmed an interview with CBS's Walter Cronkite at an undisclosed location.[48]

Before publication, the *Times* spent two months reviewing the Papers. Despite strong opposition from its longtime law firm, Lord Day & Lord (where Lewis Loeb advised the paper for almost five decades and Herbert Brownell was also a lead partner), publisher Arthur Sulzberger and executive editor Abe Rosenthal decided to go to print.[49] Rosenthal told Sheehan not to worry about opposition because "these papers belong to the American people." He rejected as "cowardly" the idea of publishing everything in one day to preempt a possible government effort to suppress.[50] So publication began on June 13, 1971, with the first article focusing on the Johnson administration's secret discussions of escalating the Vietnam War in contrast to its public statements at the time.[51] After three days of publication, the government got a court order enjoining the *Times* from further publication; the same thing happened to the *Post* after one day of publication. Within two weeks, the Supreme Court, in a 6–3 decision, lifted the injunctions.[52]

When the Pentagon Papers began to appear in print, Nixon's first reaction was glee. The stories embarrassed his Democratic predecessors. Nixon actually demanded that *more* material be leaked, particularly about the Kennedy administration's secret role in the assassination of Vietnamese president Ngo Dinh Diem. The president told his aides, "Now that it's being leaked, we'll leak out the parts we want."[53] But Henry Kissinger, appealing to Nixon's manhood, advised him that China would not respect a leader who allowed leaks. He also scared Nixon by saying "if this thing flies [in] the *New York Times*, they're gonna do the same to you next year," referring to Nixon's plans for escalating the Vietnam War.[54] Nixon promptly did a 180-degree turn, and launched a hysterical and vitriolic effort to stop publication, prosecute Ellsberg, and "destroy" him in the press.[55]

The Pentagon Papers played a major role in changing attitudes toward secrecy. From their different perspectives, H.R. Haldeman, Nixon's chief of staff, and Ellsberg spoke of the profound importance of the Papers' publication. As Haldeman—attributing the point to White House staffer Donald Rumsfeld—told Nixon:

> To the ordinary guy, all this is a bunch of gobbledygook. But out of the gobbledygook comes a very clear thing: You can't trust the government, you can't believe what they say and you can't rely on their judgment. And the implicit infallibility of presidents, which has been an accepted thing in America, is badly hurt by this, because it shows that people do things the president wants to do even though it's wrong. And the president can be wrong.[56]

Ellsberg focused on establishment newspapers' sharp break from prior practice. They were "suddenly in widespread revolt" after decades of "living happily—when it came to foreign policy and defense matters—on government handouts." The papers were defying "a solemn White House and Justice Department proclamation that they were causing irreparable harm to national security." For these "pillars of the establishment" "to contemplate challenging . . . the urgent judgment of the president and commander in chief in wartime would have been in the most literal sense unthinkable, before it happened."[57]

These effects were lasting. And so was the harm to secrecy's justification from the government's bumbling defense in the litigation. In seeking to prove how publication put national security at risk, the government looked like a gang that couldn't shoot straight, beginning when Attorney General John Mitchell warned the *Times* that continued publication would "cause irreparable injury to the defense interests of the United States," but mistakenly sent his telegram to a Brooklyn fish company.[58] Once in court, the government continued to sputter and flail. It was quickly forced to concede that two volumes of "top secret" material contained only documents already in the public domain. Still, it refused to consent to their publication.[59] Then Ben Bradlee, the *Post's* executive editor, told the court he had just read the galley proofs of

President Johnson's memoir, which contained "extensive, verbatim quotations" from classified documents in the Pentagon Papers.[60] Finally, when pressed during a secret court hearing to describe any document that was particularly harmful to national security, the government referenced a radio intercept during the Tonkin Gulf incident—an incident used to justify escalation of the Vietnam War. But the *Post*'s Pentagon reporter "stunned everyone by pulling out of his back pocket, a verbatim record of the intercept, in an unclassified transcript of Senate Foreign Relations Committee hearings."[61]

About twenty years after the Supreme Court allowed the *Times* and the *Post* to continue publication, former solicitor general Erwin Griswold, the government's Supreme Court lawyer in the case, wrote, "I have never seen any trace of a threat to the national security from the publication," adding "[i]t quickly becomes apparent to any person who has considerable experience with classified material that there is massive overclassification and that the principal concern of the classifiers is not with national security, but rather with governmental embarrassment of one sort or another."[62]

In his memoirs, Kissinger claimed publication of the Papers was a "profound shock" and "clearly intended as a weapon of political warfare," but did not say they caused harm.[63] As legal scholar David Rudenstine points out, it is revealing that Nixon's memoirs "made no claim that the publication actually injured military intelligence, defense or international affairs."[64] The Pentagon Papers episode did, however, wound the Nixon White House. Nixon's secret efforts to destroy Ellsberg "create[d] the climate that led to Watergate." According to William Safire, Nixon's former speechwriter, it escalated Nixon's paranoia, caused him to "lose all sense of balance," and led to illegal steps to harm Ellsberg and combat leaking generally, including the break-in to Ellsberg's psychiatrist's office and other acts by the White House "plumbers."[65] These contributed to dismissal of Ellsberg's criminal case, and eventually led to the Watergate debacle.

As the Haldeman and Ellsberg comments suggest, the Pentagon Papers helped bring about fundamental changes in public attitudes toward secrecy and in press responses to secrets. The Papers also highlight two overarching points: First, why should so much history be secret? This is especially relevant to war, where America's leaders ask soldiers to die for their country. Second, presidents would be wiser, and the nation better off, if presidents openly engaged in democratic persuasion and laid out the reasons and risks behind major national security and foreign policy proposals.

Turning to leaks and NSA, secrecy was vital for code-breaking and other cryptological work long before NSA was founded in 1952.[66] As mentioned earlier, one of the most irresponsible leaks in American history involved the Japanese naval code that U.S. intelligence had cracked before the battle of Midway. This was preceded a decade earlier by a massive leak about American code-breaking. In 1929, Henry Stimson, then Herbert Hoover's secretary of state, had shut down the "Black Chamber," the State Department's code-breaking division. "Gentlemen," Stimson famously said, "do not read each other's mail."[67] Suddenly out of work at the start of the Great Depression, Herbert Yardley, the division's director, wrote a bestselling book about his experience: *The American Black Chamber*.[68]

Yardley boasted of breaking the codes of at least twenty countries, including England, France, China, Germany, the Soviet Union, and Japan. On Japan, Yardley said, among other things, that at a naval conference in 1921 his outfit had read all the coded messages sent and received by the Japanese delegates. "Stud poker," Yardley bragged, "is not a very difficult game after you see your opponent's hole card."[69] Yardley's book caused a furor in Japan. In his 2010 book *Necessary Secrets*, author Gabriel Schoenfeld says Japanese militarism was "energized by the revelation of American treachery." Moreover, according to Schoenfeld, Japan tightened its communications technology after Yardley's book, preventing the United States from quickly reading some Japanese coded messages that might have provided warnings of the Japanese attack on Pearl Harbor.[70] Still, Yardley's book made a strong public case that having a code-breaking capacity was extremely valuable to America—and that, despite Stimson's aphorism, international relations are not governed by gentlemanly rules.

Code-breaking has always occupied a special place in intelligence gathering. NSA, America's largest intelligence agency, not only creates codes for the United States and breaks codes of other nations, but also intercepts vast amounts of electronic traffic. Much of NSA's work consists of legitimate secrets; its penchant for secrecy is greater even than the CIA's. Created by Truman's top-secret order, NSA's very existence was classified for years— the standing joke was that NSA stood for No Such Agency or Never Say Anything. At the time of the Church Committee's investigation in 1975, NSA's Counsel told me "the Constitution does not apply to NSA."[71] While that attitude may have changed, NSA's obsession with secrecy remains.

The importance of secrecy for much of NSA's work is clear. In 1950, Congress passed a special statute making it a crime to communicate or publish classified information relating to the "communication intelligence activities of the United States or any foreign government."[72] But what if the gist of a leak about NSA's communication intelligence activity is about illegality, or inefficiency, or overbreadth?

On December 16, 2005, the New York Times published a blockbuster article titled "Bush Lets U.S. Spy on Callers Without Courts."[73] Having been held for more than a year (during a presidential election), the article on warrantless wiretapping eventually went to press despite a final White House appeal for silence. As editor Bill Keller described the tense conclave, President Bush told the Times' top brass that if the article ran and al-Qaeda attacked again "there'll be blood on your hands,"[74] but publisher Arthur Sulzberger Jr. agreed with Keller that "nothing I heard . . . changed my mind."[75]

During the period that the Times was holding the article, an earlier draft had been shown to the Bush administration, and as a result, "some information administration officials argued could be useful to terrorists [was] omitted."[76] But such a long delay was a disservice to democracy and a blow to journalism. No justification for the lengthy delay has been provided; and very likely publication was accelerated by the Times' knowledge that James Risen, one of its reporters, was about to publish a book that included the same information as the article.[77]

The article caused a furor. Jane Harman, the lead Democrat on the House Intelligence Committee, said it had "damaged critical intelligence capabilities." CIA Director Porter Goss claimed the harm was "very severe."[78] A few years later, Schoenfeld's Necessary Secrets began and ended with an emphatic claim that the Times should have been indicted.[79] But Harman's and Goss's claims were no more concrete than Bush's warning. And Schoenfeld, whose book is generally thoughtful, was off-base in his argument for prosecution. The Bush, Goss, and Harman claims that publication would harm national security were simply conclusory. Schoenfeld's argument had more bite: "[A] highly publicized report indicating that the NSA could readily tap into calls from, say, Islamabad to Detroit might cause some al-Qaeda communications to dry up."[80] But under the publicly known FISA warrant system, al-Qaeda would already be aware that there could be taps into calls between Detroit and Islamabad that would be approved by a secret court order.

Did the article risk real harm? The place to start is with what the Times did—and did not—say. Headlined "Bush Lets U.S. Spy on Callers Without

Courts," the article began by saying "[m]onths after the Sept. 11 attacks, President Bush secretly authorized the National Security Agency to eavesdrop on Americans and others inside the United States to search for evidence of terrorist activity without the court-approved warrants ordinarily required for domestic spying. . . ." The article was based on discussions with—that is, leaks developed from—"[n]early a dozen current and former officials" who had expressed "concerns about the operation's legality and oversight." (All requested anonymity "because of the classified nature of the program.")[81] The article was *not* about how NSA picks targets or what methods it might use to decide which communications to review more closely.

Instead, the thrust of the article concerned the administration's position that a president has the right—secretly—to violate a law, specifically the Foreign Intelligence Surveillance Act, which, except for short emergency periods, prohibited eavesdropping on Americans without a secret warrant issued by a FISA court. The FISA court had almost always approved requests for warrants. Moreover, Congress had shown a willingness to update FISA to deal with technological changes in the transmission of messages. Nevertheless, the Bush administration rejected the involvement of Congress or the courts for "doctrinal" reasons. The White House, likely led by David Addington, Vice President Cheney's counsel, believed FISA had invaded what Cheney and Addington asserted was the president's *exclusive* power to decide—secretly, and with no warrant requirements or other checks—who should be wiretapped.

Isn't secretly ignoring the law precisely what the press ought to expose so the program and the law's importance can be debated in Congress and by the public? Schoenfeld implicitly sought to preempt this question by relying on another American value—representative democracy—which he introduced by characterizing Ellsberg's Pentagon Papers leak as an "assault on democratic self-governance itself." "For better or worse the American people in those years had elected Kennedy, Johnson, and Nixon; they had acted at the ballot box to make their leadership and policy preferences clear, including policies about secrecy."[82] Again, truly breathtaking. Surely no voter made "clear" a preference for the secret use of "monarchical" presidential prerogatives to ignore the law, or for suppressing a history of escalating the war in Vietnam.[83]

In developing his case against the *Times*, Schoenfeld critiqued executive editor Bill Keller's claim that the "people who invented this country" would obviously have seen an "aggressive, independent press as a protective measure against the abuse of power in a democracy, and an essential ingredient for self-government."[84] If one reads Keller as suggesting the Founders would have approved publication of all secrets, it would be fair to criticize Keller's use of history. But not if the focus is on what the article was actually about. Having just revolted against monarchical arrogance, the Founders surely would have blessed a story exposing a president's secret claim of power to violate a democratically passed law. Indeed, the *Times'* warrantless wiretapping story exposed fundamental issues facing a constitutional democracy, just as the press, at its best, should do.

Shortly after the *Times'* 2005 article on illegal NSA wiretapping, the *Baltimore Sun* ran several stories on NSA waste and inefficiency, largely based on leaks of secret information. The series, written by Siobhan Gorman, whose office was only a few miles from NSA headquarters in Fort Meade, Maryland, revealed a botched billion-dollar program code-named Trailblazer, which was "designed for sifting through an ocean of modern-day digital communications and uncovering key nuggets to protect the nation against an ever-changing collection of enemies."[85] NSA awarded the program contract to SAIC, a contractor with close ties to NSA, and assigned its oversight to a former SAIC employee who had become NSA's deputy director.[86]

Based upon comments from an NSA official "with extensive knowledge of Trailblazer," Gorman reported that since the 1990s, NSA had been "gradually 'going deaf' as unimportant communications drown out key pieces of information."[87] By the close of the twentieth century, NSA was collecting two million bits of data each hour.[88] By 2006, digital technology had sparked a data boom, and NSA's collection had grown exponentially as its spies tried to cope with the world's information output—the daily electronic equivalent of a dozen stacks of books each stretching the roughly 93 million miles from the Earth to the sun. More than 90 billion e-mail messages were sent daily by 2006. Sen. Jay Rockefeller, chair of the Senate Intelligence Committee, said NSA had "been overwhelmed" by the information explosion.[89] The severity of its management problems led Congress to bar NSA from entering into major procurement contracts without prior approval from its Defense Department superiors.[90]

Trailblazer was supposed to be a fix. But six years in and $1.2 billion later, the program was a failure. Matthew Aid, who advised three federal bodies investigating 9/11, said Trailblazer was "the biggest boondoggle going on now in the intelligence community."[91] Senator Rockefeller said the intelligence committee had "worried" about Trailblazer specifically, and "NSA acquisition practices generally."[92] Using FOIA, the *Sun* obtained an inspector general report that criticized NSA's "inadequate management and oversight."[93] Moreover, Trailblazer was developed over a less costly program called Thin-Thread, which a classified Pentagon report found was more promising and could have been more quickly deployed.[94] Ironically, the *Sun's* Trailblazer exposé emerged at roughly the same time as the warrantless wiretapping story in the *Times*. But, as Gorman observed, "although the Bush administration spent much of the past week defending the NSA's eavesdropping work as vital to keeping Americans safe from terrorism, virtually no attention has been paid to the agency's failure to deliver the system the NSA said was key to fulfilling that mission."[95]

Unlike the *Times'* warrantless wiretapping story about illegality, Gorman's inefficiency and waste stories did lead to an indictment. In 2007, the Bush administration's FBI searched the home of Thomas Drake, one of Gorman's twenty or so anonymous NSA sources.[96] Two and a half years later, the Obama administration's Justice Department hit Drake with a ten-count felony indictment. The indictment alleges Drake had talked to Gorman (referred to as "Reporter A"), but he was not charged with leaking classified information to her. Instead, he was accused of retaining classified documents on his home computer and with making false statements to the FBI about "Reporter A."[97]

Drake had joined NSA in 2001, after a ten-year career in the Air Force. At NSA, he "focused primarily on process improvements and improving efficiency within the NSA, not actual signals intelligence work."[98] In 2003, the Defense Department's Inspector General's Office asked Drake to help investigate charges of waste and fraud at NSA in developing Trailblazer instead of ThinThread.[99] Although Drake's revelations concerned only waste and inefficiency he had already complained about within the government, the indictment charged him with five felony counts of violating the Espionage Act, carrying the potential for thirty-five years in prison. It is hard to know how a Department of Justice could possibly have overreached to such an extent.

Then, on the eve of trial, the government suffered two blows. J. William Leonard, the former director of the government's Information Security Oversight Office, agreed to testify that a document the government relied upon should never have been classified and the trial judge said that at trial the government had to use the classified documents it claimed Drake improperly handled. At this point, the government dropped its overblown felony charges, and Drake pled guilty to a single misdemeanor charge of exceeding authorized use of a computer.[100] At the sentencing hearing, the judge was harshly and repeatedly critical of the thirty-month delay between the FBI search and the indictment.[101] The judge was also concerned that "other people involved with it [talking to Gorman] [were] never charged."[102] Rejecting the government's plea to "send a message" by imposing a stiff fine, the judge, with defense counsel's agreement, sentenced Drake to 250 hours of community service.[103]

Two years later, in 2013, Edward Snowden leaked the breadth of NSA information-gathering, including a program that captured and stored information about virtually every call made in the country. Even though the content of the calls was not collected, the government can paint a picture of the private lives of all Americans from the digital crumbs that are swept up in "metadata"—the calling number; the number called; the call's date, time, and duration; and the location from which the call was made—and can be reassembled to identify intimate details of a person's life: the therapist, "friend," or political figure on the other end of the line.

Much has been written about the program's legality, effect on American privacy, and effectiveness in combating terrorism. These are all vital questions, but there is a more fundamental issue that zeros in on secrecy's role in our democracy. Allowing government to capture and keep metadata about everyone's telephone communications is too great an addition to government power and too big a potential loss of privacy to be decided without democratic dialogue. What President Bush should have done when initiating the program and President Obama should have done when continuing it was to have a public discussion. The Bush administration's monarchical view of presidential power was, however, inconsistent with any public dialogue, let alone an open discussion about this (or about returning to warrantless wiretapping). And we now know that—not surprisingly—the strongest advocates after 9/11 of what they called the "President's Surveillance Program," were Dick Cheney and his then counsel, David Addington, both of whom were adamantly opposed to openness during the Bush administration.[104] But President Obama was not shackled by such monarchical views. "[T]hat's a conversation that I welcome having," Obama said, referring to the debate between privacy and security.[105] But he only said this *after* the Snowden revelations.

A public discussion need not have included details of the technology used to obtain, analyze, or store the data. It should have focused instead on the program's very existence. Even though nearly 3,000 people had been briefed on, or "read into," the program by as early as 2007, the public knew nothing.[106] The ongoing metadata program was an enormous deep secret or unknown unknown. The program affected every American, made a major change in Americans' privacy rights, and fundamentally altered the relationship between the government and the people. In a nation where the just powers of government are based on the consent of the governed, and where government is by the people, such decisions should involve the people rather than be silently imposed by their temporary leaders.

Nonetheless, during the Cold War and after 9/11 presidents became used to making fundamental, long-lasting decisions without public involvement or knowledge. But the might to decide alone does not make it right to decide alone. Similarly, formalistic notification of a handful of congressional leaders does not sanctify a broad hidden program—any more so than it would justify entering into war. Open discussion and debate before entering into such a program is vital to America's democracy. There was no strong case for secrecy for the metadata program. Terrorists presumably already believed America was attempting to harvest the content of their conversations, far more than the domestic metadata program. And even if—because of a democratic debate about the "President's Surveillance Program"—terrorists were to become more afraid of using the Internet or phones, would this be harmful? If terrorists were to go back to communication by mule or by human courier, they would lose the speed and other advantages of modern technology. With respect to details of exactly how NSA or its partner agency, the FBI, conduct communications surveillance, there is a case for secrecy to guard against behavior changes by terrorists. But for the existence and the broad outlines of these programs, secrecy served, once again, not to protect America but to keep the government's conduct secret from Americans.

The same goes for NSA's programs relating to cross-border and overseas communications. One of these programs, code-named PRISM, was supposed to target only the Internet communications of foreigners outside the United States, but program sponsors conceded that communications of Americans and permanent residents would also be captured. Authorized in an elastic interpretation of the foreign intelligence law, the mass electronic surveillance program captured photos, videos, e-mail, search history, voice and video chats, and more.[107] Analysts use search terms to determine with "at least 51 percent confidence" a target's so-called foreignness.[108] How exactly this works is unclear, but it admittedly leaves lots of room to pick up the content of Americans' conversations.

In a different program, NSA also systematically mined—without warrants—the contents of communications into and out of the country. The purpose of the program, according to intelligence officials, was to track individuals who mentioned information about foreigners who were under surveillance. But to conduct this large-scale surveillance, NSA had to temporarily copy and then sift through the contents of most e-mails and other communications that crossed the U.S. border. This also is too broad an intrusion to have been wholly shrouded in secrecy.

Compelling American companies—such as Google, Apple, Yahoo! and Microsoft—to turn over mass data cannot be good for the companies' future or, by extension, the United States. When it was revealed in the late 1960s and early 1970s that some American journalists and student leaders had relationships with the CIA, the government decided that permitting such relationships would undermine all journalists and all student leaders, and that this would damage America. (Similarly, in May 2014, the CIA announced it would not use health workers as spies because doing so undermined vaccination programs and other needed health work.) However the analysis of PRISM comes out, secrecy, once again, relieved leaders from having to think about whether a program designed to help intelligence agencies might have adverse effects on other American interests.

There is a more practical reason why the government should have opened a vigorous public debate about NSA surveillance programs. In a digital world, and with thousands of people "read into" the program, leaks were inevitable. So why act secretly at the start to set up the sure-to-come suggestion the government must have been trying to hide something wrong?

The Snowden disclosures also called attention to a new concern about the court created to hear cases under the Foreign Intelligence Surveillance Act. Known as FISC (for the Foreign Intelligence Surveillance Court), its decisions on surveillance of particular individuals are quite properly secret when made. Just as are the decisions of criminal-court judges to approve a search warrant for the property of a criminal suspect, or a wiretap on a suspect's phone. When, however, FISC is asked for broad, general rulings concerning, for example, the scope of a particular section of the Patriot Act, there is no reason why a security-cleared advocate for privacy interests should not participate to argue against the government's position.[109] And again there is a more basic point. FISC appears to be dabbling in policy choices that are not fit for the judicial branch. As revealed by the Snowden leaks and their aftermath, FISC has been used to assess and bless broad minimization and targeting policies and procedures under FISA—policy questions that should be reserved for the political branches.[110]

The Snowden revelations are now said by many, including President Obama, to have forced the nation to focus on the balance between security and liberty.[111] But the issues are broader. Snowden's revelations should also force attention to the balance between secrecy and democracy. Throughout American history, journalists have played a vital role in upholding American democracy, perhaps never more so than after 9/11. Harvard Law professor Jack Goldsmith—who earlier had trimmed some of John Yoo's excesses at the Bush administration's Justice Department's Office of Legal Counsel—advocates this view with force. While noting the press "stumbled badly" in covering the weapons-of-mass-destruction justification for the Iraq War, Goldsmith praised the press for its "hundreds of astounding journalistic successes since 9/11 in disclosing deep governmental secrets," successes that were "in part attributable to clever reporters and disgruntled leakers." Also, according to Goldsmith, "The press's many revelations about the government's conduct of the war were at the foundation of all the mechanisms of presidential accountability after 9/11. They informed the public and shaped its opinions, and spurred activists, courts, and Congress to action in changing the government's course."[112] While "publication of classified information sometimes reveals illegal or imprudent government behavior," even more important, Goldsmith said, is that "fear of leaks causes national security officials to think twice about what they are doing with little direct oversight."[113]

Moreover, for all the broadsides fired at each other, the establishment press and the government have also gradually worked out ways to reconcile their conflicting interests. Generally—at least after the Supreme Court ruled out a prior restraint in the Pentagon Papers case—establishment news outlets hear out government officials when considering publication of classified information. As Pulitzer Prize–winning journalist Barton Gellman put it, he treats classification as "a yellow light but not a red light."[114]

The general principle was described in an op-ed by the editors of the *Los*

Angeles Times and the *New York Times* a week after disclosure of a covert Bush administration program to trace international banking data: "No article on a classified program gets published until the responsible officials have been given a fair opportunity to comment."[115] Moreover, if the government argues publication would endanger national security, the papers "put things on hold and give them a respectful hearing," even letting government officials make their arguments off the record, "so they can make their case without fear of spilling more secrets onto our front pages." On occasion, the papers "withheld information because we were convinced that publishing it could put lives at risk." Similarly, they "edit[ed] out gratuitous detail that lends little to public understanding but might be useful to the targets of surveillance." In its NSA warrantless wiretapping article, for example, the *New York Times* "left out some technical details," and, in its article on secret CIA prisons, the *Washington Post* agreed not to name "specific countries" that housed the prisons.

The practical way journalists and government have worked together is better for democracy than either suppression or publication without warning. Indeed, if in the Pentagon Papers case, the Supreme Court had permitted prior restraints, the government would actually be worse off. Many such stories would still get published, but without mitigating discussions beforehand. Such discussions are healthy, but only as long as delays are not lengthy and journalists retain their vigor.

Although investigative journalism has been vital to our democracy, there are some danger signals. The question now is whether it can continue to be effective, as journalism, particularly investigative journalism, is threatened by many shifts in technology and economics. Although two grants totaling only $2,500 enabled Seymour Hersh to uncover the My Lai massacre and "leverage a whiff into a colossal stink," investigative journalism is generally expensive.[116] As Hersh himself later said, "what it takes is time and money." Moreover, he added, "I strike out one time in three." According to Alex Jones, the director of Harvard's Shorenstein Center on the Media, Politics and Public Policy, a skilled investigative reporter can cost more than $250,000 a year for only a handful of stories.[117] Even when a news organization is fed previously hidden information, the legwork required to check it can be extraordinarily expensive. Before the German newsmagazine *Der Spiegel* published information provided by WikiLeaks, it took a team of fifty nearly four months to analyze the American diplomatic cables and the so-called war logs took a team of thirty around two months.[118] Investigative journalism is expensive and often brings with it potential legal risks.[119]

In a time of belt-tightening, American media has been cutting back on investigative reporting.[120] Pinched for time and money, newsrooms devote less effort to monitoring an increasingly complex government. "Unfortunately, the problem of finding verities instead of verisimilitudes beneath the varnish has been exacerbated in recent years throughout America because there are, quite simply, fewer varnish removers," writes Charles Lewis, who founded the Center for Public Integrity.[121] Moreover, as government pours vastly more money into its public-relations budgets, journalists have become more reliant on tips and scoops from sources who too often have motives that may not be clear.[122] "One resulting paradox is that while more reporters than ever are covering Washington, we really know less about many very important things."[123] To grasp this, one need only consider media's failure in the lead-up to the Iraq War.

Erosion of investigative journalism began before the rise of the Internet and accelerated rapidly afterward. In the digital age there is no need to worry about the volume of news and opinion. In this respect, the Internet is a boon. It facilitates the diffusion of information and democratizes communication across the land, allowing ordinary citizens to hear more and to get out their views. Plus a phalanx of bloggers has also proven a formidable check on traditional newsrooms, pointing out their errors and supplying original reporting. Of course, the traditional media, too, will continue its reporting, but the abiding concern is whether most news organizations will have the resources needed to delve deeply and responsibly. As Robert Caro has said, "time equals truth."[124] And time means expense.

There are many ways to support investigative journalism, including paywalls, government subsidies, and university-commercial partnerships. Glenn Greenwald's work on the Snowden story proves that an enterprising journalist does not need a permanent affiliation to produce groundbreaking journalism that opens the door to widespread public debate.[125] In addition, in a time of big budget cuts, nonprofit organizations will likely play a central role in journalistic efforts. It is too soon to know whether the not-for-profit model will succeed, but there are some encouraging signs. Primarily relying on philanthropy, ProPublica, an investigative-news group, employs around forty journalists. Where national news has cut back, this Pulitzer Prize–winning outlet has turned out original investigations on stories about subjects ranging from surveillance to drone strikes. Launched in 2007, it has collaborated with top outlets including NPR, the *New York Times,* and the *New Yorker.* In 2012, it produced eighty "deep dive" investigative pieces with more than twenty-five partners. ProPublica's mission is to wade into the muck, and it does so with efficiency. It says 85 cents out of every $1 is spent on news, as opposed to 15 cents at traditional newspapers.[126] Many of its counterparts are similarly cost-effective, including the Center for Public Integrity.

Outside newsgathering, many policy, advocacy, and legal groups help shine light into the murky corners of government. These include the ACLU and the National Security Archive, both of which regularly use FOIA and other devices to breach the walls of secrecy. Other regular reporters on developments in the secrecy arena include the Federation of American Scientists, with Steven Aftergood running its Project on Government Secrecy and producing an online publication called *Secrecy News,* and Robert Chesney, cofounder of *Lawfare,* a national security blog. Other organizations pressing for information and pressing policy points related to secrecy include the Project on Government Oversight; the Government Accountability Project, a whistleblower advocacy organization; and Citizens for Responsibility and Ethics, which tends to do high-profile litigation and FOIA requests. More focused on rights in the digital area are the Electronic Frontier Foundation and the Center for Democracy and Technology. The existence of all these groups has helped reduce the half-life of secrets. These independent organizations help compensate for limited oversight within government, and often display a greater capacity than government to spot erroneous analysis.[127]

Watchdogs often meet with success. Two prime examples are the National Security Archive and the ACLU. Both are adept at framing demands for government information and have the time and resources to be in the struggle for a long time. The ACLU eventually prevailed over many expansive government secrecy claims, winning several important FOIA cases, including a landmark fight for documents on the torture of detainees in American custody.[128] The National Security Archive, headed by Tom Blanton, is a relentless chronicler of secret history, pushing to expand public access to information. Each year, it files roughly 1,500 FOIA and declassification requests; in 2012, it collected more than 59,000 U.S. government documents.[129] Some of the archive's more acclaimed acquisitions include transcripts of Henry Kissinger's meetings with Chinese and Soviet leaders and crucial documents on

Guatemalan human-rights abuses.[130] The archive won a decade-and-a-half lawsuit for the release of internal CIA documents from the mid-1970s known as "The Family Jewels," which described, among other things, domestic surveillance operations and assassination plots against foreign leaders.[131] In 2012, the archive uncovered a Bush-era legal memo in which a top State Department counselor said the administration's "enhanced interrogation techniques" were unlawful.[132]

In its first years, the archive was decidedly unpopular with Reagan administration officials, not least because it compiled a trove of compromising materials on their contacts with anti-Sandinista rebels and Iran. Even before Iran-Contra broke, the man at the scandal's center tried to put a stop to the archive: hanging in the archive is a note from Oliver North to Treasury Secretary Bill Simon trying to stop a Ford Foundation grant to the archive. First seen only as a challenge to U.S. national security claims, the archive now also works with officials to promote best practices for open government, even as it continues to press for the release of classified papers, netting more than 10 million pages of once-secret documents, according to its own tally. Sitting in his Washington office in the Gelman Library at George Washington University, Blanton shared an undergirding assumption of his group: "Documents aren't the truth," but they are usually the best version, he told me.[133] And by this measure, in its tireless fidelity to openness, the archive has made a remarkable contribution to the democratic process.

9

Congress I:
Investigations and Oversight

On the afternoon of September 11, 2001, James Baker, former secretary of state, White House chief of staff, and Bush family counselor, was interviewed on ABC television and blamed the Church Committee for that morning's murderous terrorist attacks. The committee, Baker said, had "unilaterally disarm[ed] . . . our intelligence capabilities." Baker further blamed the committee for spy agencies retreating from the "down-and-dirty" business of using "human intelligence" to penetrate terrorist cells.[1] The *Wall Street Journal* similarly editorialized that the intelligence services had been "reeling" ever since Church.[2]

Quick to exploit dismay and fear, these critics ignored the actual record. In fact, the Church Committee concluded that investigation of "international terrorism" was one reason "intelligence is vital to the nation's interest."[3] It urged the FBI to focus on terrorism and espionage rather than political dissent, and emphasized the need for strengthening the CIA's analytical capacities. It also emphasized the importance of the CIA using human spies as opposed to simply relying on satellites and other spying technology.[4]

The committee's critics also missed the absurdity inherent in their own claims. How could the intelligence agencies still be "reeling" after twenty-five years and six administrations? In those twenty-five years, Baker himself served as chief of staff for President Reagan for four years and for the first President Bush for five months; he also served as Reagan's treasury secretary and secretary of state under Bush I. If the committee disarmed any intelligence agencies, was Baker seriously claiming he and his bosses did not know, or that they all lacked the power to rehabilitate supposedly neutered agencies? Also, while Baker may not have known it when he appeared on ABC, the intelligence agencies, based on intelligence gathering, had repeatedly warned the Bush White House about al-Qaeda's plans for "spectacular" attacks.

Like many who never worked in Congress, Baker evinced hostility toward congressional investigations into the executive branch, which, almost by definition, explore and reveal executive-branch secrets. "If men were angels," and the executive branch always revealed all it had done, and fully and fairly explained how and why it had erred when things had gone wrong, no investigations would be necessary. But humans are, well, human. Much is kept secret. Executive explanations are rarely forthcoming, seldom complete, and at times incorrect—sometimes intentionally. Therefore, Congress must have power to investigate. In fact, it has long been argued that legislators, as the people's representatives, fulfill their most solemn obligation when uncovering matters that executives would rather not openly discuss.

Centuries ago, political philosopher John Stuart Mill said the British Parliament had more than *power* to investigate. It also had a *duty* to "throw the light of publicity on [the government's] acts" and to "compel a full exposition and justification of all of them which any one considers questionable."[5] Woodrow Wilson similarly wrote that Congress is "meant to be the eyes and the voice, and to embody the wisdom and will of its constituents." This, he stressed, was its most important role, even more important than legislation, for "[u]nless Congress have and use every means of acquainting itself with the acts and the disposition of the administrative agents of the government . . . the country must remain in embarrassing, crippling ignorance of the very affairs which it is most important that it should understand and direct."[6]

In a 1927 ruling in a case related to the Teapot Dome bribery scandal, the Supreme Court characterized congressional investigations as an "essential and appropriate auxiliary to the legislative function." The Court held that Congress had power to compel a witness to testify, saying a "legislative body cannot legislate wisely or effectively in the absence of information."[7] Yet there are restrictions. Thirty years later, in a case involving an investigation by the House Un-American Activities Committee—which the Court called a "new kind of congressional inquiry unknown in prior periods of American history . . . a broad-scale intrusion into the lives and affairs of private citizens"— the Court said congressional investigations must comply with the Bill of

Rights.[8] But the Court simply required Congress to make clear in advance why it required particular information.[9]

Judicial limits on Congress's investigative power are minimal, but practical politics often limits congressional power. Sen. Joseph McCarthy's efforts to expose Communists in government in the early years of the Cold War, for example, polarized the nation and for a while cowed public figures, even Dwight Eisenhower as a presidential candidate.[10] Despite his flash of power, however, McCarthy's investigative excess and irresponsibility eventually destroyed him politically, as he was exposed as a bully in his televised Army hearings and was censured by a bipartisan Senate committee, followed by the Senate's 67–22 censure vote.[11]

Congressional committees have investigated secret matters from the birth of the Republic.[12] Commissions have also been established either by law, such as with the 9/11 Commission, or by presidents, such as with FDR's Pearl Harbor Commission and Barack Obama's Gulf Oil Spill Commission. Regardless of the body's genesis, the common thread has been uncovering and understanding hidden information—whether it was the cause of a bloody Native American victory during the Washington administration, military contracting during the Lincoln administration, or the conduct of oil-drilling companies and the Interior Department during the Obama administration.

Some investigations perform well. Some fizzle. Some are abusive. Walter Lippmann, a usually calm commentator on American institutions, disparaged as a "legalized atrocity, the Congressional investigation, where Congressmen, starved of their legitimate food for thought, go on a wild and feverish manhunt, and do not stop at cannibalism."[13] And as Edward R. Murrow said in his famous March 1954 CBS television show targeting McCarthy, "[T]he line between investigating and persecuting is a very fine one, and the junior Senator from Wisconsin has stepped over it repeatedly."[14] But while some investigations and investigators do indeed merit criticism, or even scorn, many investigations expose fundamental problems and prompt reform.

Case Study: The Church Committee

For decades, Congress took a passive "don't ask, don't tell" attitude toward America's secret government, was afraid to look beneath J. Edgar Hoover's positive publicity, and gave the CIA a free pass.[15] But widespread distrust of government in the wake of Vietnam and Watergate fueled an appetite to learn what the government had secretly been doing. In addition, stolen FBI documents suggesting secret surveillance and harassment of dissidents, rumors of CIA assassination plots, and leaks leading to investigative articles by Seymour Hersh about "massive" CIA domestic spying directed against antiwar activists and other American dissidents provided more specific spurs to congressional action.[16]

In response, the Senate, by an 82–4 vote, created the Church Committee on January 27, 1975.[17] The committee undertook the first—and still the most wide-ranging—investigation of America's secret government. But while the increased mistrust of government and pent-up interest in what the secret government had been doing were necessary, they were not sufficient to generate and sustain the Church Committee investigation. Two other factors helped. First, Gerald Ford had recently been appointed as vice president, and therefore when he took over from the disgraced Richard Nixon, he became the nation's only unelected president.[18] While he had a problem with powerful advisors such as Henry Kissinger and Dick Cheney who opposed cooperation with the Church Committee, and therefore the committee had to push to obtain the crucial classified information,[19] Ford's more fundamental problem was that Nixon's resignation stemmed from his secret abuse of power and secret violations of the law, including trying to use the CIA to quash the FBI's investigation of Watergate and concealing the bombing of Cambodia from Congress and the public. Ford *wanted* to appear open and cooperative. He *needed* not to appear to be hiding impropriety. This helped the committee obtain the crucial information.

Second, J. Edgar Hoover, the longtime untouchable FBI director, had died in 1972. Had Hoover been alive, he would have pressed like a boa constrictor to smother disclosure and to justify the conduct concealed by his secrecy. He would have used his reputation for having caches of embarrassing information on public figures and would have pulled out all his peerless bureaucratic skills to thwart disclosure of the Bureau's embarrassing raw files. Fear of a living Hoover might have forestalled any investigation of the FBI and any disclosure of the files that hid Hoover's secrets.

Another factor in the committee's successful launch was its unusual bipartisan structure. At the time, the Senate's standard ratio for an eleven-member committee was seven Democrats and four Republicans. The Church Committee was divided 6–5. Usually, the senior member of the minority was given the largely honorific title of "ranking member." Republican senator John Tower of

Texas served as the Church Committee's vice chair, with power to preside in the absence of Senator Church. The panel also was a "select" committee, whose members were appointed by the majority and minority leaders, who deliberately selected senators who had *not* been on the panels that had exercised minimal oversight over intelligence agencies, thus excluding senators who would be most reluctant to expose previous inadequate oversight.

Many expected the Church Committee to focus on exposing additional Nixon administration abuses. But as it turned out, the committee showed that all six administrations from Franklin Roosevelt's through Richard Nixon's—four Democrats and two Republicans—had secretly abused their powers. No single man, no single party, no single administration was responsible for the abuses the committee uncovered.[20] This was probably the committee's single most important finding. The investigation's breadth and nonpartisan conclusions fostered the committee's internal cohesion and magnified its external influence.[21] Toward the end, Republican senators Barry Goldwater and John Tower dissented quite often, but there was no vote that divided the committee on a party basis.

For the committee to succeed, it had two early hurdles relating to secrecy: obtaining classified material from the White House and the intelligence agencies, and handling secrets responsibly. When the executive branch is the target of an investigation, it zealously guards its prerogatives—sometimes legitimate, but often not—to avoid turning over information, so Congress has to press for disclosure. Not to press would be to abdicate its role in delivering democracy; yet at the same time, a congressional committee must appreciate that responsible treatment of secrets is also part of its job.

The Ford administration ultimately decided it could not afford the risk of being seen as obstructionist, but it did try to delay delivering documents. Their hope was that stalling, coupled with the Senate's deadline for completing the job, would result in pallid, half-baked findings.[22] The committee's successful response had three prongs. First, Senator Church built political pressure by using the media to complain about White House foot-dragging and to stress the committee's resolve. Second, the committee repeatedly sent specific document demands to the White House and the agencies. And finally, as Senator Mondale said, "We ought to tell them we're going to keep getting extensions for the life of this committee until we finish our business." Indicating the committee's bipartisan determination, Vice Chair Tower responded with, "Amen, world without end."[23]

Even after the agencies began to cooperate, some still tried to frustrate discovery. The CIA, for example, asked the committee to specify exactly which documents it wanted to see. The committee responded it could not be that specific because it didn't know what was there. Therefore it had to examine all files and other records on particular subjects, such as the attempted assassinations of Fidel Castro or spying domestically on Americans or using drugs on unwitting subjects.

Responsible treatment of secrecy also induced cooperation from the White House and the intelligence agencies. A committee must be unyielding in *obtaining* secret information, but it should use commonsense flexibility in how it *handles* it. There must be a delicate balance in any investigation of secret government programs. Some previously classified information must be revealed, either because it should not have been stamped secret in the first place or because the benefits of disclosure to democracy outweigh national security concerns. Yet there are legitimate secrets, and investigations that are heedless of this are irresponsible—and doomed to fail.

While it retained all final disclosure decisions, the Church Committee worked out reasonable secrecy arrangements with the Ford administration. When agencies first produced documents, they could redact—or black out— names of informers or secret agents. For example, the committee would learn about the FBI's infiltration of the NAACP or feminist groups, but without getting the informants' names. If, upon review, the committee believed disclosure was important, it could press for the names. The committee also agreed that, before it issued reports, it would let agencies and the White House see final drafts so they could argue that disclosure of particular information would be unnecessarily harmful.

The committee's published reports revealed huge amounts of classified information. No improprieties were withheld, but sensible limits were placed on the details disclosed. The actual names of lower-level undercover CIA or FBI officers were withheld; those of higher-level supervisors who had issued orders for illegal or unseemly acts were included. The committee was also careful about the identity of foreign nationals who had cooperated with U.S. intelligence. For example, the preface to a report on covert action in Chile noted that: "[w]ith few exceptions, names of Chileans and of Chilean institutions have been omitted in order to avoid revealing intelligence sources and methods and to limit needless harm to individual Chileans who cooperated with the Central Intelligence Agency."[24]

These agreements did not interfere with the committee's mission. And though difficult to measure, the public's (and the administration's) trust in the committee grew because it kept its collective mouth shut. There were very few leaks, none concerning national security.[25]

The committee and the Ford administration worked out agreements with respect to all but three disclosure issues. At the last minute, the White House and the CIA tried to prevent publication of the committee's *Interim Report on Assassinations*. At 349 pages, the report was, and still is, the most comprehensive public recitation of secret covert action by any government. The administration claimed the report revealed too much. In addition, although the report used pseudonyms for lower-level CIA operatives, neither upper-level CIA officers nor high-level civilians such as members of the Mafia aiding the CIA were granted such anonymity. We believed we had drawn a proper line. But on the eve of an executive session by the Senate to discuss the report, CIA Director William Colby called in reporters and argued that a dozen names should be deleted before release.[26] We did not agree. At the Senate's executive session, the committee described the report. Though there were some comments on whether the report should be released, ultimately there was no vote.[27] We released the report (including the disputed names) as soon as the Senate session ended.

There also was disagreement about disclosure of NSA's SHAMROCK project, which lasted from 1945 to 1975 and involved telegraph companies giving NSA copies of every telegram leaving the United States.[28] Although the White House and NSA pushed to keep SHAMROCK secret, they eventually conceded the program's existence but then demanded the companies' names be withheld. Despite an appeal to the committee by Attorney General Edward Levi, a closely divided committee voted to override the administration's objections and revealed the names. I had pushed for that result because the "'companies had a duty to protect the privacy of their customers . . . they deserved to be exposed [and] if the Committee did not do it, it would become the subject of criticism itself.'"[29]

The Ford administration won the third disclosure battle. Near the end of the committee's work, when the administration's decision-makers and the political climate had changed, the administration (and the CIA) became increasingly resistant to disclosures connected to foreign intelligence.[30] While earlier reports had detailed covert actions in Cuba, the Congo, Chile, Vietnam, and the Dominican Republic, and while the committee published thoughtful analysis and many previously secret facts in its *Final Report on Foreign and Military Intelligence*, it was blocked from including in the public part of the report details about covert actions in other countries. The committee was also blocked from including in the public part the aggregate budget for the intelligence agencies. However, no data was blocked from the committee's *Final Report on Intelligence Activities and the Rights of Americans.*

In its early days, the Church Committee discussed whether it should take testimony about plots to assassinate foreign leaders in public or in executive session. The assassination testimony was dramatic, and the plots were highly colorful. For example, in trying to kill Cuba's Fidel Castro, the CIA's efforts included hiring Mafia bosses, passing a poison-pen device to a Cuban in Paris on the day JFK was shot in Dallas, and exploring rigging an exotic seashell to explode when Castro touched it while diving. In the plot to kill the Congo's Patrice Lumumba, the CIA's chief scientist concocted a deadly poison to put inside a toothpaste tube. Once past details of the colorful plots, we came to the more important question of whether Presidents Eisenhower and Kennedy had authorized them.[31] This was covered in dramatic, conflicting, and often emotional testimony from former CIA executives, national security advisors, secretaries of defense and state, and close personal aides and family members of the dead presidents.

This testimony would have made for absorbing national television, and Sen. Howard Baker—who had recently served on the Senate Watergate Committee, where he had coined the question: "[W]hat did the President know and when did he know it?"—suggested public hearings. But Senator Church, who would have garnered enormous attention from public hearings, persuaded the committee to take the assassination testimony in executive session so as not to reveal details about sources and methods that *might* deserve continued secrecy. If obtained in executive session, those sensitive details could more easily be handled appropriately in the committee's comprehensive public report. Pushing to make public the committee's first testimony-taking hearings might also derail cooperation from the Ford administration. Senator Baker did not press his point further.[32] While the issue was close, I believe Senator Church's position was correct.

After the assassinations inquiry, the committee held numerous public hearings.[33] By exposing facts about the Cold War era at home and abroad in its hearings and reports, the committee changed perceptions and cultures. The committee's testimony and reports shamed agencies that, when left to their own devices, had too often trampled on American values, the Constitution, and the law. The committee's record served as a cautionary note to presidents, national security advisors, attorneys general, other high-level executives, and members of Congress, whose predecessors had failed to exercise adequate oversight. By treating secret information responsibly, the Church Committee also showed how a congressional committee could safely investigate some of the government's most secret activities.

The evolution of the Church Committee's thinking on the responsibility of presidents and other high-ranking executive-branch officials demonstrates the value of an in-depth inquiry into facts. At the investigation's start, the role of senior executive-branch officials was not clear. In the summer of 1975, early in the investigation of assassination plots directed at Castro and others, Senator Church speculated to the press that the CIA may have acted like a "rogue elephant on a rampage," conceiving and carrying out the plots without clear authorization from presidents. Other senators, also speculating, opined that the CIA "took orders from the top."[34] But when the committee released its *Interim Report on Assassinations* in November 1975, the committee declined to adopt either theory. Instead, the interim report presented substantial evidence for both views, saying the conflicting evidence made it impossible to be certain whether or not Presidents Eisenhower and Kennedy authorized the assassination plots.[35]

In April 1976, by which time the committee had completed investigations into many other intelligence activities, covering six administrations over four decades, it was ready in its final reports to fix responsibility at the top. As the committee explained with respect to foreign actions: "On occasion, intelligence agencies concealed their programs from those in higher authority, more frequently it was the senior officials themselves who, through pressure for results, created the climate within which the abuses occurred."[36] Domestically, while intelligence agencies occasionally failed to reveal programs or acts to their superiors, the committee concluded that "the most serious breaches of duty were those of senior officials, who were responsible for controlling intelligence activities and generally failed to assure compliance with the law."[37] Fault at the top was shown by "demanding results without carefully limiting the means." Senior executive-branch officials, moreover, had enabled wrongdoing by "failing to inquire further after receiving indications that improper activities may have been occurring." They also "delegat[ed] broad authority" through open-ended mandates and vague terms such as "national security" or "subversion" but then failed to set forth adequate guidelines or procedural checks on how their wishes were being carried out. Finally, senior officials "exhibit[ed] a reluctance to know about secret details of programs."[38]

The committee's conclusions on responsibility evolved due to the clarity produced by exposure to the massive record. Specific agency acts, examined in isolation, sometimes suggested an agency acted on its own and even misled political superiors. But the fuller record of many years and many agencies made clear that ultimate responsibility was properly fixed with presidents, attorneys general, and other senior executive-branch officials. Looking backward at the Church Committee investigation some forty years later, there are at least three further reasons to place ultimate responsibility with higher authorities. It is crystal clear that presidents, national security advisors, and other high-ranking executive-branch officials exploited plausible deniability. Therefore, even if they did not know about particular actions, their willful ignorance cannot absolve them of responsibility. And although Hoover's power meant attorneys general exercised, at most, only weak oversight of the FBI, the attorneys general knew that was happening, and so must receive a measure of responsibility even for acts they did not see. Finally, presidents and other high-level executive-branch officials knew that intelligence activities were smothered by layers of excess secrecy. They knew Congress and the courts played no meaningful checking role. And they knew—or should have known—that excessive secrecy, nonexistent or weak checks and balances, and fuzzy or open-ended authorizations were invitations for excess and abuse. This remains equally true today.

The committee's work also led to concrete reforms, including the creation of permanent Senate and House Intelligence Committees to oversee the intelligence agencies, passage of the Foreign Intelligence Surveillance Act, and a ten-year limit on the FBI director's tenure. The committee's recommendations also bolstered the independence and strength of inspectors general for intelligence agencies.[39] After the committee's revelations, Attorney General Levi issued guidelines that for the first time controlled FBI investigations. While not as strong as a law because they could be amended by future attorneys general—as they have been—and while somewhat weaker than the committee's scores of FBI recommendations,[40] Levi's guidelines nevertheless moved in the direction the committee had urged.[41]

The Church Committee approached its job believing that understanding must rest upon a bed of facts and that there would be no groundswell for reform unless we revealed shocking secret abuses to the American people. To understand the past and to propose guidance for the future, a congressional committee must investigate past wrongdoing and mistakes. As the committee said, an investigation has to "determine what particular individuals appear to have done and, on occasion, to make judgments on their responsibility." Nonetheless, a congressional committee is "not a prosecutor, a grand jury or a court." Recognizing those limitations, the committee expressed the hope its reports would "provoke a national debate not on 'Who did it?', but on 'How did it happen and what can be done to keep it from happening again?'"[42]

The committee's view was that the nation would benefit from that debate if informed by public disclosure of the disturbing facts the committee had uncovered:

> Despite our distaste for what we have seen, we have great faith in this country. The story is sad, but this country has the strength to hear the story and to learn from it. We must remain a people who confront our mistakes and resolve not to repeat them. If we do not, we will decline; but, if we do, our future will be worthy of the best of our past.[43]

Lessons from Other Committees

Investigations generally fall into three categories. Some stem from defeats or disasters. Congress launched its first investigation after the 1791 rout of Gen. Arthur St. Clair's army by a coalition of Indians in Ohio Territory, and later investigations looked into the burning of Washington in the War of 1812, racial violence after the Civil War, the stock-market crash of 1929 and the Great Depression that followed, Pearl Harbor, 9/11, and Hurricane Katrina.

As government grew, waste and corruption also garnered more congressional attention. This led to investigations of, for example, military procurement at the start of the Civil War; the Credit Mobilier scandal in the 1870s, in which the Union Pacific Railroad bribed members of Congress who approved federal subsidies for railroad construction; munitions purchases during World War I; the Teapot Dome scandal in the 1920s in which oil barons bribed the interior secretary for leases on public land; military procurement before and during World War II; and aspects of Watergate involving contributions to Nixon's reelection campaign from companies fearing regulation or indictment.

A third type of investigation uncovers secret abuses of power. As presidential power, the federal bureaucracy, and classification all grew, there were more investigations that exposed secret violation of legal or constitutional restraints. Elements of Watergate (the "Plumbers" and efforts to frustrate or corrupt lawful government investigations), as well as the Church Committee and the counterpart House Committee, and the Iran-Contra hearings focused on executive abuses. Similarly, Congress investigated the weapons-of-mass-destruction justification for the Iraq War.

Congressional investigators should not act either as journalists pressing for the first story or historians waiting years to compile an encyclopedic tome. Investigations have been marred because they came too soon, or undermined because they came too late. The Joint Congressional Committee on the Conduct of the War, for example, investigated battles and generals while the Civil War was still under way.[44] (Confederate general Robert E. Lee later said these investigations were worth two divisions to him—a remark Sen. Harry Truman frequently cited as a caution when he chaired the committee investigating World War II procurement.)[45] The same month as the Pearl Harbor attacks, FDR appointed a commission to investigate the attack. It was led by Republican Supreme Court Justice Owen Roberts, who had investigated the Teapot Dome scandal before he joined the Court, and whose 1937 vote on the Court to uphold a minimum-wage law is famously known as the "switch in time [that] saves nine."[46] The commission issued its report just two months later. The investigation was rushed and shallow; its members did not have access to many secrets later obtained by a congressional investigation conducted shortly after the war's end.[47] At the other extreme, a 1912 Senate investigation of possible campaign-finance corruption in the election of 1904 was marred by the passage of time. Of course, it is not inherently inappropriate that an investigation go back a number of years. Indeed, the Church Committee's investigation gained credibility by going back almost four decades. But it did so to cover six administrations, not to target one.

Brazenly partisan congressional committee investigations are usually less respected and have less impact. An example is the Senate committee that concentrated on corporate contributions to Theodore Roosevelt in the 1904 presidential election. The effect of campaign contributions certainly merits investigation. But this investigation took place eight years after the election, when Roosevelt was running an insurgent campaign to recapture the presidency. Formed to explore Roosevelt's "Machiavellian shenanigans," the committee squabbled and split on partisan grounds. Despite taking lots of testimony, the committee did not issue a report. "What had been a political bang ended with a silent report."[48]

During the Clinton administration, congressional inquiries—including the investigations of Whitewater, a failed land development venture in Arkansas; the suicide of Deputy White House Counsel Vince Foster; and the impeachment tied to the president's conduct with Monica Lewinsky—also suffered from an aura of partisanship.

Conversely, nonpartisan investigations enjoy increased credibility at the time and fare better in history's light. Two investigations into wartime waste and corruption make the point. The first occurred early in the Civil War. Abraham Lincoln's first secretary of war was GOP boss and Pennsylvania senator Simon Cameron, who helped Lincoln win the presidential nomination. Soon after Cameron's appointment, newspapers ran stories of widespread waste and corruption in War Department contracts. In July 1861, the House, led by Republicans in Lincoln's party, appointed a committee to investigate. Seven months later, its 1,100-page report detailed frauds in the purchase of weapons, horses and cattle, and wagons.[49] A similar and better-known investigation into government waste in wartime came when a committee led by Harry Truman investigated military procurement before and during World War II. At the time, the Senate was overwhelmingly Democratic, and Truman was a loyal member of President Roosevelt's party. Nonetheless, the Truman Committee, with five Democrats and four Republicans, exposed much waste and some corruption in an applauded effort. "It is particularly significant that in four years of operation no committee member ever dissented from any report," said *Harper's*. "Truman achieved this surprising unanimity by tireless search for all the facts, and then by consultation—no matter how tedious—until a set of conclusions was hammered out on which everyone could agree."[50]

During both investigations, the president's party dominated Congress. In contrast, during the Iraq and Afghanistan Wars, Congress was closely divided, and its investigations into government procurement were less memorable.[51] It is likely that a closely divided Congress reduces the likelihood of a successful nonpartisan investigation. Each party is more partisan because it sees a chance to take, or lose, power in the next election. This may also explain why Congress ducked any investigation of the causes of the recent Great Recession, opting instead for a rather weak independent commission.[52]

The vigor, persuasiveness, and character of committee members (and staff) plays an obvious but huge role in determining an investigating committee's effectiveness. Committee balance matters as well. Both the House committee that paralleled the Church Committee and the 9/11 Commission got off to bad starts when their initial choices for chair were accused of being too close to the investigation's subjects. Congressman Lucien Nedzi resigned as chair of the House committee after it was disclosed that, when he had been chair of an Armed Services Subcommittee, he had been briefed on improper and secret CIA activities but had done nothing.[53] Henry Kissinger, George W. Bush's initial choice for chair of the 9/11 Commission, was forced to step aside because victims' families and others thought Kissinger's long membership in the national security priesthood would taint his judgment and because he refused to disclose the clients of his lucrative consulting business.[54]

But with new leadership, the 9/11 Commission went on to deal effectively with issues that were emotional and fraught with political consequences. Its internal effectiveness and its external credibility benefited from its ten members being evenly divided between Republican and Democratic appointees. In a creative arrangement, commissioners sat not in party blocs but in alternating seats. This was not merely cosmetic; it sent a signal that the commission sought to be nonpartisan. In contrast, it is likely the 9–4 split between Democrats and Republicans on the House committee parallel to the Church Committee was a factor in its overly partisan rhetoric and perhaps its irresponsibility with secrets. Poor selections for some committee members contributed as well.

Committee size can hamper cohesion and effectiveness. When the Senate and the House combined forces to investigate Iran-Contra, they created a twenty-six-member panel, with eleven from the Senate and fifteen from the House. This large size made it hard for the committee to coalesce and for all members to participate. But a joint committee need not be ungainly. The postwar Joint Congressional Committee on Pearl Harbor had only ten members (six Democrat and four Republican).

The Iran-Contra Committee was hobbled by a structural problem that derived from the relative roles of committee counsel and committee members. This was evident during the committee's defining event—the television coverage of Oliver North's testimony.

While working at the National Security Council in the Reagan White House, North had played a key role in selling weapons to Iran and evading a congressional ban on funding Nicaragua rebels by diverting money from those sales to the Contras. Although a Marine Lieutenant Colonel, North wore civilian clothes as a White House worker. But when facing television cameras, he dressed in his full Marine uniform, with medals and ribbons across his chest. The chief counsels of the House and Senate committees, John Nields and Arthur Liman, both skilled trial lawyers, spent nearly four days cross-examining North. (North's lawyer, Brendan Sullivan, had negotiated an agreement that North would not have to give a pre-hearing deposition, pushing the lawyers at the public hearing to pose rather routine exploratory questions.) Counsel's questioning brought out unsavory facts about North. He had lied to Congress, shredded and falsified documents, and accepted money for a $14,000 security fence around his Virginia home from an Iran-Contra arms profiteer. But North turned the tables with charismatic appeals to patriotism, and emotional testimony that the security system was needed to protect his eleven-year-old daughter from a notorious terrorist.[55] As Sens. William Cohen and George Mitchell said in their book about the investigation, "[N]o sentiment went untapped by North, no role untried."[56]

Liman and Nields pressed for facts—some big, some small. North answered some questions, dodged others, and preached patriotism and moral values throughout. North's values and patriotism prevailed publicly. According to the *Washington Post*, North's defense was "compelling."[57] His face was "America's face."[58] Indeed, "if the Emmy were a medal, and there were any more room on Ollie North's chest, he would be a shoo-in."[59] As Senators Cohen and Mitchell later put it, "'Olliemania' swept the nation."[60] On one day the *Post* ran twenty-three pictures of him.[61] North became a "national hero."[62]

Arthur Liman was an esteemed Manhattan lawyer. But as senators later concluded, he was not made for television.[63] During his examination of former general Richard Secord, according to Cohen and Mitchell, "thousands of letters, telegrams and phone calls started flooding [the committee's] offices" as viewers around the country "complained about Liman's hair, abrasiveness, and religion. Secord was a patriotic Anglo-American. Liman was a nasty New York lawyer—translate as 'New York Jew.'"[64] The same kind of criticism was lodged in even greater volume during North's subsequent testimony. But the irrelevance of counsel's hair and the inappropriateness of the focus on his religion missed the main point. The real problem was that

Liman and Nields's questioning went on much too long, and this blocked committee members from promptly countering North with alternative views of American values and patriotism. Yes, counsel could do that. But only through asking questions, not by rhetorical flights to counter North's monologues. In any event, counsel's task in taking testimony—as opposed to drafting reports—is to lay a factual groundwork for the committee's elected members (and the public) by exposing secrets that reveal departures from American values and abandonment of the rule of law.

Counsel has played a dominant role in some investigations. One example is Ferdinand Pecora's investigation for the Senate Banking and Currency Committee, which examined the conduct of Wall Street tycoons before and during the Great Depression.[65] The Wall Street moguls—whose secret cupidity, selfishness, and duplicity were exposed by Pecora—had no refuge in patriotism. So Pecora's superior knowledge of the detailed and sordid facts properly took center stage.

Forceful investigators, such as Sen. Hugo Black, stress the "enormous pains that the investigators must go to to get at the facts."[66] Because there is "no substitute for facts," successful public hearings are "preceded by a long period of extensive research."[67] Counsel sometimes obtain vital testimony without aid from secret documents. A prime example is Alexander Butterfield, a Nixon assistant, revealing the Nixon White House taping system during the Senate Watergate Committee's hearings. But planning for such testimonial surprises is feckless.

Investigation targets are well aware of the importance of documents. A piece of paper or a recording will say the same thing on Tuesday that it said on Monday. Words in a document are not "revised or extended" or recollections "refreshed." This is one reason the executive branch commonly resists and stalls document production, often relying on secrecy. President Nixon's last line of defense during the Watergate investigation was to keep the White House tapes secret. When the Supreme Court rejected his constitutional privilege claims, the tapes were produced, and Nixon promptly resigned.

The post–World War II investigation of Pearl Harbor by a joint Senate/ House committee further demonstrates the centrality of secret documents. Japan's surprise attack on December 7, 1941, had maimed the U.S. Navy. FDR's rushed Roberts Commission had blamed the local commanders, Admiral Kimmel and General Short, but then, in 1944, Congress required the

Army and the Navy to investigate Pearl Harbor.[68] Both subsequent reports blamed officials above the local commanders, including Army Chief of Staff George Marshall.[69] After the Japanese surrender in August 1945, President Truman released the two reports but withheld much of the Army report. When asked about this, Truman said the information "should not be divulged [and] . . . has nothing to do with the Pearl Harbor situation. It is the system by which we get information. We need that source of information now as we needed it then." Truman added he did not think the deletions would ever be made public.[70]

Eventually, the joint committee gained access to the hidden information, which concerned an issue we have seen before: breaking Japanese codes.[71] The slim distribution list for the pre–Pearl Harbor Japanese messages did not include the general and admiral in Hawaii. They were not sent copies of relevant decoded cables, some of which suggested possible Japanese attacks on Western interests; other cables, shortly before the attack, revealed that Japanese embassies were ordered to destroy code machines. The most revealing cable was a request made to a Japanese agent in Hawaii for the exact location of Navy ships in Pearl Harbor. Contrary to Truman's assertion, this secret information was highly relevant to the committee's work.

Despite lots of evidence, the joint committee's conclusions were mushy. Partisan splits may explain this, as the political stakes were enormous. Republicans generally hoped blame could be pinned on President Roosevelt and the secretaries of war and the Navy (Henry Stimson and Frank Knox). Democrats hoped for low-level responsibility, but also feared a party split would suggest the "investigation was a Democratic whitewash."[72] Eventually, the chair, Kentucky senator Alben Barkley (who became Truman's vice-presidential candidate in 1948), persuaded the two Republicans from the House to join the final report, which criticized the defense system but did not blame any specific people in Washington and reduced the critique of the admiral and general to "errors of judgment."[73]

Truman's effort to keep decoded Japanese cables secret from investigators is a good example of pushing secrecy too far. So was the Bush administration's effort to limit the access of 9/11 commissioners to the warnings of al-Qaeda attacks. Still, if investigations fail to recognize legitimate secrets, they suffer. The best example is the House counterpart to the Church Committee, known as the Pike Committee, named for its eventual chair, Long

Island congressman Otis Pike. The Pike Committee could have made a solid contribution with its focus on the quality of CIA intelligence. However, it floundered at the outset and foundered at the end on issues of secrecy.[74] The committee refused to allow any redactions (such as informers' names) from the initial production of agency documents. It gave inadequate opportunity to the executive branch to review reports. It leaked like a sieve. After the House voted to bar publication of its final report, the report was leaked to the *Village Voice*. CBS reporter Daniel Schorr acknowledged he gave the report to the *Voice*, but his source was never revealed.[75]

There are times when a decision not to investigate speaks as loudly as disclosures of hidden information. Early in his first term, President Barack Obama squelched a drive to investigate the post-9/11 antiterror policies of the Bush-Cheney administration. This left many questions unanswered. Were the policies consistent with American values? Were they lawful? Did they harm America's standing in the world? Did they thwart terrorism? Or did they fuel terrorist recruitment instead? Should so many of these actions have been concealed? What don't we know at all?

An investigation free from retribution and focused on the big questions could have helped America learn from its recent secret past. Two days after he won reelection in 1864, Abraham Lincoln suggested such a prudent approach, saying, "In any future great national trial, compared with the men of this, we shall have as weak, and as strong; as silly and as wise; as bad and good. Let us, therefore, study the incidents of this history as philosophy to learn wisdom from and none of them as wrongs to be revenged."[76] But while President Obama released the Bush administration's torture memos, and banned torture's future use,[77] Obama said he was "more interested in looking forward than . . . looking backwards."[78] In response, Patrick Leahy, Senate Judiciary Committee chair, quipped, "We need to be able to read the page before we turn it."[79] Obama's view prevailed.

Someday, however, there will be—and should be—a comprehensive investigation of the post-9/11 period. Most likely, it will reveal more than we know and be worse than we thought. Moreover, when this investigation comes, it will cover more than one administration and more than one party. That greater breadth will make an investigation more likely. It also will make its results more convincing.

Oversight

While investigations are episodic, oversight is meant to be more sustained.[80] A history of the CIA by its inspector general noted that after the Church Committee, "Virtually everything changed once the [Senate and House] select committees [on intelligence] were created."[81] Instead of oversight of intelligence agencies being superficial and sporadic, at its best it became regular, and sometimes rigorous. Instead of being handled individually by a few congressional barons, oversight became collegial, by committee. While the new oversight still has significant limits, "the two intelligence committees have, since their inception, provided the only significant check and balance outside the executive branch" of covert action by the CIA.[82]

The two intelligence committees deal with sensitive secrets all the time. They review agencies' classified budgets and programs and assess their effectiveness. Although the committees have generally been kept informed, members sometimes express frustration or anger about lack of disclosure by the executive branch. For example, Peter Hoekstra, then the Republican chair of the House Intelligence Committee, wrote President George W. Bush that Congress "simply should not have to play Twenty Questions to get the information that it deserves under our Constitution."[83] Two decades earlier, when CIA Director William Casey withheld information from the Senate Intelligence Committee about the mining of Nicaraguan harbors in 1984, Chair Barry Goldwater (generally a close CIA ally), exploded with anger, writing Casey that he was "pissed off."[84]

Even when all members of the intelligence committees are informed about a secret program by the executive branch, members express frustration about not being able to convey concerns beyond the committee. Moreover, by law or custom, there are times when only four or eight members of Congress are notified of especially sensitive covert actions, or new programs. These members are known as the "Gang of Eight" or the "Gang of Four."[85] The Gang of Eight consists of the majority and minority leader of the Senate, the Speaker and House minority leader, and the chair and ranking minority member of the House and Senate Intelligence Committees. The Gang of Four, which is sometimes briefed on what an administration regards as potentially sensitive non-covert-action intelligence activities, consists of the chairs and ranking minority members of the two intelligence committees.

There are two gang problems. The first concerns how the gangs are notified, the second concerns what they can do with what they are told. In both cases, secrecy is served but oversight suffers. Gang members are notified orally and individually—without note-taking, or opportunity for collegial discussion. Expert staff are not present or permitted to be informed.[86] The other members of the intelligence committees are not involved. Technically, gang members are *notified* of something. But in reality, they are not *informed*.[87] When matters covered by a secret, oral briefing become public—as many eventually do—the informal nature of the gang process and human nature inevitably lead to conflicting accounts about what was actually revealed.[88]

To the extent these briefings involve extremely sensitive covert operations where secrecy is vital to save lives, there is a good case for limited notification— but only if it is sufficiently meaningful to give the gang members opportunity to provide input. In such a case, there would already be a general consensus that action is appropriate if success is likely and such a covert action is immediate, not ongoing. But what about such covert actions as the overthrow of a foreign government? Unlike a case of rescuing captured Americans, there is no general acceptance of such actions. Take, for example, the overthrow of elected governments in Iran, Guatemala, and Chile, where it is contended that long-term harm to American interests exceeded supposed short-term benefits. Our country would be better served by some meaningful discussions about sense, sensibility, and long-term consequences. At the very least, Congress or a committee should have a role in advising on whether such a covert action should proceed.

There are also notification problems when an administration embarks on a new secret program. The Bush administration's decisions to use torture and to return to warrantless wiretapping on Americans are good examples. In each case, some members of Congress were notified to some degree. Later, when the programs became public, there were disputes about the clarity of that notification. But it is undisputed that the members of Congress were not told that there were substantial legal questions, or that the administration arrived at the decisions without consulting relevant people—in the case of torture, the military, the State Department, and the FBI. Also, in denying that Edward Snowden served the nation by revealing the breadth of NSA surveillance, President Obama said that Snowden should have taken his concerns to the intelligence committees.[89] The committees, however, already had the information, or much of it. As Sen. Ron Wyden had already indicated, eventually the American people would be "stunned" when they found out how the government was using its power. But Wyden and other concerned senators, such as Mark Udall, felt unable to do anything with the specific information they had.[90]

The culture of super-secrecy means congressional oversight and advice is often preempted by papering over problems with a formalistic notification but with little real information and even less opportunity for input. There may be difficult constitutional issues in defining Congress's precise role with respect to secret executive actions. But Congress has some role to play. The current system nods to congressional power but, in fact, the executive branch shares little power with Congress. The current system shuts out congressional wisdom even though meaningful oversight would better serve the needs of presidents, Congress, and the nation.

That the congressional oversight system is being frustrated is shown by delays in release of the Senate Intelligence Committee's review of the Bush administration's torture regime. The Committee began with a 6,000-page report—reflecting work that started in 2009. The report apparently showed that the CIA had both gone beyond what the Justice Department had authorized and exaggerated—or lied about—its success. In December 2012 the committee voted 9–6 to release the report, with ex officio committee member Sen. John McCain saying he "totally agree[d] with the report and . . . hope[d] it can be made public as soon as possible."[91]

The CIA did not respond until June 2013, when it provided a 122-page rebuttal.[92] But the process got bogged down because the CIA would not make clear whether it had specific objections to declassification of particular items in the draft report. Then came a nasty public confrontation when Sen. Dianne Feinstein, the committee chair, accused the CIA of spying on committee staff, and the CIA's acting general counsel accused committee staff of illegally removing documents from the CIA facility, where the staffers had been reviewing them.[93] Underlying this dispute was the Senate staff's discovery of a CIA internal memorandum that apparently agreed with the committee's conclusions about the torture program. The CIA had not, however, produced the document in response to the committee's document demand. CIA Director John Brennan initially reacted to Senator Feinstein's attack by claiming that the accusations would be proved wrong. However, a subsequent CIA Inspector General's report concluded that the Agency had in fact spied on committee staff.[94]

In April 2014, the committee voted to release the report's executive summary and conclusions, which totaled more than 500 pages.[95] A week later, even though the president had not responded to the committee's disclosure vote and the committee had not moved forward on release, the report's conclusions were anonymously leaked to the McClatchy news service. Despite the committee's vote and the unauthorized leak, the report's executive summary and conclusions remained classified and officially undisclosed as the Obama administration undertook declassification review, giving ample opportunity for the administration to delay its release. The administration announced the end of its inexcusably long delay right after the story leaked that the CIA had improperly monitored the conversations of the Senate staff assigned to oversee it. But what President Obama cleared for release still redacted information the committee said was essential for its report. Another unnecessarily long battle further delaying information vital to public understanding seemed likely.[96]

Commentary about the delays echoed the conventional wisdom that "the White House, in consultation with the CIA, has the final say over what portions of the summary are made public and which are redacted."[97] Senator Feinstein's transmittal letter to the president also assumed his unilateral power: "I request that you declassify these documents . . . with minimal redactions."[98]

But all this commentary is wrong. Senate rules permit the committee and the Senate to disclose classified information. The Senate resolution establishing the committee allows any member to compel a vote to determine whether the "public interest would be served" by disclosure. There are, of course, checks and balances built into the system. If the information is classified and the executive branch requests it be kept secret, the committee is barred for five days from disclosing it. During that time, the committee must notify the president of its disclosure vote, and the president may object personally, and in writing, that the threat of disclosure to the national interest is of "such gravity that it outweighs any public interest in disclosure." If the president objects, the majority and minority leaders may jointly decide to refer the disclosure decision to the entire Senate, or the committee may do so. The Senate then may choose to permit disclosure, prohibit disclosure, or refer final decision back to the committee.[99] In no case is the Senate prohibited outright from disclosing information the president refuses to declassify.

So the rule makes two things clear: first, the committee can force the president personally to take responsibility for the administration's position.

Second, the Senate, either through its committee or as a body, may make the final decision to disclose even if material is still classified.

A believable threat to use this power should deter administration stalling of the sort there has been with the torture report.

It is a truism that oversight bodies in both the public and the private sphere tend to be coopted by becoming too close to those they oversee. But truisms are often true. It is striking that gang members—or members of the intelligence committees generally—do not usually make waves or challenge the exclusivity of their super-secret access to secret information or their presumed lack of power to do anything about it. Once again, this shows secrecy's seduction. After all, being an intelligence committee member, and, beyond that, a gang member, means that you—above all your congressional colleagues— are trusted with what are deemed the nation's most important secrets. With that special distinction, human nature may make it more difficult to take the position that the system pushes the boundaries of secrecy too far.

This seduction has been strengthened by the elimination of term limits for intelligence committee members. Earlier, all intelligence committee members had term limits, which were thought to inhibit excessive coziness with intelligence agencies. But now the limits are gone for the entire Senate committee and for House committee leadership.[100] While the change may add to expertise, it also risks adding to the seduction of being a super-trusted insider and to the danger of becoming too cozy with the agencies.

10

Congress II: The Freedom
of Information Act

In 1955, Charles Wilson, Eisenhower's secretary of defense, told government officials and defense contractors that no information should be made public unless it would make a "constructive contribution" to the Defense Department.[1] This was an extraordinary statement, one that implied the world's most powerful military organization had no obligations to inform the public about its activities. Yet when uttered, the statement provoked relatively little controversy. In the 1950s, the Administrative Procedure Act allowed government officials to hide anything as long as doing so was "in the public interest" or for "good cause." Such sweeping and vague exceptions allowed the executive branch to use a law originally intended to enhance openness as a shield for secrecy.[2] It was against this background of routine secrecy that Congress enacted the Freedom of Information Act (or FOIA) in 1966.

Although it falls short of its objectives, FOIA remains the most powerful law ever created for revealing what is hidden. FOIA was the result of more than a decade of congressional investigations, and in passing it Congress addressed the fundamentals of democracy with an almost constitutional tone.[3] FOIA's evolution also illuminates the pervasiveness and strength of the secrecy culture.

Because secrecy is entrenched, reform often takes a long time. But then it can come with great speed. It took fifty-seven years from the nation's first freedom of information law (in Florida) to FOIA's enactment in 1966. Similarly, California congressman John Moss ran investigations of government secrecy for eleven years before he assembled a bipartisan coalition to pass FOIA in 1966.[4] Further multiyear congressional investigations of how FOIA was, and was not, working led to its amendment in 1974. But that amendment was also accelerated by the abuses of secrecy revealed by Watergate.

The struggle to pass and amend FOIA dramatizes secrecy's seduction. Bureaucrats thought "'they own their desks and they own their file cabinets and they own the papers that are in them.'"[5] This attitude was also rooted in self-protection because a bureaucrat faces real legal and reputational risks for improper releases but "no sanction at all if he illegally withholds information from the public."[6] The dominant bureaucratic attitude in the mid-1950s was, when in doubt, classify. Or, as Congressman Moss derided it, "If in doubt, don't give out."[7] But the problem went beyond classification. In fact, disclosure was actually turned upside down. As the Charles Wilson directive illustrates, the question became not what should remain confidential, but what, if anything, should be public.

Frustrated by secrecy,[8] in 1954 Moss pushed to be named as chair of a Subcommittee on Government Operations to study information-withholding by executive-branch officials.[9] Over the course of the next eleven years, Moss held numerous hearings. They began with press witnesses such as James Reston, then chief of the *New York Times* Washington bureau, and then moved on to government witnesses.[10] One witness, Trevor Gardner, ex-chief of Air Force research and development, testified that at least half of classified documents at the time were improperly stamped secret.[11] The previous year, the subcommittee discovered some thirty new classification categories devised by agencies to withhold information.[12] The subcommittee also reported on a slew of instances of questionable withholding, such as when a commanding general at the Air Force Missile Test Center in Cape Canaveral, Florida, was prohibited from admitting a missile had been test-fired, even though thousands of onlookers could see it from outside the test center.[13] The National Science Foundation ruled it was not in the "public interest" to release cost projections submitted by unsuccessful contractors in connection with a multimillion-dollar deep-sea study. The secretary of the Navy withheld telephone directories because, as he wrote to Moss, phone books fell in "the category of information relating to the internal management of the Navy."[14]

Despite the record his investigation built, Moss was unable to develop a winning coalition for FOIA until House Minority Leader Gerald Ford and other Republican leaders attacked the Johnson administration for opposing secrecy reform. Republicans then decided to back FOIA although they had been "silent on the issue during the Eisenhower administration."[15]

The House Committee on Government Operations supported the bill with language that drew on the substance, if not the eloquence, of the convictions of Jefferson, Madison, and Lincoln, stating, "A democratic society requires an informed, intelligent electorate, and the intelligence of the electorate varies as the quantity and quality of its information varies."[16] When the bill went to the House for debate, Moss began with a reminder that "our system of government is based on the participation of the governed." Indeed, "[i]nherent in the right of free speech and of free press is the right to know." Moss contended these principles required removing "every barrier" to information about government activities that is consistent with our security.[17]

Today it may seem surprising that the bill's co-sponsor and the principal Republican speaker in the House was Donald Rumsfeld, then a thirty-four-year-old congressman from the Chicago suburbs. Referring to the bill as one of the "most important measures" to be considered by Congress since World War II, Rumsfeld said "No matter what party" has controlled the executive branch, "there have been attempts to cover up mistakes and errors." Moreover, Rumsfeld continued, "the growing complexity of Government itself makes it extremely difficult for a citizen to become and remain knowledgeable enough to exercise his responsibilities as a citizen; without Government secrecy it is difficult, with Government secrecy it is impossible."[18]

Before the bill passed the House by 308 to 0, Moss voiced his "hope" that placing the burden on federal agencies to justify withholding "will be a moderating influence on those officials who, on occasion, have an almost proprietary attitude toward their own niche in Government."[19] Rumsfeld voiced his intent that "the courts interpret this legislation broadly."[20] But Moss's hope was frustrated, and Rumsfeld's intent was not realized. FOIA was hamstrung by foot-dragging of federal officials who seemed to share LBJ's private view of "the fucking thing." The Supreme Court interpreted FOIA narrowly. Both the foot-dragging and the Court decision necessitated amendments designed to add life to the law.[21]

Most of the amendments passed in 1974 were procedural responses to the federal bureaucracy's "delaying tactics."[22] The "failure of the act to realize fully its lofty goals" was due to "agency antagonism to its objectives."[23] Even administration officials conceded a need "to improve agency compliance with [FOIA's] letter and spirit."[24]

On May 30, 1974, Ted Kennedy began the Senate debate on amendments to strengthen FOIA by observing that "[t]he people can judge public officials better by knowing what they are doing, rather than only by listening to what they say."[25] Indeed, the rights of a free people "may gradually slip away, silently stolen when decisions which affect their lives are made under the cover of secrecy."[26] As Florida congressman Dante Fascell put it, as in the 1960s, "under a Democratic President," so too in the 1970s "every single witness from the Federal bureaucracy—this time under a Republican President—has again opposed the bill."[27] And once again, there were unusual bedfellows supporting reform. Conservative South Carolina senator Strom Thurmond agreed with liberal lion Ted Kennedy. More surprisingly, Thurmond echoed consumer advocate Ralph Nader in urging Congress to insure that ordinary citizens could use FOIA to the "same extent as the giant corporations with large legal staffs."[28] Thurmond's observation that "unjustifiable delay renders the information useless" paralleled Nader's testimony that "[a]bove all else, time delay and the frequent need to use agency appeal procedures make the public's right to know, as established by [FOIA], a hollow right."[29]

Delays, excessive charges for document production, and other burdens on information seekers led to a number of procedural reforms, including reduction of search and copy fees, expedition of appeals, shorter court deadlines, allowance of attorneys' fees against the government, sanctions of officials responsible for unreasonable withholding, and public identification of government officials who deny information requests. The amendments also made clear that if the exempt portion of a record was "severable," the nonexempt portions should be disclosed.[30]

A Supreme Court decision also spurred Congress to act. In July 1971, President Nixon refused to provide Rep. Patsy Mink with a copy of a study the president reportedly received recommending whether to proceed with an upcoming underground nuclear test. Mink and thirty-two other representatives instituted a FOIA case, but the administration claimed the information was classified and thus exempt from FOIA. In *EPA v. Mink*, the Supreme Court held that if documents relating to national defense or foreign policy were stamped classified they could not be examined by a court.[31] As Senator Kennedy said, the Supreme Court decided FOIA "does not permit an attack on the merits of the classification decision."[32] Nonetheless, all the Justices, on both sides of *Mink*, said too much was being kept secret. Justice Byron White, who wrote the majority opinion, said FOIA sought to give access to information "long shielded unnecessarily from public view." Justices William Brennan and Thurgood Marshall, in dissent, said documents are "indiscriminately classified" when there is no "need for secrecy." Justice William O. Douglas, also dissenting, called classification a "tool of suppression" that covered "for decades the footprints of a nervous bureaucrat or a wary executive." Justice Potter Stewart joined the opinion but, in effect, invited Congress to override it. The withheld documents, describing controversy within the executive branch about nuclear testing, were, said Stewart, precisely what should be "considered by the people" and "evaluated by the Congress," or else—with both in ignorance—"the democratic process is paralyzed." But, Stewart added, Congress wrote the exemptions to leave no room to question a decision to stamp a document secret, "however cynical, myopic, or even corrupt that decision might have been."[33]

The first proposed response to *Mink* was not much of a cure. A bipartisan Senate report supported a House amendment that said a judge could *examine* requested documents, but could *overrule* the agency's denial of access only if convinced there was no reasonable basis for classification.[34] But then Maine senator Edmund Muskie, joined by a wide coalition from both parties, proposed an amendment to increase judicial power. The reasonable-basis standard would, he said, make judicial review "meaningless," abandon FOIA's placement of the burden of proof on the government, and "foster the outworn myth" that only government officials "can have the expertise" to consider classification.[35] Senator Philip Hart of Michigan more clearly illuminated the weakness of the reasonable-basis standard by supposing that five prior secretaries of defense and the CIA director all said a certificate by the current secretary of defense that claimed a reasonable basis was nonsense. "The court may agree with them," but under the reasonable basis language, "[the judge] is handcuffed."[36]

The Muskie amendment allowed federal judges to conduct *de novo* reviews—brand-new examinations—in FOIA cases, and to examine documents *in camera*, or in private. Moreover, it delegated to the court discretion over whether to consider an *ex parte* showing, in which government would make its case without other parties present.[37] The amendment, which pared back the undue weight given to executive claims and gave judges the power to decide, passed with bipartisan support.

Because the Senate and House bills differed, a conference had to resolve the differences. The House accepted the Senate amendments, including

Muskie's. However, the conference report's comments on judicial review of documents classified on the basis of national security or foreign policy looked in two different directions. On the one hand, while examination by a court "need not be automatic, in many situations it will plainly be necessary and appropriate." Before a court orders inspection in its chambers, the government should be given an opportunity to establish that the documents are "clearly exempt from disclosure." But "[t]he burden remains on the Government."[38] On the other hand, the conference report said agencies responsible for defense and foreign affairs have "unique insights into what adverse affects (sic) might occur as a result of public disclosure of a particular classified record." Therefore, the conferees "expect" that courts, in making decisions under the national security and foreign policy exemption "will accord substantial weight to an agency's affidavit concerning the details of the classified status of the disputed record."[39]

Gerald Ford, now the president, vetoed the amended act in October 1974, arguing in his veto message the bill gave the courts too much power. Ford recognized that a "determination by the secretary of defense that disclosure of a document would endanger our national security would, even though reasonable, have to be overturned by a district judge who thought the plaintiff's position just as reasonable,"—admitting that whatever weight was given to an agency affidavit, a court could reject it.[40] Both houses overrode Ford's veto by substantial bipartisan majorities.[41] The override debates included passionate pleas about secrecy's abuse, particularly in national security matters. Override supporters emphasized recent secrecy abuses involving Nixon and Watergate as well as Vietnam and the Pentagon Papers. Republican Hugh Scott of Pennsylvania, the Senate minority leader, also reached back more than three decades to his election to the House in 1941 to say, "I have been in Congress a long time [and] have seen Presidents of both political parties misuse secrecy."[42]

After 1974, Congress took additional steps to strengthen FOIA and tailor it to new media. In 1996, Congress supplemented FOIA with the Electronic FOIA Amendments. These placed affirmative obligations on agencies to compile and place on the Internet information of general interest to the public.[43] Nonetheless, after 1974, executive-branch agencies have still not leapt to comply with FOIA and the courts have been reluctant to enforce FOIA when agencies raise national security objections.[44]

FOIA has freed millions of documents from secrecy's cage. In the year 2012 alone, FOIA requests resulted in the release of records in more than 400,000 cases, split about evenly between full and partial disclosures.[45] FOIA has been an invaluable tool for informing citizens about the activities of their government. It has allowed the public to learn of post-9/11 excesses both at home and abroad.[46] Nonetheless, FOIA is frequently frustrated especially by disclosure delays.

David Barstow, a *New York Times* reporter and two-time Pulitzer Prize winner, colorfully expressed his frustration at FOIA delays: "Nothing makes my blood boil more than the federal Freedom of Information Act." When pushing federal government officials for information, they often will show "a little smile" and say "Well—you could always file a Freedom of Information Act request," adding, "[T]hey know they are condemning me to Siberia."[47] Expressing similar concerns, a *Wall Street Journal* reporter decided against filing a national security request under FOIA because of "opportunity costs," "bureaucratic black-holes," and "time-consuming lawsuit[s], a prospect publishers don't relish."[48] Barstow contrasted his experience under FOIA with his earlier experience under Florida's Sunshine Act when working for the *St. Petersburg Times*. There, he said, he could almost "walk into the mayor's office and say I'd like to read the emails on your computer today and he would have to let me sit down and do so or he would be in big trouble."[49]

There is some good news. In 2007, Congress gave FOIA its first significant lift in a decade with the OPEN (Openness Promotes Effectiveness in our National) Government Act. To start, its amendments streamline how agencies track and process FOIA requests and require each to install a public-liaison officer to assist in disputes. The law establishes the Office of Government Information Services within the National Archives and Records Administration to oversee FOIA compliance throughout government and provide mediation services to resolve disputes. It allows citizens to more easily recover legal costs in FOIA litigation if they win and expands the definition of "news media" to be more inclusive of nontraditional outlets.[50] Despite these constructive, commonsense changes, federal agencies still drag their feet, causing major problems, particularly for journalists.

In an indirect way, Antonin Scalia highlighted the harm to journalists. In 1982, Scalia, then a law professor, wrote an article about FOIA for the American Enterprise Institute. Using his zest for colorful language, Scalia said FOIA had "no clothes"; it was the "Taj Mahal of the Doctrine of Unanticipated Consequences."[51] Scalia admitted the original FOIA had been a "relatively toothless beast" that had been "sometimes kicked about shamelessly by the agencies," which "delayed responses to requests for documents, replied with arbitrary denials, and overclassified documents to take advantage of the 'national security' exemption." But then Scalia switched gears and attacked—as "going to absurd extremes"—the 1974 amendments, which had in fact been designed to address those very problems but which he had urged Ford to veto.[52] Scalia added that while FOIA was "promoted as a boon to the press, the public interest group, the little guy," it actually had been used most frequently by corporate lawyers, "a far cry from John Q. Public finding out how his government works."[53]

Here Scalia fell into a trap: recognizing a symptom of a disease but ignoring its cause. The reason that big institutions like business corporations made relatively great use of FOIA—more than the press, the public interest group, or the little guy—is that they could better afford the time and expense of challenging the federal bureaucracy's obstruction. Moreover, because government knows this, it is less likely to be obstructive when challenged by big institutions.

There have been FOIA victories even in national security cases. The National Security Archive, for decades, and the ACLU, particularly since 9/11, have had major victories.[54] Nonetheless, because of government intransigence, a major FOIA success can take far too long and cost far too much. Take Seth Rosenfeld's recent book *Subversives* about the FBI's "war on student radicals" in California, an account based "primarily" on confidential FBI files released only after a lengthy FOIA legal fight, a fight that took twenty-seven years and led ultimately to the release of "more than 300,000 pages" of FBI records.[55] Rosenfeld was able to press his five cases against the FBI only because of pro bono assistance from a San Francisco civil-rights lawyer, Thomas Steel. The enormous cost of this lengthy effort is shown by the FBI ultimately paying Steel $600,000 for his legal fees. The FBI also had its own legal costs, and claimed to have spent $900,000 in processing records.[56]

Executive-branch delay, defiance, and overuse of exemptions continue to limit FOIA. One reason these hurdles remain standing is the undue deference courts generally have given to government secrecy claims under FOIA, one of the subjects covered in the next chapter.

11

The Courts and Secrecy

When it comes to challenges to secrets, courts generally bend over backward to accommodate executive-branch demands. True, the Supreme Court ruled against the government in the Pentagon Papers case (although that case also involved the First Amendment) and against the president in the Nixon tapes case (although there the government's special prosecutor was pushing for disclosure). But in Freedom of Information Act cases where the government resists production of documents on "national security" grounds, the government almost always wins. The same is true when the government seeks to dismiss litigation because it claims moving forward will expose "state secrets." Moreover, since 9/11, courts have more frequently closed hearings, sealed court papers, and issued opinions portions of which are cloaked from public view.[1]

The courts' deference to government secrecy claims is not limited to national security. While known primarily for requiring President Nixon to turn over the White House tapes to the Watergate special prosecutor, *United States v. Nixon* also created a presumption of long-term secrecy—an executive privilege—for White House discussions.[2] *Nixon* led to the fall of a sitting president, but its more lasting impact has been to increase the power of future presidents and other executive-branch officials to resist requests for release of information.

Numerous academic studies show courts have "tilted sharply" toward secrecy; the "government almost always wins." Respected judges have observed that judicial review of government secrecy claims is generally "perfunctory" and courts are "far too deferential" in deciding FOIA cases.[3] Therefore, instead of providing a long litany of cases in which the courts have sided with the government to preserve secrecy, it is more useful to show how cramped and ahistorical the courts have been in considering government secrecy cases, examine only a few cases, and then consider *why* the judiciary so often accedes to the executive branch.

Two factors are relevant. Often courts fear they lack sufficient expertise to weigh government claims of harm to national security and worry that a "wrong" decision might endanger the nation. No judge wants to be accused of aiding the enemy. The second factor is intangible but equally important: while courts generally tilt in favor of openness in the judicial process, they tend to have an institutional bias toward secrecy with respect to their own work. Judges, by training and experience, are receptive to the notion that exposure can cause damage. And all of this subtly, perhaps even unconsciously, buttresses the inclination of courts to support secrecy decisions made by the executive branch.

Upon closer examination, what is striking is not just the results in government secrecy cases, but what the courts have *not* done in reaching their decisions. "Perfunctory" is kind. An almost willful ignorance of history—both recent and long-term—is a more accurate characterization. Courts routinely ignore the overwhelming historical record that demonstrates the overuse and misuse of secrecy. Courts have paid no attention to decades of commission reports, congressional investigations, and historical and journalistic accounts that have shown repeatedly that secrecy is often not only unnecessary but also has been used as an excuse to hide mistakes, abuse, or illegality. Even more surprising, courts have also overlooked the extensive record of the executive branch making false or misleading claims concerning national security to the courts themselves. And rarely, if ever, do judges expressly consider that openness is a pillar of American democracy.

Of course, neither the government's long record of perfidy in national security matters nor the overwhelming evidence of secrecy's overuse nor the virtues of transparency in a democracy should necessarily decide any particular case. But they all should be part of the picture courts consider before deciding secrecy cases. They rarely are.

Ignoring the Experience of the Courts Themselves

In 1973, the Supreme Court denied FOIA disclosure to members of Congress who had requested EPA classified documents related to government disputes about a scheduled underground nuclear test. Nevertheless, at that time, every Justice recognized the overuse of secrecy, with Justice Potter Stewart, in effect, urging Congress to narrow FOIA's national security exemption, which the Court had held barred disclosure of classified documents no matter how "cynical, myopic, or even corrupt" the classification decision had been.[4] But in later years—even after Congress did narrow the exemption—courts have paid *less* attention to the long and growing history of secrecy's overuse and misuse.

The Supreme Court understood the problem in 1973. Did judges later forget what they once knew? Or did they react to changes in the public mood between the 1970s—a time of substantial national concern about the overuse of secrecy—and the period after 9/11? Advocates have also failed to develop for the courts the broad history of secrecy's overuse and of government exaggeration of the need for secrecy. There have been no effective "Brandeis briefs" marshaling evidence from outside the record to explain the problems underlying the specific matter before a court.[5] Courts have also not learned from, or apparently even considered, their *own* history, which shows courts themselves have often been misled by claims of risks to "national security" that later turned out to be overblown, or even false, as shown by at least the four Supreme Court decisions that follow.

In *Korematsu v. United States*, during World War II, a divided Supreme Court upheld military orders of Gen. John DeWitt that had forced some 117,000 Japanese Americans on the West Coast to leave their homes for "relocation camps." The Court relied on General DeWitt's "military exigency" justification, based on his report of dangers posed by Japanese Americans.[6] Neither the Supreme Court nor lower courts dug beneath DeWitt's report. Had they done so, a stain on America would have been avoided, as would the harm to the reputations of President Franklin Delano Roosevelt and the Supreme Court itself.

Decades after *Korematsu*, facts were uncovered that showed the executive branch had knowingly concealed from the Court vital facts that undermined General DeWitt's assertion of military exigency. The Federal Communications Commission and the FBI had both contradicted DeWitt's report that

Japanese Americans were communicating by radio with the Japanese Navy. Justice Department lawyers drafted a footnote in their Supreme Court brief alerting the Court to these facts, but the War Department objected. Justice Department supervisors then diluted the footnote to obscurity.[7] It was also later discovered that DeWitt's original report had not relied on any specific military risk but instead had relied on racial "traits peculiar to citizens of Japanese ancestry."[8]

Based on these discoveries, the convictions of Fred Korematsu and another detainee for violating DeWitt's order were vacated. And in 2011, the acting U.S. solicitor general took the unprecedented step of apologizing for the conduct of his office in defending the internments before the Supreme Court.[9]

A decade after *Korematsu*, in 1953, the Supreme Court created the modern "state secrets" doctrine in another seminal case: *Reynolds*.[10] An Air Force B-29 bomber had crashed in Georgia while testing secret electronic equipment. Three widows of civilian observers on the plane sued, claiming government negligence. They sought to see the accident report. The Air Force Secretary initially said to release the report would not be in the public interest because it had been prepared under regulations that encouraged collection of information about aircraft accidents. After the trial court rejected this justification, the secretary and the Air Force judge advocate general switched gears and made a new claim predicated on the notion that furnishing the report would harm "national security . . . and the development of highly technical and secret military equipment."[11]

The trial judge ordered the government to produce the report so the judge could see if it related to such secrets, and, if so, whether any such references could be excised.[12] The government refused. The trial judge said the government could not have it both ways: it could not declare relevant evidence was off limits and claim no liability. So the trial judge held negligence by the government should be assumed.

A unanimous three-judge panel of the U.S. Court of Appeals for the Third Circuit upheld the trial court. In light of later applications of the state-secrets privilege, Judge Albert Maris's opinion was prophetic: "[W]e regard the recognition of such a sweeping [secrecy] privilege . . . as contrary to a sound public policy. . . . It is but a small step to assert a privilege against any disclosure of records merely because they might prove embarrassing to government officials. Indeed, it requires no great flight of imagination to realize that if the Government's contentions in these cases were affirmed, the privilege against disclosure might gradually be enlarged . . . until, as is the case in some nations today, it embraced the whole range of governmental activities. . . ."

Maris explicitly recognized the role of the judiciary in checking the power of the executive to withhold information:

> The Government of the United States is one of checks and balances. One of the principal checks is furnished by the independent judiciary. . . . Neither the executive nor the legislative branch of the Government may constitutionally encroach upon the field which the Constitution has reserved for the judiciary. . . . Nor is there any danger to the public interest in submitting the question of privilege to the decision of the courts. The judges of the United States are public officers whose responsibility under the Constitution is just as great as that of the heads of the executive departments.[13]

A divided Supreme Court reversed, saying the report was privileged simply because the military claimed it contained sensitive material—and because there was a "possibility" that this was the case. The Supreme Court did not itself look at the report and it ruled no lower court judge should do so to check the claim. Chief Justice Fred Vinson's majority opinion makes no sense. He began by saying the flight's purpose was to test secret electronic equipment, that air power is a potent weapon of defense, and that newly developed electronic devices greatly enhance air power. Therefore, such "electronic devices must be kept secret if their full military advantage is to be exploited."[14] All obviously correct. Vinson added, that even though "[t]here is nothing to suggest the electronic equipment in this case had any causal connection with the accident," there was a "possibility" military secrets were involved in the accident report.[15] Fair enough.

But then Vinson wandered away from both logic and law. Vinson said the district judge should *not* examine the accident report to see whether there were, in fact, references to the secret electronic equipment, and, if so, whether these could be excised to allow the three widows' lawyers to learn whether negligence caused the accident. Vinson added that courts should be cautious in disagreeing with the executive on national security claims. Also fair enough. But this was no reason simply to blindly rely on the executive's assertion of sensitive national security issues or to ignore whether any such information might be redacted from the document. Unfortunately, the three dissenters,

Justices Black, Frankfurter, and Jackson, chose not to take Vinson head-on. Their one-sentence dissent merely said they agreed with Maris's appellate court opinion.[16]

When the report was publicly released four decades later, there was in fact no connection to any military secret; but there was evidence of negligence.[17] Moreover, although no one outside the military knew this at the time, it was learned later that before the case reached the Court, the accident report was no longer classified as "secret." Its classification level had been reduced to "restricted."[18]

When judges dismiss cases on state-secrets grounds, they routinely cite *Reynolds,* but they ignore the cautionary tale that *Reynolds* tells. Judges never mention the Supreme Court's lack of reasoning. They overlook subsequent research showing the government report did not mention national security risks. They blot out the stark injustice to the widows.[19]

The Pentagon Papers case of 1971 is probably the best-known case dealing with government national security claims. When a divided Supreme Court rejected the executive branch's effort to restrain the *New York Times* and *Washington Post* from publishing portions of the top-secret history of America's involvement in Vietnam and the escalation of that war, the issue before the Court was the constitutionality of a "prior restraint" against the papers.[20] The Supreme Court's opinion had no meaningful analysis of the government's case for secrecy. In the district courts, however, there had been two trials: in New York for the *Times,* in Washington for the *Post.* In these expedited trials, it became clear the executive branch had, once again, exaggerated the need for secrecy and had taken liberties with the facts in claiming the need for secrecy. Some twenty years after the Supreme Court decision, Erwin Griswold, who as solicitor general had argued the government's case in the Court, admitted he had "never seen any trace of a threat" to security from publication, adding, more generally, that "there is massive over-classification."[21]

When, in a crucial Supreme Court case about national security secrecy with the largest factual record of any such case, the government began by grossly exaggerating the risk of harm, failed to prove harm at trial, and the government's chief lawyer subsequently conceded massive overclassification, one would hope courts would remember what happened, and in future secrecy cases would look closely at the material underlying government claims of harm. But in later cases courts have generally done nothing to check government claims that total secrecy is required, usually not looking at the underlying material at all.

More than four decades after the Pentagon Papers case, the Supreme Court decided *Clapper*.[22] James Clapper was sued as director of national intelligence by American lawyers and human-rights, legal, labor, and media organizations. They challenged the constitutionality of amended provisions of the Foreign Intelligence Surveillance Act that focused on communications from within the United States to non-U.S. targets located abroad. Plaintiffs claimed they believed their communications with, for example, clients of the lawyers and sources of the reporters would be subject to surveillance, and that they had changed their behavior and used costly and burdensome communication alternatives to avoid surveillance, including traveling overseas rather than talking on the telephone to a foreign client or source.

By a 5–4 vote, the Supreme Court agreed with the government that plaintiffs lacked standing to sue because they had not made a sufficient showing of harm. The Court said it was "highly speculative" that the government would "target" communications to which the plaintiffs were a party.[23] The four dissenters, in an opinion by Justice Stephen Breyer, made powerful counter-arguments on the law of standing.[24] But the point here is more basic. The government argued that plaintiffs "have not established that communications involving them have been or ever will be incidentally collected" under the statute and that plaintiffs' claims were "based on speculation" that the government could take harmful action.[25] The subsequent Snowden revelations, however, have taught us more about the breadth of NSA's collection. When all the facts come out we will know still more; based on experience, it seems fair to predict that when this happens, plaintiffs' "speculation" will turn out to be correct.

Certainly the lead defendant, James Clapper, as director of national intelligence, knew how very broad NSA surveillance was. So did his co-defendant Keith Alexander, the director of NSA. So presumably did NSA's general counsel and associate general counsel who worked on the government's brief. Whether the solicitor general knew, or just failed to ask, we do not yet know. But we do know that—to put it charitably—Clapper himself played fast and loose with the facts when he testified to Congress in March 2013 about NSA surveillance. Senator Ron Wyden, a staunch critic of the National Security Agency's domestic surveillance, asked Clapper if the Agency collected "any type of data at all on millions, or hundreds of millions, of Americans." Clapper responded "No, sir." Then he added, "Not wittingly." When the

Snowden leaks revealed NSA's massive "metadata" program a few months later, Clapper said he did not lie, he just testified in the "least untruthful manner."[26] At the time of *Clapper*, NSA and government lawyers also knew that the super-secret FISA Court had at least twice rebuked government lawyers and NSA for misleading that court.[27]

In coming years, the public is likely to learn much more about how the government and its Department of Justice handled *Clapper*, just as the public eventually learned more about the truth underlying *Korematsu* and *Reynolds*. It is likely that by then we will know that the government of the United States believed it was proper in a secrecy case to wriggle away from a decision on the constitutionality of a government program by telling the Supreme Court that plaintiffs were only speculating about what the government itself knew was true. That does not sound like doing justice.[28]

Tunnel Vision

In considering secrecy claims, courts generally don't acknowledge that openness is one of America's founding values. They turn a blind eye to all the history this book lays out. Judge Maris's *Reynolds* opinion was an exception. In it, he quoted Edward Livingston, who had served in the House and Senate, been mayor of New York, and was Andrew Jackson's secretary of state: "'No nation ever yet found any inconvenience from too close an inspection into the conduct of its officers, but many have been brought to ruin, and reduced to slavery, by suffering gradual imposition and abuses, which were imperceptible, only because the means of publicity had not been secured.'"[29]

American democracy depends upon citizens having full information about the acts of their government and the character of their leaders. One would suppose this principle would find its way into judicial deliberations in secrecy cases, not to provide a conclusive answer but at least to be part of how a court weighs the issues. Nevertheless, in deciding government-secrecy cases, courts do not mention this basic principle. Their failure to do so is particularly telling when contrasted with the frequency with which judges tip their judicial hats to other founding values, particularly checks and balances and separation of powers. Democracy and its sister, openness, deserve their proper place along with those other founding values. Indeed, democracy actually had a preferred place at the Founding. As Madison made clear in Federalist 51, separation of powers and checks and balances were secondary to voting as a check on government. Checks and balances were *auxiliary* precautions," while the vote was the most important check: "A dependence on the people is, no doubt, the *primary* control on the government."[30]

Again, the importance of openness to democracy should at least be part of judicial deliberations in all secrecy cases. The failure to do this is especially egregious in FOIA cases, since Congress, in enacting the 1974 FOIA amendments, specifically harked back to that fundamental value when it increased judges' power to review classified documents and decisively overrode President Ford's veto.[31] But even Congress's recent emphasis on the value of openness to democracy is ignored by the courts.

In evaluating government secrecy claims, courts have also failed to consider the tilt in favor of classification that permeates executive orders on classification. A document can be stamped as secret (or top secret) if it "reasonably *could*" be expected to cause serious damage (or exceptionally grave damage) to national security.[32] The executive branch appropriately emphasizes protection of secrets, and because damage is always a prediction, this justifies saying "could" cause rather than "will" cause. But the courts should see *their* role as checking and balancing the executive branch, particularly given the instructions of Congress in the 1974 FOIA amendments, and also given the requirement of "reasonableness" now in the executive orders.[33] Instead the courts have generally blindly accepted the secrecy claims of the executive branch.[34]

President Nixon Falls—But the Court Increases the Power of Future Presidents to Withhold Information

In *Nixon v. United States*, Leon Jaworski, the special prosecutor empowered to investigate Watergate, subpoenaed secretly recorded White House tapes of conversations between President Nixon and his aides.[35] After District Court Judge John Sirica rejected Nixon's challenge to the subpoena, Nixon appealed directly to the Supreme Court, arguing that confidential conversations among a president and his advisors were absolutely privileged—and that the president had the exclusive power to decide the question, leaving no role for the courts. Nixon's claim was akin to the later claims he made, first to the Church Committee and then to British television talk-show host David Frost, that, despite laws enacted by Congress, the president can decide what is or is not legal. As Nixon famously said to Frost, "When the president does it, that means that it is not illegal."[36]

The Supreme Court rejected Nixon's arguments and required him to produce the tapes; within days Nixon resigned. The Court said it was "the province and duty of this Court 'to say what the law is,'" adding that, in the context of the Watergate criminal case, it was important that relevant evidence be made available.[37] That was all the Court needed to say to decide the actual case. However, it went on to offer sweeping but superficial conclusions about issues that were not necessary to decide. While rejecting presidential secrecy in the particular case, the Court blessed presidential secrecy broadly, saying there was a need to protect communications between presidents—indeed all "high Government officials"—and those who advise them.[38] That was "too plain to require further discussion," the Court wrote, because "human experience teaches that those who expect public dissemination of their remarks may well temper candor with a concern for appearances and for their own interests to the detriment of the decision making process."[39] Similarly, "candid, objective and even blunt or harsh opinions" expressed "in a way many would be unwilling to express except privately" need protection.[40]

The Court's musings about human experience and candor were unsupported by anything in the opinion and are, at best, dubious. The job of all public officials is to provide their best advice. That is how they should be evaluated. Being craven or cowardly are not qualities to be sought or expected. If a presidential advisor would temper his or her advice based on fear of eventual public exposure, it is likely the advisor would not be acting in the public interest. What human experience really teaches is that a guarantee of lasting secrecy is, if anything, more likely to lead to bad advice, and to bad decisions.[41]

In any event, whatever the Supreme Court assumed, all advisors—particularly presidential advisors advising on momentous matters—actually already know that lasting secrecy for their advice is *not* guaranteed. Their boss or one of their colleagues is likely to reveal it. A prime recent example was the revelation after Osama bin Laden was killed that some high-level presidential advisors had opposed the more risky raid that President Obama favored. Bob Woodward's books on momentous national security decisions by presidents are filled with other examples, as is Defense Secretary Robert Gates's recent memoir.

The *Nixon* Court compared the supposed White House expectations of confidentiality with "the claim of confidentiality of judicial deliberations."[42] But it did not suggest judges themselves would otherwise be craven or cowardly in talking with one another as they deliberate. Did the Supreme Court justices really believe *they* would not be candid, or blunt, or harsh with one another in judicial conferences unless guaranteed lasting secrecy? This is hardly likely. Therefore, a crucial and current actual "human experience" of the Justices cut against their unsupported musings.

Nobody suggests that meetings in the Oval Office or other meetings of executive officers with their advisors should be available to C-SPAN or otherwise held in the open. The problem with the Supreme Court's musings upon human experience is that they have been used to create a presumption of an executive privilege that provides *lasting* protection for executive-branch conversations.

In *Nixon*, the Supreme Court, again without any briefing, also suggested a president might have an *absolute* right to withhold conversations that were said by the president to concern "military, diplomatic or sensitive national security secrets."[43] Once again, the Court ignored all the real-world experience that such claims are often exaggerated, and sometimes mendacious.

Shutting the Door to Redress for Torture and Other Post 9/11 Actions

In state-secrets cases, courts have been prone to dismiss an entire case when the executive claims a national security risk, even in situations where a wrong has been publicly disclosed—and indeed when a gross injustice had already been described in detail in other forums. And in FOIA cases in which the executive relies on a national security exception, courts have generally declined even to look at the documents. This defies Congress, which made clear that courts in FOIA cases can examine the documents in camera to see if they really endanger national security, and, if so, whether any threatening parts could be excised.[44]

Under the Bush administration, the United States resorted to torture. This stained our country's honor. It fouled the traditions of Washington and Lincoln. It violated U.S. laws and treaties.[45] And the courts further dishonored America by using the state-secrets doctrine and other procedural devices to dismiss innocent victims' claims of torture and extraordinary rendition to torture.[46]

Khalid El-Masri, a German citizen of Lebanese descent, was detained by Macedonian authorities because he was mistaken for an al-Qaeda agent with a similar name. He was handed over to a CIA rendition team that beat, sodomized, and shackled him, before flying him with his head in a bag to a hidden prison in Afghanistan. There he was tortured by the CIA. El-Masri made these allegations in a Virginia lawsuit, which was dismissed on state-secrets grounds by the district court and the Fourth Circuit Court of Appeals.[47] But El-Masri's case had already been publicly addressed by authorities in Europe. An extensive investigation of extraordinary renditions had been ordered by the Council of Europe and conducted by Sen. Dick Marty of Switzerland. Among many other findings, Marty's 2006 report detailed its conclusion that El-Masri was "the victim of abduction and ill-treatment amounting to torture."[48]

In the teeth of this evidence from lengthy proceedings, the American courts shut the door at the government's insistence, claiming that to hear the case risked revealing some secret. Similarly, a divided Ninth Circuit Court of Appeals dismissed the case of Binyam Mohamed on state-secrets grounds.[49] Binyam was an Ethiopian who was a legal resident of the United Kingdom. As in El-Masri's case, the facts about his treatment had been exposed in another forum, in this case an American court, where, in a habeas corpus case involving another Guantánamo inmate, Judge Gladys Kessler evaluated the credibility of Binyam Mohamed's statements implicating the other inmate. She rejected use of his statements based on the two-year "trauma" he suffered. "During that time, he was physically and psychologically tortured. His genitals were mutilated. He was deprived of sleep and food. He was summarily transported from one foreign prison to another. Captors held him in stress positions for days at a time. He was forced to listen to piercingly loud music and the screams of other prisoners while locked in a pitch-black cell. All the while, he was forced to inculpate himself and others in various plots to imperil Americans. The Government does not dispute this evidence."[50]

Despite such facts having been laid bare in the earlier habeas case, the government pushed to dismiss Binyam Mohamed's own case on state-secrets grounds. The government won. The court's dissent contended the state-secrets doctrine is "so dangerous as a means of hiding governmental misbehavior under the guise of national security, and so violative of common rights to due process, that courts should confine its application to the narrowest circumstances that still protect the government's essential secrets."[51] The majority, however, went in the opposite direction.

Likewise, a divided Second Circuit dismissed the claim of Maher Arar, a joint Canadian and Syrian citizen.[52] (The court door was shut to Arar based on a vaguely expressed "hesitation" to hear his claim of a constitutional violation.) Arar had alleged that on his way back from Switzerland to his home in Canada, he was seized at Kennedy Airport, mistreated by American officials, misled by American authorities, and then shipped to Syria, where he was tortured. State Department reports had regularly said that Syria used torture.[53] And once again, another nation's detailed and lengthy official report publicly supported Arar's version of the facts. A Canadian Commission found that the Canadian Royal Mounted Police had given U.S. officials terrorism-related information about Arar, "although they did not consider him a suspect or a target." However, with "no basis," the Mounties also described Arar as an "Islamic Extremist . . . suspected of being linked to the al-Qaeda terrorist movement," knowing the "potential consequences of labeling someone an Islamic extremist in post-9/11 America." Americans said the United States relied on Canadian information in sending Arar to Syria. According to the Canadian Commission, in Syria, Arar was "interrogated and tortured." The torture "fit squarely" within the State Department's reports of Syrian torture practices. Subsequent investigations, including cooperation "with American agencies," did not turn up any evidence against Arar. In Syria, "Maher Arar had lived through a nightmare."[54]

Based on Commissioner O'Connor's report, Canadian prime minister Stephen Harper sent letters to Syria and the United States formally objecting to Arar's treatment. He also apologized to Arar and his wife and family for Canada's part in his "terrible ordeal," paying them $10.5 million plus legal costs.[55] Yet, with all this disclosed, the United States did not apologize. Instead, at the request of the United States Department of Justice, the courts refused to hear Arar's case. In a dissenting opinion, Judge Barrington D. Parker wrote it was a "miscarriage of justice" to leave a torture victim without any remedy in American courts. There is, Parker added, an "enormous difference between being deferential and being supine in the face of governmental misconduct."[56]

These cases all allege extraordinary rendition to torture. Before the cases were dismissed, the post-9/11 programs of extraordinary rendition and torture were no longer secret. In addition, many raw details had already been disclosed, including the mistreatment of the three plaintiffs where official proceedings in other forums exposed detailed facts and found the plaintiffs had been tortured. In that context, it is hard to imagine what secrets were so damaging that the courts decided the cases had to be shut down before they even started. An ugly picture is painted of American justice when it silences the voice of torture victims claiming constitutional and statutory violations that caused severe physical and mental harm.

At a minimum, the claims were clearly plausible. Faced with gross injustice, courts should be creative in doing justice. But in these secrecy cases, the courts used no creativity, simply bowing to the executive branch's argument that cases involving torture—even of innocents—would somehow reveal some dangerous secret. In years to come, these cases will be remembered as dark smears on America's system of justice.[57] But the failure is not that of the courts alone. All the branches, and America as a whole, have failed to do justice, have failed to recognize the pain we caused by torture. After more time, and after more secrets are dug up, this sad failure will be lamented.

What explains the courts' behavior? Certainly, fear is a factor. Fear that judges might turn out to be wrong and harm the nation, and fear that judges may lack the competence to evaluate secrecy claims based on national security. But as Professor Stephen Schulhofer has shown, courts decide all sorts of cases that come before them without the judge having prior experience in a particular field.[58] That is part of their job. They do it by learning from the parties' arguments and often by learning from experts or a special master.

The FOIA amendments of 1974 specifically authorize courts to use a special master experienced in classification to help with substance, and to relieve burdens of requiring a judge to do the initial review of the thousands of documents involved in some FOIA cases. Judge Louis Oberdorfer of the federal district court in Washington, D.C., took advantage of a special master in a case involving a *Washington Post* reporter's FOIA request for thousands of Defense Department documents connected to the failed 1980 Iran hostage rescue operation. The Department resisted production of approximately 2,000 documents totaling 14,000 pages, and relied on the national security exemption. Oberdorfer appointed D.C. attorney Kenneth C. Bass III—formerly counsel for intelligence policy at the Justice Department, where he had a top-secret clearance—to prepare a "representative sample" and analysis of each claimed exemption for the judge to review. After Bass's comments, the Defense Department turned around and released about 85 percent of the documents it had originally withheld.[59]

Despite this graphic proof of how a special master can help the court, and the ensuing benefits to the public interest, Oberdorfer appears to be the only judge who has used a special master in a FOIA case.[60] A creative court could also appoint security-cleared counsel to support the side opposing the government in state-secrets or FOIA cases. Revealingly, such appointments are made routinely in cases where it is the *government* that wants to use classified information in a trial. An example is when the government wants to prosecute someone for misuse, or theft, of classified information. Then, under CIPA—the Classified Information Procedure Act—cleared counsel is appointed to represent the interests of the defendant, and there are special procedures to protect classified information, allowing trials to proceed.[61]

Perhaps no nation has had more experience with security dangers than Israel. But when a plaintiff in Israel claims violations of human rights, the courts regularly allow the case to move forward.[62] Echoing Francis Biddle's warning against "mystic clichés," an Israeli High Court Justice warned that government secrecy claims have no "magical power." While the courts should not "intervene in [such cases] lightly," where a case involves violations of human rights the court should examine the reasonableness and proportionality of the government's action.[63]

In the United States, it is suggestive that several federal judges who have decided national security secrecy cases against the government had previous experience with the security system and its flaws. Judge Marilyn Hall Patel, who decided Seth Rosenfeld's FOIA case against the FBI, had earlier vacated Korematsu's conviction on the ground that the government had misled the Supreme Court about the secret evidence.[64] The two trial judges in the Pentagon Papers litigation—Gerhard Gesell in Washington and Murray Gurfein in New York—had previous experience with secrecy: Gesell as a staff member on the joint congressional committee investigating Pearl Harbor and Gurfein in Army Intelligence in World War II.[65] Judge Alvin Hellerstein, who has firmly and courageously presided over the ACLU's FOIA cases seeking documents relating to torture, was likely affected by his long exposure to government overreaching in those cases and possibly by his youthful service in the Army's Judge Advocate Corps.

The Interagency Security Classification Appeals Panel (ISCAP)—which is part of the executive branch—is another example of how fear dissipates and decisions overriding secrecy claims become more likely when decision makers *do* have experience in the national security field. ISCAP was created in 1995 by President Clinton as part of an improved process of "Mandatory Declassification Review," which allows members of the public to request agency declassification of documents without a FOIA request.[66] ISCAP is involved only when agencies resist disclosure. Its members come from the Departments of State, Defense, and Justice; the National Archives; the Office of the Director of National Intelligence, and the National Security Advisor; and from the CIA if its documents are involved.[67] While there are not many ISCAP cases, it is revealing that when a secrecy dispute is reviewed by officials with secrecy experience, they rule *against* secrecy, at least in part, some 70 percent of the time.[68]

The Secrecy Culture of the Courts Themselves

Two aspects of the judicial culture may also foster a judicial psychology that creates empathy for the executive position on secrecy: opposition to television coverage of Supreme Court arguments, and judges' ownership of "their" documents. Supreme Court Justices have been passionate in their opposition to television coverage of oral arguments. Even some who favored television coverage before they were confirmed later came out against it.[69] While arguments against television coverage of jury trials may have more weight, the Supreme Court's resistance to TV coverage of its arguments is heartfelt but misguided.[70] Supreme Court advocates want to win their cases; they know mugging for the cameras would not help. Justices already appeal to newspapers, radio, and the Internet by asking colorful questions during oral argument; questioning by individual Justices already drowns out the advocates arguing before them. It is unrealistic to think Justices would change their behavior with television coverage.

Justice Anthony Kennedy—who in closely divided cases has been the Court's regular "swing vote"—makes an argument about television coverage that suggests an added reason courts might bend toward the executive branch's secrecy arguments. Kennedy said Congress should accept the Court's decision on television in light of "the deference and etiquette that should apply between the branches."[71] The courts have shown similar deference to the executive branch's position in secrecy cases. Many Justices also relish their personal privacy and might believe a regular presence on television would cost them some of it. Some may worry that coverage would focus on sound bites that might detract from the Court's majesty.

But Justices are public servants. And Supreme Court arguments are public events about the public's business. Television coverage of a key public part of the work of the third branch of government would add to public knowledge about government. This should be sufficient to overcome all the heartfelt counterarguments from the Court.

Supreme Court Justices' passionate opposition to television coverage of the arguments made before the Court contains a whiff of elitism reminiscent of the British attorney general's warning to Thomas Cooper in the 1790s. According to the British AG, it was permissible for Cooper to reveal secret parliamentary debates in an expensive tome directed to "that class of readers who may consider it coolly." Today, the Supreme Court similarly says it is permissible for its arguments to be seen only by the select few who can afford to take time off and manage to get into its majestic courtroom, sometimes paying large sums to do so. Of some four hundred courtroom seats available for a particularly important case, about half are reserved for friends of the Justices and the news media. At the two days of arguments on same-sex marriage issues in March 2013, members of the Bar got a few more than hundred seats, and there were only seventy seats set aside for the public (plus thirty seats for people limited to a three-to-five minute peek at the argument). One seat for those arguments was reportedly bought for $6,000.[72] Insiders now pay a line-standing service to hold a place in the long line that forms outside the Court long before dawn. The service costs $50 per hour.

Just as the British AG announced it would be his duty to prosecute if Cooper published information about Parliament "cheaply for dissemination among the populace," so the Supreme Court today feels duty-bound to ban television broadcasts of its arguments that could be seen readily and cheaply by the people. So money changes hands so some can enter America's temple of justice to be among the privileged few to view the oral arguments.

The judicial culture also includes the understandable conviction that deliberations among judges before a court issues a decision are, and should be, confidential. Secrecy continues, however, long after cases have been decided and the judges have issued their opinions. Indeed, the judicial culture supports judges retaining *perpetual* control over "their" judicial papers, including those relating to deliberations, even though those papers were produced while judges were paid by the people to perform the people's business.

The Supreme Court itself cares deeply about the privacy of its deliberations. "The most confidential proceeding in all of government is probably the conference of the Justices of the Supreme Court," where the justices privately discuss and cast preliminary votes on cases heard by the Court.[73] Devotees of open government should not be offended. In normal cases, before judges deliberate, arguments are publicly presented by the parties in briefs and oral arguments. And after judges deliberate, a public decision is issued that gives the result and lays out the underlying reasoning.[74] Moreover, inside information about what the Court may be considering doing could lead to financial and other speculation. Predecision disclosure would not serve any interest other than curiosity.

The conferences are held just off the Chief Justice's chambers. No one is present besides the Justices themselves. When the Justices emerge from their conference and opinion writing begins, secrecy remains the rule until the Court issues its opinions. Law clerks are sworn to secrecy. Nonetheless, even the Supreme Court has had leaks about its work—but almost never about the results of decisions before they are issued, although there was a leak to *Time* magazine of the result in the forthcoming decision in *Roe v. Wade*.[75]

The most significant leak occurred in 1979, when Bob Woodward and Scott Armstrong published *The Brethren*. That book infuriated, and embarrassed, the Justices by using anonymous leaks—from more than 170 former law clerks and some Justices themselves—to describe secret communications, including conference deliberations, during the early years that Warren Burger was Chief Justice.[76] Such leaks, and the more recent leaks about conservative Justices' anger at Chief Justice John Roberts's upholding Obamacare, are extremely rare. Relatively common, however, are later revelations authorized by individual Justices themselves about the Justices' conferences and about back-and-forths among the Justices as opinions are drafted. These revelations come when individual Justices themselves choose to release their papers after retirement or death, or permit an authorized biographer to examine them.

So judges treat the official papers they generated when they are paid by the taxpayers to work on public business as their perpetual private property. Judges can withhold their papers for as long as they wish, or destroy them, as presidents did from George Washington to Richard Nixon.[77] The post-Nixon commission established by Congress and chaired by former Attorney General Herbert Brownell to consider policy changes governing the records and documents of federal officials unanimously recommended that the papers of *all* federal officials created in the discharge of their official duties be public property to be released at specific later dates.[78] In a bar journal article calling for congressional action, Brownell particularly emphasized the importance of treating judicial working papers as public papers. Indeed, he said, treating judges' working papers as private "weakens" judicial accountability. Brownell agreed with testimony from D.C. circuit judge Carl McGowan who testified that "there is no mystique about the functioning of the judicial process" that should make judges' papers immune.[79] Nonetheless, Congress exempted itself and the judiciary, once more proving the seduction of secrecy.

Before Barack Obama became president, he wondered in *The Audacity of Hope* whether by placing so much "reliance on the courts to vindicate not only our rights but also our values, progressives had lost too much faith in democracy."[80] In this, Obama joined with a robust group of thinkers, including Learned Hand—often described as the most able judge of the twentieth century not to have been appointed to the Supreme Court—who said "Liberty lies in the hearts of men and women, when it dies there, no constitution, no law, no court can save it."[81] Or, as Harvard Law School professor James Bradley Thayer said more than a century ago, "[T]he tendency of a common and easy resort" to judicial review is to "dwarf the political capacity of the people, and to deaden its sense of moral responsibility."[82]

But now, at the same time as courts have generally moved away from being at the forefront of articulating new rights[83]—a practice that Hand, Thayer, Obama, and others have said possibly had undermined democracy—the courts are again undermining democracy. The danger in court-secrecy decisions is that they undermine democracy by discounting the relationship between American democracy and citizens' access to information about what their government is doing.

Strengthening that connection to our founding national values is imperative to cure the culture of secrecy and overcome the seductions of secrecy that push our democracy into the dark.

PART FOUR

Conclusion: Getting to Secrecy Reform

The United States has a secrecy problem. But it can be remedied.

The current conversation about government secrecy continues a centuries-long debate about the nature of American democracy and the role citizens should play in it. The debate concerns American ideals, but it also raises practical questions. Government policy is mired in an old order of paper and typewriters, but the world has evolved into a digital world, one of increasing dependency on personal computers, e-mail, the Internet, and the cloud. Many of our policies regarding information—and how much, when, and to whom it should be disclosed—date from early Cold War days. Technological advances enable the government to collect, store, and use more information than ever before. But by seeking to keep secret so much for so long, the secrecy system cheapens and undermines vital secrets. One encouraging sign that change is possible is that some security professionals have reached the same conclusion and believe that in light of new technology the overreach of the current secrecy system is actually making it harder to protect legitimate, crown-jewel secrets. It is also encouraging that concerns about secrecy often cross partisan lines, even in our hyperpartisan era.

Debate about citizens' role in governing has continued since America's founding. The Founders rejected Britain's hierarchical model in which citizens were treated largely as passive bystanders between elections. Instead, this country charted a new course, where the public was regularly informed about government affairs. Is it still part of America's belief that to participate in democracy the people should be informed to the maximum extent possible? Do we still agree with Lincoln that there should be "confidence in the ultimate justice of the people"? Is there any better or equal hope in the world?[1] Or has America come to accept Walter Lippmann's view that an average citizen is like "a deaf spectator in the back row" of a sporting event who "lives in a world which he cannot see, does not understand and is unable to direct."[2]

Defenders of today's secrecy system are not likely to voice Lippmann's contempt, however much they might agree. But according to Leslie Gelb—who directed the Pentagon Papers project when working at the Defense Department and later was an assistant secretary of state, a *New York Times* reporter, and president of the Council on Foreign Relations—the national security establishment has endorsed a Lippmann-like view that the issues are "too subtle and sophisticated for the common man." The "pattern of concealment and half truths" is rooted, in part, in "rank paternalism. It is the courtly conviction that the American people cannot appreciate the problems and have to be 'brought along.'"[3]

Call it contempt, paternalism, or both, these traits have been institutionalized. Today's pervasive secrecy infantilizes the public. We should not naively overstate citizens' ability to wrestle with hard issues. But American democracy depends upon our being given the chance. Moreover, the public includes reporters, commentators, bloggers, former government officials, and others who could offer additional perspectives and wisdom on hard issues if there were more openness.

Hidden contempt for citizens and their ability to wrestle with tough issues becomes a self-fulfilling prophecy. Lack of civic literacy makes citizens less knowledgeable.[4] This encourages elitist beliefs that there is no need to involve, and no point in involving, average people in hard decisions. This in turn encourages more secrecy, which, to complete the vicious circle, further reduces civic literacy.

Eventually, most secrets see the light of day. And when they do, the light often focuses on previously unknown illegal or embarrassing acts. Paranoia by government then leads to paranoia about government.[5] Excessive secrecy leads to government deception, or even outright lying, which, when the truth emerges, makes government leaders look either malevolent or ridiculous. This has been a constant throughout the Secrecy Era. A recent reminder followed the Snowden leaks about NSA surveillance: the director of national intelligence, James Clapper, had to apologize for deceiving Congress about spying on Americans; NSA's director, Gen. Keith Alexander, was exposed for falsely telling Congress that NSA did not hold data on U.S. citizens; and, two judges on the FISA court released opinions chastising NSA and its lawyers for lying to the Court.[6] NSA has some vital secrets, but protection of critical information is not a license to lie. Perhaps there are still people within NSA who believe what its general counsel told me in 1975: "The Constitution does not apply to NSA."

For more than six decades, far too much has been kept secret for far too long. Policy makers consider the risks of disclosure but often ignore the benefits of openness. Despite repeated calls for change, it is often easier for officials not to act than to act. Members of the executive branch, Congress, and courts all fear making mistakes and releasing something precious. But the central problem is the failure to recognize, and to value sufficiently, that openness is vital for democracy; the harm to democracy caused by our overly broad secrecy regime is pervasive. The necessary first step to secrecy reform is, therefore, to understand, and then to reaffirm, the American creed that democracy depends upon providing citizens with maximum information about their government. The debate about government secrecy must be framed in terms of values.

Reforming the secrecy system requires three additional elements: more knowledge, a change in culture, and a better understanding of how and where to draw the line between legitimate and illegitimate secrets.

One of my goals in this book is to increase awareness of government secrecy and the problems it poses. Shocking facts and revealing quotations about secrets, and clearer and deeper analysis of secrecy, reinforced by a renewed emphasis on American values, will drive reform. But to achieve reform the nation also needs to understand and address all the cultural and psychological seductions of secrecy.

Cultural change is often slow in coming. But when it comes it can arrive suddenly. The civil-rights and gay-marriage movements are two examples. The same is true inside government. Back in 1954, Sen. Mike Mansfield called for congressional scrutiny of the CIA, warning that "[o]nce secrecy becomes sacrosanct, it invites abuse."[7] Nothing happened for twenty-one years. Secrets were off-limits. Congress preferred to remain in the dark about the activities of the FBI, the CIA, and other intelligence agencies. But growing concern about the nation's course increased the appetite for learning about the secret government. The nation's culture suddenly changed. So did

Congress's. And then, in 1975, Majority Leader Mansfield led the way in creating the Church Committee.

In biology, the notion of relatively rapid change is called "punctuated equilibrium." Under that theory of evolutionary change, long periods of minimal change are interrupted by short periods of rapid change.[8] In 2008, referring to this part of evolutionary theory, a CIA official charged with thinking about the new world of technology, declared that "[i]n 15 years there will be no more secrets." Later, at a conference of intelligence experts, the CIA official joined a more nuanced consensus, not that there will be "no more secrets," but that there soon will be vastly fewer secrets with much shorter half-lives.[9]

Of course, in earlier times, technological change often led to reduction in the information monopolies of the powerful. Invention of the movable-type printing press is an example. But back then change in the sources, the amount, and the dissemination of information played out over decades or centuries. Change occurs faster now. Digital information creation, storage, retrieval, and transmission all spark more rapid evolution.

If the United States is to correct the harm caused by the current secrecy culture, advocates who favor greater government openness must acknowledge that there are legitimate secrets. Transparency proponents must better understand the rationales for legitimate secrets—and the limits of those rationales. Secrecy that aims to hide embarrassment or illegality is obviously out of bounds. So is secrecy meant to deprive the American people of information, rather than denying it to an enemy. But line drawing is also more subtle.

There is a qualitative difference between hiding the details of a government program's operation and hiding the very existence of the government program. Such "deep secrets" can be particularly troublesome. Disclosures about NSA during the past few years make this clear. It is one thing to keep secret which warrantless wiretaps NSA obtained but quite a different matter to hide that NSA had secretly returned to the old regime of warrantless wiretaps. Similarly, to conceal the very existence of a program designed to capture logs of every phone call in the United States stretches both presidential power and secrecy beyond proper limits.

Another fundamental distinction between legitimate and illegitimate secrets is fuzzier but just as important. Secret programs that sully American values and violate U.S. laws and traditions are on the illegitimate side of the secrecy line. The slide to torture after 9/11 is one recent example. The FBI's

COINTELPRO program to harass and attempt to destroy law-abiding dissidents is an earlier example. One hopes neither could have survived an open democratic debate. But that aside, such programs are too fundamental to be snuck into government policy without real public deliberation.

The slogan during World War II that "loose lips sink ships" reminded Americans of the danger of talking about military matters, especially ship movements, when German submarines patrolled the North Atlantic. In today's terms, it would have been indefensible to reveal the coming raid on bin Laden's hideout, or to reveal a planned drone attack on a key terrorist's lair. But a government program to kill terrorist leaders overseas, and the legal justifications for drone attacks—including ones targeting Americans—are legitimate matters for public debate.

During the Vietnam War, it would not have been proper to reveal the exact target of a particular forthcoming U.S. bombing mission. Yet Richard Nixon and Henry Kissinger distorted this principle to blanket their massive bombing raids on neutral Cambodia. As was dryly noted at the time, the secret bombing was hardly a secret to the Cambodians, or to the Viet Cong. Rather, the real—and improper—aim of the secrecy was to stifle consideration by Americans of American policy.

Usually, military weakness is properly kept secret. George Washington hid his shortages of troops and ammunition when he fought the British in Boston early in the Revolution. Deception also often supports legitimate secrecy, as when General Washington grappled with his "grave problem" of a gunpowder shortage by circulating "the fiction that he possessed eighteen hundred barrels of powder."[10] But more than two centuries later, when improvised explosive devices (IEDs) on the roads of Iraq killed or maimed American soldiers because of inadequate vehicle armor and body armor, candid disclosure of the problem would not have told the enemy anything it did not already know. But disclosure would have moved Congress and the American people to push sooner and harder for improvements to protect soldiers.[11]

Protecting the identity of informants and agents is both moral and practical. Revealing their identities jeopardizes their lives and also makes it harder to recruit future informants. But these basic truisms can be abused, as when J. Edgar Hoover made misleading claims about the scope of an informant's information to help him push the Kennedy brothers to let him wiretap Martin Luther King Jr. and his colleagues. Four decades later, the road to the Iraq War was greased by the Bush administration's withholding from Congress (and the world) details about the credibility of "Curveball," the Iraqi defector who claimed Saddam Hussein was working on biological weapons of mass destruction. Not only had U.S. intelligence agents never spoken to Curreball—he had been debriefed only by German intelligence—there were substantial questions about his information.[12] Although intelligence officials routinely claim they will never disclose or discuss sources, this was a case in which a discussion about the source, and negative information about his credibility (without using his real name), was essential for fully informed deliberation about going to war. But George W. Bush and Dick Cheney were set on their course, one that found expression in Secretary of State Colin Powell's February 5, 2003, speech to the United Nations, a speech that relied for specifics almost entirely on information coming from Curveball.[13] Had there been a broader analysis about Curveball's allegations and credibility, Powell might well not have given the speech, thus avoiding tarnish on his reputation for integrity.

And we might not have gone to war.

Most of these examples test lines about whether something should be secret at the outset. Equal attention needs to be given to how long items are kept secret. Everybody knows there is a serious problem, but the will to address it effectively is lacking. What is needed is recognition that making sensible future decisions generally means documents should, on average, remain secret for much shorter periods of time. The aim should be to get as much information to the public as soon as possible, in time for elections where citizens provide their consent to government. With goodwill and effort, a great deal of secret information can be made public much more quickly.

To address the secrecy problem, the limitations on legitimate secrecy discussed in Chapter 3 must also be absorbed. The case against secrecy is usually not made in the first place (exemplified by 9/11); once secrecy is established, its continuation is not usually revisited (exemplified by the Cuban Missile Crisis); and extra care needs to be taken to subject momentous—properly secret—internal governmental decisions to continuing internal analysis (exemplified by the case of where to drop the first atom bomb).

Government officials must also begin to calibrate secrecy decisions on a more granular scale. Entire documents are often classified when in fact only part of the document merits protection. Classification rules already say distinctions should be drawn between which portions of documents should be secret and which should be open. But doing so requires extra work. A cultural change and a change in incentives are needed if leaders are to enforce the rules and workers are to observe them.

The power of the national security state, genuine national security threats, continuing fear, and the fact that the secrecy culture has prevailed for more than six decades all stand as obstacles to change. Almost 86 percent of Americans have lived their entire lives during the Secrecy Era. And less than 2 percent of Americans alive today reached voting age before 1950. President Eisenhower warned us a half century ago about the power of the "military-industrial complex," but today the United States has a military, industrial, *and* intelligence complex.[14] Dana Priest and many others have revealed the vast number and size of commercial interests that work for the government on secret matters.

Despite these obstacles, there remain reasons for optimism about the possibility of changing the pervasive secrecy culture. More time has passed since 9/11. Younger people are used to having ready access to information. Changes within government have made it harder to hide improprieties or illegality. The press is more aggressive in pursuing secrets (although widespread investigative journalism is at risk), and bloggers are often additional vehicles for disclosures. These factors contribute to the fact that the shelf life of secrets—at least big secrets—is shortening.

The possibility of a nonpartisan approach to excessive secrecy and emerging technology that makes it harder to protect so many secrets for so long supply additional bases for optimism about reform possibilities.

What can be the sources of reform? Executive action is a starting place, since the secrecy regime is governed largely by executive orders. Barack Obama ended torture and made public the Bush administration's torture memos. He also disclosed more information on our nuclear arsenal and intelligence spending. In fact, a president, as head of the classification system, can instantly declassify anything without going through any formal process. Yet presidents are not free from partisan constraints. The executive branch also has the greatest parochial interest in limiting change in the secrecy regime because it is an element of the national security state that maximizes presidential power over defense and foreign policy.

The contrast between Barack Obama's rhetoric on secrecy before and after he became president shows that, once in office, a president is subject to many new and powerful pressures. These include reliance on the good work of the intelligence community in helping a president live up to the awesome responsibility of keeping the nation safe. A president, therefore, has positive pressures to support the intelligence community as well as negative pressures to avoid confronting it on issues such as secrecy that traditionally have been seen as going to its core. It seems far harder to take a long-term view of secrecy once in the Oval Office.[15]

While presidents must be a factor in change, wider and more lasting change requires a broader consensus in Congress and among the public. It was enormously helpful to the Church Committee—both internally and externally—that the committee concluded the secret government had abused its power under six administrations, both Democratic and Republican. Today, the fact there has been an administration of each party since 9/11, each of whom has engaged in excessive secrecy, makes it easier to form a bipartisan consensus.

Impatience with excessive secrecy spans the ideological spectrum. Conservatives are concerned about unchecked government power; libertarians are concerned about privacy and civil liberties; and liberals tend to worry about everything. As far back as the 1980s, Democratic senator Pat Moynihan and Republican senator Barry Goldwater both expressed frustration with the intelligence community and the way it handled secrecy.[16] Republican Tom Kean and Democrat Lee Hamilton fostered a nonpartisan spirit on the 9/11 Commission. In 2004, GOP senator Trent Lott, a staunch conservative, and Sen. Ron Wyden, a liberal Democrat, complained in an op-ed that secrecy has become "so pervasive" that "it's often unclear whether facts are classified for legitimate security reasons or simply for political protection of agencies and officials." Their frustration arose in the context of CIA efforts to delete extensive sections of a Senate report on flawed intelligence about Iraq.[17]

When Edward Snowden's leaks prompted concern about the scope of NSA's domestic surveillance, a coalition of 94 House Republicans and 111 Democrats quickly came close to passing a measure to rein in NSA; the measure was sponsored by the pro-gun, pro-life, and anti-tax junior GOP representative Justin Amash and cosponsored by John Conyers Jr., a twenty-four-term liberal member from Detroit.[18] Republican representative James Sensenbrenner, a primary author of the Patriot Act and its extensions, said he and his colleagues had not intended to permit NSA's widespread scooping up of data about American communications.[19] And Sensenbrenner and Democratic senator Patrick Leahy, chair of the Senate Judiciary Committee, joined forces to propose a bill to curb NSA surveillance.[20] Action, however, was slow in the paralyzed Congress. The House passed a bill in May 2014, but transparency groups withdrew their support because the White House had watered it down. Senator Leahy introduced a stronger bill in his Judiciary Committee, but by the time Congress recessed for the midterm elections of 2014 nothing had happened in the full Senate.

Conservative Republicans have colorfully expressed distaste for secrecy's overuse. Laurence Silberman—now a judge on the U.S. Court of Appeals for the D.C. Circuit, and known as a thoughtful conservative—said his reading of J. Edgar Hoover's secret and confidential files when Silberman was acting attorney general in the mid-1970s "was the single worst experience in my long governmental service."[21] And Peter Hoekstra, when he was the GOP chair of the House Intelligence Committee, angrily criticized the Bush administration for requiring the committee to "play twenty questions" to break through secrecy to get necessary information.[22]

The public is beginning to awaken to concerns about excessive secrecy. When security professionals also start to say that too much secrecy gets in the way of protecting the nation and makes it harder to protect the most important secrets, it should be easier to form a bipartisan coalition in favor of secrecy reform. This is not the first time observers have noted that trying to protect too many secrets undermines all secrecy. A Supreme Court Justice said, "[W]hen everything is classified, then nothing is classified."[23] A future national security advisor warned if we guard "our toothbrushes and our diamond rings with equal zeal, we usually lose fewer toothbrushes but more diamond rings."[24] Security professionals have begun to express similar concerns. A 2010 conference of national security experts held by the Office of the National Counterintelligence Executive and an American Bar Association Committee on Law and National Security concluded there is a "real risk that the Intelligence Community is squandering its resources attempting to keep non-secrets secret."[25] The conference reached a consensus that technology has outpaced the nation's defensive posture; that connectedness and information access provide greater benefits than secrecy; that governments need to learn to operate with far fewer secrets because the world is increasingly transparent; and that if everything is a tightly held secret, then nothing is.[26]

As the conference correctly observed, new technologies have also considerably raised the stakes. "The most damaging threat to both government and the private sector has traditionally been from insiders stealing information for personal use or for sale to the highest bidder." But with "advancing cyber capabilities and better technology, the insider threat only becomes more dangerous." CIA and FBI officials such as Aldrich Ames and Robert Hanssen, who sold secrets to the Soviet Union, did "significant damage to the United States. However, with today's technologies, they could have removed gigabytes of information rather than hundreds of pages."[27]

New technology makes American secrets more vulnerable not only to individual traitors but also to lone hackers, to insiders such as Edward Snowden concerned about agency conduct, and, most dangerously, to the sophisticated and relentless digital frogmen of foreign governments who can hack into America's secret databases. An excellent 2011 book by Joel Brenner, who had been, among other things, NSA's inspector general and the national counterintelligence executive in the Office of the Director of National Intelligence, asserts that America is "under relentless cyber assault . . . bleeding military secrets, commercial secrets, and technology that drive our standard of living and create our power as a nation."[28] When the Chinese hacked into the Pentagon's electronic data, they stole what, had it been on paper, would have taken "miles and miles of moving vans lined up nose to tail to cart it away."[29]

The world now stores its data electronically on computer networks for two reasons. First, there is much more data, unimaginable even to try to handle without computer capacity. The head of supercomputer development at IBM estimated that all the information from the beginning of human history until 2003 totaled five exabytes. By 2011, that much data was created every two days; by now the estimate is that much data is being produced every ten minutes.[30] Second, the high speed of computer processing—and our ability to find and use the nuggets in all this data—is now "the coin of the realm," more so than secrecy.[31]

But the "more widely and quickly you make information available the more trouble you have protecting it," as Brenner explained in describing his concerns about the vulnerability of America's secrets. Brenner brought to life the new thinking by secrecy professionals about secrecy, adding that electronic information is liquid, and liquid leaks; and when secrets are replicated and portable they will be duplicated and lost.[32] Therefore, Brenner argues, "organizations must learn to live in a world where less and less information can be kept secret, and where secret information will remain secret for less and less time." Plus, he reminds readers, "most of what is worth knowing in the world is not classified, and technol[ogy] . . . will make this axiom truer than ever." In addition, classification is "a drag on how [governmental agencies] communicate, whom they communicate with, and how they do business."[33]

The United States is witnessing only the beginning of support for secrecy reform from insiders. As time passes, more veteran insiders will likely turn away from the current secrecy culture. Young recruits to security services already spring from a culture that leans toward openness. The movement to reform an entrenched system will require a broad consensus based on a mix of concerns. Some secrecy insiders will not emphasize implementing the ideals of democracy. But those who do focus on reducing secrecy to implement those democratic ideals should also want secrecy to be limited to help protect crown-jewel secrets.

More than fifty years ago, when I was working for the Nigerian government as a young man, I heard the expression "I don't care who writes the laws as long as I can write the songs."[34] Of course, to create change you want both songs and laws, always remembering that laws are midwifed by public sentiment.[35] For secrecy reform, the songs start with America's revered hymns: the Declaration of Independence and the Gettysburg Address. They continue through our historical experience. We have learned much about the harm done by secret programs and the obsessive secrecy culture. There is more to do to let the public know the truth and learn the lessons. That is why I continue to recommend the creation of a nonpartisan committee or independent commission to investigate national counterterrorism policies.

Returning to a more open America will honor our democratic values. It will reduce mistakes and limit harm. The need to return to a more open America also reflects a triumph of American technology and ingenuity. For sixteen decades—before the atomic bomb, the Cold War, and 9/11—America was largely shielded from fear by the sheltering arms of the oceans. Then, due substantially to American ingenuity and technology, those sheltering arms shrank. We became more vulnerable, more fearful, and, as a result, driven to more secrecy. But today—again substantially driven by American innovation and coupled with a worldwide spread of skills—technology is undermining the secrecy that many thought was necessary to our nation's defense. We need to move beyond reliance on secrecy's static stone walls and moats. In today's new, more integrated world, speed of spreading information is a better defense. New technology also creates the opportunity for a new information revolution in which government can, once again, foster much wider distribution to the public of more information about its own plans and actions, thereby strengthening our democracy.

America—the greatest democracy on Earth—will not thrive in a secrecy culture. We have a choice. Will we continue down secrecy's path of silence and darkness? Or will we let the light shine in?

Author's Note:
Personal Encounters with Secrecy

Many of the Church Committee's discoveries illustrate broader points the book makes about secrets and secrecy. Although the Introduction describes my first visits to the CIA and the FBI at the start of my Church Committee work, I have not described how I came to be chief counsel, how I felt in doing the job, or how I continued to develop my interests in secrecy through the Cold War and after 9/11.

When asked about my interest in the committee job, I leapt at it. After clerking and then working for a year for one of the three regions of the newly independent nation of Nigeria, in 1963 I had gone to work for Cravath, Swaine & Moore, a leading New York City establishment law firm. I chose Cravath because I believed that there, more than elsewhere, I would be judged by the quality of my work and not by extraneous factors. This proved correct, most notably in 1965 when I helped lead an antiapartheid boycott against six American banks that had supported the South African regime when it was in financial trouble after massacring scores of peaceful black demonstrators. In that campaign, I wrote an early magazine article highlighting Apartheid's cruelty and arguing against American companies doing business in South Africa.[1] One of the banks was one of Cravath's largest clients.

Six years after arrival, I became a Cravath partner, an ambition partially driven by my father's success as a private lawyer who eventually became head of Davis Polk—another big establishment New York City law firm. Along with a desire to succeed in private practice, I had an equally powerful desire to play a role in controversial and important public issues. So when Burke

Marshall called to ask if I would be interested in becoming chief counsel of the Church Committee, my immediate answer was yes. I had gotten to know Burke when he was IBM's general counsel (after he served as assistant attorney general for civil rights in the Kennedy administration). Representing IBM in the U.S. government's massive computer-monopoly case had become my major Cravath assignment. I also worked with Burke when he chaired the Vera Institute of Justice, an innovative criminal-justice-reform group.

After a simple interview, mostly with Senator Church, I was offered the job. I felt joyful; hungry to work. Apart from recruiting and organizing an excellent nonpartisan staff (along with Bill Miller, the committee's thoughtful staff director), I saw my job as helping to obtain secret information, then to put before the senators, and the public, clear information about secret wrongdoing, and the resulting harm to the nation. Much of what we discovered shocked and revolted me. Particularly revolting was the FBI's treatment of Martin Luther King Jr., whose speech at the March on Washington I had attended. Many comments about the Committee suggest our main focus was on the CIA. To me, however, the exposure of FBI wrongdoing was most important. The way I simplified it was to describe FBI wrongdoing as threatening American democracy and CIA wrongdoing as undermining America's reputation in the world.

Still, while shocked and disgusted by what we uncovered, I did not dislike most of the people whose acts we revealed and criticized. I understood most were driven by a passion to protect the nation. Fairness also required empathy for most of the men and women working in intelligence. During the Cold War, facing a ruthless enemy, presidents and other high-level officials gave them assignments that were impossible to fulfill. They were expected to predict or prevent every possible crisis, respond immediately with information on any question, and anticipate and respond to the incessant demands of presidents and other leaders of the national security establishment. Under that pressure, no wonder some cut corners. Nonetheless, it seemed to me that while empathy was appropriate, distance was also required. Many oversight bodies stumble by becoming too close to the agencies they oversee. Both empathy for and distance from the agencies are essential.

While working for the committee, it was a joy to see what today seems archaic: a nonpartisan approach to tough issues. And while often shocked and disappointed by the secrets we discovered, I stayed optimistic, convinced that, in the words of the Church Committee, America has "the strength to hear the story and to learn from it," and that if we "confront our mistakes and resolve not to repeat them . . . our future will be worthy of the best of our past."[2]

One of my early roles was to push to center our work on "the extent, if any, [of] illegal, improper or unethical activities."[3] Others urged us to emphasize "wise men" opining on what was wrong with the intelligence agencies and what reforms were needed. My view was that unless we showed shocking secret abuses to the American people, there would be no groundswell for reform. We took the debate to Senator Church, who sided with an aggressive investigation.[4]

Before coming to the Church Committee, I knew nothing about the secret world of intelligence. Nevertheless, my years as a litigator did teach me some important lessons about how to "know the truth," which—as the CIA's huge entrance lobby says—"will make you free." Facts drive cases and thus the truth, and a key way to discover the facts is to get documents. Even after the Ford administration began to cooperate, I believed we still had to press for details and documents. This is how we started our hearings when CIA Director William Colby—our first witness—appeared in executive session to testify about CIA assassination attempts. That day, I pushed Colby to produce specific categories of documents relating to the assassination attempts, believing that testimony without documents risked being shallow.

Some ten minutes before that first hearing, Senator Church told me I would generally start the questioning of all witnesses. Doing so was professionally fulfilling. At the same time, working with relevant staff, I prepared packages of material concerning each witness for the senators to use in preparing their questions and comments. Another particularly fulfilling piece of preparatory work was a daylong preliminary statement describing for the senators and the public the evidence to come during the hearings on the FBI.

Working to make committee reports fact-based, credible, and readable was another source of satisfaction. My principal work was on the *Interim Report on Assassinations* (our first report), on our *Final Report on Intelligence Activities and the Rights of Americans* (Book II), and on the *Supplementary Detailed Staff Reports on Intelligence Activities and the Rights of Americans* (Book III).[5] One emotional high at the Senate's secret session to discuss the committee's assassinations report was the applause that followed Senator Church's reading of the report's epilogue, which I had written the day before the report was printed. Part of that epilogue still, I believe, echoes today:

> The United States must not adopt the tactics of the enemy. Means are as important as ends. Crisis makes it tempting to ignore the wise restraints that make [us] free. But each time we do so, each time the means we use are wrong, our inner strength, the strength which makes us free, is lessened.[6]

In addition to obtaining and releasing information at its hearings and in its reports, the Church Committee had an excellent record in avoiding leaks. Leaks of secret information can be used to undermine the leakers, as the White House did to the House investigation proceeding at the same time as the Church Committee. But the weapon can misfire, as when the new CIA director, George H. W. Bush, accused the Church Committee of causing the assassination of Richard Welch, the CIA's station chief in Greece. Shortly after Bush became director, he testified in executive session about the committee's ideas for reform. I remember looking down at him at the witness table when an aide whispered in his ear. Out of the blue, Bush then blurted out that "you" (the committee) were responsible for Welch's assassination. This was false. In fact, the committee took great care to protect agents' names. Indeed, Bush had to come back to admit that no evidence supported the accusation that congressional inquiries had any "adverse impact on Mr. Welch's cover or any relationship to his tragic death."[7] Bush—widely regarded as having been a successful CIA director—had made a careless and false accusation. And not just careless and false but stupid, because it was deeply insulting to the entire committee, including the five Republican senators (as well as to me).

Secret government files contain much private personal information. The FBI, for example, had collected too much personal information about too many people for too long. The committee was careful not to release material about government wrongdoing in a way that might injure innocent victims. With one glaring exception, this policy was not controversial. The one exception involved Martin Luther King Jr. Sen. Barry Goldwater had at the outset expressed concern that investigating the FBI's treatment of Dr. King might stir up racial unrest. ("They" might riot as after King's assassination.) But after we had finished investigating, and before our public FBI hearings, I told the senators that the proof would be much worse than anticipated, giving as one example the FBI trying to push King to commit suicide by sending him a composite tape of recordings made by warrantless bugging of his hotel rooms. I told the senators I had chosen not to listen to the tape, nor had I let any staff member do so. Listening was not necessary to make our point, and doing so would further violate the King family's privacy. Senator Goldwater said I was wrong—indeed that we should play the tape on national television. Goldwater's reaction was surprising and disappointing, particularly from one who was often a libertarian and a defender of privacy rights.

After the committee, I continued not only to deal with secrets, but also to think more about secrecy. When I returned to Cravath in mid-1976, I picked up all our major litigation for Time, Inc. While this included the case that led to female reporters being admitted to sports locker rooms, my main work was defending libel cases across the country.[8] One libel case reinforced views I developed during the Church Committee about the harm caused by unchecked power coupled with secrecy. Synanon was a California drug and alcohol rehab facility founded by a charismatic former alcoholic, Chuck Dederich. It had, at least at the outset, substantial success in helping former addicts, all living together in a tight-knit community. Later, starting with benign demands, Dederich moved toward indefensible ones—the same mission creep the Church Committee had repeatedly uncovered. Dederich first ordered all members to stop smoking, and all male members to get crew cuts. Reasonable, or pretty mild. But Dederich then went on to urge male members to get a vasectomy and (after his wife died and he acquired a new female consort) said members would benefit from changing partners. A *Time* investigative reporter cut through Synanon's secrecy to expose abuses of Dederich's unchecked power.[9] In response, Synanon and Dederich brought a $76 million libel case. After extensive argument, a California judge granted us summary judgment on forty-two of the forty-four counts. The remaining two were dismissed by Synanon after we discovered secret tape recordings showing Synanon had destroyed relevant documents.[10]

Two stints in New York City's government also sharpened my understanding of secrecy and the benefits of openness. From 1982 through 1986, I served as the city's head lawyer (the "corporation counsel") during Ed Koch's mayoralty. The job evolved far beyond strictly legal matters.[11] What struck me about policy meetings with the mayor was how he welcomed debate, was willing to change his mind based upon the exchanges he clearly relished, and would listen to a wide range of low- as well as high-ranking officials. Openness served Koch and the city well. Then, shortly after Koch left office, Columbia University commissioned an oral history of his administration. The mayor urged us to hold nothing back. I told Koch he was like Oliver Cromwell, who told the portrait painter, "Paint me warts and all." Of course, Koch believed there would be more "all" than "warts." But still, what a refreshing attitude, as opposed to government policies bottling up secrets for ages.

In 1989, while back again at Cravath, I chaired the commission that extensively rewrote New York City's constitution—or "Charter."[12] This required thinking about a different element of secrecy than with the Church Committee, where my principal focus had been on exposing illegal or improper secret conduct. With the charter, I had to decide whether the commission's discussions should be open or closed, and along with the commission's counsel and staff director, Eric Lane, I decided we would benefit by allowing the public to see all our work. Initially, some commission members were wary, wondering whether they could speak as fully in public as in private. But we went ahead with only open meetings. In retrospect, openness helped us— first in resolving issues within the commission, and later in winning the hard-fought charter referendum vote battle. In a contentious city, sharply divided along racial and geographic lines, allowing, and encouraging, public observation of our wrestling with hard issues demystified what we were doing and diminished any sense that we were "acting upon" rather than "for" the public. Openness did not restrain debate within the commission. In fact, the constant public feedback we received helped sharpen debate.

Later, my views about the value of openness were reinforced as a board member of Atlantic Philanthropies, a huge foundation that has given away billions of dollars. Before 1996, Atlantic was anonymous. But then, because of litigation, the foundation's existence could be discovered. Therefore, we gave the *New York Times* an exclusive on the foundation's history, but very few other details.[13] Even after this "unveiling," Atlantic continued to make its grants anonymously. A few years later, I wrote a report that persuaded Atlantic's board to abandon anonymity altogether. The reasons echo concerns about excessive government secrecy: "a foundation that donates a lot of money wields a lot of power"; "experience teaches that outside scrutiny or constructive advice, while sometimes naïve or painful, or even unjust, is, nonetheless, often helpful"; "the only outside discipline on foundations is assessment by outsiders of their work, its results, and the activities and donees that they choose to support, or not support."[14] Moreover, as with government secrecy inhibiting knowledge sharing between agencies, Atlantic's anonymity policy had prevented donees in a common field from learning from one another.

Shortly after 9/11, I began to think more about government secrecy and did a little work, including reading the report by Senator Moynihan's commission on secrecy. However, I set aside sustained research because of other work I was then doing at the Brennan Center for Justice at NYU Law School, including three trials, a Supreme Court argument, and writing, along with Aziz Z. Huq, *Unchecked and Unbalanced: Presidential Power in a Time of Terror.*[15] Working on that book increased my interest in the dangers of excessive secrecy. Indeed, it is striking to see in *Unchecked and Unbalanced* the greater emphasis on the dangers and harms of secrecy as compared to my Church Committee work.

In January 2009, in casting about for the topic of a speech to give after I received the New York State Bar Association's Gold Medal, I selected secrecy. In the speech, titled "Abuses of Presidential Power: Where Do We Go from Here, Addressing the Culture of Secrecy," I said: the "hard work has just begun. We must move beyond curing symptoms (like Guantánamo) to addressing root causes. A central root cause of our recent move toward harmful excesses of presidential power is excessive secrecy."[16] Since that speech, a very substantial portion of my time at the Brennan Center has been devoted to researching and writing this book.

Acknowledgments

Antrina Richardson began working with me as my number-two daytime secretary/assistant soon after she had started her first job working at New York City's Law Department and I was New York City Corporation Counsel. She has been a friend and a great help to me ever since—for thirty years. This book could not have been produced without her typing all my (horribly hard to read) handwritten first drafts of the book chapters. Thereafter, as I edited constantly, Trina did much of that retyping work as well, aided by Helen Sikorski and by Cravath night secretaries, including Arlene Greeno (who also became a specialist in my handwriting) and proofreader Ron Weiss. This night work was supervised by Lenny Tropp, Diane Konsky, and Rosemarie Hartdorn.

I have always been lucky to work with extremely talented colleagues, for example, at the Church Committee, Cravath, the City of New York, the Charter Revision Commission, the Campaign Finance Board, and the Brennan Center for Justice at NYU Law School. Over the course of the past five years, I did an enormous amount of research for this book, and I was aided by a number of talented young people at the Brennan Center to whom I gave focused assignments. These included Vishal Agraharkar, Emmanuel Arnaud, Jonathan Backer, Jacob Frackman, Scott Greenberg, Emily Harris, Ben Levander, Mary McCullough, and Dana Roizen. In addition, two PhD candidates were helpful part-time research assistants: David Viola and Kathryn Montalbano (who was particularly helpful on journalism and on the "Who Owns History?" section of Chapter 5). Finally, Kyle Alagood worked with me on research subjects and on the endnotes from 2010, when he started at the Brennan Center, through his first two-plus years at law school. Kyle was a great help on every part of the book. He should have a great future as a lawyer, a public policy analyst, or both.

For all my professional life, I have welcomed and benefited from editorial suggestions. For this book, two friends from college, Dan Morgan and Ed Burlingame, gave me useful structural and conceptual comments. Jim Lyons has a great eye and ear for writing and gave me editorial suggestions and comments on every part of the book. Others who made helpful suggestions on the whole book include Michael Waldman, Steven J. Schulhofer, Loch K. Johnson, Eric Lane, Sidney Rosdeitcher, Aziz Huq, David Pozen, and Jeanine Plant-Chirlin. People who gave me useful comments on parts of the book include Jack Rosenthal, Max Frankel, Robert S. (Stan) Norris, Burt Neuborne, Norman Dorsen, Emily Berman, Burt Wides, Elizabeth Goitein (who also suggested the title *Democracy in the Dark*), Rachel Levinson-Waldman, Bob Rifkind, Melissa Ludtke, Eric Schwarz, Harry Martin, and Laurie Perera. Obviously, errors or omissions in the book are mine alone.

I tried out early ideas and versions of chapter drafts on several occasions: at the 2009 New York State Bar Association Gold Medal award ceremony; at a speech given in 2010 at the John F. Kennedy Institute for North American Studies at the Free University of Berlin titled "The Expansion of Democracy in America"; in receiving the Henry Award at the University of Oklahoma Law School in 2012 ("Access to Government Information Is a Foundation of American Democracy—But the Courts Don't Get It"); at the 2012 conference "From the Pentagon Papers to WikiLeaks" at the Heidelberg Center for American Studies; and in receiving the Ridenhour Courage Award in Washington, D.C., in 2014. I am grateful to each institution for the opportunity.

After the book draft went to The New Press, very helpful comments were provided by Diane Wachtell and by Susan Lehman. Subsequently, Rachelle Mandik did careful copyediting, and Sarah Fan put the book together. Jed Bickman and Diane Wachtell were crucial to the publishing process.

The Brennan Center is a welcoming place for those interested in transformative ideas coupled with effective action. To work here is a pleasure and a privilege. Its board members are smart, committed, and caring. Its staff keeps me stimulated. At the Brennan Center, I have had the opportunity not only to write this book and an earlier one but also to try three cases, argue in the Supreme Court, write numerous articles and speeches, help guide our governance, and try to give helpful advice.

Finally, my beloved wife, Ricky (Professor Frederica Perera), not only read each part of the book with helpful suggestions but also supported and loved me throughout, particularly during the nine months of 2013 and 2014 when I was hobbled and homebound by three leg surgeries—but kept busy working on this book.

Notes

Citations marked SEE WEBSITE can be found at thenewpress.com/democracy-in-the-dark-endnotes.

The notes generally use short forms for sources cited more than once within a chapter. The following is a list of citations that appear frequently and short forms used to reference those materials.

Books, Newspapers, and Compilations of Presidential Papers

America the Vulnerable	Joel Brenner, *America the Vulnerable: Inside the New Threat Matrix of Digital Espionage* (Penguin Press, 2010)
Danger and Survival	McGeorge Bundy, *Danger and Survival: Choices About the Bomb in the First Fifty Years* (1988; Vintage, 1990)
Federalist No. ##	Clinton Rossiter, ed., *The Federalist Papers* (Mentor Books, 1961)
Moynihan, *Secrecy*	Daniel Patrick Moynihan, *Secrecy: The American Experience* (Yale University Press, 1998)
My Fellow Americans	Michael Waldman, *My Fellow Americans: The Most Important Speeches of America's Presidents, from George Washington to Barack Obama*, 2d ed. (Sourcebooks MediaFusion, 2010)

Unchecked and Unbalanced	Frederick A.O. Schwarz Jr. and Aziz Z. Huq, *Unchecked and Unbalanced: Presidential Power in a Time of Terror* (The New Press, 2007)
NYT	*The New York Times*
WSJ	*The Wall Street Journal*
WPost	*The Washington Post*
Papers of Thomas Jefferson	Julian P. Boyd et al., eds., *The Papers of Thomas Jefferson*, 40 vols. (Princeton University Press, 1955–2013)
Collected Works of Abraham Lincoln	Roy P. Basler, ed., *Collected Works of Abraham Lincoln*, 8 vols. (Rutgers University Press, 1953)

Presidential papers other than Jefferson's and Lincoln's are too widely dispersed to have a single source.

Government Reports (in Chronological Order)

Farrand's Records	I.M. Farrand, ed., *The Records of the Federal Convention of 1787*, 3 vols. (Yale University Press, 1911)
Elliot's Debates	Jonathan Elliot, ed., *The Debates in the Several State Conventions, on the Adoption of the Federal Constitution, as Recommended by the Federal Convention at Philadelphia in 1787*, 5 vols. (1836–45)
Annals of Cong.	*Annals of Congress*, 42 vols. (Gales & Seaton, 1834–56)
Church Comm. Assassinations	*Senate Select Committee to Study Governmental Operations with Respect to Intelligence Activities, Interim Report: Alleged Assassination Plots Involving Foreign Leaders*, S. Rep. No. 94-465 (1975)
Church Comm. Bk. #	*Senate Select Committee to Study Governmental Operations with Respect to Intelli-*

gence Activities, S. Rep. No. 94-755, 6 vols. (1976)

> *Bk. I: Foreign and Military Intelligence*
>
> *Bk. II: Intelligence Activities and the Rights of Americans*
>
> *Bk. III: Supplementary Detailed Staff Reports on Intelligence Activities and the Rights of Americans*

Church Comm. FBI Hearings	*Federal Bureau of Investigation: Hearings Before the Senate Select Committee to Study Governmental Operations with Respect to Intelligence Activities*, 94th Cong. (1975)
Iran-Contra Report	*Report of the Congressional Committees Investigating the Iran-Contra Affair*, S. Rep. No. 100-216, H. Rep. No. 100-433 (Government Printing Office, 1987)
Iran-Contra Minority Report	*Report of the Congressional Committees Investigating the Iran-Contra Affair*, S. Rep. No. 100-216, H. Rep. No. 100-433 (Government Printing Office, 1987), 431–636
9/11 Comm'n	*The 9/11 Commission Report: Final Report of the National Commission on Terrorist Attacks Upon the United States*, official government edition (Government Printing Office, 2004)

Introduction

1. *Church Comm. Assassinations*, Epilogue, 285.
2. James Madison, *Federalist No. 51*, 322.
3. *Iran-Contra Minority Report*, 444, 445, 450, 515, 532. (These comments are quoted in full and elaborated in Chapter 4, pp. 79–80.)

Part I: History

1. For historical background, SEE WEBSITE.

1: From the Garden of Eden to America's Founding

1. Gen. 1:1; Gen. 3:1–24; Gen. 11:1–9 (King James Version). "In the beginning" begins Genesis.

2. Robert Wright, *The Evolution of God* (Little, Brown, 2009), 52, 75; Lynn V. Foster, *Handbook to Life in the Ancient Maya World* (Oxford University Press, 2005), 178; Bruce G. Trigger, *Early Civilization: Ancient Egypt in Context* (American University in Cairo Press, 1993), 102.

3. John Baines, "Literacy and Ancient Egyptian Society," *Man* 18, no. 3 (1983): 572, 577.

4. John Burrow, *A History of Histories: Epics, Chronicles, Romances, and Inquiries from Herodotus and Thucydides to the Twentieth Century* (Vintage, 2009), 3–10 (quoting Herodotus, *Histories* 2.77, trans. A. de Selincourt [Penguin, 2003]). For additional scholarship, SEE WEBSITE.

5. Burrow, *History of Histories*, xiii. Homer had used the word *histor* to denote one who judged based upon facts from inscriptions. Ibid. For additional scholarship, SEE WEBSITE.

6. Burrow, *History of Histories*, 20 (characterizing Herodotus's description of the Persian court). See also Christopher Tuplin, "Herodotus on Persia and the Persian Empire," in *The Landmark Herodotus: The Histories*, trans. Andrea L. Purvis and ed. Robert B. Strassler (Pantheon, 2007), 792–97.

7. Herodotus, *Histories*, 5.78. See also Peter Krentz, "The Athenian Government in Herodotus," in *Landmark Herodotus*, 723–26.

8. Thomas Mitchell, "Athenian Democracy: Origin and Ideas," Annual Helen F. North Lecture at Swarthmore College, March 3, 2011, 35 (on file with author); Russell Meiggs, *The Athenian Empire* (Clarendon Press, 1972), 18–19, 235.

9. See Josiah Ober, *Democracy and Knowledge: Innovation and Learning in Classical Athens* (Princeton University Press, 2008), 212–26. For additional scholarship, SEE WEBSITE.

10. Thucydides, *The Peloponnesian War*, 2.36–40 (setting forth the speech by Pericles, with quoted material at 2.36.4, 2.37.1, 2.40.1, and 2.40.2). References to *The Peloponnesian War* refer to *The Landmark Thucydides: A Comprehensive Guide to the Peloponnesian War*, ed. Robert B. Strassler, (Free Press, 1996). For additional scholarship, SEE WEBSITE.

11. Ober, *Democracy and Knowledge*, 17, 40, 121–23.

12. Aristotle, *Politics* 1326b. References to *Politics* refer to *The Politics and the Constitution of Athens*, ed. Stephen Everson, Texts in the History of Political Thought (Cambridge University Press, 1996). For additional scholarship, SEE WEBSITE.

13. James Madison, *Federalist No. 10*, 81. See Gordon S. Wood, *The Idea of America: Reflections on the Birth of the United States* (Penguin, 2011), 191. See generally Meyer Reinhold, *Classica Americana: The Greek and Roman Heritage in the United States* (Wayne State University Press, 1984).

14. See Anthony Everitt, *Augustus: The Life of Rome's First Emperor* (Random House, 2007), 199–211 (discussing Augustus keeping the form of a republic). See also D.C.A. Shotter, "Elections Under Tiberius," *Classical Quarterly* 16, no. 2 (1966): 321–32 (discussing how Tiberius, Augustus's successor and stepson, also kept the form of a republic).

15. Everitt, *Augustus*, xi–xiii.

16. Cornelius Tacitus, *Histories* 1.1; Wood, *Idea of America*, 66 (discussing Jefferson on Tacitus). For additional scholarship, SEE WEBSITE.

17. Cassius Dio, *The Roman History: The Reign of Augustus*, 53.19ff. Citations to *The Roman History* refer to *Cassius Dio: The Roman History: The Reign of Augustus*, trans. Ian Scott-Kilvert (Penguin, 1987). See Everitt, *Augustus*, xii; Burrow, *History of Histories*, 124.

18. Andrew Wallace-Hadrill, "The Imperial Court," in *The Augustan Empire, 43 B.C.–A.D. 69*, Cambridge Ancient History, vol. 10 (Cambridge University Press, 1996), 284. Palatine gave rise to the word "palace"—places where decision-making has often been hidden behind closed doors.

19. Ibid., 286.

20. Everitt, *Augustus*, 247–48.

21. See Margaret Deanesly, *The Lollard Bible and Other Medieval Biblical Versions* (Cambridge University Press, 1966), 59–61 (discussing death by fire of Waldensians [German language]), 363–71 (discussing death by fire of Lollards [English language]). For additional scholarship, SEE WEBSITE.

22. S.H. Steinberg, *Five Hundred Years of Printing*, ed. John Trevitt (Oak Knoll Press, 1996), 18 (quoting from Duke Federigo of Urbino, in *The Vespasiano Memoirs: Lives of Illustrious Men of the XVth Century*, trans. William George and Emily Waters [Dial Press, 1926], 104).

23. Alexandra Walsham, "Unclasping the Book? Post-Reformation English Catholicism and the Vernacular Bible," *Journal of British Studies* 42, no. 2 (2003): 165 (quoting Andrew Marvell, who was satirizing the views of a prelate) (internal quotations and citation omitted).

24. See generally Steinberg, *Five Hundred Years of Printing*; Elizabeth L. Eisenstein, *The Printing Press as an Agent of Change: Communications and Cultural Transformations in Early-Modern Europe* (Cambridge University Press, 1979); Michael Clapham, "Printing," in *From the Renaissance to the Industrial Revolution, A History of Technology*, vol. 3, ed. Charles Singer et al. (Oxford University Press, 1957), 377–411; Paul Starr, *The Creation of the Media: Political Origins of Modern Communications* (Basic Books, 2004); Paul F. Grendler, "The Conditions of Enquiry: Printing and Censorship," in *The Cambridge History of Renaissance*

Philosophy, ed. Charles B. Schmitt and Quentin Skinner (Cambridge University Press, 1988), 25–53.

25. See, e.g., Norman Davies, *Europe: A History* (Harper Perennial, 1998), 260–445.

26. Alasdair Roberts, *Blacked Out: Government Secrecy in the Information Age* (Cambridge University Press, 2006), 9; Robin J. Ives, "Political Publicity and Political Economy in Eighteenth Century France," *French History* 17, no. 1 (2003): 13–17.

27. Jean Bodin, *Six Books of the Commonwealth,* trans. M.J. Tooley (Basil Blackwell, 1955), 77.

28. Armand DuPlessis, Cardinal Duke de Richelieu, *Political Will and Testament,* ed. T.E.H., trans. unknown, part 2, (1695), 8.

29. Louis XIV, *Memoires for the Instructions of the Dauphin,* ed. Paul Sonnino (Free Press, 1970), 36; Jacob Soll, *The Information Master: Jean-Baptiste Colbert's Secret State Intelligence System* (University of Michigan Press, 2009), 59–60.

30. Ibid., 44. For an additional comment, SEE WEBSITE.

31. Ernst H. Kantorowicz, "Mysteries of State: An Absolutist Concept and Its Late Medieval Origins," *Harvard Theological Review* 48, no. 1 (1955): 68 (internal parentheses removed).

32. See David Zaret, *Origins of Democratic Culture: Printing, Petitions, and the Public Sphere in Early-Modern England* (Princeton University Press, 2000), 56 (quoting royal proclamation drafted by Francis Bacon for James I in 1620).

33. See Vernon Bogdanor, *The Monarchy and the Constitution* (Oxford University Press, 1995), 1–14 (reviewing the Glorious Revolution and limits on the power of English monarchs). See also Patrick Dillon, *The Last Revolution: 1688 and the Creation of the Modern World* (Jonathan Cape, 2006) (the Glorious Revolution more generally).

34. Joyce Appleby, *Capitalism and a New Social Order: The Republican Vision of the 1790s* (New York University Press, 1984), 60. See Charles F. Himes, "Life and Times of Judge Thomas Cooper," Lectures Before the Dickinson School of Law, 1918.

2: More Openness to More Secrecy: America from the Founding to the Secrecy Era

1. U.S. Representatives argued that limiting franking—subsidizing mailing information to constituents—was to risk "treading on dangerous ground to take any measures that may stop the channels of public information." *Annals of Cong.,* vol. 3, 252–55. See ibid., 252–54, 275–8, 282–98.

2. Paul Starr, *The Creation of the Media: Political Origins of Modern Communications* (Basic Books, 2004), 97–99.

3. Arthur M. Schlesinger Jr., *The Imperial Presidency* (Houghton Mifflin, 1973).

4. George Washington to Patrick Henry, February 24, 1777, in *Revolutionary War Series*, ed. Frank E. Grizzard, vol. 8, *The Papers of George Washington* (University Press of Virginia, 1998), 437; Ron Chernow, *Washington: A Life* (Penguin, 2010), 198–200. *Elliot's Debates*, vol. 3, 170 (Henry's speech to Virginia Ratifying Convention, June 9, 1788). Henry added the Constitution's provisions allowing for secrecy for Congress's "common routine" were "an abomination." Ibid.

For general works discussing secrecy and the Founders, see Daniel N. Hoffman, *Governmental Secrecy and the Founding Fathers: A Study in Constitutional Controls* (Greenwood Press, 1981); Gabriel Schoenfeld, *Necessary Secrets: National Security, the Media, and the Rule of Law* (W.W. Norton, 2010), 54–82; Rahul Sagar, *Secrets and Leaks: The Dilemma of State Secrecy* (Princeton University Press, 2013), 1–50.

5. See, e.g., Gordon S. Wood, *Empire of Liberty: A History of the Early Republic, 1789–1815* (Oxford University Press, 2009); Sean Wilentz, *The Rise of American Democracy: Jefferson to Lincoln* (W.W. Norton, 2005).

6. U.S. Declaration of Independence, para. 2.

7. Thomas Jefferson to Edward Carrington, January 16, 1787, in *Papers of Thomas Jefferson*, vol. 11, 49.

8. Thomas Jefferson to John Adams, August 30, 1787, in ibid., vol. 12, 69.

9. See Charles Warren, *The Making of the Constitution* (Little, Brown, 1928), 135.

10. James Madison to Thomas Jefferson, June 6, 1787, in *Papers of Thomas Jefferson*, vol. 11, 401. A few days later, Madison referred to the rule as being a "prudent one" that would "effectually secure the requisite freedom of discussion" and "save both the Convention and the Community from a thousand erroneous and perhaps mischievous reports." Madison to James Monroe, June 10, 1787, in *The Papers of James Madison*, ed. Robert A. Rutland et al., vol. 10 (University of Chicago Press, 1977), 43. For a later Madison comment, SEE WEBSITE.

11. "Notes of Major William Pierce on the Federal Convention of 1787," *American Historical Review* 3, no. 2 (1898): 324–25.

12. Chernow, *Washington*, 531.

13. See Starr, *Creation of the Media*, 71.

14. Madison, *Federalist No. 40*, 252. See also James Wilson's stress on ratification because the Constitution's drafters "exercised no power at all," and the Constitution was "laid before" the "citizens of the United States" with no more status than "a production of the same nature would claim, flowing from a private pen." *Elliot's Debates*, vol. 2, 470 (remarks at Pennsylvania Ratifying Convention).

15. Abraham Lincoln, "Gettysburg Address," in *My Fellow Americans*, 56. The Civil War Amendments refer to the Thirteenth, Fourteenth, and Fifteenth Amendments, which abolished slavery; granted citizenship, due process, and equal protection; and prohibited limiting the right to vote based on race.

16. U.S. Constitution, art. I, sec. 8, cl. 7.

17. U.S. Constitution, art. I, sec. 5, cl. 3. The First Amendment's clause protecting

the right of the "people" to "petition the Government for a redress of grievances," implies people will have information about what the government is doing. And the ban on abridgements of the freedom of the press implies the importance of information.

18. Under the Articles of Confederation of 1781, art. IX, sec. 7, the Congress "shall publish the journal of their proceedings monthly, except such parts thereof relating to treaties, alliances, or military operations. . . ." Nevertheless, the Continental Congress met behind closed doors until after the Constitution's ratification, when the Continental Congress became the Federal Congress. "Introduction," in *Documentary History of the First Federal Congress of the United States of America, 1789–1791*, ed. Charlene Bangs Bickford et al., vol. 15 (Johns Hopkins University Press, 2004), xi. For additional history, SEE WEBSITE.

19. John Adams to Abigail Adams, April 19, 1789, in *Adams Family Correspondence*, ed. Margaret A. Hogan et al., vol. 8 (Belknap Press of Harvard University Press, 2007), 333. See Donald A. Ritchie, *Press Gallery: Congress and the Washington Correspondents* (Harvard University Press, 1991).

20. Michael Emery, Edwin Emery, and Nancy L. Roberts, *The Press and America: An Interpretive History of the Mass Media*, 9th ed. (Allyn and Bacon, 2000), 83–84.

21. Gerald L. Grotta, "Philip Freneau's Crusade for Open Sessions of the U.S. Senate," *Journalism Quarterly* 48 (Winter 1971): 667–71. For additional scholarship, SEE WEBSITE.

22. Grotta, "Philip Freneau's Crusade," 669–70 (quoting from *National Gazette*, February 13, 1793).

23. Daniel N. Hoffman, *Governmental Secrecy and the Founding Fathers*, 88. See *Annals of Cong.*, vol. 4, 46 (Senate's resolution to end its general closed-door policy). For additional scholarship, SEE WEBSITE.

24. John Jay wrote that in the "negotiation of treaties," "perfect *secrecy* and immediate *dispatch* are sometimes requisite." John Jay, *Federalist No. 64*, 392 (emphasis in original).

25. John Jay to Rufus King, December 22, 1793, in *Documentary History of the Supreme Court of the United States, 1789–1800*, ed. Maeva Marcus et al., vol. 2 (Columbia University Press, 1988), 434–35.

26. Jerald A. Combs, *The Jay Treaty: Political Battleground of the Founding Fathers* (University of California Press, 1970), 151 (quoting *The Autobiography of Colonel John Trumbull*, ed. Theodore Sizer [Yale University Press, 1953], 181).

27. Note, however, that the "Senate's executive sessions (to consider nominations and treaties) were usually closed until 1929." Betsy Palmer, *Secret Sessions of the House and Senate: Authority, Confidentiality, and Frequency* (Congressional Research Service, 2011), 3 (citing Senate Historian's Office).

28. Combs, *Jay Treaty*, 150–55, 161.

29. Todd Estes, *The Jay Treaty Debate, Public Opinions, and the Evaluation of Early American Political Culture* (University of Massachusetts Press, 2006), 34.

30. Combs, *Jay Treaty*, 162.

31. George Cabot to Rufus King, July 27, 1795, in *Life and Letters of George Cabot*, ed. Henry Cabot Lodge (Little, Brown, 1878), 82–83. See Combs, *Jay Treaty*, 162.

32. Hoffman, *Governmental Secrecy and the Founding Fathers*, 138.

33. Ibid., 71–75. Hoffman relies on extensive archival sources and provides a narrative of and sources for the St. Clair episode.

34. Ibid., 105–6.

35. Ibid., 165–66. See *Annals of Cong.*, vol. 5, 759–68 (1796) (House Resolution calling for the president to share Jay Treaty papers with the House, with Washington's letter refusing, and congressional discussion.)

36. Hoffman, *Governmental Secrecy and the Founding Fathers*, 194. All Adams failed to provide were the names of the French X, Y, and Z. See *Annals of Cong.*, vol. 7, 535–36 (1798).

37. See Hoffman, *Governmental Secrecy and the Founding Fathers*, 101.

38. *Annals of Cong.*, vol. 4, 151 (1793).

39. Hoffman, *Governmental Secrecy and the Founding Fathers*, 126–27.

40. See, e.g., Geoffrey R. Stone, *Perilous Times: Free Speech in Wartime from the Sedition Act of 1798 to the War on Terrorism* (W.W. Norton, 2004), 16–78 (discussing the Sedition Act); John Chester Miller, *Crisis in Freedom: The Alien and Sedition Acts* (Little Brown, 1951).

41. Opposition newspapers actually increased under the Sedition Act. See Jeffrey L. Padey, *The Tyranny of Printers: Newspaper Politics in the Early American Republic* (University of Virginia Press, 2001), 126 ("[T]he pace of newspaper creation sped up"; opposition papers by 1800 were "two thirds again more than there had been before the Sedition Act was introduced"). Wood, *Empire of Liberty*, 262 ("The longer the persecution campaign lasted, the more Republican newspapers appeared.").

42. Thomas Cooper, *An Account of the Trial of Thomas Cooper of Northumberland* (John Bioren, 1800), 39; also quoted in Stone, *Perilous Times*, 58.

43. *Annals of Cong.*, vol. 8, 2110, 2164 (1798). For more information on Gallatin, see Raymond Walters, *Albert Gallatin: Jeffersonian Financier and Diplomat* (University of Pittsburgh Press, 1957).

44. *Annals of Cong.*, vol. 8, 2140, 2145, 2105–6 (July 1798).

45. "Madison's Report on the Virginia Resolutions," *Elliot's Debates*, vol. 4, 570 (also known as *The Madison Report, The Report of 1800*, and *The Report on the Alien and Sedition Acts*).

46. James Morton Smith, "The 'Aurora' and the Alien and Sedition Laws: Part I: The Editorship of Benjamin Franklin Bache," *Pennsylvania Magazine of History and Biography* 77 (January 1953), 4, 6.

47. Cooper, *Account of the Trial of Thomas Cooper*, 20.

48. Thomas Jefferson, "First Inaugural Address," March 4, 1801, in *My Fellow Americans*, 20–21. For Washington's related comment, SEE WEBSITE.

49. James Madison, *The Debates on the Federal Convention of 1787*, ed. Gaillard Hunt and James Brown Scott (Oxford University Press, 1920), 538. Morris wrote most of the Constitution's Preamble. For more on Morris, SEE WEBSITE.

50. *Farrand's Records*, vol. 1, 514. See Anne Cary Morris, ed., *The Diary and Letters of Gouverneur Morris*, vol. 2 (Charles Scribner's Sons, 1888), 540 (remarks in 1812). (Benjamin Franklin's remarks at the Convention urging defeat of Morris's property qualification for voting are at *Farrand's Records* vol. 2, 204–5.)

51. John Taylor, *An Inquiry into the Principles and Policy of the Government of the United States* (Green and Cady, 1814), 200. See also Arthur M. Schlesinger Jr.'s preface to Steven L. Katz, *Government Secrecy: Decisions Without Democracy* (People for the American Way Foundation, 1987), 6.

52. James Madison to W.T. Barry, August 4, 1822, in *The Writings of James Madison*, ed. Gaillard Hunt, vol. 9 (G.P. Putnam's Sons, 1910), 103. For context of Madison's letter, SEE WEBSITE.

53. James Madison, *Federalist No. 51*, 320–22.

54. Ibid. (emphasis added).

55. Thomas Jefferson to John Taylor, June 4, 1798, Alexander Calvin and Ellen Morton Washburn Autograph Collection, Massachusetts Historical Society. For additional information about Jefferson's use of "delate," SEE WEBSITE.

56. Benjamin Rush to Richard Price, May 25, 1786, in *Letters of Benjamin Rush*, ed. L.H. Butterfield, vol. 1 (Princeton University Press, 1951), 388. See also Rush to Charles Nisbet, December 5, 1783, 316 (describing the new country's changing nature); Alan Brodsky, *Benjamin Rush: Patriot and Physician* (St. Martin's Press, 2004).

57. When Washington took office in 1789, the federal government was a skeleton. The only agencies and offices existing were those the Constitution established. At Mount Vernon, the Washington family slaves numbered around two hundred. See generally Mary V. Thompson, "The Lives of Enslaved Workers on George Washington's Outlying Farms," talk for the Neighborhood Friends of Mt. Vernon, June 16, 1999; George Washington, entry for February 18, 1786, in *Diaries*, ed. Donald Jackson and Dorothy Twohig, vol. 4, *The Papers of George Washington* (University Press of Virginia, 1978), 277–83. In contrast, Congress had only eighty-one members, but there were seventy-five post offices, most or all of which employed a postmaster.

58. Richard R. John, *Spreading the News: The American Postal System from Franklin to Morse* (Harvard University Press, 1995), 51.

59. James Madison, "Public Opinion," *National Gazette*, December 19, 1791, 59, reproduced in *The Papers of James Madison*, ed. Robert A. Rutland et al., vol. 6 (University Press of Virginia, 1983), 170.

60. John, *Spreading the News*, 36–42; Timothy E. Cook, *Governing with the*

News, 2nd ed. (University of Chicago Press, 2005), 38–44; Wood, *Empire of Liberty*, 478–79.

61. Alfred McClung Lee, *The Daily Newspaper in America: The Evolution of a Social Instrument* (Macmillan, 1937), 711; Wayne E. Fuller, *The American Mail: Enlarger of the Common Life* (University of Chicago Press, 1972), 112; John, *Spreading the News*, 38. See Wesley Everill Rich, *The History of the United States Post Office to the Year 1829* (Harvard University Press, 1924); Wood, *Empire of Liberty*, 250, 307–8 (partisanship in newspapers and the subsidies' importance).

62. Thomas Jefferson to Edward Carrington, January 16, 1787, in *Papers of Thomas Jefferson*, vol. 11, 49.

63. Thomas Jefferson to M. Pictet, February 5, 1803, in *Papers of Thomas Jefferson*, vol. 39, 457. Thomas Jefferson to Thomas McKean, February 19, 1803, in ibid., 553. See Joseph J. Ellis, *American Sphinx: The Character of Thomas Jefferson* (Alfred A. Knopf, 1997), 215–19.

64. Alexis de Tocqueville, *Democracy in America*, ed. Phillips Bradley, vol. 2 (Alfred A. Knopf, 1980), 107, 111; ibid., vol. 1, 186–87.

65. Ibid., vol. 2, 106, 109, 112.

66. Francis J. Grund, *The Americans, in Their Moral, Social, and Political Relations* (Marsh, Capen and Lyon, 1837), 112, 117–18. See Holman Hamilton and James L. Crouthamel, "A Man for Both Parties: Francis J. Grund as Political Chameleon," *Pennsylvania Magazine of History and Biography* 97, no. 4 (1973): 465–84 (reviewing Grund's life and influence in America).

67. In 1848, President John Tyler was criticized for trying to keep secret the treaty for annexing Texas. Arthur M. Schlesinger Jr. preface to Katz, *Government Secrecy*, i.

68. Abraham Lincoln, "The War with Mexico," January 12, 1848, in *Appendix to Congressional Globe*, 30th Cong., 1st sess. (Blair and Rives, 1848), 93–95 (emphasis in original).

69. For profound discussions of both lying and secrecy, see Sissela Bok's *Lying: Moral Choice in Public and Private Life* (Pantheon, 1978) and *Secrets: On the Ethics of Concealment and Revelation*, rev. ed. (Vintage Books, 1989).

70. William H. Herndon and Jesse W. Weik, *Abraham Lincoln: The True Story of a Great Life*, vol. 2 (D. Appleton, 1895), 269. See *Lincoln*, DVD (Walt Disney, 2013); Doris Kearns Goodwin, *Team of Rivals: The Political Genius of Abraham Lincoln* (Simon & Schuster, 2005), 688.

71. Aaron W. Marrs, "Lincoln's P.R. Coup," *Disunion* (blog), *NYT*, December 1, 2011.

72. See U.S. Department of State, "Foreign Relations of the United States: 1861 to Date," press release, June 1, 1995. For additional information on *FRUS*, SEE WEBSITE.

73. Woodrow Wilson, *The New Freedom* (Doubleday, Page, 1913), 113–14, 130 (collecting Wilson's campaign speeches in 1912).

74. See Stone, *Perilous Times*, 136–77 (discussing Wilson and World War I courts on these issues, generally); David Pietrusza, *1920: The Year of the Six Presidents* (Carroll and Graf, 2007), 262–81, 397–417 (Debs and the 1920 election). For Supreme Court cases involving Wilson's prosecution of critics, and more on the Vermont minister case, SEE WEBSITE.

75. Woodrow Wilson, "Address to Congress on Peace Terms," January 8, 1918, in *My Fellow Americans*, 90.

76. See Ernest Marshall, "Press Presents Claims," *NYT*, January 17, 1919, 1; "Senators Assail Secret Diplomacy," *NYT*, January 17, 1919, 2; "London Journals Condemn Secrecy," *NYT*, January 17, 1919.

77. See Sherrill Halbert, "The Suspension of the Writ of Habeas Corpus by President Lincoln," *American Journal of Legal History* 2 (1958): 95–116; Stone, *Perilous Times*, 80–93. For additional scholarship, SEE WEBSITE.

78. See Lee, *Daily Newspaper in America*, 715–17, 725–26.

79. Richard Hofstadter, *The Age of Reform: From Bryan to F.D.R.* (Vintage Books, 1955), 232–33.

80. Theodore Roosevelt, "Speech in Osawatomie, Kansas," August 31, 1910, in *My Fellow Americans*, 68–76.

81. Louis D. Brandeis, "What Publicity Can Do," in *Other People's Money and How the Bankers Use It* (Frederick A. Stokes, 1914), 92–108. Originally published in *Harper's Weekly*, December 20, 1913. But see Samuel D. Warren and Louis D. Brandeis, "The Right to Privacy," *Harvard Law Review* 4 (1890): 193.

82. Ferdinand Pecora, *Wall Street Under Oath: The Story of Our Modern Money Changers* (Simon & Schuster, 1939), 130.

83. Florida Statutes, ch. 5942, sec. 1, Laws of 1909 ("[A]ll State, county and municipal records shall at all times be open for a personal inspection of any citizen of Florida, and those in charge of such records shall not refuse this privilege to any citizen.") For Sweden as the first [1766] foreign nation, SEE WEBSITE.

84. An Act to Prohibit the Making of Photographs, Sketches, or Maps of Vital Military and Naval Defense Installations and Equipment, and for Other Purposes, 75 Pub. L. 418, 52 Stat. 3 (1938).

85. Exec. Order No. 8381 (March 22, 1940), 5 Fed. Reg. 1147. See Jennifer K. Elsea, *The Protection of Classified Information: The Legal Framework* (Congressional Research Service, 2011).

86. An Act to Expedite the Prosecution of the War Effort, 55 U.S. Stat. 838 (1941); Exec. Order 8985 (December 19, 1941), 6 Fed. Reg. 6625; Michael S. Sweeney, *Secrets of Victory: The Office of Censorship and the American Press and Radio in World War II* (University of North Carolina Press, 2001), 40–42 (detailing history of the Office of Censorship).

87. See generally Robert S. Norris, *Racing for the Bomb: General Leslie R. Groves: The Manhattan Project's Indispensable Man* (Steerforth, 2002); Garry Wills, *Bomb Power: The Modern Presidency and the National Security State* (Penguin, 2010). *Bomb*

Power argues that "the Bomb altered our subsequent history down to its deepest constitutional roots." Wills posits that the bomb was "the seed" for growing executive powers. A better expression would have been "a" seed.

88. For the 1940s dollar costs, see Stephen I. Schwartz, ed., *Atomic Audit: The Costs and Consequences of U.S. Nuclear Weapons Since 1940* (Brookings Institution, 1998), 60. For additional scholarship, SEE WEBSITE.

89. Joe Martin, *My First Fifty Years in Politics*, as told to Robert J. Donovan (McGraw-Hill, 1960), 100–01. See Norris, *Racing for the Bomb*, 278; David McCullough, *Truman* (Simon & Schuster, 1992), 291.

90. Leslie R. Groves, *Now It Can Be Told: The Story of the Manhattan Project* (Harper, 1962), 362–63; Norris, *Racing for the Bomb*, 278.

91. Harry S. Truman, *Memoirs*, vol. 1 (Doubleday, 1955), 10–11. See McCullough, *Truman*, 289.

92. Harry S. Truman to Hon. Lewis B. Schwellenbach, July 15, 1943, Harry S. Truman Library, Presidential and Vice Presidential Papers. See also McCullough, *Truman*, 289–90.

93. See William L. Laurence, *Men and Atoms: The Discovery, the Uses and the Future of Atomic Energy* (Simon & Schuster, 1959), 50. For additional scholarship, SEE WEBSITE.

94. "Biggest Secret," *Editor and Publisher*, August 11, 1945, 40, quoted in Patrick S. Washburn, "The Office of Censorship's Attempt to Control Press Coverage of the Atomic Bomb During World War II," *Journalism Monographs* 12 (1990): 1.

95. See Washburn, "Office of Censorship's Attempt" (discussing the leaks and their seriousness). See also Gabriel Schoenfeld, *Necessary Secrets*, 149–53.

96. These included articles such as one in the *Washington Post* discussing the difficulty in getting a wage increase of an "atom-smasher," a man whose military job was of a "secret nature" and who "ha[d] been studying much of his life on the matter of blowing up nations with an atom." Jean Craighead, "Just an Atom-Smasher: He Can't Get a Raise—Hasn't Accomplished Anything," *WPost*, October 31, 1943, L1. An article in the *New York Times* reported on destruction of a Nazi "heavy-water" plant in Norway and, more generally, potential use of heavy water in "disintegrating the atom . . . [to] release a devastating power." "Nazi 'Heavy Water' Looms as Weapon," *NYT*, April 4, 1943, 18. See also Washburn, "Office of Censorship's Attempt."

97. Herbert M. Merrill, letter to the editor, *Schenectady* (NY) *Gazette*, July 27, 1943, quoted in Washburn, "Office of Censorship's Attempt," 7–8.

98. "Secret Project's Wash," *Business Week*, July 31, 1943, 85.

99. "The Periscope," *Newsweek*, June 11, 1945, 28. The magazine predicted lifting of censorship. General Groves predicted great harm from the article. See Washburn, "Office of Censorship's Attempt," 23–24.

100. Ernest Lindley, "Germany's Last Hopes," *WPost*, August 11, 1943, 11; Jerry Kluttz, "The Federal Diary: Per Diems Won't Get Yule Time-and-a-Half," *WPost*, December 10, 1943, B1.

101. Washburn, "Office of Censorship's Attempt," 11.

102. Richard Wilson, "Washington Memo," *Minneapolis Tribune*, August 24, 1944, 1. See Washburn, "Office of Censorship's Attempt," 14.

103. Arthur Hale, *Confidentially Yours*, Mutual Broadcasting System, radio broadcast, August 15, 1944, in K.R.M. Short, "Radio's Scoop of the War," *Historical Journal of Film, Radio, and Television* 5, no. 1 (1985), 104–8. "Shortly after" *Confidentially Yours* aired, the FBI "swooped down" on broadcast offices and "impounded scripts," "destroyed programme recordings," and interrogated "those involved in any way" with Hale's broadcast. Ibid., 101

104. See Irving M. Klotz, "Captives of Their Fantasies: The German Atomic Bomb Scientists," *Journal of Chemical Education* 74, no. 2 (1997): 204–9. The Japanese had engaged in a "minuscule" effort to build an atomic bomb. Martin Flacker, "Fukushima's Long Link to a Dark Nuclear Past," *NYT*, September 5, 2011, A10.

105. Even during World War II, a Russian Air Force lieutenant in 1942 wrote the chairman of the Soviet Scientific-Technical Council that Western journals had stopped publishing articles on nuclear fission. The lieutenant inferred correctly that ceasing publication meant the West was working on an atomic bomb. See Thomas B. Cochran, Robert S. Norris, and Oleg A. Bukharin, *Making the Russian Bomb: From Stalin to Yeltsin* (Westview Press, 1995), 5–7. For additional inferences that could be drawn today, SEE WEBSITE.

106. James S. Pope, "Foreword," in Harold I. Cross, *The People's Right to Know: Legal Access to Public Records and Proceedings* (Columbia University Press, 1953), vii–viii.

107. James S. Pope, "The Suppression of News," *Atlantic Monthly*, July 1951, 50.

108. Herbert Brucker, *Freedom of Information* (Macmillan, 1949). While credited with early use of "freedom of information," this book has little about government controlling information. It is mostly about the importance of a free press. For information on first use of "right to know," SEE WEBSITE.

109. See Exec. Order No. 10290 (September 24, 1951), 16 Fed. Reg. 9795. (The Navy had a cabinet secretary, while the Army was part of the Department of War.)

110. "Tight Lid on News Aim of New Order," *NYT*, September 22, 1951, 34.

111. "U.S. Adds Controls on Security Data," *NYT*, September 26, 1951, 17.

112. "O.P.S. Bans 'Embarrassing' News, Truman Quickly Rescinds Order," *NYT*, September 28, 1951, 1.

Part II: Legitimate Secrets, and Secrecy's Dangers, Harms, Culture, and Seduction

1. Dwight D. Eisenhower, "Chance for Peace," April 16, 1953, in *Public Papers of the Presidents of the United States: Dwight D. Eisenhower, 1953* (Government Printing Office, 1960), 182. Eisenhower expressed hope the Soviets would change their

positions. If not, the worst outcome of no change from the current "dread road," would be atomic war; the best would be a life of perpetual fear and tension.

2. See National Archives and Records Administration, *Information Security Oversight Office, Annual Report to the President, Fiscal Year 1979* (1980), 2, 15.

3. For Clinton's reform and large-scale release of national security information, see Exec. Order No. 12958 (April 17, 1995), 60 Fed. Reg. 19825; Exec. Order No. 12937 (November 10, 1994), 59 Fed. Reg. 59097 (bulk declassification of National Archives documents); Exec. Order 12951 (February 22, 1995), 60 Fed. Reg. 10789 (release of spy satellite images). For Moynihan, see *Report of the Commission on Protecting and Reducing Government Secrecy*, S. Doc. No. 105-2 (1997); Moynihan, *Secrecy*, 9–11, 14, 16, 62–63, 143, 217–18; *Restoring the Rule of Law: Hearing Before the Subcomm. on the Constitution of the S. Comm. on the Judiciary*, 110th Cong., 39–41 (statement of John Podesta).

4. Frank Church, interview by Lawrence Spivak, *Meet the Press*, NBC, August 17, 1975.

3: Appropriate Secrecy and Its Limits: 9/11, the Cuban Missile Crisis, and Where to Drop the First Atomic Bomb

1. Central Intelligence Agency, "Bin Ladin [*sic*] Determined to Strike in U.S.," *President's Daily Brief*, August 6, 2001; Douglas Jehl and David E. Sanger, "Secret Briefing Said That Qaeda Was Active in U.S.," *NYT*, April 11, 2004, 1; Philip Shenon, "9/11 Panel Threatens to Issue Subpoena for Bush's Briefings," *NYT*, February 10, 2004, A22. For the text of the August 6 PDB, see *9/11 Comm'n Report*, 261–62.

2. *9/11 Comm'n Report*, 259 ("blinking red"), 254–77 (discussing pre-9/11 intelligence reports).

3. Loch K. Johnson, "Glimpses into the Gems of American Intelligence: The *President's Daily Brief* and the National Intelligence Estimate," *Intelligence and National Security* 23, no. 3 (2008): 336; *9/11 Comm'n Report*, 533n2; Loch K. Johnson, *The Threat on the Horizon: An Insider's Account of America's Search for Security in the Aftermath of the Cold War* (Oxford University Press 2011), 26.

4. *9/11 Comm'n Report*, 255–56.

5. Ibid., 256–59. The full text of the documents was not made available to the commission. Except for the August 6 PDB, these reports were nonspecific as to location. As the *9/11 Commission Report* noted, "We cannot say for certain whether these [other] reports, as dramatic as they were, related to the 9/11 attacks." Ibid., 263. But they did not *exclude* the United States. In July, a CIA report said that Khalid Sheikh Mohammad was "recruiting people to travel to the United States to meet with colleagues already there so that they might conduct terrorist attacks on bin Laden's behalf." Ibid., 277.

6. See Office of the Inspector General of the Department of Justice, *A Review of the FBI's Handling of Intelligence Information Related to the September 11 Attacks*

(2004), 180; *9/11 Comm'n Report*, 257–58; Associated Press, "Bush Faced Threat of Airborne Attack at G-8," *Commercial Appeal* (Memphis, TN), September 26, 2001, A9. For additional information, SEE WEBSITE.

7. "Bin Ladin [*sic*] Declares Jihad on Americans," in *Compilation of Osama Bin Ladin [sic] Statements: 1994–January 2004*, FBIS Report (January 2004), 13–28; "Text of Fatwa Urging Jihad Against Americans," in ibid., 56–58.

8. See Benjamin Weiser, "The Terror Verdict: The Violence and Its Aftermath," *NYT*, May 30, 2001, 1; John F. Burns, "No Special Alert for Cole Before Bombing," *NYT*, October 25, 2000, 10. See also *9/11 Comm'n Report* (discussing rise of al-Qaeda and pre-9/11 attacks). See generally Lawrence Wright, *The Looming Tower: Al-Qaeda and the Road to 9/11* (Alfred A. Knopf, 2006); Ali H. Soufan, *Black Banners: The Inside Story of 9/11 and the War Against al Qaeda* (W.W. Norton, 2011).

9. The threat to the United States by al-Qaeda was mentioned in a July 2, 2001, FBI Counterterrorism Division message to federal, state, and local officials. But the FBI downplayed it: "'The FBI has no information indicating a credible threat of terrorist attack in the United States.'" *9/11 Comm'n Report*, 258, 273; *Review of the FBI's Handling of Intelligence Information*, 120–21.

10. For general discussion of the Moussaoui case, see *9/11 Comm'n Report*, 273–76. The "extremist preparing" quotation comes from a Minneapolis FBI agent describing the Moussaoui facts and seeking a search warrant. Ibid. For a play-by-play of developments in Minneapolis and FBI headquarters, see *Review of the FBI's Handling of Intelligence Information*, 101–222. For additional information, SEE WEBSITE.

11. *9/11 Comm'n Report*, 221–22. For additional information, SEE WEBSITE.

12. Ibid., 276. The commission added "publicity about Moussaoui's arrest and a possible hijacking threat might have derailed the plot." Ibid.

13. *America the Vulnerable*, 222 (describing the "gold standard" for testing cyberdefense: NSA's assembling a "red team of professional cyberburglars who are really good guys, and set them to work against one of our own systems"). For additional information, SEE WEBSITE.

14. Clare Nullis, "Hijackers Intended Jet to Become Flying Bomb," *Times-Picayune* (New Orleans, LA), December 28, 1994, A1.

15. *9/11 Comm'n Report*, 274.

16. John F. Burns and Craig Pyes, "Radical Islamic Network May Have Come to U.S.," *NYT*, December 31, 1999, A16. The arrest on December 14 followed the Clinton administration's decision to issue a public warning of "specific and credible information" of terrorist attacks abroad in connection with the millennium. Stephen Labaton, "National Security Adviser Warns of Risk of Terrorism," *NYT*, December 19, 1999, A30. For additional information, SEE WEBSITE.

17. See *9/11 Comm'n Report*, 4. For pre-9/11 hijacking planning, see ibid., 82–86. For additional information, SEE WEBSITE.

18. The 9/11 Commission said institutional imagination might have led to the leap in judgment that would have pushed the United States to prepare for suicide air-

craft bombs. The commission noted al-Qaeda had already used truck bombs, then boats, so aircraft were not out of the realm of imagination. Moreover, it would not really have been a leap; previous threat reports had mentioned "the possibility of using an aircraft filled with explosives . . . to fly . . . into a U.S. city" Ibid., 344–48.

19. *9/11 Comm'n Report*, xvi.

20. Ibid., 277.

21. Ibid., 417.

22. Ibid., 533n2. For additional information, SEE WEBSITE.

23. For the Cuban Missile Crisis generally, see Michael Dobbs, *One Minute to Midnight: Kennedy, Khrushchev, and Castro on the Brink of Nuclear War* (Alfred A. Knopf, 2008); Sheldon M. Stern, *The Cuban Missile Crisis in American Memory: Myths Versus Reality* (Stanford University Press, 2012); James A. Nathan, *Anatomy of the Cuban Missile Crisis* (Greenwood Press, 2001); Max Frankel, *High Noon in the Cold War: Kennedy, Khrushchev, and the Cuban Missile Crisis* (Presidio Press, 2004) and *The Times of My Life and My Life with the Times* (Random House, 1990), 247–51; *Danger and Survival*, 392–462.

24. Kennedy's speechwriter, Theodore "Ted" Sorensen, wrote the speech Kennedy ultimately delivered on October 22, 1962, calling for a blockade. For additional information, SEE WEBSITE.

25. For a general overview of the last days of the missile crisis, see Frankel, *High Noon in the Cold War*, 147–63; Laurence Chang and Peter Kornblush, eds., *The Cuban Missile Crisis, 1962: A National Security Archive Documents Reader* (New Press, 1998), 373–89. For the deal to trade missiles in Turkey, see Anatoly Dobrynin to the USSR Foreign Ministry, top-secret cable, October 27, 1962; Robert F. Kennedy to Dean Rusk, top-secret memorandum, October 30, 1962. These and other original documents from the missile crisis and atomic bomb decision-making process are available through the National Security Archive at George Washington University (henceforth "Nat'l Sec. Archive"). See also Robert F. Kennedy, *Thirteen Days: A Memoir of the Cuban Missile Crisis* (W.W. Norton, 1971), 87. Kennedy's posthumous memoir (by Ted Sorensen), however, does not accurately reflect the October 27 meeting and deal.

26. *Danger and Survival*, 32. The three others who met in the Oval Office were Undersecretary of State George Ball, Undersecretary of Defense Roswell Gilpatric, and former ambassador to the Soviet Union Llewellyn Thompson. In his memoir, Ted Sorensen said that JFK's decision "to limit attendance [in the Oval Office] implied to those of us present" that the other members of EXCOMM "did not need to know." Sorensen, *Counselor*, 302.

27. Dean Rusk, Robert McNamara, George W. Ball, Roswell L. Gilpatric, Theodore Sorensen, and McGeorge Bundy, "The Lessons of the Cuban Missile Crisis," *Time*, September 27, 1982, 89.

28. The phrase "eyeball to eyeball" stems from staring contests in Rusk's home state of Georgia. Rusk's comment was made before the final resolution—when

Soviet ships heading for Cuba stopped, following the announcement of a U.S. quarantine. But Rusk's comment continued to be used as a metaphor for the crisis's resolution. Dean Rusk, *As I Saw It*, ed. Daniel S. Papp (W.W. Norton, 1990), 237.

29. "The Backdown," *Time*, November 2, 1962, 33.

30. Walter Trohan, "Report from Washington," *Chicago Tribune*, October 27, 1962, 4.

31. Richard Rovere, "Letter from Washington," *New Yorker*, November 3, 1962, 118–23 (praising JFK's "steady nerves" and adding Khrushchev was "no longer asking us to dismantle our Turkish base").

32. William Manchester, *One Brief Shining Moment: Remembering Kennedy* (Little, Brown, 1983), 215.

33. Stewart Alsop and Charles Bartlett, "In Times of Crisis," *Saturday Evening Post*, December 8, 1962, cover page, 15–21.

34. Ibid., 21. The "non-admiring official" was said to have "learned" of Stevenson's proposal, suggesting the official was not part of Excomm.

35. Frankel, *High Noon in the Cold War*, 161. Moreover, the administration did not reveal that had the crisis not been resolved when it was, the president had authorized Rusk to arrange for UN Secretary General U Thant to make a public proposal for a missile trade to settle the crisis.

36. *Briefing on Cuban Developments: Hearing Before the Subcomm. on American Republics Affairs of the S. Comm. on Foreign Relations*, 88th Cong. 105–06 (1963).

37. *Hearings on H.R. 2440 (S. 843) Before the S. Comm. on Armed Services*, 88th Cong. 313–14 (1963).

38. McGeorge Bundy, interview by Ned Brooks, *Meet the Press*, NBC, December 16, 1962.

39. John F. Kennedy, excerpt from press conference, September 12, 1963, Papers of President Kennedy, John F. Kennedy Presidential Library and Museum, National Security Files (hereinafter JFK Library NSF), Box 61, Cuba: Guidelines for Public Testimony, Presidential Comments, 10/20/62–10/31/63. The questioner had referred to Sen. Barry Goldwater, having hinted "you made secret agreements" concerning Cuba. For additional information, SEE WEBSITE.

40. The conversation was triggered by Khrushchev referring to the Turkish deal in a letter to JFK via Dobrynin to RFK. Anatoly Dobrynin, *In Confidence: Moscow's Ambassador to America's Six Cold War Presidents 1962–1986* (Times Books, 1995), 90. The Excomm members who knew of the deal agreed to return the letter "as though it had never been opened." Center for Science and International Affairs, *Back to the Brink: Proceedings of the Moscow Conference on the Cuban Missile Crisis, January 27–28, 1989*, ed. Bruce J. Allyun, James G. Blight, and David A. Welch (University Press of America, 1992), 80–81, 92–93.

41. *Back to the Brink*, 92–93. See Kennedy, *Thirteen Days*, 86 (as edited by Sorensen) "(I said [to Dobrynin] that there could be no quid pro quo or any arrange-

ment made under this kind of threat or pressure regarding our removing the missiles from Turkey.").

42. In an article published after my first draft of this chapter, Leslie Gelb wrote "The Myth That Screwed Up 50 Years of U.S. Foreign Policy," *Foreign Policy*, November 2012, 24–26. Gelb refers to America's "triumphant myth" of no compromise, contending this myth about the missile crisis "strengthened [Americans'] scorn" for compromise, and adding the impact continues today when it would be "near political suicide to publicly suggest letting Iran enrich uranium up to an inconsequential 5 percent with strong inspections, though the Nuclear Non-Proliferation Treaty permits it."

43. *Danger and Survival*, 454.

44. See Eric Alterman, *When Presidents Lie: A History of Official Deception and its Consequences* (Viking, 2004), 90–159 (focusing on the missile crisis resolution at 142–51).

45. Leslie Gelb notes after the 1968 Tet Offensive, when LBJ ordered an "'A to Z' review of U.S. policy toward Vietnam . . . [the reviewers] weren't even permitted to study possible compromises with Hanoi." Gelb, "The Myth," 26.

46. See, most recently, Robert A. Caro, *The Years of Lyndon Johnson: The Passage of Power* (Alfred A. Knopf, 2012), 208–29, 375.

47. See, e.g., *Danger and Survival*, 434 ("There was no leak. As far as I know, none of the nine of us told anyone else what had happened."). Even if something is found to suggest President Johnson was told, it would still be relevant to know if he was told the whole truth—that there was a "deal," not the partial truth later told in the joint letter to *Time*.

48. For members of the Interim Committee, SEE WEBSITE.

49. Notes of the Interim Committee Meeting, May 31, 1945, in *Documentary History of the Truman Presidency*, gen. ed. Dennis Merrill (University Publications of America, 1995), 22–38.

50. Ibid., 34–35.

51. Notes of the Interim Committee Meeting, June 1, 1945, in ibid., 39–48. For additional information on attendees, SEE WEBSITE.

52. Ibid., 8–9.

53. Stimson, "The Decision to Use the Atomic Bomb," 100–101. The chapter on "The Atomic Bomb and the Surrender of Japan," in Henry L. Stimson with McGeorge Bundy, *On Active Service in Peace and War* (Harper, 1947), uses extensive quotes from the *Harper's* article in describing decisions on use of the bomb. The one difference was the article's summary of the Interim Committee's review was truncated to: "should be used against Japan, without specific warning, as soon as possible, and against such a target as to make clear its devastating strength."

54. John J. McCloy, memorandum of conversation with General Marshall, May 29, 1945, Nat'l Sec. Archive Electronic Briefing Book No. 162 (hereinafter NSA-EBB 162), doc. 11 (conversation on "Objectives toward Japan and methods of concluding war with minimum casualties").

55. Scientific Panel of the Interim Committee to Henry L. Stimson, "Recommendations on the Immediate Use of Nuclear Weapons," June 16, 1945, in NSA-EBB 162, doc. 19.

56. Ibid.

57. For Groves's role in building and targeting the bomb, see Robert S. Norris, *Racing for the Bomb: General Leslie R. Groves, the Manhattan Project's Indispensable Man* (Steerforth, 2002); Stanley Goldberg, "Groves Takes the Reins," *Bulletin of the Atomic Scientists* 48, no. 10 (1992): 32–39.

58. See J.A. Derry and N.F. Ramsey to L.R. Groves, "Summary of Target Committee Meetings on 10 and 11 May 1945," May 12, 1945, in *Documentary History of the Truman Presidency*, 5.

59. Secretary Stimson ruled out Kyoto because of its cultural, religious, and historic significance, not because of its large civilian population (more than a million). Stimson, "Decision to Use the Atomic Bomb," 105. For additional information on Stimson's position, SEE WEBSITE.

60. See Groves, *Now It Can Be Told*.

61. Notes of the Interim Committee meeting, May 31, 1945, in *Documentary History of the Truman Presidency* 22–38.

62. Groves, *Now It Can Be Told*, 267, 327.

63. See Derry and Ramsey to Groves, "Summary of Target Committee Meetings on 10 and 11 May 1945," 5–14. Later, just before Stimson vetoed Kyoto, the memorandum supporting Kyoto mentioned military benefits, but Groves again stressed the huge population of Kyoto. Groves, *Now It Can Be Told*, 274.

64. L.R. Groves to the Secretary of War, July 18, 1945 in *Documentary History of the Truman Presidency*, 130 (discussing "The Test").

65. Ibid., 124.

66. Henry Lewis Stimson, "Diary entry, July 21, 1945, concerning report on successful testing of the atomic bomb," Box 77, Folder 52 (on file at Yale University, Manuscripts and Archives); see also Groves to the Secretary of War, July 18, 1945, 122 ("The test was successful beyond the most optimistic expectations of anyone.").

67. While General Groves always believed two bombs would end the war, he worked to ensure more would be available. See Norris, *Racing for the Bomb*, 405–6, 413, 416, 424. See L.R. Groves to Chief of Staff [George C. Marshall], July 30, 1945, United States National Archives, Record Group 77, Manhattan Engineer District Records, Top Secret Documents, File no. 5 (Groves discussing production rate of bombs through the end of 1945 as being "three or four" per month) (duplicated by the Nat'l Sec. Archive). The memorandum from Groves to Marshall is in line with a schedule Groves prepared for Gen. Thomas Handy, which called for use of atomic bombs in Japan at the rate of one every ten days through the end of October. Norris, *Racing for the Bomb*, 413. Initially, the third bomb was scheduled for use by August 24; later this was advanced to August 17. Ibid., 416, 424. See Groves to Marshall, July 30, 1945. In his autobiography, Groves said "our production facilities were operating

at such an accelerating rate" and that after Nagasaki "the next bomb would be ready for delivery to the field momentarily." Groves, *Now It Can Be Told*, 352. Another relevant fact is the invasion of Japan—avoiding the casualties from which was a major aim of using the bomb—was not scheduled until November. See Stimson, *On Active Service*, 618–20. See also "Minutes of Meeting Held at the White House, June 18, 1945," in *Documentary History of the Truman Presidency*, 49–57.

68. Stimson, "The Decision to Use the Atomic Bomb," 101.

69. For information on Hiroshima's industrial facilities, see Strategic Bombing Survey, *The Effects of the Atomic Bombs on Hiroshima and Nagasaki* (Government Printing Office, 1946). Hiroshima and Nagasaki had military facilities, but these were dwarfed by their civilian population. Moreover, the bomb target at Hiroshima was the center of the city, where civilian and military populations were intermingled, not a specific military facility. See Ibid. See also *Danger and Survival*, 77–81.

70. Five factories on Hiroshima's outskirts were responsible for half the city's industrial output. Only one suffered more than "superficial damage," and the Army estimated that within a month, 75 percent of Hiroshima's industry would have resumed normal operations. Strategic Bombing Survey, *Effects of the Atomic Bombs*, 8. The immediate death toll in Hiroshima was increased because the severely wounded could not be treated. Most doctors were dead or disabled. "Of 1,780 nurses, 1,654 were dead or too badly hurt to work." In the largest remaining hospital, "only six doctors out of thirty were able to work, and only ten nurses out of more than two hundred." Later, radiation caused many more deaths, plus damaged lives. John Hersey, *Hiroshima* (Vintage Books, 1985), 24. Nagasaki added around 50,000 deaths.

71. But see Tsuyoshi Hasegawa, *Racing the Enemy: Stalin, Truman, and the Surrender of Japan* (Belknap Press, 2006) (arguing the Japanese surrendered because the Soviet Union had entered the war, ending Japanese hopes the USSR might mediate a softer peace with the United States). See also Gareth Cook, "The Deterrent That Wasn't," *Boston Globe*, August 7, 2011, K1.

72. Curtis E. LeMay with MacKinley Kastor, *Mission with LeMay* (Doubleday, 1965), 387. See Max Hastings, *Retribution: The Battle for Japan, 1944–45* (Vintage Books, 2009), 318.

73. For example, on the night of March 9, 1945, LeMay sent scores of B-29 bombers to firebomb Tokyo, killing 100,000 people and leaving a million homeless. For additional information on the destruction of Tokyo, SEE WEBSITE.

74. Harry S. Truman, *Year of Decisions*, vol. 1 of *Memoirs of Harry S. Truman* (Doubleday, 1955), 10, 11, 87. For Truman's approving the targets, see ibid., 418–21. After the second bomb was dropped on Nagasaki on August 9, just before the Japanese surrendered, the president "was inserting himself back into the chain of command" if any more bombs were to be used. Norris, *Racing for the Bomb*, 424 (discussing General Marshall's response to Groves's memo describing "an improved timetable for the next bomb" by replying "it is not to be released over Japan without express

authority from the President," thus revoking Groves's previous authority to drop bombs "as made ready").

75. Harry S. Truman handwritten diary entry, July 25, 1945, in *Documentary History of the Truman Presidency*, 155–56. For additional information on changing American views on killing civilians, SEE WEBSITE.

76. Ibid. In his subsequent autobiography, Truman moderated his diary rhetoric and said simply that the targets had been "approved as proper for military purposes." Truman, *Year of Decisions*, 420.

77. *Danger and Survival*, 79–80; David McCullough, *Truman* (Simon & Schuster, 2002), 537. Hastings is starker: "impossible to interpret this passage as anything but a self-conscious attempt by Truman to create a record which would serve his reputation in the eyes of history." Hastings, *Retribution*, 469.

78. Groves, *Now It Can Be Told*, 265.

79. Ibid., 267.

80. Norris, *Racing for the Bomb*, 256.

81. Leslie Groves, speech to the Washington Club, November 5, 1946, excerpted in Norris, *Racing for the Bomb*, 659n80.

82. Stimson, "The Decision to Use the Atomic Bomb," 100–101.

4: Building Power Through Secrecy:
J. Edgar Hoover and Dick Cheney

1. James Madison, *Federalist No. 51*, 322.

2. *Iran-Contra Minority Report*, 465 (emphasis added). This acceptance of standards of seventeenth-century British monarchs remained hidden in plain sight in Cheney's 202-page dissent until it was featured on page 1 of *Unchecked and Unbalanced*. Other portions of the *Iran-Contra Minority Report* were contemporaneously excerpted in newspapers. See, e.g., "Reports of the Iran-Contra Committees: Excerpts from the Minority View," *NYT*, November 17, 1987, A6; Gary Thatcher, "Minority Report Takes Strong Issue," *Christian Science Monitor*, November 19, 1987, 36. "Excerpts from Minority Report: 'Mistakes . . . and Nothing More,'" *WPost*, November 19, 1987, 31.

3. See *Unchecked and Unbalanced*, 65–199.

4. For biographical material on J. Edgar Hoover, see Richard Gid Powers, *Secrecy and Power: The Life of J. Edgar Hoover* (Free Press, 1987); Curt Gentry, *J. Edgar Hoover: The Man and the Secrets* (W.W. Norton, 1991); David J. Garrow, *The FBI and Martin Luther King, Jr.: From Solo to Memphis* (W.W. Norton, 1981). Hoover plays a recurring role in Taylor Branch's *America in the King Years* trilogy: *Parting the Waters: America in the King Years 1954–63* (Simon & Schuster, 1988); *Pillar of Fire: America in the King Years 1963–65* (Simon & Schuster, 1999); and *At Canaan's Edge: America in the King Years 1965–68* (Simon & Schuster, 2006). See also *Church Comm. Bk. II*, passim; *Bk. III*, 79–184; *FBI Hearings*, passim; *Unchecked and Unbalanced*, 26–49.

5. David Halberstam, *The Fifties* (Random House, 1993), 341.

6. William Preston, *Aliens and Dissenters: Federal Suppression of Radicals, 1903–1933*, 2nd ed. (University of Illinois Press, 1994), 221. For the Palmer Raids generally, see *Church Comm. Bk. III*, 382–88; and R.G. Brown et al., *To the American People: Report Upon the Illegal Practices of the United States Department of Justice* (National Popular Government League, 1920). For additional information on the league, SEE WEBSITE.

7. See *Church Comm. Bk. III*, 389 (citing Donald O. Johnson, *The Challenge to American Freedoms: World War I and the Rise of the American Civil Liberties Union* [University of Kentucky Press, 1963], 174–75).

8. Preston, *Aliens and Dissenters*, 219, 224–25. See *Church Comm. Bk. III*, 384; Brown et al., *To the American People*, (citing memoranda from Hoover to Antony Caminetti, January 22, 1920; February 2, 1920; and April 6, 1920). Hoover continued to spy on the ACLU, even while currying Baldwin's favor. See "'They Never Stopped Watching Us': A Conversation Between Roger Baldwin and Alan F. Westin," *Civil Liberties Review* 4 (November/December 1977): 25.

9. *Church Comm. FBI Hearings* (quoting Attorney General Stone to Hoover, memorandum, excerpted in "An Analysis of FBI Domestic Security Intelligence Investigations: Authority, Official Attitudes, and Activities in Historic Perspective," October 28, 1975, 6). For more on Stone's standard, see *Church Comm. Bk. II*, 3, 20, 23–24, 35, 165–66, 169, 172, 318; *Church Comm. Bk. III*, 388–89, 395–96.

10. *Church Comm. Bk. III*, 391 (quoting Hoover to Attorney General William DeWitt Mitchell, January 2, 1932). For additional information on Hoover's public statements versus secret acts, SEE WEBSITE.

11. See generally Hoover biographical material; Christopher Lydon, "J. Edgar Hoover Made the F.B.I. Formidable with Politics, Publicity and Results," *NYT*, May 3, 1972, 52.

12. Lydon, "J. Edgar Hoover Made the F.B.I. Formidable." See Powers, *Secrecy and Power*, 196–214; Curt Gentry, *J. Edgar Hoover: The Man and His Secrets*, 218.

13. This was one of the first documents discovered by the activists who, in 1971, broke into and stole documents from the FBI office in Media, Pennsylvania. See Betty Medsger, "Stolen Documents Describe FBI Surveillance Activities," *WPost*, March 24, 1971, A1.

14. Robert H. Jackson, *The Supreme Court in the American System of Government* (Harper & Row, 1963), 71. See also *Church Comm. Bk. III*, 412. Similarly, Representative Hale Boggs warned, "Our society . . . cannot survive a planned and programmed fear of its own Government bureaus and agencies." Boggs also expressed concern that "[o]ur apathy in this Congress, our silence in this House, and our very fear of speaking out in other forums has watered the roots and hastened the growth of a vine of tyranny which is ensnaring that Constitution and Bill of Rights which we are each sworn to defend and uphold." 117 Cong. Rec. 11562 (1971) (statement of Rep. Hale Boggs [D-LA.] on J. Edgar Hoover).

15. See *Church Comm. Bk. III*, 225–40, 274–75. *Church Comm. FBI Hearings*, 158–65 (statement of John Elliff). For examples of Hoover's gossip peddling, see Exhibit 35 in *Church Comm. FBI Hearings*, 455–69.

16. Alexander Charns and Paul M. Green, "Playing the Information Game: How It Took Thirteen Years and Two Lawsuits to Get J. Edgar Hoover's Secret Supreme Court Sex Files," in *A Culture of Secrecy: The Government Versus the People's Right to Know*, ed. Athan G. Theoharis (University Press of Kansas, 1998), 103.

17. See Charns and Green, "Playing the Information Game," 97–114.

18. Ibid., 105n32 (citing DeLoach to Hoover, July 24, 1967, Hoover's O&C Files, folder 71).

19. The Church Committee discovered the letter in FBI files during investigation of plots to assassinate Fidel Castro. For the letter and volume of calls between the White House and Campbell, see *Church Comm. Assassinations*, 129–30. The president's secretary, Evelyn Lincoln, said she would have shown the president the letter. The committee—correctly, in the view of the author, who took her testimony—concluded Campbell did not serve as a liaison between the Chicago Mafia boss and the president on the Castro plots. Indeed, the committee concluded she knew nothing about it.

20. Gentry, *J. Edgar Hoover*, 487.

21. *Church Comm. Assassinations*, 130.

22. For that information, SEE WEBSITE.

23. *Church Comm. Bk. II*, 158–59, 272–73. See Garrow, *FBI and Martin Luther King, Jr.*, 78–80. Garrow's book is an in-depth discussion of Hoover's obsession with King. For more on Hoover, King, and Kennedy, see Branch, *Parting the Waters*, 853–58, 906–14 and *Pillar of Fire*, 154–54, 160–61; Powers, *Secrecy and Power*, 370–73; Gentry, *J. Edgar Hoover*, 501–3, 527–29.

24. See *Church Comm. Bk. III*, 95 (quoting Hoover to Kennedy, January 8, 1962); Garrow, *FBI and Martin Luther King, Jr.*, 26.

25. J. Edgar Hoover to Attorney General Robert F. Kennedy, April 13, 1962, in *FBI Vault*, "Stanley Levison: Part 9" (emphasis added), available at vault.fbi.gov/Stanley%20Levison/Stanley%20Levison%20 Part%2009%20of%20109/view.

26. Garrow, *FBI and Martin Luther King, Jr.*, 61.

27. Branch, *Parting the Waters*, 852.

28. By the 1960s, if not earlier, a substantial number of Party "members" were affiliated with the FBI. Powers, *Secrecy and Power*, 340. See also Garrow, *FBI and Martin Luther King, Jr.*, 41, citing internal New York office memo, July 25, 1956, 100-111180-679, for Levison's lack of Communist Party activity.

29. Garrow, *FBI and Martin Luther King, Jr.* 42–43; J. Edgar Hoover to SAC New York, March 22, 1957, in *FBI Vault*, "Stanley Levison: Part 8," available at vault.fbi.gov/Stanley%20Levison/Stanley%20Levison%20Part%2008%20of%20109/view; memoranda between Hoover and SAC New York from November 1959 to February 1960, in ibid.

30. Branch, *Parting the Waters*, 697 (citing *NY Report to Hoover*, February 21, 1963 (FL-189). As a last-ditch effort, Hoover instructed agents to interview Louis Budenz, a former top editor at the *Daily Worker* who broke with the Party in the mid-1940s. He did not know Stanley Levison. Ibid.

31. Ibid., 46 (citing Hoover to Attorney General Kennedy, memorandum, March 6, 1962 (returned several days later with the attorney general's signature).

32. *Church Comm. Bk. III*, 111–12.

33. See ibid., 81–86, 161. The FBI offered to play the tapes from bugging King's hotel rooms for reporters. They did not bite. Ibid.

34. See Clarence Jones, *Behind the Dream: The Making of the Speech that Transformed a Nation* (Palgrave Macmillan, 2011). For additional information, SEE WEBSITE.

35. Before King's June 22, 1963, meeting with President Kennedy, Assistant Attorney General Burke Marshall told King that, according to the FBI, Stanley Levison and Jack O'Dell were Communists. Kennedy told King to get rid of both, but King wanted proof, especially as to Levison. Branch, *Parting the Waters*, 835–38. O'Dell had been on the administration's radar for past affiliation with Communism, including work organizing for the National Maritime Union, attendance at party meetings in Louisiana, and writing an article in a party publication. Ibid., 675. King ultimately fired O'Dell. Arthur M. Schlesinger Jr. *Robert Kennedy and His Times* (Houghton Mifflin, 2002), 358. Proof on Levison, however, never came, and he continued to work with King. When called before the Senate Subcommittee on Internal Security (the Eastland Committee), Levison testified, "To dispose of a question causing current apprehension, I am a loyal American and I am not now and never have been a member of the Communist Party." Levison invoked his Fifth Amendment privilege against self-incrimination on the rest of the subcommittee's questions, which inquired about whether Levison was a spy or had gotten funds from the Soviet Union to fund the Communist Party USA. Ibid., 354–58. No evidence showed Levison's association with communism after he became King's advisor.

36. Garrow, *FBI and Martin Luther King, Jr.*, 61.

37. *Church Comm. Bk. II* (describing campaign to undermine King); *Church Comm. Bk. III*, 133–46 (detailing the same).

38. William Sullivan to Alan Belmont, September 25, 1963, Exhibit 11 in *Report of the Department of Justice Task Force to Review the FBI Martin Luther King, Jr., Security and Assassination Investigations* (January 11, 1977); Alan Belmont to William Sullivan, August 30, 1963, Exhibit 8 in ibid.: *Church Comm. Bk. III*, 83, 180.

39. *Church Comm. Bk. II*, 11–12 (citing FBI Headquarters to all SACs, Memorandum, March 4, 1968). Actually, King was introduced to nonviolence through conversations with an advisor King would have called a Negro: Bayard Rustin, who led King to the writings of an Indian, Gandhi.

40. *Church Comm. Bk. II*, 11, 220–21; *Church Comm. Bk. III*, 158–60. For additional support for the induce-suicide interpretation, SEE WEBSITE.

41. See *Church Comm. Bk. II*, 7–8, 179–80; *Church Comm. Bk. III*, 412–22. While, during Roosevelt's administration, few investigations were based on the "subversion standard," an early example was secret infiltration of informers into the NAACP. Acting at the Navy's request after protests against racial discrimination by "fifteen colored mess attendants," the FBI opened an investigation. *Church Co. BK. III*, 416 (quoting *Report of Washington, D.C., Office*, March 11, 1941). The FBI was told NAACP Director-Counsel Thurgood Marshall was "a loyal American," who "would not permit anything radical to be done." Ibid. (quoting *Report of Savannah, Georgia, Field Office*, October 29, 1943). But the investigation lasted for more than twenty-five years despite never finding any evidence of illegality. See generally Patricia Sullivan, *Lift Every Voice: The NAACP and the Making of the Civil Rights Movement* (New Press, 2009).

42. *Church Comm. Bk. II*, 233n40 (citing Dillon Anderson to Maxwell Rabb, Memorandum January 16, 1956). Ibid., 250, n151a (citing J.W. Anderson, *Eisenhower, Brownell, and the Congress: The Tangled Origins of the Civil Rights Bill of 1956–57* [University of Alabama Press, 1964], 34).

43. *Church Comm. Bk. II*, 150 (citing *Hearings before House Appropriations Subcommittee*, 88th Cong., 2d sess. [1964], 309) (emphasis added).

44. Ibid., 251 (citing Hoover to FBI officials, Memorandum, April 28, 1965).

45. Seth Rosenfeld, *Subversives: The FBI's War on Student Radicals and Reagan's Rise to Power* (Farrar, Straus and Giroux, 2012), 230.

46. Ibid., 240–41.

47. Rosenfeld v. U.S. Dep't of Justice, 761 F. Supp. 1440 (N.D. Cal. 1991), *aff'd in part, rev'd in part*, 57 F.3d 803 (9th Cir. 1995).

48. *Church Comm. Bk. II*, 65–95 (COINTELPRO generally); *Church Co. Bk. III*, 176 (the same). See also Tim Weiner, *Enemies: A History of the FBI* (Random House, 2012), Gentry, *J. Edgar Hoover*; Ciara Carolyn Torres, "The Construction of Probable Cause: An Analysis of the Congressional Testimony of J. Edgar Hoover 1959–1972," (BA thesis, Harvard University, 1997) (on file with author).

49. But SEE WEBSITE.

50. See *Church Comm. Bk. II*, 211–24; *Church Comm. Bk. III*, 1–78.

51. Ibid. See generally Rosenfeld, *Subversives*, and Robert Cohen and Reginald E. Zelnik, eds., *The Free Speech Movement: Reflections on Berkeley in the 1960s* (University of California Press, 2002).

52. *Church Comm. Bk. II*, 213.

53. *Church Comm. Bk. III*, 7–8, 16–27, 188, passim; *Church Comm. Bk. II*, 216–19.

54. *Church Comm. Bk. II*, 271–72n20 (quoting Chicago Field Office to FBI headquarters, Memorandum January 18, 1969).

55. *Church Comm. Bk. II*, 218 (quoting San Diego Field Office to FBI headquarters, Memorandum, September 15, 1969).

56. *Church Comm. Bk. II*, 156 (quoting the *FBI Manual of Rules and Regulations* for "embarrass the Bureau").

57. Weiner, *Enemies*, 267–68; William C. Sullivan to Cartha B. DeLoach "Re: Black Bag Jobs," July 16, 1966, in *Church Comm. FBI Hearings*, 359.

58. See *Huston Plan: Hearings Before the S. Select Comm. to Study Governmental Operations with Respect to Intelligence Activities*, 94th Cong. (1975). See also J. Edgar Hoover, "Special Report, Interagency Committee on Intelligence (Ad Hoc)," (1970) (the *Huston Report*); *Church Comm. Bk. III*, 921–82; Loch K. Johnson, *A Season of Inquiry: The Senate Intelligence Investigation* (University Press of Kentucky, 1985), 78–88.

59. Gentry, *J. Edgar Hoover*, 560–61; Weiner, *Enemies*, 291. President Johnson exempted the FBI director from mandatory retirement for an "indefinite period of time," putting Hoover on a short leash that could theoretically be "yanked any time he damn well pleased." Gentry, *J. Edgar Hoover*, 561. Since President Nixon gave only oral approval to the Huston Plan, the program would have had to be carried out on Hoover's own authority. *Church Comm. Bk. III*, 932 (citing staff summary of Louis Tordella [deputy director of the NSA] interview, 6/16/75).

60. See Barton Gellman, *Angler: The Cheney Vice Presidency* (Penguin, 2008); Dick Cheney, *In My Time: A Personal and Political Memoir* (Simon & Schuster, 2011); Peter Baker, *Days of Fire: Bush and Cheney in the White House* (Doubleday, 2013); Ron Suskind, *The One Percent Doctrine: Deep Inside America's Pursuit of its Enemies Since 9/11* (Simon & Schuster, 2006); Jane Mayer, *The Dark Side: The Inside Story of How the War on Terror Turned into a War on American Ideals* (Doubleday, 2008).

61. Charles Mohr, "New Chief Assistant: Richard Bruce Cheney," *NYT*, November 5, 1975, 20.

62. Lou Cannon, "Stepping Out of Rumsfeld's Shadow," *WPost*, November 6, 1975, 3.

63. *The Ford White House: A Miller Center Conference Chaired by Herbert J. Storing* (University Press of America, 1986), 91.

64. Gellman, *Angler*, 86 (citing Notes, "11/19 Cheney," James A. Baker III Papers, Seely G. Mudd Manuscript Library, Princeton University, Series 6H, box 66, folder 9).

65. Terry Sullivan, ed., *The Nerve Center: Lessons in Governing from the White House Chiefs of Staff* (Texas A&M University Press, 2004), 128–29 (citing "Interview with Richard Cheney," White House 2001 Project, White House Interview Program, Martha J. Kumar, July 29, 1999, Dallas, TX.).

66. Leslie H. Gelb, "Ford's Timetable Upset in Shakeup," *NYT*, November 4, 1975, 1.

67. Seymour M. Hersh, "Submarines of U.S. Stage Spy Missions Inside Soviet Waters," *NYT*, May 25, 1975, 1: Kathryn S. Olmstead, *Challenging the Secret Government: The Post-Watergate Investigations of the CIA and FBI* (University of North Carolina Press, 1996), 75–76.

68. Cheney's recommendations are contained in handwritten notes. See "What

Does the Law Say?," *Frontline*, February 13, 2007. Cheney also added a "do nothing" option. Ibid. The notes are at the Ford Presidential Library.

69. "What Does the Law Say?"

70. Bob Woodward, "Cheney Upholds Power of the Presidency," *WPost*, January 20, 2005, A7.

71. Barton Gellman and Jo Becker, "'A Different Understanding with the President,'" *WPost*, June 24, 2007, A1.

72. James Carney, "7 Clues to Understanding Dick Cheney," *Time*, December 30, 2002, 104.

73. *Joint Hearings Before the H. Select Comm. to Investigate Covert Arms Transactions with Iran and the S. Select Comm. on Secret Military Assistance to Iran and the Nicaraguan Opposition*, 100th Cong. 38–40 (1987) (testimony of John M. Poindexter). See *Iran-Contra Report*, 271–72.

74. *Iran-Contra Report*, 9–10, 305–21; *Iran-Contra Minority Report*, 448, 563–65, 643–47.

75. Helen Dewar and Edward Walsh, "Hill Sees Policy in 'Disarray'; Members of Both Parties Express Shock, Plan Probes," *WPost*, November 6, 1986, A1.

76. David S. Broder, "Secrecy Trips a President; Iran-Contras Imbroglio May Be Long-Term Trouble," *WPost*, November 26, 1986, A1.

77. See *Iran-Contra Report*, xv–xvi.

78. Mary McCorry, "Hill to Reagan: All Is Forgiven," *WPost*, August 4, 1987, A2.

79. *Iran-Contra Minority Report*, 449; *Iran-Contra Report*, 17, 142.

80. See, e.g., Philip Shenon, "G.O.P. Iran Report Defends President," *NYT*, November 17, 1987, A1; Gary Thatcher, "Minority Report Takes Strong Issue," *Christian Science Monitor*, November 19, 1987, 36.

81. *Iran-Contra Minority Report*, 557.

82. Ibid., 526.

83. Ibid., 525 (citing then CIA deputy director Robert M. Gates, "The CIA and the Making of American Foreign Policy," speech delivered at Princeton University, September 29, 1987, 23). Gates also wrote that intelligence information can be "highly misleading" because of intelligence officials' "personal agendas or biases," or because policy makers may "selectively use or misstate intelligence to influence public debate." Robert M. Gates, "The CIA and Foreign Policy," *Foreign Affairs* 66 (Winter 1987–88): 219.

84. *Iran-Contra Minority Report*, 536.

85. Ibid., 450.

86. Ibid., 444, 515.

87. Ibid., 445, 515.

88. Ibid., 532 (emphasis added).

89. Ibid., 515 (emphasis added). In addition to none of these earlier statements by Cheney ever being used to contrast with his conduct as vice president, this statement and the one covered by the next endnote were the only portions of what the

text highlights from the *Iran-Contra Minority Report* covered contemporaneously. See Thatcher, "Minority Report Takes Strong Issue."

90. Ibid., 444, 515.

91. Bob Woodward, "Cheney Upholds Power of the Presidency," *WPost*, January 20, 2005, 7.

92. Dick Cheney, "Vice President's Remarks to the Traveling Press," December 20, 2005. Cheney said the report was "authored by a guy working for me, for my staff." Ibid. See Sean Wilentz, "Mr. Cheney's Minority Report," op-ed, *NYT*, July 9, 2007, A17; Michael J. Malbin, "The Iran-Contra Minority Redux: Executive Power Disputes Resurface," *Weekly Standard*, July 16, 2007.

93. Gellman, *Angler*, 82–90. George W. Bush, "A Comprehensive National Energy Policy," speech in Saginaw, Michigan, September 29, 2000, in *In Their Own Words: Sourcebook for the 2000 Presidential Election* (Political Communication Lab, Stanford University, 2000) chap. 2. See also Eric Pianin and Amy Goldstein, "Bush Drops a Call for Emissions Cuts," *WPost*, March 14, 2001, A1; "Text of a Letter from the President to Senators Hagel, Helms, Craig, and Roberts," March 13, 2001.

94. Gellman, *Angler*, 292–326.

95. Thomas M. DeFrank, *Write It When I'm Gone: Remarkable Off-the-Record Conversations with Gerald R. Ford* (Penguin, 2007), 92.

96. Jeffrey Goldberg, "Breaking Ranks: What Turned Brent Scowcroft Against the Bush Administration?," *New Yorker*, October 31, 2005, 54.

97. Bob Woodward, "Ford Disagreed with Bush About Invading Iraq," *WPost*, December 28, 2006, 1.

98. *Joint Hearings Before the H. Select Committee to Investigate Covert Arms Transactions with Iran and the S. Select Committee on Secret Military Assistance to Iran and the Nicaraguan Opposition*, 100th Cong. 264 (1987) (closing remarks, Rep. Dick Cheney).

99. Simon Schama, *Citizens: A Chronicle of the French Revolution* (Alfred A. Knopf, 1989), xiii.

5: Six Secrecy Stories: From Slavery to Science

1. See Gary B. Nash, "Introduction," in Benjamin Quarles, *The Negro in the American Revolution* (University of North Carolina Press, 1996), xiii–xxvi (referring to the "thin" record and "gaping lacunae" in histories by noted white historians writing before the 1930s). For additional scholarship, SEE WEBSITE.

2. See Quarles, *Negro in the American Revolution*, 94–95 (referencing Lafayette's praise for the slave, dated November 21, 1784). For additional scholarship, SEE WEBSITE.

3. Nash, "Introduction," xix. After defeat, the British honored their commitment by moving thousands of American Blacks to Nova Scotia and elsewhere. See Simon Schama, *Rough Crossings: Britain, the Slaves and the American Revolution* (HarperCollins, 2006); Quarles, *The Negro in the American Revolution*, 177–81.

4. See U.S. Constitution Art. I, sec. 2, cl. 3 (providing for apportionment of seats in the House and for direct taxes, "three fifths of all *other Persons*" in a state shall be added to "the whole Number of free Persons, including those bound to Service for a Term of Years, but excluding Indians not taxed"); U.S. Constitution Art. I, sec. 9, cl. 1 (providing importation of *"such Persons"* that an existing state shall think proper shall not be prohibited by Congress prior to 1808); U.S. Constitution Art. IV, sec. 2, cl. 3 (providing "No *Person* held to Service or Labour" in one state shall be discharged from service by "escaping" to another state, but shall rather be "delivered up" to "the Party to whom such Service or Labour may be due"). For additional scholarship, SEE WEBSITE.

5. Abraham Lincoln, "Speech at Peoria, Illinois," October 16, 1854, in *Collected Works of Abraham Lincoln*, 274. Lincoln claimed the Constitution also contained the "promise, nevertheless, that the cutting may begin at the end of a given time"— presumably a rather bold reading of the Importation Clause. For a scathing analysis of how slavery affected the Constitutional Convention, see Paul Finkelman, *Slavery and the Founders: Race and Liberty in the Age of Jefferson* (M.E. Sharpe, 1996), 1–33 (Chapter 1: "Making a Covenant with Death: Slavery and the Constitutional Convention"). "Covenant with Death" was William Lloyd Garrison's phrase. Garrison's doubts about the Constitution solidified to scorn after Madison's Convention notes were released from secrecy in 1837. Ibid., 1.

6. Benjamin Franklin, Memorial from the Pennsylvania Society for Promoting the Abolition of Slavery, February 3, 1790, in *Annals of Cong.*, vol. 1, 1239–40. See Richard S. Newman, "Prelude to the Gag Rule: Southern Reaction to Antislavery Petitions in the First Federal Congress," *Journal of the Early Republic*, 16, no. 4 (1996): 571–99. For the broader context, see Joseph J. Ellis, *Founding Brothers: The Revolutionary Generation* (Random House, 2000), 81–119.

7. "Report of the Committee of the Whole House," *Annals of Cong.*, vol. 2, 1524.

8. See Ellis, *Founding Brothers*, 102.

9. Samuel Johnson, *The Works of Samuel Johnson*, vol. 10 (J. Buckland et al., 1787), 142.

10. James Madison, "Notes for the *National Gazette* Essays," in *Congressional Series*, ed. Robert A. Rutland et al., vol. 14, *The Papers of James Madison* (University Press of Virginia, 1983), 163.

11. A photocopy of George Washington's will is available through the Fairfax County (VA) Clerk of Court's website web.archive.org/web/20121016131412/http://www.fairfaxcounty.gov/courts/circuit/pdf/george-washington-will.pdf. See "George Washington's Last Will and Testament," July 9, 1799, in *Retirement Series*, ed. W.W. Abbot, vol. 4, *The Papers of George Washington* (University Press of Virginia, 1999), 479–99. For additional scholarship on Washington and slaves, SEE WEBSITE.

12. See An Act for the Gradual Abolition of Slavery, passed March 1, 1780, *Pennsylvania Statutes at Large, 1686–1801*, vol. 10 (1904), 67–73. For use of the word "believed," see n14, infra.

13. See Ron Chernow, *Washington: A Life* (Penguin, 2010), 638.

14. George Washington to Tobias Lear, April 12, 1791, in *Presidential Series*, ed. Mark A. Mastromarino, vol. 8, *The Papers of George Washington* (University Press of Virginia, 1999), 85. See also Edward Lawler Jr., "Washington, the Enslaved and the 1780 Law," President's House in Philadelphia, web.archive.org/web/20131029194637 /http://www.ushistory.org/presidentshouse/slaves/washingtonand8.htm (citing this letter as one of a series of letters on slavery between Lear and Washington). Attorney General Edmund Randolph's slaves had obtained freedom under the Pennsylvania law. He warned Washington through Lear. Washington thought his situation was "somewhat different" because Randolph had become a Pennsylvania citizen so he could practice private law. The law exempted members of Congress, foreign ministers, and consuls from the six-month rule. When the federal government was established by the Constitution, however, the Pennsylvania law was not amended to exempt members of the executive branch.

15. George Washington to the Secretary of the Treasury [Oliver Wolcott Jr.] (Private), September 1, 1796, in *The Writings of George Washington*, ed. John C. Fitzpatrick, vol. 35 (Government Printing Office, 1940), 201–2.

16. See Richard R. John, *Spreading the News: The American Postal Service from Franklin to Morse* (Harvard University Press, 1995), 247–83 (discussing Southern— and the New York City—postmasters and federal postmasters general generally); Clement Eaton, "Censorship of the Southern Mails," *American Historical Review* 48, no. 2 (1943): 266–80. "[I]ncendiary" publications that were banned included not only abolitionist tracts but also Horace Greeley's *New York Tribune*. Ibid., 276.

17. See William Miller, *Arguing About Slavery: The Great Battle in the United States Congress* (Alfred A. Knopf, 1996).

18. See Paul C. Nagel, *John Quincy Adams: A Public Life, A Private Life* (Alfred A. Knopf, 1995) (covering gag rule at 355–56, 364–65, 385 and 402–3).

19. See Carl Sandburg, *Abraham Lincoln: The War Years*, vol. 2 (Harcourt, Brace, 1936), 201 (Stowe's recollection). But see Daniel R. Vollaro, "Lincoln, Stowe, and the 'Little Woman/Great War' Story: The Making, and Breaking, of a Great American Anecdote," *Journal of the Abraham Lincoln Association* 30, no. 1 (Winter 2009): 18–34.

20. Miller, *Arguing About Slavery*, 333. See David S. Reynolds, *Mightier Than the Sword: Uncle Tom's Cabin and the Battle for America* (W.W. Norton, 2011) (covering Stowe's influence on slavery and the coming of the Civil War); Annette Gordon-Reed, "The Persuader: What Harriet Beecher Stowe Wrought," *New Yorker*, June 13, 2011, 120–24.

21. Stowe wrote two other bestselling books exposing even more Americans to slavery's cruelty. See Harriett Beecher Stowe, *The Key to Uncle Tom's Cabin* (John P. Jewett, 1853), which sold 100,000 copies within a year, and *Dred: A Tale of the Great Dismal Swamp* (Phillips, Sampson, 1856). Theatrical plays about Uncle Tom spread its message further. See Reynolds, *Mightier Than the Sword*, 145–47.

22. Written and compiled by the husband-and-wife team of Theodore Weld and Angelina Grimke in 1839, available on the Internet from the University of North Carolina library's Documenting the American South project at web.archive.org /web/20121225074041/http://docsouth.unc.edu/neh/weld/weld.html and reprinted by Ayer Company, Salem, New Hampshire in 1991.

23. Jean Fagan Yellin, "Doing It Herself: *Uncle Tom's Cabin* and Woman's Role in the Slavery Crisis," in *New Essays on Uncle Tom's Cabin*, ed., Eric J. Sundquist (University of Cambridge Press, 1993), 85–105 (citing an unpublished manuscript by Sara Weld discussing "reminisces of her mother, Angelina Grimke Weld," in Gilbert Hobbs Barnes, *The Antislavery Impulse, 1830–44* [Harcourt, Brace, and World, 1964], 231).

24. For the disputed derivation of the expression, SEE WEBSITE.

25. Jacob Riis is best known for *How the Other Half Lives: Studies Among the Tenements of New York* (Charles Scribner's Sons, 1890), which documented in words and photographs the squalid conditions in which New York City's poor lived and worked. See generally Tom Buk-Swienty, *The Other Half: The Life of Jacob Riis and the World of Immigrant America* (W.W. Norton, 2008). Lewis Hine was a photographer for the National Child Labor Committee, and used photography to document harm from child labor, among other things. See Deborah L. Smith-Shank, "Lewis Hine and His Photo Stories: Visual Culture and Social Reform," *Art Education* 56, no. 2 (2003): 33–37; Peter Seixas, "Lewis Hine: From 'Social' to 'Interpretive' Photographer," *American Quarterly* 39, no. 3 (1987): 381–409.

26. See Robert Siegel, "Jacob Riis: Shedding Light on NYC's 'Other Half,'" *NPR*, June 30, 2008, web.archive/org/web/20140329072349://www.npr.org/templates/story /story.php?storyId=91981589; Riis, *How the Other Half Lives*. And see National Archives and Records Administration, "Portfolio: Lewis Hine," *Preserving the Century: One Hundred Years of Photography from the National Archives*, web.archive.org /web/20111025065303/http://www.archives.gov/exhibits/picturing_the_century /text/port_hine_text.html.

27. "They Fight a Fire That Won't Go Out: The Spectacle of Racial Turbulence in Birmingham" *LIFE*, May 17, 1963, 22–24, 29–36. See Michael S. Durham, *Powerful Days: The Civil Rights Photography of Charles Moore* (University of Alabama Press, 1991), 23–30, 90–119.

28. Arthur M. Schlesinger Jr. *The Cycles of American History* (Houghton Mifflin, 1986), 410. See also David Margolick, "Through a Lens, Darkly," *Vanity Fair*, September 24, 2007.

29. Mark Mazzetti, "U.S. Says the CIA Destroyed 92 Tapes of Interrogations," *NYT*, March 3, 2009, A16.

30. See Susan D. Moeller, *Shooting War: Photography and the American Experience of Combat* (Basic Books, 1989) (comprehensive treatment of wartime photography, covering Vietnam at 325–413). See also Bernd Huppauf, "The Emergence of Modern War Imagery in Early Photography," *History and Memory* 5, no. 1 (1993): 130–51.

31. *News Policies in Vietnam: Hearings Before the S. Comm. on Foreign Relations*, 89th Cong. 89 (1966) (statement of Sen. Gale W. McGee). McGee preceded "spill the blood" by saying Americans were "deeply troubled" by Vietnam, as "the first war they have ever fought themselves in the living room." After McGee, the witness, Arthur Sylvester, assistant secretary of defense for public affairs, said, "Right." For people's pockets, see David Carr, "War Horror at Your Fingertips, Fast and Straight from the Gut," *NYT*, July 28, 2014, A1.

32. See Moeller, *Shooting War*, 366–67 (providing eleven examples of Vietnam War photos). For additional details on the photos, SEE WEBSITE.

33. As Shana Alexander wrote in critiquing "outraged letters deploring the display of horror for its own sake," "if we had been able to print early pictures of the Nazi destruction of the Jews, millions might have been saved." Shana Alexander, "The Feminine Eye: What Is the Truth of the Picture?," *LIFE*, March 1, 1968, 19. For comments on the failures of print journalism, SEE WEBSITE.

34. See Paul G. Cassell, "Restrictions of Press Coverage of Military Operations: The Right of Access, Grenada, and 'Off-the-Record Wars,'" *Georgetown Law Journal* 73 (1984): 943; Phil Gailey, "U.S. Bars Coverage of Grenada Action: News Groups Protest," *NYT*, October 27, 1983, A1; Robert Hanley, "U.S. Defends Warning About Grenada Radios," *NYT*, October 28, 1983, A13; William E. Farrell, "U.S. Allows 15 Reporters to Go to Grenada for Day," *NYT*, October 18, 1983, A13.

35. Office of the Secretary of Defense Crisis Coordination Center, "Public Affairs Guidance—Operation Desert Storm Casualty and Mortuary Affairs," February 6, 1991.

36. Department of Defense, "Instruction Number 1300.18: Department of Defense (DoD) Personnel Casualty Matters, Policies, and Procedures," January 8, 2008, updated to incorporate Change 1, August 14, 2009). See Elisabeth Bumiller, "Defense Chief Lifts Ban on Pictures of Coffins," *NYT*, February 27, 2009, A-13; Robert M. Gates, *Duty: Memoirs of a Secretary at War* (Alfred A. Knopf, 2014), 306–8.

37. The case centered on the Army withholding twenty-one photographs of detainee abuse in Afghanistan that had been referenced in Army investigations. For additional information, SEE WEBSITE.

38. Protected National Security Documents Act of 2009, Pub. L. 111-83, 123 Stat. 2142 (2009), codified at 5 U.S.C. § 552 note (2012) (allowing secretary of defense to withhold records based on secretary's certification disclosure would "endanger" U.S. citizens, Armed Forces, or government employees outside the United States). The act only covers photographs or videos taken on or between September 11, 2001, and January 22, 2009, that "relate[] to the treatment of individuals engaged, captured, or detained after September 11, 2001, by the Armed Forces of the United States in operations outside of the United States." §§ (B) (1)-(2).

39. Petition for a Writ of Certiorari 12, Department of Defense v. American Civil Liberties Union, 558 U.S. 1042 (2009).

40. Jeff Zeleny and Thom Shanker, "Obama Reversal on Abuse Photos," *NYT*, May 14, 2009, A1.

41. Barack Obama, interview by Steve Kroft, *60 Minutes*, CBS News, May 15, 2011, transcript available at web.archive.org/web/20140213083905/http://www.cbsnews.com/news/obama-on-bin-laden-the-full-60-minutes-interview.

42. Ibid.

43. Ibid.

44. Johnson revealed his scar to journalists in 1965 outside the hospital where the surgery occurred. See Charles Tasnadi, "Johnson Surgery Scar," October 20, 1965, EBSCO, AP Images Collection, Image ID no. 651020015.

45. By the time he was president, Washington had only one tooth left. Washington's letters from the capital in Philadelphia to his dentist in New York were sent by messenger, not entrusted to the mail, and even then referenced his dental problems only indirectly. Chernow, *Washington*, 642–43.

46. See generally John D. Feerick, *From Failing Hands: The Story of Presidential Succession* (Fordham University Press, 1965) (describing the history and debate on presidential succession before the Twenty-Fifth Amendment).

47. Amendment 25, sec. 4, first para. For additional information, SEE WEBSITE.

48. See Ira Rutkow, *James A. Garfield* (Times Books, 2006) 115–39; Candice Millard, *Destiny of the Republic: A Tale of Madness, Medicine and the Murder of a President* (Anchor, 2012).

49. Matthew Algeo, *The President Is a Sick Man: Wherein the Supposedly Virtuous Grover Cleveland Survives a Secret Surgery at Sea and Vilifies the Courageous Newspaperman Who Dared Expose the Truth* (Chicago Review Press, 2011), 110–11. See Leonard Schlup, "Presidential Disability: The Case of Cleveland and Stevenson," *Presidential Studies Quarterly* 9, no. 3 (1979): 303–10.

50. Algeo, *The President Is a Sick Man*, 150 (describing the operation, secrecy, exposure, and denial); W.W. Keen, "The Surgical Operations on President Cleveland in 1893," *Saturday Evening Post*, September 22, 1917, 24, 55 (Cleveland's surgeon confessing concealment). See Feerick, *From Failing Hands*, 149–51.

51. Siddhartha Mukherjee, *The Emperor of All Maladies: A Biography of Cancer* (Scribner, 2010), 26.

52. Jimmie C. Holland and Sheldon Lewis, *The Human Side of Cancer: Living with Hope, Coping with Uncertainty* (Harper, 2000), 8–9.

53. Joseph P. Tumulty, *Woodrow Wilson As I Know Him* (Doubleday, Page, 1921), 435.

54. See John Milton Cooper Jr., *Woodrow Wilson: A Biography* (Alfred A. Knopf, 2000), 535–42. Edith Wilson insisted on keeping details about Wilson's condition hidden by allowing only general statements about the president's health. The White House physician, Adm. Cary T. Grayson, denied the president's condition was grave. Ibid., 536–42.

55. Edith Bolling Wilson, *My Memoir* (Bobbs-Merrill, 1938), 289–90.

56. Jean Edward Smith, *FDR* (Random House, 2007), 603–5.

57. "Whispering Drive Seen by Hannegan," *NYT*, October 14, 1944, 8 (quoting Roosevelt's personal physician, Vice Admiral Ross T. McIntire).

58. Robert Dallek, "The Medical Ordeals of JFK," *The Atlantic*, December 2002, 50.

59. See ibid., 49–61. See generally Robert Dallek, *An Unfinished Life: John F. Kennedy, 1917–1963* (Little, Brown, 2003).

60. Jeffrey Kelman, MD, interview by Ray Suarez, *NewsHour*, PBS, November 18, 2002, transcript available at web.archive.org/web/20140522201323/www.pbs.org /newshour/bb/health-july-dec02-jfk_11-18.

61. See Dallek, *Unfinished Life*, 260–63. See also Robert A. Caro, *The Years of Lyndon Johnson: The Passage of Power* (Alfred A. Knopf, 2012), 42–43 (providing a glimpse of JFK's bravery in facing his health problems).

62. Lawrence K. Altman, "Hasty and Ruinous 1972 Pick Colors Today's Hunt for a No. 2," *NYT*, July 24, 2012, A1; Douglas E. Kneeland, "Behind Eagleton's Withdrawal: A Tale of Confusion and Division," *NYT*, August 2, 1972, 1.

63. Lawrence K. Altman, interview by author, November 7, 2012.

64. See Lawrence K. Altman, "Many Holes in Disclosure of Nominees' Health," *NYT*, October 20, 2008, A1. Both 2008 presidential candidates disclosed information about their medical history, but McCain's records contained "inconsistencies in medical opinions about the severity of his melanoma," and Barack Obama released only a one-page letter from his physician, noting he was in good health.

65. Advertisement, *NYT*, October 3, 2008, A7.

66. See Curt Gentry, *J. Edgar Hoover: The Man and the Secrets* (W.W. Norton, 1991), 467–71, 485–94 (describing FBI knowledge re: Kennedy liaisons and claiming disclosure could have cost him reelection).

67. Raymond Hernandez, "In Chaotic Scene, Weiner Quits Seat in Scandal's Wake," *NYT*, June 17, 2011, A1. Two years later, Weiner joined the NYC mayoral race, doing well for a time before being crushed by news of his continuing electronic sexual self-promotion.

68. Raymond Hernandez, "New York Congressman Quits After E-Mail Exchange Is Posted Online," *NYT*, February 10, 2011, A19.

69. Adam Nossiter, "A Senator's Moral High Ground Gets a Little Shaky," *NYT*, July 11, 2007, A11; Adam Nossiter, "Senator Apologizes Again for Prostitution Link," *NYT*, July 17, 2007, A14.

70. U.S. Constitution, Art. I, sec. 9, cl. 7. See generally Louis Fisher, "Presidential Budgetary Duties," *Presidential Quarterly* 42, no. 4 (2012): 755–58.

71. Frank J. Smist Jr., *Congress Oversees the United States Intelligence Community: 1947–1989* (University of Tennessee Press, 1990), 5. The Central Intelligence Agency Act of 1949 establishing administrative and fiscal guidelines for the Agency, and arguably authorizing concealment of CIA fiscal information, was not openly debated by Congress due to its "highly confidential nature." The law was enacted

without members "knowing what all its provisions meant." Tim Wiener, *Blank Check: The Pentagon's Black Budget* (Warner Books, 1990), 118–19.

72. *Farrand's Records*, vol. 2, 618–19 (Madison's notes on dialogue at the Convention).

73. *Elliot's Debates*, vol. 3 (1836), 460.

74. See United States v. Richardson, 418 U.S. 166 (1974). For dissents, SEE WEBSITE.

75. *Richardson*, 418 U.S. at 178n11. All Burger found was that in opposing the "ambiguous expression" "from time to time," Mason conceded "there might be some matters which might require secrecy." Secrecy was "necessary sometimes" as to military operations and foreign negotiations. But Mason also said this did not justify concealing "receipts and expenditures of the public money." *Farrand's Records*, vol. 3, 326 (statement of George Mason). In addition, Burger cited *Farrand's Records*, vol. 2, 618–19 (debating Mason's amendment to require annual accounting but compromising to add "from time to time" instead); and *Elliot's Debates*, vol. 3, 462 (statement of Patrick Henry).

76. U.S. Constitution, Art. I, sec. 5, cl. 3 (emphasis added). The State of the Union Clause says the president "shall from time to time give to the Congress Information on the State of the Union." Art. II, sec. 3. Obviously, no one would claim this means presidents could delay providing information for years—or decades.

77. An Act Providing the Means of Intercourse Between the United States and Foreign Nations, 1 Stat. 128–29 (1790). Congressional actions in the nation's early years are given weight in interpreting the Constitution. See Chief Justice John Marshall in Cohens v. Virginia, 19 U.S. 264, 6 Wheat 264, 418 (1821).

78. Remarks by Edward I. Koch at a conference on government secrecy on May 18–19, 1973, in Albert Gore Sr., "Legislative Secrecy," *None of Your Business: Government Secrecy in America*, ed. Norman Dorsen and Stephen A. Gillers (Penguin, 1974), 147.

79. *Church Comm. Bk. I*, 469. For additional comments by the committee, SEE WEBSITE.

80. 143 Cong. Rec. H4981 (1997) (statement of Professor Robert F. Turner on constitutional implications of authorizing and appropriating funds for intelligence operations without publicly disclosing the aggregate amount of funds). For history, SEE WEBSITE.

81. Tim Weiner, "The Worst-Kept Secret in the Capital," *NYT*, July 21, 1994, B10.

82. Richard A. Best Jr. and Elizabeth B. Bazen, *Intelligence Spending: Public Disclosure Issues* (Congressional Research Service, 2007), 15.

83. Dana Priest and William M. Arkin, "A Hidden World, Growing Beyond Control," *WPost*, July 19, 2010, A1; Priest and Arkin, "National Security, Inc.," *WPost*, July 20, 2010, A1; Priest and Arkin, "The Secrets Next Door," *WPost*, July 21, 2010, A1.

84. Central Intelligence Agency, "DCI [Director of Central Intelligence George

Tenet] Statement on FY97 Intelligence Budget," press statement, October 15, 1997, available at web.archive.org/web/20140401161433/https://www.cia.gov/news information/press-releases-statements/press-release-archive-1997-1/pr101597.html.

85. *9/11 Comm'n Report*, 416. "Availability to Public of Certain Intelligence Funding Information," 50 U.S.C. §415c (2012) (codifying §601 "Implementing Recommendations of the 9/11 Commission Act of 2007," Publ. L. 110-53 (2007). No other intelligence budget figures were released under Bush II.

86. The National Intelligence Program is a term for funding the U.S. Intelligence Community in six federal departments, the Central Intelligence Agency, and the Office of the Director of National Intelligence. See *The Budget of the United States Government, Fiscal Year 2014* (Government Printing Office, 2013), 74.

87. Congress did not mandate the release of MIP Top Line numbers in the Implementing Recommendations of the 9/11 Commission Act, only the NIP.

88. See *Budget of the United States Government, Fiscal Year 2014*, 76 ("Reflecting the Administration's commitment to transparency and open government, the Budget continues the practice begun in the 2012 Budget of disclosing the President's aggregate funding request for the NIP. However, the details regarding the NIP budget remain classified, so the Budget highlights key NIP-funded activities, but does not publicly disclose detailed funding requests for intelligence activities.").

89. For the NIP and MIP numbers, see *Budget of the United States Government, Fiscal Year 2014*, 75 (National Intelligence Program); Department of Defense, "DOD Releases Revised Military Intelligence Program (MIP) Request for Fiscal Year 2014," news release, April 10, 2013, available at web.archive.org/web/20130712184645/http://www.defense.gov/releases/release.aspx?releaseid=16124 ("The total [MIP Fiscal Year 2014] request . . . is $18.6 billion.) For comparisons with some other federal agencies, SEE WEBSITE.

90. In 1981, the Air Force estimated the cost to build 132 Stealth bombers was $22 billion. The actual cost was around $44.7 billion for 21. Tim Weiner, "The $2 Billion Stealth Bomber Can't Go Out in the Rain," *NYT*, August 23, 1997, A5. See John R. Kasich, "The Stealth Boondoggle," op-ed, *NYT*, September 19, 1997, A31. In 1998, the National Reconnaissance Office contracted to create a spy satellite program called the Future Imagery Architecture for $5 billion. By the time the project was killed, the FIA had launched no satellites and had cost the government an estimated $18 billion. Philip Taubman, "Death of a Spy Satellite Program," *NYT*, November 11, 2007, A1.

91. After choosing this subtitle, I came across Barton J. Bernstein's article with the same name, discussing the controversy when Henry Kissinger embargoed 33,000 pages of transcripts and summaries of his Nixon-era taped phone calls. Kissinger gave the papers to the Library of Congress, permitting access to only himself and related researchers for twenty-five years. A group of scholars sued for access and won at trial. See Barton J. Bernstein, "Who Owns History?," *Inquiry*, May 1, 1978, 6–8. However, the Supreme Court reversed in Kissinger v. Reporters Committee for

Freedom of the Press, 445 U.S. 136 (1980), holding Kissinger did not have to turn over the transcripts because once removed from the State Department, the documents were no longer within the department's control for FOIA purposes, and even if removal to a private residence and then the Library of Congress was improper, government records laws provided no private right of action to compel transfer back to the State Department. 445 U.S. at 137–38.

92. Nixon's tax deduction for "his" pre-presidential papers totaled $576,000. Vice President Humphrey, and Presidents Johnson, Eisenhower, and Truman all claimed deductions for gifts of "their" papers. Matthew G. Brown, "The *First* Nixon Papers Controversy: Richard Nixon's 1969 Prepresidential Papers Tax Deduction," *Archival Issues* 26, no. 1 (2001): 10. See Russell W. Fridley, "Should Public Papers Be Private Property?," *Minnesota History* 44 (1974): 37–39. For additional scholarship, SEE WEBSITE.

93. Dorothy S. Eaton, "Introduction," in *Index to the George Washington Papers*, Library of Congress Presidents' Papers Index Series (Government Printing Office, 1964), vi.

94. George Washington to James McHenry, April 3, 1797, *Retirement Series*, ed. W.W. Abbot, vol. 1, *The Papers of George Washington* (University Press of Virginia, 1998), 71–72.

95. Eaton, "Introduction," xiii. See also *An Act to Enable the Secretary of State to Purchase the Papers and Books of General Washington*, 9 Stat. 712 (1834), 712; "George Washington's Last Will and Testament."

96. Library of Congress, "About the Manuscript Division," web.archive.org /web/20130731002542/http://www.loc.gov/rr/mss/mss_abt.html.

97. See, e.g., Ellis, *Founding Brothers* (giving examples of such worries by Founders).

98. See Walter R. Borneman, *The War That Forged a Nation* (HarperCollins, 2004) (discussing the War of 1812 generally). For material on movement of historic documents, SEE WEBSITE.

99. Jefferson, for example, paid his French steward directly, and paid more than $16,500 for wine served during his two terms in the White House. John Hailman, *Thomas Jefferson on Wine* (University Press of Mississippi, 2006), 255–56.

100. Gilson Willets, *Inside History of the White House* (Christian Herald, 1908), 158.

101. Alexis de Tocqueville, *Democracy in America*, ed. Philips Bradley, vol. 1 (Alfred A. Knopf, 1980), 211–12.

102. Eaton, "Introduction," xvi (quoting George Washington Parke Custis to John Pickett, April 17, 1857, George Washington's Estate, Museum, and Gardens Library Manuscript Collection).

103. For discussion of whether presidents taking "their" papers with them was a tradition or a right, SEE WEBSITE.

104. There was a surge in interest in America's past during the centennials of

key events in the Revolutionary War. See David B. Little, *America's First Centennial Celebration* (Houghton Mifflin, 1961) (describing huge turnout for celebrations at Lexington and Concord). The Centennial of the Declaration of Independence in Philadelphia also drew huge crowds. See Dorothy Gondos Beers, "The Centennial City, 1865–1876," in *Philadelphia: A 300-Year History*, ed. Russell F. Weigley (W.W. Norton, 1982), 417–70, 466 (quoting a *New York Herald* report).

105. Information, organized by president, about harms is collected in a number of places. The most convenient is the historical appendix to Nixon v. United States, 978 F.2d 1269 (D.C. Cir. 1992), 1287–99. This is derived from the longer history in the *Final Report of the National Study Commission on Records and Documents of Federal Officials* (Government Printing Office, 1977). See also Arnold Hirshon, "The Scope, Accessibility and History of Presidential Papers," *Government Publications Review* 1, no. 4 (1974), 363–90; Carl McGowan, "Presidents and Their Papers," *Minnesota Law Review* 68 (1983): 1409–37.

106. George Santayana, *The Life of Reason: Or the Phases of Human Progress* (Charles Scribner's Sons, 1920), 284 (emphasis added).

107. All of John Tyler's and Zachary Taylor's papers were destroyed by fire during the Civil War. Earlier, when his family house burned down, William Henry Harrison's papers, though limited, were destroyed. *Nixon* v. U.S., 978 F.2d at 1290–91.

108. For example, Martin Van Buren destroyed incoming correspondence while in office. He then "began sorting and selecting papers to archive, reportedly burning those he did not wish to keep." While Millard Fillmore was careful to organize his papers for a "future historian or biographer," his son, to whom the papers were bequeathed in his will, directed they be destroyed. Most were. Franklin Pierce "destroyed virtually all of his presidential papers." Between the time he was shot and his death, President Garfield "reputedly" destroyed many of his records. *Nixon* v. U.S., 978 F.2d at 1291–92.

109. *Nixon* v. U.S., 978 F.2d at 1279.

110. Among many examples, Madison "gave selections from his presidential papers to family members for mementos"; President Grover Cleveland, who "apparently had little interest in preserving a record," widely "dispersed" his papers "among those seeking presidential memorabilia." *Nixon* v. U.S., 978 F.2d at 1288, 1293.

111. Eaton, "Introduction," ix (quoting Lafayette to Bushrod Washington, December 15, 1811, George Washington's Estate, Museum, and Gardens Library Manuscript Collection). The papers remained in France until after World War I, when bought by an American collector who gave them to Lafayette College in Easton, Pennsylvania. Ibid., n28 (citing *The Letters of Lafayette to Washington*, ed. Louis Gottschalk (H.F. Hubbard, 1944), xxiv–xxv).

112. John McDonough, "Introduction," in *Index to the Andrew Jackson Papers*, Library of Congress Presidents' Papers Index Series (Government Printing Office, 1967), v.

113. See L.H. Butterfield, ed., *Diary and Autobiography of John Adams* (Belknap

Press, 1962) xxiii–xxxvii; *Index to the Abraham Lincoln Papers*, Library of Congress Presidents' Papers Index Series (Government Printing Office, 1960), v–vii; David C. Mearns, "The Lincoln Papers," *Abraham Lincoln Quarterly* 4, no. 8 (1948): 374–75.

114. Ulysses S. Grant, *Personal Memoirs*, 2 vols. (Charles L. Webster, 1886); Harry S. Truman, *Memoirs*, 2 vols. (Doubleday, 1955); Dwight D. Eisenhower, *Mandate for Change: 1953–1956* (Doubleday, 1963); Dwight D. Eisenhower, *The White House Years: Waging Peace 1956–1961* (Doubleday, 1965); Lyndon B. Johnson, *The Vantage Point: Perspectives on the Presidency, 1963–1969* (Holt, Rinehart and Winston, 1971). Grant's *Memoirs*, posthumously published by Mark Twain, generated around $450,000 for Grant's widow. Craig E. Miller, "Give the Book to Clemens," *American History* 34, no. 1 (1999): 40–46. Truman received $675,000 for his memoirs but paid two-thirds in tax. After paying his assistants, he claims to have netted $37,000. Robert H. Ferrell, *Harry S. Truman: A Life* (University of Missouri Press, 1994), 387. Johnson and his wife received $1.2 million for their memoirs. Robert Dallek, *Flawed Giant: Lyndon Johnson and His Times* (Oxford University Press, 1998), 609.

115. See John Marshall, *The Life of George Washington*, 5 vols. (C.P. Wayne, 1804–7); Jared Sparks, *The Life of George Washington* (Ferdinand Andrews, 1839); John George Nicolay and John Hay, *Abraham Lincoln: A History*, 10 vols. (Century, 1890–1909). Nicolay and Hay had been President Lincoln's secretary and assistant secretary, respectively.

116. Bushrod Washington to James Madison, September 14, 1819, *Retirement Series*, ed. David B. Mattern et al., vol. 1, *The Papers of James Madison* (University Press of Virginia, 2009), 513.

117. Purdue University professor Peter Aschenbrenner has analyzed *Farrand's Records* to create a chart of each instance where Constitutional Convention secrecy was broken. See Peter J. Aschenbrenner, "Secrecy Broken: Reports of the Delegates Following the Federal Convention," *Our Constitutional Logic*, part 2, 164 (2013), together with Table Annexed. Aschenbrenner gives 117 examples, dated and labeled in six ways from "very minor" to "severe." George Washington's during the Jay Treaty dispute with the House was characterized as "blatant." Table, 3/30/1796. For additional scholarship, SEE WEBSITE.

118. See "Introduction," in *The Papers of James Madison*, ed. William T. Hutchinson and William M.E. Rachal, vol. 1 (University of Chicago Press, 1962), xvii; Eaton, "Introduction," in *Index to the James Madison Papers*, v; "Purchase and Publication of the Papers of James Madison," The Dolley Madison Digital Edition, ed. Holly C. Shulman (Univ. Press of Virginia), web.archive.org/web/20130622022502/http://rotunda.upress.virginia.edu/dmde/editorialnote.xqy?note=all#n4.

119. See Finkelman, *Slavery and the Founders*, 1–33 (discussing Madison's notes and slavery); James H. Hutson, "Riddles of the Federal Constitutional Convention," *William and Mary Quarterly* 44, no. 3 (1987), 412–15 (delay of the notes and constitutional interpretation generally); and James H. Hutson, "The Creation of the

Constitution: The Integrity of the Documentary Record," *Texas Law Review* 65, no. 1 (1986): 24–35 (scholarly debates about Madison's Convention notes). The most extreme critic of Madison's Convention notes was University of Chicago Law School professor William Crosskey, whose three-volume *Politics and the Constitution in the History of the United States*, 3 vols. (University of Chicago Press), argued Madison doctored his notes to line up with his political views. See Hutson, "Creation of the Constitution," 24–35 and accompanying footnotes.

120. SEE WEBSITE for information on the papers of Grover Cleveland, Benjamin Harrison, Theodore Roosevelt, William Taft, Woodrow Wilson, Warren Harding, Calvin Coolidge, and Herbert Hoover.

121. See R.D.W. Connor, "The Franklin D. Roosevelt Library," *American Archivist* 3, no. 2 (1940): 81–92.

122. *Joint Resolution to Provide for the Establishment and Maintenance of the Franklin D. Roosevelt Library, And for Other Purposes*, Pub. L. 76-194, 53 Stat. 1062 (1939).

123. 84 Cong. Rec. 9053 (1939) (Rep. Dewey Short's speech calling Roosevelt an "egocentric megalomaniac"). For additional information on the vote in Congress, SEE WEBSITE.

124. Remarks of Franklin D. Roosevelt at the dedication of the Franklin D. Roosevelt Library at Hyde Park, New York, June 30, 1941, in *The Public Papers and Addresses of Franklin D. Roosevelt*, comp. Samuel I. Rosenman, 1941 vol. (Random House, 1941).

125. Presidential Libraries Act of 1955, Pub. L. 84-373, 69 Stat. 695 (1955). (Herbert Hoover, who preceded FDR, also took advantage of the act.)

126. Presidents from Hoover to Carter, with the exception of Nixon, by virtue of the donors' deeds of gift, were able to control access to "their" documents. Congress passed the Presidential Recordings and Materials Preservation Act, Pub. L. 93-526 (1974), which covered Nixon's materials. Beginning with Reagan, access to presidential documents has been governed by the Presidential Records Act of 1978, 44 U.S.C. §§ 2201-07 (2012). See Nancy Kegan Smith and Gary M. Stern, "A Historical Review of Access to Records in Presidential Libraries," *Public Historian* 28, no. 3 (2006): 79–116. Volume 28, issue 3 of the *Public Historian* (2006), is dedicated to presidential libraries and provides detailed scholarship on many issues related to the libraries and their contributions to public knowledge. See also Herbert Brownell, "Who Really Owns the Papers of Departing Federal Officials?," *NY State Bar Journal* 50, no. 3 (1978): 193.

127. R.W. Apple Jr., "Nixon Tapes Must Be Kept 3 Years for Use in Court," *NYT*, September 9, 1974, A1. For additional information, SEE WEBSITE.

128. See Appendix A in Nixon v. Sampson, 389 F. Supp. 107, 160-62 (D.D.C. 1975).

129. Ibid.

130. See Presidential Recordings and Materials Preservation Act, Pub. L. 93-526,

88 Stat. 1695 (1974). See also Smith and Stern, "A Historical Review of Access to Records in Presidential Libraries."

131. See Nixon v. Administrator of General Services, 408 F. Supp. 321 (D.D.C. 1976).

132. Nixon v. Administrator of General Services, 433 U.S. 425 (1977).

133. Ibid. at 453.

134. *Nixon v. Administrator*, 408 F. Supp. at 349–50. Judge McGowan also pointed out that while some materials "may never be needed by any historian, member of the public, or branch of government . . . adequate foresight does not exist to permit anyone today to determine what materials may acquire importance . . . over time. Virtually any item might be needed by a historian, depending upon what subjects seem fit for study some years from now." 408 F. Supp. at 355.

135. *Nixon v. Administrator*, 433 U.S. at 452.

136. *Nixon v. Administrator*, 408 F. Supp. at 348.

137. *Nixon v. Administrator*, 433 U.S. at 504, 515.

138. Brownell, "Who Really Owns the Papers of Departing Federal Officials?" On one issue, Brownell dissented, believing there should be no delay in applying FOIA to all government records—the majority said there should be a fifteen-year delay before presidential papers were made available under FOIA. For a critical review of the commission, see Anna Kasten Nelson, "The Public Documents Commission: Politics and Presidential Records," *Government Publications Review* 9, no. 5 (1982): 443–51.

139. 44 U.S.C. §2202 (2012).

140. The act defines presidential records as all documentary materials that "relate to or have an effect upon the carrying out of the constitutional, statutory, or other official or ceremonial duties of the President." 44 U.S.C. §2201(2) (2012). It covers the president and his staff and any unit or individual in the Executive Office of the President who advise him. § 2201(2). It also covers "political activities" where they "relate to or have a direct effect" on carrying out the president's duties. § 2201(2)(A).

141. 44 U.S.C. § 2204 (2012).

142. 44 U.S.C. §§ 2204(a)(1)(A) (a)(6) (2012). For additional information about the act, SEE WEBSITE.

143. See Armstrong v. Executive Office of the President, 90 F.3d 553 (D.C. Cir. 1996), *cert. denied*, 530 U.S. 1229 (1997).

144. Public Citizen v. Burke, 843 F. 2d 1473 (D.C. Cir. 1988).

145. See, e.g., Bruce P. Montgomery, "Presidential Materials: Politics and the Presidential Records Act," *American Archivist* 66, no. 1 (2003), 103; Ben Gose and Dan Curry, "Historians Attack Bush Executive Order on Presidential Records," *Chronicle of Higher Education*, November 16, 2001, 27; Bruce Craig, "Draft Presidential Records Act Executive Order: A 'Disaster' for History," National Coordinating Committee for the Promotion of History, *Washington Update* 7, no. 45 (2001); Robert D.

Putnam and Robert J. Spitzer; "American Political Science Association Response to Executive Order 13233," *Presidential Studies Quarterly*, 32, no. 1 (2002): 190–92.

146. Executive Order No. 13489, January 21, 2009, 74 Fed. Reg. 4669 (revoking Exec. Order No. 13233).

147. Ibid. (emphasis added).

148. *From the Department of Justice to Guantanamo Bay: Administration Lawyers and Administration Interrogation Rules (Part III): Hearings Before the Subcomm. on the Constitution, Civil Rights, and Civil Liberties of the H. Comm. on the Judiciary,* 110th Cong. 67 (2008).

149. John Donne, "XVII Meditation," in *John Donne: The Major Works*, Oxford World Classics rev. ed., ed. John Carey (Oxford University Press, 2000) 344. For additional scholarship, SEE WEBSITE.

150. Isaac Newton to Robert Hooke, February 5, 1675/6, in *The Correspondence of Isaac Newton*, vol. 1, ed. H. W. Turnbull, (Cambridge University Press, 1959), 416.

151. For additional scholarship, SEE WEBSITE.

152. Gordon R. England, "Remarks at the MILCOM 2006 Conference," October 25, 2006, available at web.archive.org/web/20121231232705/http://www.defense.gov/speeches/speech.aspx?speechid=1059.

153. See, e.g., Wade Rowland: *Galileo's Mistake: A New Look at the Confrontation Between Galileo and the Church* (Arcade Publishing, 2001). For additional scholarship, SEE WEBSITE.

154. Andrew C. Revkin, "Climate Expert Says NASA Tried to Silence Him," *NYT*, January 29, 2006, A1. See also James Gustave Speth, letter to the editor, "The Globe Is Warming. Why Aren't We Marching?," *NYT*, February 24, 2006, A22.

155. See Robert S. Norris, *Racing for the Bomb: General Leslie R. Groves, The Manhattan Project's Indispensible Man* (Steerforth, 2002).

156. Vincent C. Jones, *United States Army in World War II, Manhattan: The Army and the Atomic Bomb* (U.S. Army Center of Military History, 1985), 270–71; Norris, *Racing for the Bomb*, 267; *Atomic Energy: Hearings Before the Special Comm. on Atomic Energy*, 79th Cong. 290–91 (1945) (testimony of Leó Szilárd).

157. *Government Secrecy: Hearings Before the Subcomm. on Intergovernmental Relations of the S. Comm. on Government Operations*, 93rd Cong. 253–54 (1974).

158. Albert Einstein, "'The Real Problem Is in the Hearts of Men': Professor Einstein Says a New Type of Thinking Is Needed to Meet the Challenge of the Atomic Bomb," interview by Michael Amrine, *NYT Magazine*, June 23, 1946, 44. See also Jessica Wang, "Scientists and the Problem of the Public in Cold War America, 1945–1960," *Osiris* 17 (2002): 323–47.

159. Gabriel Schoenfeld, *Necessary Secrets: National Security, the Media, and the Rule of Law* (W.W. Norton, 2010), 157. The first draft of the Atomic Energy Act is reproduced in the Congressional Record at *Atomic Energy Act of 1946: Hearings Before the S. Special Comm. on Atomic Energy*, 79th Cong. 1 (1946) (S. 1717

introduced into the record). The act signed by President Truman became Public Law No. 79-585 60 Stat. 755 (1946). The changed language discussed here is Sec. 1(b)(2).

160. Howard Morland, "Born Secret," *Cardozo Law Review* 26, no. 4 (2005): 1401–8. Moynihan, *Secrecy*, 156.

161. Commission on Government Security, *Report Pursuant to Public Law 304, 84th Congress, As Amended* (1957), xx.

162. Office of the Director of Defense Research and Engineering, *Report of the Defense Science Board Task Force on Secrecy* (1970), iv, v, 4–6, 9. Books by Sissela Bok and Senator Moynihan expressed special concern about secrecy's impact on science. See Bok, *Secrets: On the Ethics of Concealment and Revelation* (Vintage Books, 1989), 25, 151–56, 285 ("[T]he damage is perhaps especially noticeable in science because of its reliance on reasoning and creativity."); Moynihan, *Secrecy*, 174–76.

163. National Research Council, *Science and Security in a Post 9/11 World: A Report Based on Regional Discussions Between the Science and Security Communities* (National Academies Press, 2007). National Research Council, *Beyond Fortress America: National Security Controls on Science and Technology in a Globalized World* (National Academies Press, 2009) (hereinafter *Beyond Fortress America*).

164. *Science and Security*, 5.

165. *Beyond Fortress America*, 1–5, 13, 24. See National Science Board, *Science and Engineering Indicators* (2014), statistics showing while still the world's leader in science, the U.S. share of leadership indicators is steadily declining).

166. *Beyond Fortress America*, 1–5, 13, 24–28.

167. *Science and Security*, 20, 27. See National Research Council, *Seeking Security: Pathogens, Open Access, and Genome Databases* (National Academies Press, 2004) (earlier study of pathogens).

168. See Ronald G. McNeil Jr. and Denise Grady, "How Hard Would It Be for Avian Flu to Spread?," *NYT*, January 3, 2012, D1.

169. *Biological Security: The Risk of Dual-Use Research: Hearing Before the S. Comm. on Homeland Security*, 112th Cong. 38 (2012) (written statement of Dr. Anthony S. Fauci, Director, National Institute of Allergy and Infectious Diseases).

170. Howard Markel, "Don't Censor Influenza Research," op-ed, *NYT*, February 2, 2012, A27. Markel is a professor of medical history at the University of Michigan and author of *When Germs Travel: Six Major Epidemics That Have Invaded America Since 1900 and the Fears They Have Unleashed* (Pantheon, 2004). See also Yoshihiro Kawaoka, "H5N1: Flu Transmission Work Is Urgent," *Nature* 482 (2012): 155. Kawaoka is a medical researcher and part of the group whose research was submitted to *Nature*.

171. World Health Organization, *Report on Technical Consultation on H5N1 Research Issues* (2012). For additional scholarship, SEE WEBSITE.

172. Masaki Imai et al., "Experimental Adaptation of an Influenza H5 HA Confers Respiratory Droplet Transmission to a Reassortant H5 Ha/H1N1 Virus in Fer-

rets," *Nature* 486 (2012): 420–28; Colin A. Russell et al., "The Potential for Respiratory Droplet-Transmissible A/H5N1 Influenza Virus to Evolve in a Mammalian Host," *Science* 336 (2012): 1541–47.

173. Bruce Alberts, "Introduction: H5N1," *Science* 336 (2012): 1521. See Sander Herfst et al., "Airborne Transmission of Influenza A/H5N1 Virus Between Ferrets," *Science* 336 (2012), 1521; Anthony S. Fauci and Francis S. Collins, "Benefits and Risks of Influenza Research: Lessons Learned," *Science* 336 (2012): 1522 (noting, among other things, that as a result of public debate over publication, "major gaps in our knowledge of influenza became painfully obvious").

174. Donald G. McNeil Jr., "Bird Flu Paper Is Published After Debate," *NYT*, June 22, 2012, A7.

175. Bruce Schneider, "Securing Medical Research: A Cyber Security Point of View," *Science* 336 (2012): 1527–28 (arguing that openness in virology would be more beneficial than harmful to science, based on prior experience with secrecy in the national security cryptology field).

6: Cultures of Secrecy

1. This was generally true for my work on the Church Committee, where I paid less attention to harm done by *secrecy* than to the need to discover and responsibly expose *secrets*. For occasions where I did mention the harm from secrecy, SEE WEBSITE. (The Church Committee's report on foreign and Military Intelligence, for which Bill Miller was the principal staff drafter, does have some thoughtful comments about the importance of secrecy.)

2. *Church Comm. Bk. II*, 165; *Church Comm. Bk. III*, 391–406.

3. *Church Comm. Bk. II*, 165.

4. *Church Comm. Bk. III*, 398 (quoting Hoover memo enclosed with letter from [Attorney General Homer S.] Cummings to the president [FDR], October 20, 1938); ibid. (quoting Cummings to Roosevelt, October 20, 1938). See also *Church Comm. Bk. II*, 36 (Roosevelt directing Cummings to limit approval of FBI wiretaps against people suspected of undertaking "subversive activities" "insofar as possible to aliens"); *Church Comm. Bk. II*, 28 (discussing breadth of the FBI's authority to investigate subversion). For Attorney General Jackson's later derision of the bredth of "subversive," SEE WEBSITE.

5. *Church Comm. Bk. III*, 278–79. The Supreme Court case was Nardone v. United States, 302 U.S. 379 (1937); 308 U.S. 338 (1939), interpreting 47 U.S.C. § 605 *et seq.*

6. *Church Comm. Bk. III*, 279 (quoting Franklin D. Roosevelt, Attorney General [Robert H. Jackson], Confidential Memorandum, May 21, 1940).

7. The Bureau was less intrusive than later. However, it was, for example, used by the White House to investigate supporters of Charles Lindbergh, one of FDR's leading critics. See generally *Unchecked and Unbalanced*, 16–17.

8. Irvine v. California, 347 U.S. 128, 132 (1954) (Jackson, J., for a plurality).

9. *Church Comm. Bk. II*, 162–63 (quoting Attorney General [Brownell] to the Director, FBI [Hoover], Memorandum, May 20, 1954).

10. National Security Act of 1947, Pub. L. No. 80-253 § 102(B)(2)(d), 61 Stat. 495 (1947). For certain subsequent changes in the act, SEE WEBSITE.

11. *NSC 10/2: National Security Council Directive on Office of Special Projects* (June 18, 1948), Document 292 in *Foreign Relations of the United States, 1945–1950: Emergence of the Intelligence Establishment* (Government Printing Office, 1996), 713–15. For further information on the directive, SEE WEBSITE.

12. *Church Comm. Bk. II*, 14, 141 (quoting Sullivan's testimony of November 1, 1975, 92–93). *The National Security Agency and Fourth Amendment Rights: Hearings Before the S. Select Comm. to Study Government Operations with Respect to Intelligence Activities*, 94th Cong. (1975) (quoting Buffham's testimony). See Walter F. Mondale with David Hage, *The Good Fight: A Life in Liberal Politics* (Simon & Schuster, 2010), 148–49.

13. See *Unchecked and Unbalanced*, 151–99.

14. *Huston Plan, Hearings Before the S. Select Comm. to Study Governmental Operations with Respect to Intelligence Activities*, 94th Cong. 45 (1975) (hereinafter *Church Comm. Huston Plan Hearings*) (Senator Church quoting Tom Charles Huston testimony from executive session before public hearings). For the Huston Plan generally, see *Church Comm. Bk. II*, 111–16; *Church Comm. Bk. III*, 921–83; *Church Comm. Huston Plan Hearings*, passim; Loch K. Johnson, *A Season of Inquiry: Congress and Intelligence* (Dorsey Press, 1988), 78–88.

15. *Church Comm. Bk. III*, 279 (quoting Franklin D. Roosevelt, Attorney General, Confidential Memorandum, May 21, 1940). See also *Church Comm. Bk. III*, 282–83 (quoting Tom C. Clark, Attorney General, to the President [Truman], July 17, 1946).

16. *Church Comm. Bk. I*, 394.

17. See *Church Comm. Bk. II*, 208–9.

18. *Church Comm. Bk. III*, 765–76. See generally L. Britt Snider, "Recollections from the Church Committee's Investigation of NSA: Unlucky SHAMROCK," *Studies in Intelligence* 40 (Winter 1999).

19. *Church Comm. Bk. II*, 212n7 (quoting William Sullivan's testimony of November 1, 1975). *Church Comm. FBI Hearings*, 23–24 (opening statement of Curtis R. Smothers, minority counsel).

20. Ali Soufan, *The Black Banners: The Inside Story of 9/11 and the War Against al-Qaeda* (W.W. Norton, 2011), 464–66, 483.

21. Executive Order No. 13526 (December 29, 2009), Federal Register 75, no. 2 (2010), 707. See generally Elizabeth Goitein and David M. Shapiro, *Reducing Overclassification Through Accountability* (Brennan Center for Justice, 2011) (discussing proliferation of classification).

22. See *Church Comm. Assassinations*, 91–106. Eight former or current CIA of-

ficials testified McCone was not told. Richard Helms would not admit he was not, nor testify that he was. When Helms was pushed about his subordinate's testimony that he and Helms had "agreed" not to brief McCone, Helms said, "I frankly don't recall having agreed to [not briefing McCone]" but then added "this was, you know, not a very savory effort." Ibid., 103 (quoting from Helms testimony, June 13, 1975).

23. See *Church Comm. Bk. II*, 8, 179–80.

24. *Church Comm. Bk. III*, 139.

25. Ibid., 112.

26. "Transcript: Defense Department Briefing," *News from the Washington File*, 12 February 2002 (Office of International Information Programs, U.S. Department of State), available at web.archive.org/web/20131212195408/http://www.defense.gov /transcripts/transcript.aspx?transcriptid=2636; "Rumsfeld Urges NATO to Transform Alliance Militaries," *News from the Washington File*, June 7, 2002 (Office of International Information Programs, U.S. Department of State), available at web.archive .org/web/20140315134732/http://www.nato.int/docu/speech/2002/s020606g.htm. For "oft-ridiculed," see, e.g., L. Gordon Crovitz, "Information Age: Rumsfeld: Know the Unknowns," *WSJ*, April 4, 2011, A15 (referencing Rumsfeld's winning the Plain English Institute's Gobbledygook Award)—actually the "Foot in Mouth Award" for "the worst spoken gobbledygook." Rumsfeld won in 2003. Plain English Campaign, "Foot in Mouth Awards: Past Winners," web.archive.org/web/20140528182051/http://www. plainenglish.co.uk/campaigning/awards/2001-2010-awards/2003-awards/811-foot-in-mouth-award-2003.htm. For an excellent article on unknown unknowns, or "deep secrets," see David Pozen, "Deep Secrecy," *Stanford Law Review* 62, no. 2 (2010).

27. For evasion, see the press conference texts at ibid. For "enigmatic language" and the weak example, see Donald Rumsfeld, *Known and Unknown: A Memoir* (Sentinel, Penguin Group, 2011), xiv. But a major attack from al-Qaeda was imagined, as was the possibility that airplanes could be used as suicide bombs.

28. *Church Comm. Bk. I*, 385–422; *Church Comm. Bk. II*, 57–58. For military and Atomic Energy Commission, see generally Advisory Committee on Human Radiation Experiments, *Final Report of the Advisory Committee on Human Radiation Experiments* (Government Printing Office, 1995).

29. See *Church Comm. Bk. I*, 394–99 (detailing CIA's experiment with LSD on Dr. Frank Olson).

30. *Church Comm. Bk. I*, 394 (quoting memorandum for Deputy Director of Central Intelligence from Deputy Director for Plans, December 17, 1963, 2–3).

31. *Church Comm. Bk. I*, 389 (quoting CIA Inspector General to Director, Memorandum, July 26, 1963).

32. *Church Comm. Bk. I*, 394 (quoting page 217 of the 1957 *Inspector General Survey of the Technical Services Division*).

33. O.G. Haywood Jr. to Dr. Fidler, memorandum, "Medical Experiments on Humans," April 17, 1947, available at web.archive.org/web/20140413193730/http://www2 .gwu.edu/~nsarchiv/radiation/dir/mstreet/commeet/meet3/brief3.gfr/tab_f/br3flj.tx.

34. See, e.g., George Orwell, "Politics and the English Language," in *Why I Write* (Penguin, 2005), 102–21.

35. Frederick A.O. Schwarz Jr., "Intelligence Activities and the Rights of Americans," *Record of the Association of the Bar of the City of New York*, no. 1 (1977): 43, 45–46.

36. *Church Comm. Bk. II*, 271n20 quoting Chicago Field Office to FBI Headquarters, Memorandum, January 12, 1969) ("violent type") and the FBI's summary of that memorandum ("hopefully drive a wedge").

37. *Church Comm. Bk. II*, 110–11, 148n48. The assistant FBI director in charge of the Intelligence Division testified to the committee that "his job was to ensure that Bureau programs were being operated efficiently, not constitutionally." Ibid., 155. See ibid., 12–13, 147 (discussing CIA mail opening and "flap potential"). *Church Comm. Bk. III*, 608–11.

38. *Iran-Contra Report, 3–11.*

39. Maj. Gen. Antonio M. Taguba, *Article 15-6 Investigation of the 800th Military Police Brigade* (2004), 16.

40. Robert Rogalski, Director of Security, Deputy Undersecretary of Defense (Counterintelligence and Security) to the Federation of American Scientists, October 29, 2004, available at www.fas.org/sgp/news/2004/10/dod102904.pdf; "Pentagon Acknowledges, Combats Overclassification," *Secrecy News*, November 1, 2004.

41. *Church Comm. Bk. II*, 210. And see *Church Comm. Bk. III*, 477.

42. *Church Comm. Bk. II*, 205, 208.

43. See *Church Comm. Bk. II*, 44; *Church Comm. Bk. III*, 574; Alexander Charns, *Cloak and Gavel: FBI Wiretaps, Bugs, Informers, and the Supreme Court* (University of Illinois Press, 1992), 18.

44. *Church Comm. Bk. II*, 168.

45. Conversation between Richard M. Nixon and John Dean, March 21, 1973, Nixon Presidential Library and Museum, Nixon White House Tapes, Conversation No. 886-8, Cassette Number E-7 Segment 1 (Exhibit 12 in United States v. John N. Mitchell, et al.), 73–74, available at web.archive.org/web/20140316065055/http://www.nixonlibrary.gov/forreseachers/find/tapes/watergate/trial/exhibit_12.pdf.

46. Egil Krogh, "Statement of Defendant on the Offense and His Role," January 3, 1974, 9–12, reprinted in *Watergate Special Prosecutors: Judiciary Committee's Impeachment Inquiry (April 30, 1973–July 1, 1974): Hearings Before the H. Comm. on the Judiciary*, 93rd Cong. 910–21 (1974).

47. Youngstown Sheet & Tube Co. v. Sawyer, 343 U.S. 579, 646–47 (1952) (Jackson, J., concurring).

48. Francis Biddle, *In Brief Authority* (Doubleday, 1962), 226 (emphasis added).

49. President George W. Bush, "Humane Treatment of al Qaeda and Taliban Detainees," Memorandum, February 7, 2002, reprinted in Mark Danner, *Torture and Truth: America, Abu Ghraib, and the War on Terror* (New York Review Books, 2004), 105–6 (emphasis added).

50. William Safire, "On Language: Waterboarding," op-ed, *NYT Magazine*, March 9, 2008, 16.

51. Moynihan, *Secrecy*, 73.

52. See *Church Comm. Assassinations*, 120–21.

53. CIA Inspector General, *Inspector General's Survey of the Cuban Operation and Associated Documents* (October 1961), 77–80, available at web.archive.org/web /20140413234645/http://foia.cia.gov/sites/default/files/document_conversions/89801/DOC_0000129914.pdf. For another fanciful covert plan, SEE WEBSITE.

54. Dana Priest and William M. Arkin, "A Hidden World, Growing Beyond Control," *WPost*, July 19, 2010, A1; Dana Priest and William M. Arkin, *Top Secret America: The Rise of the New American Security State* (Little, Brown, 2011), 29.

55. Tim Weiner, *Enemies: A History of the FBI* (Random House, 2012), 145, 189.

56. See, e.g., Soufan, *Black Banners*, 464–66, 512–17.

57. S. Select Comm. to Study Government Operations with Respect to Intelligence Activities, *Final Report: The Investigation of the Assassination of President John F. Kennedy: Performance of the Intelligence Agencies*, S. Rep. No. 94-755, vol. 5, 67–68.

58. Moynihan, *Secrecy*, x–xii.

59. *Church Comm. Bk. II*, 259.

60. Glenn Greenwald and Ewen MacAskill, "Boundless Informant: The NSA's Secret Tool to Track Global Surveillance Data," *The Guardian*, June 8, 2013, web. archive.org/web/20140516070605/http://theguardian.com/world/2013/jun/08/nsa-boundless-informant-global-datamining.

61. David E. Sanger, "N.S.A. Leaks Make Plan for Cyberdefense Unlikely," *NYT*, August 13, 2013, A6.

62. James Bamford, "The Black Box," *Wired*, April 2012, 78.

63. *Law Enforcement and the Intelligence Community: Hearing Before the National Commission on Terrorist Attacks Upon the United States*, Panel 2 (April 13, 2004), 52 (testimony of Janet Reno, former U.S. Attorney General): Weiner, *Enemies*, 445; S. Comm. on Appropriations, *Departments of Commerce and Justice, Science, and Related Agencies Appropriations Bill, 2006*, S. Rep. No. 109-88 (2005), 26 ("The Committee is concerned that only one-third of FBI employees have access to the Internet through the FBI's sensitive but unclassified network [SBUNet]").

64. *Church Comm. Bk. I*, 141.

65. *Church Comm. Assassinations*, 277. For other instances of plausible deniability, see *Iran-Contra Report*, 16–17, 375–84; *Unchecked and Unbalanced*, 38–43, 57, 67, 73, 82, 85–87, 107, 116.

66. *Church Comm. Assassinations*, 277.

67. Ibid., 278.

68. *Church Comm. Bk. I*, 16. See ibid., 156–57 (discussing covert actions' effect on democratic government).

69. *Iran-Contra Report*, 17.

70. For example, Cheney helped orchestrate the administration's torture policy with virtually no input from the president. See Barton Gellman, *Angler: The Cheney Vice Presidency* (Penguin, 2008), 174–93.

71. George W. Bush, interview by Matt Lauer, *Decision Points*, NBC News Special (November 8, 2010), transcript available at www.nbcnews.com/id/40076644/ns /politics-decision_points/#.UkTVWhb5hUQ. See *Unchecked and Unbalanced*, 192–99.

72. See, e.g., Nicholas deB. Katzenbach and Frederick A.O. Schwarz Jr., "Release Justice's Secrets," *NYT*, November 20, 2007, A23. See also *Unchecked and Unbalanced*, 212–14.

73. See New York Times v. United States Dept. of Justice, 13 Civ. 13-422, 2014 WL 2838861, __ F.3rd __ (2d. Cir., June 23, 2014), and ibid., 2014 WL 3397065, __ F.3rd __ (2d Cir., July 10, 2014).

74. Jack Goldsmith, *The Terror Presidency: Law and Judgment Inside the Bush Administration* (W.W. Norton, 2007), 144–45, 151.

75. See Philip Zelikow, "Codes of Conduct for a Twilight War," *Houston Law Review* 49, no. 1 (2012): 1. For Bush administration efforts to hide Zelikow's opinion, SEE WEBSITE.

76. For an overview of the hostage crisis, see David R. Farber, *Taken Hostage: The Iran Hostage Crisis and America's First Encounter with Radical Islam* (Princeton University Press, 2005). Roosevelt's role and the coup are discussed at 55–58. The coup, consequences, and the hostage crisis are overviewed at 1–34. See also Robert A. Divine, *Eisenhower and the Cold War* (Oxford University Press, 1981), 75–78; Jean Edward Smith, *Eisenhower in War and Peace* (Random House, 2012), 623–33. For a favorable gloss, see Kermit Roosevelt, *Countercoup: The Struggle for Control of Iran* (McGraw-Hill, 1979).

77. *Church Comm. Huston Plan Hearings*, 51–93; David C. Martin, *Wilderness of Mirrors* (Harper & Row, 1980), 190–214; Tom Mangold, *Cold Warrior: James Jesus Angleton: The CIA's Master Spy Hunter* (Simon & Schuster, 1991). Angleton, who recommended the CIA expand its fledgling mail-opening program and oversaw the program from 1956 until it was terminated in 1973, testified he believed the program was illegal but allowed it to continue. *Church Committee Huston Plan Hearings*, 19–22; *Church Comm. Bk. II*, 143; *Church Comm. Bk. III*, 569–70.

78. John Yoo to the Attorney General, memorandum, November 2, 2001, available at web.archive.org/web/20140410153305/http://www.aclu.org/files/assets/NSA_ Wiretapping_OLC_Memo_Nov_2_2001_Yoo.pdf; John Yoo to William J. Hayes II, memorandum, "Re: Application of Treaties and Laws to al Qaeda and Taliban Detainees," January 9, 2002, available at web.archive.org/web/20120310075143/http:// www.torturingdemocracy.org/documents/20020109.pdf; John Yoo to Alberto R. Gonzales, Counsel to the President, August 1, 2002, available at web.archive.org /web/20120310075708/http://www.torturingdemocracy.org/documents/20020801 3.pdf; Office of Legal Counsel to Alberto R. Gonzales, Counsel to the President,

memorandum, "Re: Standards of Conduct for Interrogation under 18 U.S.C. §§ 2340-2340A," August 1, 2002 (OLC adopting Yoo's opinion), available at web.archive. org/web/20120310075110/http.//www.torturingdemocracy.org /documents/20020801-1.pdf; John Yoo to William J. Haynes II, General Counsel of the Department of Defense, memorandum, March 14, 2003, available at web.archive .org/web/20121025194417/http://www.torturingdemocracy.org/documents /20030314.pdf. For the widespread derision of Yoo's opinions once they were revealed, see *Unchecked and Unbalanced*, 187–99; Offices of the Inspectors General of the Department of Defense et al., *Unclassified Report on the President's Surveillance Program*, Report No. 2009-0013-AS (2009). See also Jay S. Bybee to John Rizzo, Memorandum, "Interrogation of al Qaeda Operative," August 1, 2002, available at web.archive.org/web/20140113010446/http://www.justice.gov/olc/docs/memo bybee2002.pdf.

79. Olmstead v. United States, 277 U.S. 438, 479 (1928).

7: The Seduction of Secrecy

1. Daniel Ellsberg, *Secrets: A Memoir of Vietnam and the Pentagon Papers* (Penguin, 2003), 233–38.

2. Ibid., 237–38.

3. Ibid., 347. Kissinger neglected to mention Ellsberg in his nearly 1,500-page autobiography of his time as Nixon's national security advisor, even in discussion of the Pentagon Papers. See Henry Kissinger, *White House Years* (Little, Brown, 1979). Indeed, when the Pentagon Papers were discussed in the White House, Kissinger shocked H.R. Haldeman by making "beyond belief" charges against Ellsberg for having "weird sexual habits, us[ing] drugs, and enjoy[ing] helicopter flights in which he would take potshots at the Vietnamese below." H.R. Haldeman and Joseph DiMona, *The Ends of Power* (Times Books, 1978), 110. Kissinger did not tell his White House colleagues he had reached out to Ellsberg for advice.

4. Ellsberg, *Secrets*, 348.

5. Gerald R. Ford, "Remarks at the Ford Foundation Journalism Awards for Presidential and National Defense Reporting," C-SPAN video, June 2, 1997, available at www.c-span.org/video/?86382-1/gerald-r-ford-journalism-award, quoted material at 32:10–33:54.

6. Richard Gid Powers, "Introduction," in Moynihan *Secrecy*, 8–9.

7. Moynihan, *Secrecy*, 195–98. See *Estimating the Size and Growth of the Soviet Economy: Hearing Before the S. Comm. on Foreign Relations.*, 101st Cong. (1990).

8. Peter Eisler, "Today's Spies Find Secrets in Plain Sight," *USA Today*, April 1, 2008, A1.

9. Arthur S. Hulnick, "The Dilemma of Open Source Intelligence: Is OSINT Really Intelligence?," in *The Oxford Handbook of National Security Intelligence*, ed. Loch Johnson (Oxford University Press, 2010), 230.

10. *America the Vulnerable*, 209. Joel Brenner had been NSA's inspector general and senior counsel, and had served as National Counterintelligence Executive in the Office of the Director of National Intelligence from 2006 to 2009.

11. Ibid., 183–87.

12. Ibid., 207. See generally Commission on Intelligence Capabilities of the United States Regarding Weapons of Mass Destruction, *Report to the President of the United States* (2005).

13. Stephen E. Ambrose, "Eisenhower and the Intelligence Community in World War II," *Journal of Contemporary History*, 16, no. 1 (January 1981): 158 (citing "Synthesis of Experience in the Use of Ultra Intelligence," compiled by Telford Taylor, who led the U.S. group relaying Ultra information to field commanders).

14. Ted Gup, *Nation of Secrets: The Threat to Democracy and the American Way of Life* (Anchor Books, 2007), 46 (quoting Harold Relyea).

15. Stansfield Turner, *Secrecy and Democracy: The CIA in Transition* (Houghton Mifflin, 1985), 254.

16. Dana Priest and William M. Arkin, *Top Secret America: The Rise of the New American Security State* (Little, Brown, 2011), 81 (citing a "senior intelligence officer").

17. Loch K. Johnson, "Glimpses into the Gems of American Intelligence: The *President's Daily Brief* and the National Intelligence Estimate," *Intelligence and National Security* 23, no. 3 (June 2008): 336. Today PDBs are prepared by the intelligence community, coordinated by the director of national intelligence.

18. Dana Priest and William M. Arkin, "Top Secret America: A Hidden World Growing Beyond Control," *WPost*, July 19, 2010, A1.

19. Anita Huslin, "If These Walls Could Talk," *WPost*, May 28, 2006, D1.

20. Max Frankel, "Word and Image: Top Secret," *NYT Magazine*, June 16, 1996, 20.

21. Richard Harris Smith, *OSS: The Secret History of America's First Central Intelligence Agency* (Lyons Press, 2005), 18.

22. *9/11 Comm'n Report*, 355–56, 417.

23. Ali Soufan, *The Black Banners: The Inside Story of 9/11 and the War Against Al-Qaeda* (W.W. Norton, 2011), 439–63.

24. Max Weber, "Bureaucracy," in *From Max Weber: Essays in Sociology*, trans. H.H. Garth and C. Wright Mills (Oxford University Press, 1946), 233–34. Senator Moynihan used Weber to illustrate bureaucracies' "tendency to amass official secrets," Moynihan, *Secrecy*, 142–43.

25. Nicholas deB. Katzenbach, "Foreign Policy, Public Opinion and Secrecy," *Foreign Affairs* 52, no.1 (1973): 14.

26. 121 Cong. Rec. 1434 (1975). See Frank J. Smist Jr., *Congress Oversees the United States Intelligence Community, 1947–1989* (Univ. of Tennessee Press, 1990), 4–9 (other examples of the "less they knew the better").

27. Manu Raju, Elana Schor, and Ilan Wurman, "Few Senators Read Iraq NIE

Report," *The Hill*, June 17, 2007, web.archive.org/web/20140522003828/http://the hill.com/homenews/news/12304-few-senators-read-iraq-nie-report.

28. *Report on the U.S. Intelligence Community's Prewar Intelligence Assessments on Iraq*, S. Rep. 108-301 (2004), 295.

29. Charles Fried and Gregory Fried, *Because It Is Wrong: Torture, Privacy, and Presidential Power in the Age of Terror* (W.W. Norton, 2010). Among other things, Charles Fried was Ronald Reagan's solicitor general. See also Albie Sachs, *The Strange Alchemy of Life and Law* (Oxford University Press, 2009).

30. *Unchecked and Unbalanced*, 67–72.

31. George Washington to Samuel Blachley Webb, January 8, 1777, in *Revolutionary War Series*, ed. Frank E. Grizzard Jr., vol. 8, *The Papers of George Washington* (University Press of Virginia, 1998), 16.

32. "Instructions for the Government of Armies of the United States in the Field," U.S. War Department, Office of the Adjutant General, Order No. 100 (1863), in *The War of the Rebellion: A Compilation of the Official Records of the Union and Confederate Armies*, series 3, vol. 3, H. Doc. 56-287 (Government Printing Office, 1899), 148–64 (referred to as the "Lieber Code" for its drafter, Francis Lieber). Lincoln approved the Lieber Code during the Civil War, forbidding Union soldiers using "torture to extort confessions." Ibid., 150. See generally Charles Fried, "Humanity in War," review of *Lincoln's Code: The Laws of War in American History* by John Fabian Witt, *New Republic*, December 31, 2012, 35.

33. Raymund T. Yingling and Robert W. Ginnane, "The Geneva Conventions of 1949," *American Journal of International Law* 46, no. 3 (1952): 396, 413, 427.

34. Evan Wallach, "Waterboarding Used to Be a Crime," *WPost*, November 4, 2007, B1; Jane Mayer, *The Dark Side: The Inside Story of How the War on Terror Turned into a War on American Ideals* (Doubleday, 2008), 157–58. See also Soufan, *Black Banners*, 464–65.

35. Soufan, *Black Banners*, 439–508.

36. James C. Thomson Jr., "How Could Vietnam Happen? An Autopsy," *Atlantic Monthly* 221, no. 4 (1968), 47–53 (emphasis in original).

37. John Ashcroft to the Heads of All Federal Departments and Agencies, memorandum, October 12, 2001, available at web.archive.org/web/20140413130758/http://www.justice.gov/archive/oip/011012.htm.

38. Richard Nixon, "Statement on Establishing a New System for Classification and Declassification of Government Documents Relating to National Security (EO 11652)," March 8, 1972, available at web.archive.org/web/20121031021652/https://www.fas.org/irp/offdocs/eo/eo-11652.htm.

39. Michael Lemov, *People's Warrior: John Moss and the Fight for Freedom of Information and Consumer Rights* (Farleigh Dickinson University Press, 2011), 53. For additional scholarship, SEE WEBSITE.

40. Bill Moyers, *Moyers on America: A Journalist and His Times* (Anchor Books, 2005), 157.

41. Merle Miller, *Plain Speaking: An Oral Biography of Harry S. Truman* (Berkley Medallion Books, 1974), 286.

42. National Archives and Records Administration, Information Security Oversight Office, *2012 Annual Report to the President*, (2013), 1; see Peter Galison, "Removing Knowledge," *Critical Inquiry* 31, no. 1 (2004):229.

43. Office of the Director of National Intelligence, *2012 Report on Security Clearance Determinations* (2013), 3.

44. National Archives and Records Administration, *Information Security Oversight Office, 2012 Annual Report to the President*, 1. From 2011 to 2012, the number of "original" classification decisions dropped by 42 percent to 73,477.

45. Ibid., 1.

46. Elizabeth Goitein and David M. Shapiro, *Reducing Overclassification Through Accountability* (Brennan Center for Justice, 2011), 2–3, 21–32.

47. *Report to the Secretary of Defense by the Committee on Classified Information* (1956), 3, available at web.archive.org/web/20060715194832/http://www.thememo ryhole.org/foi/coolidge_committee.pdf.

48. Availability of Information from Federal Departments and Agencies (Department of Defense), H.R. Rep. No. 85-1884 (1958), 158.

49. *9/11 Comm'n Report*, 417.

50. Goitein and Shapiro, *Reducing Overclassification*, 21.

51. But see ibid., 33–49. After noting many of the problems discussed here, the authors suggest reforms to change classification incentives.

52. *9/11 Comm'n Report*, 403.

53. Ibid., 416.

54. Department of Defense, *Report to the Secretary*, 6; Commission on Government Security, *Report Pursuant to Public Law 304, 84th Congress, As Amended* (1957), 174–75; Special Government Information Subcomm., *Availability of Information from Federal Departments and Agencies (Department of Defense)*, H.R. Rep. No. 85-1884 (1958), 4; Office of the Director of Defense Research and Engineering, *Report of the Defense Science Board Task Force on Secrecy* (1970), 2; U.S. Department of Defense, *Keeping the Nation's Secrets: A Report to the Secretary of Defense by the Commission to Review DoD Security Policies and Practices* (1985), 49; Joint Security Commission, *Redefining Security: A Report to the Secretary of Defense and the Director of Central Intelligence* (1994), 6; Commission on Protecting and Reducing Government Secrecy (Moynihan Commission), *Report Pursuant to Public Law 236, 103rd Cong., S. Doc. No. 105-2* (1997), xxi; Lance Gay, "9/11 Panel Says Too Many Documents Are Being Stamped Secret," Scripps Howard News Service, May 14, 2004 (quoting 9/11 Commission Chair Thomas Kean). See also Goitein and Shapiro, *Reducing Overclassification*.

55. Niccolo Machiavelli, *The Prince*, trans. Peter Constantine (Modern Library, 2008), 13.

Part III: Exposing Secrets and Checking Secrecy

1. See Alfred Lord Tennyson, "The Brook: An Idyll," in *The Poetical Works of Alfred Tennyson* (Ticknor and Fields, 1857), 500–506.

2. "Navy Had Word of Jap Plan to Strike at Sea: Knew Dutch Harbor Was a Feint," *Chicago Daily Tribune*, June 7, 1942, 1. See Gabriel Schoenfeld, *Necessary Secrets; National Security, the Media, and the Rule of Law* (W.W. Norton, 2010), 123–40 and sources cited therein. See generally Dina Goren, "Communication Intelligence and the Freedom of the Press: The *Chicago Tribune*'s Battle of Midway Dispatch and the Breaking of the Japanese Naval Code," *Journal of Contemporary History* 16, no. 4 (1981): 663–90.

3. See Henry F. Schorreck, "Battle of Midway, 4–7 June 1942: The Role of COMINT in the Battle of Midway," Naval History and Heritage Command, May 11, 2009.

4. Clay Blair Jr., "*Silent Victory: The U.S. Submarine War Against Japan* (Naval Institute Press, 2001), 424. See Schoenfeld, *Necessary Secrets*, 124.

5. See, e.g., Condoleezza Rice, interview by Wolf Blitzer, *Late Edition*, CNN, September 8, 2002 ("The problem here is that there will always be some uncertainty about how quickly [Saddam Hussein] can acquire nuclear weapons. But we don't want the smoking gun to be a mushroom cloud.") For the *New York Times* story, see Michael R. Gordon and Judith Miller, "U.S. Says Hussein Intensifies Quest for A-Bomb Parts, " *NYT*, September 8, 2002, A1.

8: Leaks, Investigative Journalism, and Nonprofit Watchdogs

1. There are a number of books and articles about leaks. See, e.g., Gabriel Schoenfeld, *Necessary Secrets: National Security, the Media, and the Rule of Law* (W.W. Norton, 2010); Elie Abel, *Leaking: Who Does It? Who Benefits? At What Cost?* (Priority Press Publications, 1987); Geoffrey Stone, *Top Secret: When Our Government Keeps Us in the Dark* (Rowman & Littlefield, 2007) (legal issues). David E. Pozen, "The Leaky Leviathan: Why the Government Condemns and Condones Unlawful Disclosure of Information," *Harvard Law Review* 127 (2013): 512; and Rahul Sagar, *Secrets and Leaks: The Dilemma of State Secrecy* (Princeton University Press, 2013). There are also many books and articles discussing particular leaks.

2. Conor Friedersdorf, "Edward Snowden's Other Motive for Leaking," *The Atlantic*, May 13, 2014.

3. Suetonius, *Lives of the Caesars*, trans. Catharine Edwards (Oxford University Press, 2000), 78.

4. Sarah Palin's Facebook page, November 29, 2010; William Kristol, "Whack WikiLeaks," *The Blog*, *Weekly Standard*, November 30, 2010.

5. Bernard Bailyn, *The Ordeal of Thomas Hutchinson* (Belknap Press of Harvard University Press, 1974), 221–73; William B. Willcox, "Franklin's Last Years in

England: The Making of a Rebel," in *Critical Essays on Benjamin Franklin*, ed. Melvin H. Buxbaum (G.K. Hall and Company, 1987); Gordon S. Wood, *The Americanization of Benjamin Franklin* (Penguin, 2004), 139–47, 158; H.W. Brands, *The First American: The Life and Times of Benjamin Franklin* (Anchor Books, 2002), 1–5, 452–54, 459–60, 466–75.

6. Charlie Savage and Emmarie Huetteman, "Manning Sentenced to 35 Years for a Pivotal Leak of U.S. Files," *New York Times*, August 22, 2013, A1. See also a redacted copy of Manning's court statement, see U.S. v. Private First Class (PFC) Bradley E. Manning (U), January 29, 2013, www.fas.org/sgp/jud/manning/022813 -statement.pdf.

7. My friend Doron Gopstein asked this question in reaction to the Snowden disclosures.

8. William H. Young and Nancy K. Young, *Music of the World War II Era* (Greenwood Press, 2008), 18–19; "Harlem Hit Parade," *Billboard*, September 25, 1943, 12.

9. Theodore Roosevelt, "Dedication of the House Office Building," April 15, 1906, in *My Fellow Americans*, 65. For Roosevelt's source for "muck-rake," and his close relationship with muckrakers, SEE WEBSITE.

10. Richard Hofstadter, *The Age of Reform: From Bryan to FDR* (Vintage Books, 1955), 192.

11. Harold S. Wilson, *McClure's Magazine and the Muckrakers* (Princeton University Press, 1970); Willa Cather, *The Autobiography of S. S. McClure* (University of Nebraska Press, 1997), 207–66; Peter Lyon, *Success Story: The Life and Times of S. S. McClure* (Scribner, 1963), 111–338 (at part 3).

12. Wilson, *McClure's*, 64–65.

13. *McClure's Magazine* 20, no. 3 (1903).

14. Lincoln Steffens, "The Shame of Minneapolis," *McClure's Magazine* 20 (1903), 227–39.

15. Ray Stannard Baker, "The Right to Work," *McClure's Magazine* 20 (1903), 323–36.

16. Ida Tarbell, "The Oil War of 1872: Chapter III of the History of the Standard Oil Company," *McClure's Magazine* 20 (1903), 248–60.

17. For some later writings by muckrakers, see Ida M. Tarbell, *The History of the Standard Oil Company* (Macmillan, 1904), based on her *McClure's* articles; Lincoln Steffens, *The Shame of the Cities* (McClure, Phillips, 1904); Upton Sinclair, *The Jungle* (Doubleday, Page, 1906); David Graham Phillips, *The Treason of the Senate* (Quadrangle Books, 1964) (based on articles Phillips wrote for *Cosmopolitan* beginning in February 1906).

18. See Standard Oil Co. of New Jersey v. United States, 221 U.S. 1 (1911).

19. See Ron Chernow, *Titan: The Life of John D. Rockefeller, Sr.* (Random House, 1998), 750. See also Steven Weinberg, *Taking on the Trust: The Epic Battle of Ida Tarbell and John D. Rockefeller* (W.W. Norton, 2008).

20. "Concerning Three Articles in This Number of McClure's, and a Coincidence That May Set Us Thinking," editorial, *McClure's Magazine* 20 (1903), 336.

21. Amos Pinchot, "Two Revolts Against Oligarchy," *McClure's Magazine* 35, no. 5 (1910), 586.

22. By 1911, many of the renowned writers at *McClure's* had gone into freelance work, including Tarbell, who had earlier left to join *American Magazine*. Both periodicals were sold that year. See Wilson, *McClure's*, 320–21.

23. Michael Schudson, *The Power of News* (Harvard University Press, 1995), 165.

24. James S. Pope, "The Suppression of News," *Atlantic Monthly* 188, no. 1 (1951), 50.

25. See D.D. Guttenplan, *American Radical: The Life and Times of I. F. Stone* (Northwestern University Press, 2012).

26. See, e.g., Affidavit of Theodore Sorensen at 5, United States v. Russo & Ellsberg, Crim. No. 9373 (WMB) Cal., dismissed May 11, 1973, reprinted as Exhibit A in *Nomination of Theodore C. Sorensen: Hearing Before the S. Select Comm. on Intelligence*, 95th Cong. (1977). For Sorensen's supporting information and its limitations, SEE WEBSITE.

27. For an early recognition of the correlation between changes in respect for government leaders and the amount of leaking, see Nicholas de B. Katzenbach, "Foreign Policy, Public Opinion and Secrecy," *Foreign Affairs* 52 (October 1973): 17.

28. Sol Stern, "A Short Account of International Student Politics and the Cold War with Particular Reference to the NSA, CIA, etc.," *Ramparts*, March 1967, 29–38. For a general view of *Ramparts*, see Peter Richardson, *A Bomb in Every Issue: How the Short, Unruly Life of Ramparts Magazine Changed America* (The New Press, 2009). The CIA funding story is told at 79–81. See also Nicholas deB. Katzenbach, John W. Gardner, and Richard Helms, *Report to the President; Outline of a New Policy for United States Funding of Voluntary Organizations* (1967), Document XIII-3 in *American Foreign Policy: Current Documents, 1967* (Government Printing Office, 1969), 1214. Seymour M. Hersh, "Lieutenant Accused of Murdering 109 Civilians," *St. Louis Post-Dispatch*, November 13, 1969, 1; Seymour M. Hersh, "Hamlet Attack Called 'Point-Blank' Murder," *St. Louis Post-Dispatch*, November 20, 1969, 1; Seymour M. Hersh, "Ex-GI Tells of Killing Civilians at Pinkville," *St. Louis Post-Dispatch*, November 25, 1969. William Beecher, "Raids in Cambodia by U.S. Unprotested," *NYT*, May 9, 1969, 1.

29. For whether Kennedy actually was the source, SEE WEBSITE.

30. Affidavit of Max Frankel at 3, 9, United States v. New York Times Co., 328 F. Supp. 324 (S.D.N.Y. 1971). For a recent study of reasons why government itself often depends on leaks, see Pozen, "Leaky Leviathan."

31. Affidavit of Max Frankel, *US v. New York Times*, 2.

32. Ibid., 3.

33. Ibid., 12. See George Christian, *The President Steps Down: A Personal Memoir of the Transfer of Power* (Macmillan, 1970) 34, 69–70, 88–90, 109, 131–36, 152.

34. Affidavit of Chalmers M. Roberts, 2, *United States v. Washington Post Co.,* No. 71-cv-1235 (D.D.C. 1971). A decade later, Richard Halloran, an experienced military reporter, described leaks as "oil in the machinery of Government"—"a political instrument wielded almost daily by senior officials within the Administration to influence a decision, to promote policy, to persuade Congress and to signal foreign governments." See Richard Halloran, "A Primer on the Fine Art of Leaking Information," *NYT,* January 14, 1983, A16.

35. I.F. Stone, "Arrest of 'the Six,'" *The Nation,* June 16, 1945, 666–67. For the context and outcome, see Guttenplan, *American Radical,* 202–5.

36. I.F. Stone, "Opinion: What's Behind the Arrest of the Six?," *P.M.,* June 8, 1945, 2.

37. *White House Procedures for Safeguarding Classified Information: Hearing Before the H. Comm. on Oversight and Government Reform,* 110th Cong. 67 (2007) (testimony of Rep. Henry Waxman).

38. Michael Isikoff, "'Double Standard' in White House Leak Inquiries?," NBC News, October 18, 2010.

39. Mark Mazzetti, Helene Cooper, and Peter Baker, "Behind the Hunt for Bin Laden," *NYT,* May 3, 2011, A1; Peter Bergen, *Manhunt: The Ten-Year Search for Bin Laden from 9/11 to Abbottabad* (Crown, 2012); Nicholas Schmidle, "Getting Bin Laden," *New Yorker,* August 8, 2011, 34–45.

40. Affidavit of Max Frankel, *US v. New York Times,* 7.

41. David Wise, "Pressures on the Press," in *None of Your Business: Government Secrecy in America,* ed. Norman Dorsen and Stephen Gillers (Viking Press, 1974), 233.

42. See Harrison E. Salisbury, *Without Fear or Favor: The New York Times and Its Times* (Times Books, 1980); Sanford J. Ungar, *The Papers and the Papers: An Account of the Legal and Political Battle over the Pentagon Papers* (Columbia University Press, 1989); Ben Bradlee, *A Good Life: Newspapering and Other Adventures* (Simon & Schuster, 1995), 310–23; David Rudenstine, *The Day the Presses Stopped: A History of the Pentagon Papers Case* (University of California Press, 1996); Max Frankel, *The Times of My Life and My Life with The Times* (Random House, 1999), 321–46; Floyd Abrams, *Speaking Freely: Trials of the First Amendment* (Penguin, 2006), 6–61; Floyd Abrams, *Friend of the Court: On the Front Lines with the First Amendment* (Yale University Press, 2013), 135–58; James C. Goodale, *Fighting for the Press: The Inside Story of the Pentagon Papers and Other Battles* (CUNY Journalism Press, 2013). Ellsberg's own writings are comprehensive. See, e.g., Daniel Ellsberg, *Secrets: A Memoir of Vietnam and the Pentagon Papers* (Penguin, 2003). See also "Ellsberg Talks: Why He Leaked the Pentagon Papers," *Look,* October 5, 1971, 31–42; James C. Goodale, ed., *The New York Times Company vs. United States: A Documentary History* (Arno Press, 1971); John Prado and Margaret Pratt Parker, eds., *Inside the Pentagon Papers* (University Press of Kansas, 2004).

For the papers themselves, see Neil Sheehan et al., eds., *The Pentagon Papers:*

The Secret History of the Vietnam War (Bantam, 1971); Department of Defense, *The Pentagon Papers: The Defense Department History of United States Decisionmaking on Vietnam*, 5 vols., Senator Gravel ed. (Beacon Press, 1971–72). For the opening articles in the *Times*, see Neil Sheehan, "Vietnam Archive: Pentagon Study Traces 3 Decades of Growing U.S. Involvement," *NYT*, June 13, 1971, 1; Neil Sheehan, "Vietnam Archive: A Consensus to Bomb Developed Before '64 Election, Study Says," *NYT*, June 14, 1971, 1. For the *Washington Post*, see Chalmers M. Roberts, "Documents Reveal U.S. Effort in '54 to Delay Viet Election," *W Post*, June 18, 1971, A1; Murrey Marder, "Viet Study Says Bombing Lull Pressure Move," *W Post*, June 19, 1971, A1.

43. McNamara was worried that key documents might disappear because as "time goes on and administrations change, internal policy papers and the ideas that are expressed in them are inevitably dispersed." Ungar, *The Papers and the Papers*, 26.

44. The Pentagon Papers' authors ended the study by opining—prematurely, as it turned out—that "the first step on what would undoubtedly be a long and tortuous road to peace had apparently been taken."

45. It relied "by and large" on the documents. See Department of Defense, *The Pentagon Papers*, vol. 1, xv–xvi.

46. The term "sensitive" was not "authorized by statute or executive order. . . . It signaled the information contained in the document might cause bureaucratic and political embarrassment, apart from any effect that its disclosure might have on national security. [Morton] Halperin and [Leslie] Gelb [who managed writing the History,] feared that [President] Johnson or [National Security Advisor Walt] Rostow would destroy the study if they learned of it," Rudenstine, *The Day the Presses Stopped*, 30–31.

47. Earlier, Ellsberg leaked materials to Sheehan on Gen. William C. Westmoreland's request for more troops in Vietnam. See Neil Sheehan, "U.S. Undervalued Enemy's Strength Before the Offensive: C.I.A. Reports Forces Were Significantly Larger than Intelligence Estimates," *NYT*, March 19, 1968, 1; Ellsberg, *Secrets*, 20.

48. For the Cronkite interview, see Ungar, *The Papers and the Papers*, 129–30, 239; Ellsberg, *Secrets*, 400–402; and Rudenstein, *The Day the Presses Stopped*, 252.

49. As a former attorney general, Brownell said that he could not defend publication. Loeb also opposed publication. Their firm was replaced by Cahill Gordon, giving Floyd Abrams his start as a renowned First Amendment lawyer.

50. Author's notes of remarks by Neil Sheehan as keynote speaker at a May 2012 conference, "From the Pentagon Papers to WikiLeaks: A Transatlantic Conversation on the Right to Know," at the Heidelberg Center for American Studies, Germany. See also Rudenstine, *The Day the Presses Stopped*, 60, and Goodale, *Fighting for the Press*, 55–57.

51. Sheehan, "Pentagon Study Traces 3 Decades."

52. New York Times Co. v. United States, 403 U.S. 713 (1971).

53. Ellsberg, *Secrets*, Nixon conversation with H.R. Haldeman, Ron Ziegler, and

Henry Kissinger, Nixon Tapes, Oval Office conversation no. 523-6 (June 16, 1971, 5:24 p.m.). See Ellsberg, *Secrets*, 424. For Nixon's subsequent orders, SEE WEBSITE.

54. Nixon conversation with Henry Kissinger, Nixon Tapes, Oval Office conversation no. 520-4 (June 15, 1971, 10:39 a.m.).

55. See Ellsberg, *Secrets*, 429–38, 454–57 (the indictment and its dismissal); ibid., 422–43 (more Oval Office conversations).

56. Nixon conversation with H.R. Haldeman, Nixon Tapes, Oval Office conversation no. 519-1 (June 14, 1971, 8:49 a.m.).

57. Ellsberg, *Secrets*, 398–99.

58. Salisbury, *Without Fear or Favor*, 240–41.

59. See Rudenstine, *The Day the Presses Stopped*, 175.

60. Russell Sackett, "Publishing Secrets: Trials Not Likely," *Newsday* [July] 29, 1971, 4; see Rudenstein, *The Day the Presses Stopped*, 202 (citing unpublished memorandum by Judge Gesell, filed June 18, 1971).

61. Bradlee, *Good Life*, 320. See also Rudenstine, *The Day the Presses Stopped*, 347; Ungar, *The Papers and the Papers*, 204.

62. Erwin N. Griswold, "Secrets Not Worth Keeping: The Courts and Classified Information," op-ed, *WPost*, February 15, 1989, A25. See Erwin N. Griswold, *Ould Fields, New Corne: The Personal Memoirs of a Twentieth Century Lawyer* (West Publishing, 1992), 312. See also Rudenstine, *The Day the Presses Stopped*, 245 (discussing concessions made by Griswold in court).

63. Henry Kissinger, *White House Years* (Little, Brown, 1979), 729–30.

64. Rudenstine, *The Day the Presses Stopped*, 327–28. Nixon's memoir *The Memoirs of Richard Nixon* (Grosset and Dunlap, 1978) does make one "undocumented and unexplained claim" that publication caused a secret contact to dry up. (See Rudenstine, *The Day the Presses Stopped*, 327.)

65. William Safire, *Before the Fall: An Inside Account of the Pre-Watergate White House* (Da Capo Press, 1975), 358, 552.

66. For NSA generally, see James Bamford: *The Shadow Factory: The Ultra-Secret NSA from 9/11 to the Eavesdropping on America* (Anchor Books, 2009); *Body of Secrets: Anatomy of the Ultra-Secret National Security Agency* (Doubleday, 2001); *The Puzzle Palace: Inside the National Security Agency, America's Most Secret Intelligence Organization* (Penguin, 1983). See also Matthew M. Aid, *The Secret Sentry: The Untold History of the National Security Agency* (Bloomsbury Press, 2009).

67. Henry L. Stimson and McGeorge Bundy, *On Active Service in Peace & War* (Harper, 1947), 188. For the Black Chamber and its shutdown, see David Kahn, *The Reader of Gentlemen's Mail: Herbert O. Yardley and the Birth of American Codebreaking* (Yale University Press, 2004); Schoenfeld, *Necessary Secrets*, 112–15.

68. Herbert O. Yardley, *The American Black Chamber* (Aegean Park Press, 1931).

69. Ibid., 313.

70. Schoenfeld, *Necessary Secrets*, 119. But see his chap. 5, 107, discussing Japanese codes that *were* broken before Pearl Harbor.

71. Author's recollection.

72. *18 U.S.C. 798 (2012). See Harold Edgar and Benno C. Schmidt Jr., "The Espionage Statutes and Publication of Defense Information," *Columbia Law Review* 73 (1973): 1064–69.

73. James Risen and Eric Lichtblau, "Bush Lets U.S. Spy on Callers Without Courts," *NYT*, December 16, 2005, A1. See also Eric Lichtblau and James Risen, "Bank Data Is Sifted by U.S. in Secret to Block Terror," *NYT*, June 22, 2006, A1; Dean Baquet and Bill Keller, "When Do We Publish a Secret?," *NYT*, July 1, 2006, A15: ("A few days ago, Treasury Secretary John Snow said he was scandalized by our decision to report on the bank-monitoring program. But in September 2003 the same Secretary Snow invited a group of reporters from our papers, The *Wall Street Journal* and others to travel with him and his aides on a military aircraft for a six-day tour to show off the department's efforts to track terrorist financing. The secretary's team discussed many sensitive details of their monitoring efforts, hoping they would appear in print and demonstrate the administration's relentlessness against the terrorist threat.")

74. Eric Lichtblau, *Bush's Law: The Remaking of American Justice* (Pantheon, 2008), 208.

75. Ibid.

76. Risen and Lichtblau, "Bush Lets U.S. Spy on Callers."

77. See James Risen, *State of War: The Secret History of the CIA and the Bush Administration* (Free Press, 2006), 39–60.

78. Representative Jane Harman, "Harman Statement on NSA Electronic Surveillance Program," news release, December 21, 2005, web.archive.org/web /20060114045436/http://www.house.gov/Harman/press/releases/2005/1221PR_ nsa.html; *Current and Projected National Security Threats to the United States: Hearing Before the S. Select Comm. on Intelligence*, 109th Cong. 50 (2006) (testimony of Porter Goss, CIA Director). Harman's statement was not unequivocal: She expressed "deep[] concern[] . . . that this program in fact goes far beyond the measure to target Al Qaeda," about which she had been briefed.

79. Schoenfeld, *Necessary Secrets*, 11–26, 248–75.

80. Ibid., 32.

81. Risen and Lichtblau, "Bush Lets U.S. Spy on Callers."

82. Schoenfeld, *Necessary Secrets*, 187.

83. For Cheney's reference to "monarchical" presidential prerogatives, see *Iran-Contra Minority Report*, 465.

84. Bill Keller, "Letter from Bill Keller on the *Times*'s Banking Records Report," *NYT*, June 25, 2006.

85. Siobhan Gorman, "System Error," *Baltimore Sun*, January 29, 2006, A1. In addition to the articles cited below, see the following articles by Gorman in the *Baltimore Sun*: "Computer Ills Hinder NSA," February 26, 2006, A1; "NSA Killed System That Sifted Phone Data Legally," May 18, 2006, A1; "Hacker Attacks Hitting

Pentagon," July 2, 2006, A1; "Costly NSA Initiative Has Shaky Takeoff," February 11, 2007, A1.

86. Siobhan Gorman, "Little-Known Contractor Has Close Ties with Staff of NSA," *Baltimore Sun*, January 29, 2006, A13.

87. Gorman, "System Error."

88. Ibid.

89. Siobhan Gorman, "Chief of NSA Urges Action," *Baltimore Sun*, March 10, 2007, A1.

90. Gorman, "System Error." See Bamford, *Shadow Factory*, 45–47, 329–31 (discussing Trailblazer and Thin Thread); Jane Mayer, "The Secret Sharer: Is Thomas Drake an Enemy of the State?," *New Yorker*, May 23, 2011, 46.

91. Gorman, "System Error," 1.

92. Ibid.

93. Ibid.

94. Ibid. See Office of the Inspector General of the Department of Defense, *Requirements for the Trailblazer and Thinthread Systems* (2004), available at web.archive.org/web/20140125122704/http://www.fas.org/irp/agency/dod/ig-thinthbread.pdf.

95. Gorman, "System Error," 1.

96. Ellen Nakashima, "Judge Slams Prosecutors' Handling of Leak Suspect," *WPost*, July 30, 2011, A2.

97. See Indictment, United States v. Thomas Andrews Drake, 10-CR-181. See also the sentencing transcript cited in infra n101.

98. Indictment of Thomas Andrew Drake, 3.

99. Defendant's Motion to Dismiss Counts 1-5 of the Indictment, February, 25, 2011, in *United States v. Thomas Andrews Drake*, 10-CR-181, 4.

100. Drake pled guilty to exceeding authorized use of a government computer in violation of 18 U.S.C. 1030.

101. See Sentencing Proceeding Transcript, *United States v. Thomas A. Drake*, 10-CR-181 (D. Md. 2011).

102. Ibid., 15.

103. Ibid., 44–46. See also Judgment at 4, *United States v. Thomas A. Drake*, 10-CR-181 (D. Md. 2011).

104. See NSA Inspector General, top-secret "working draft of the review of the President's Surveillance Program," March 24, 2009, 3, 4, 6–7, 21, 22, 38, available at web.archive.org/web/20140314135250/https://www.aclu.org/files/natsec/nsa/20130816/NSA%201G%20Report.pdf.

105. Barack Obama, "Remarks by President Obama and President Xi Jinping of the People's Republic of China After Bilateral Meeting," June 8, 2013, web.archive.org/web/20131019191020/http://www.whitehouse.gov/the-press-office/2013/09/06/remarks-president-obama-and-president-xi-peoples-republic-china-bilatera.

106. See NSA Inspector General, top secret working draft, 28.

107. Barton Gellman and Laura Poitras, "U.S. Mines Internet Firms' Data, Documents Show," *WPost*, June 7, 2013, A1.

108. Ibid.

109. See Robert Chesney, "The President's Surveillance Reform Initiatives: A Section-by-Section Analysis," *Lawfare* (blog), August 9, 2013, web.archive.org /web/20130816022951/http://www.lawfareblog.com/2013/08/the-presidents-surveillance-reform-initiatives-a-section-by-section-analysis.

110. For a similar thought, see Privacy and Civil Liberties Oversight Board, Workshop Regarding Surveillance Programs Operated Pursuant to Section 215 of the USA PATRIOT Act and Section 702 of the Foreign Intelligence Surveillance Act, July 9, 2013, 33–37 (statement of former judge James Robertson).

111. See, e.g., White House, "Remarks by the President (Obama) in a Press Conference," August 9, 2013, available at web.archive.org/web/20140509103645/http:// www.whitehouse.gov/the-press-office/2013/08/09/remarks-president-press-conference.

112. Jack Goldsmith, *Power and Constraint: The Accountable Presidency After 9/11* (W.W. Norton, 2012), 56–57.

113. Jack Goldsmith, "Just Ignore Him," op-ed, *WPost*, February 11, 2011, A19.

114. Barton Gellman, "Secrecy, Security and Self-Government: How I Learned Secrets and Why I Print Them," unpublished lecture, Woodrow Wilson School, Princeton University, October 9, 2003, 1 (on file with author).

115. Baquet and Keller, "When Do We Publish a Secret?" See also Walter Pincus, "Secrets and the Press: An Essay About Ted Gup's Book 'Nation of Secrets: The Threat to Democracy and the American Way of Life,'" *Nieman Reports* 62, no. 1 (2008): 83–85.

116. John Hyde, "When a Few Dollars Made a Big Difference: The Fund for Investigative Journalism Enabled Seymour Hersh to Report on the My Lai Massacre," Nieman Reports 62, no. 1 (2008): 38.

117. Alex S. Jones, *Losing the News: The Future of the News That Feeds Democracy* (Oxford University Press, 2009), 7.

118. Information provided to author by Marcel Rosenbach of *Der Spiegel* in discussion of his paper "WikiLeaks: Lessons Learned," delivered at a May 2012 Conference at the Heidelberg Center for American Studies, Germany. Rosenbach added that before publishing, *Der Spiegel* reacted to two rounds of "wishes" from the State Department.

119. Jones, *Losing the News*, 7 130.

120. See, e.g., Robert W. McChesney and John Nichols, *The Death and Life of American Journalism: The Media Revolution That Will Begin the World Again* (Nation Books, 2010).

121. Charles Lewis, "Seeking New Ways to Nurture the Capacity to Report," *Nieman Reports* 62, no. 1 (2008): 24.

122. See John Sullivan, "True Enough: The Second Age of P.R.," *Columbia Journalism Review*, May/June 2011, 34–39 ("the muscles of public relations are

bulking up" while those of journalism are weakening," as shown by in 1980 there being 0.45 PR workers per 100,000 population versus 0.36 journalists, but by 2008 the ratio was 0.90 versus 0.25).

123. Florence Graves, "Watchdog Reporting: Exploring Its Myth," *Nieman Reports* 62, no. 1 (2008): 33.

124. Stephen Harrigan, "The Man Who Never Stops," *Texas Monthly* 18, no. 4 (1990): 100.

125. See Glenn Greenwald, *No Place to Hide: Edward Snowden, the NSA and the U.S. Surveillance State* (Henry Holt, 2014), including references to Greenwald's relationship to The *Guardian*.

126. Peter Osnos, "In Praise of ProPublica," *The Atlantic*, May 22, 2012, web. archive.org/web/20140225083045/http://www.theatlantic.com/national/archive/2012 /05/in-praise-of-propublica/257514.

127. See, generally, Alasdair Roberts, "National Security and Open Government," *Georgetown Public Policy Review* 9 (2004): 75; *Emerging Threats: Overclassification and Pseudo-Classification: Hearing Before the Subcomm. on National Security, Emerging Threats, and International Relations of the H. Comm. on Government Reform*, 109th Cong. (2005).

128. For ACLU legal cases, see ACLU on national security letters, Doe v. Ashcroft, 334 F. Supp. 2d 471 (S.D.N.Y. 2004), *vacated sub nom.* Doe v. Gonzales, 449 F.3d 415 (2d Cir. 2006); on warrantless wiretapping, ACLU v. National Security Agency, 493 F.3d 644 (2007); on publicly available but still classified documents, ACLU v. Department of State, 878 F. Supp. 2d 215 (D.D.C. 2012); on drone strike data, ACLU v. CIA, 710 F.3d 422 (D.D.C. 2013); and on bulk collection of phone logs, ACLU v. Clapper, F. Supp. 2d 724 (S.D.N.Y. 2013). See also Scott Shane, "A.C.L.U. Lawyers Mine Documents for Truth About Detainees and Interrogations," *NYT*, August 30, 2009, A4.

129. National Security Archive: *Annual Report for 2012* (2013), available at web. archive.org/web/20140113000806www2.gwu.edu/~nsarchiv/nsa/2012_Annual_ Report.pdf.

130. See *Death Squads, Guerrilla War, Covert Operations, and Genocide: Guatemala and the United States, 1954–1999* in the National Security Archive's database partnership with ProQuest, Digital National Security Archive.

131. Peter Carlson, "Eyes Only," *WPost*, May 8, 2008, C1. For the "family jewels" report, see the National Security Archive's digital copies of originals, available at web.archive.org/web/20140413001438/http://www.gwu.edu/~nsarchiv/NSAEBB /NSAEBB222/family_jewels_full_ocr.pdf.

132. See Andrew Rosenthal, "Bush-Era Torture: A Dissenting View," *Taking Note* (blog), *NYT*, April 9, 2012, (referring to Philip Zelikow) web.archive.org/web /20130403123608/http://www.takingnote.blogs.nytimes.com/2012/04/09/bush era-torture-a-dissenting-view/.

133. Interview by author.

9: Congress I: Investigations and Oversight

1. James Baker, interview by Peter Jennings, *America Under Attack*, 3 *p.m.*, ABC News, September 11, 2001.

2. "Unspooking Spooks," *WSJ*, editorial, September 18, 2001, A22.

3. *Church Comm. Bk. II*, v.

4. See, e.g., *Church Comm. Bk. II*, passim, and Preface, v–x; Introduction and Summary, 18; Conclusion and Recommendations, 289–342. See also *Bk. I* passim and e.g. 1, 123–36, 364–84, 437–38. James Baker would also have benefited from reading GOP senator Howard Baker's comment at the end of the Church Committee's work that, while the short term might be hard, "a responsible inquiry, as this has been, will in the long run result in a *stronger and more efficient intelligence community*" (*Bk. II*, separate views of Howard H. Baker, 373) (emphasis added).

5. John Stuart Mill, *Considerations on Representative Government* (Prometheus Books, 1991), 115–16.

6. Woodrow Wilson, *Congressional Government: A Study in American Politics* (Houghton Mifflin, 1885), 303.

7. McGrain v. Daugherty, 273 U.S. 135, 174–75 (1927).

8. Watkins v. United States, 354 U.S. 178 195 (1957). Clearly bothered by the House Committee's inquiries into personal political beliefs, the Court reversed a conviction for contempt of Congress because the witness had refused to answer whether union associates had been Communist Party members.

9. *Watkins*, 354 U.S. at 217 (Frankfurter, J., concurring). A more substantive Bill of Rights limit on congressional investigations is the Fifth Amendment ban on coercing incriminating testimony. Before becoming Justices, Felix Frankfurter and Hugo Black stressed the importance of congressional investigations. See Felix Frankfurter, "Hands Off the Investigations," *New Republic* 38, no. 25 (1924), 329; Hugo L. Black, "Inside a Senate Investigation," *Harper's Monthly*, February 1936, 275.

10. For an early book critical of McCarthy, see Richard H. Rovere, *Senator Joe McCarthy* (Harcourt, Brace, Jovanovich, 1959) ["in many ways the most gifted demagogue ever bred on these shores," 3]. Eisenhower's most notorious cave to McCarthy was removing praise for George Marshall from a presidential campaign speech in Wisconsin in October, 1952. See, e.g., Jean Edward Smith, *Eisenhower in War and Peace* (Random House, 2012), 543–44.

11. See S. Res. 301, 83rd Cong., 2nd sess., Cong. Rec. (December 2, 1954): S 16392-16393. See also Senate Select Committee to Study Censure Charges, *Report Pursuant to the Order on S. Res 301 and Amendments: A Resolution to Censure the Senator from Wisconsin, Mr. McCarthy*, S. Rep No. 83-2508 (November 8, 1954). The committee chair was Republican Senator Arthur Watkins; McCarthy was censured for "obstructing" the Watkins Committee, rather than misbehavior in the Army hearings.

12. See Paul C. Light, *Government by Investigation: Congress, Presidents, and the*

Search for Answers, 1945–2012 (Brookings Institution Press, 2013) (analyzing one hundred investigations since 1945). Light concludes that while "[i]t is impossible to single out one investigation . . . as the best of the best . . . I often return to the Church Committee's 1975 investigation of intelligence agency abuses as a model of the high-impact investigation." Ibid., 193. See also Roger A. Bruns, Daniel L. Hostetter, and Raymond W. Smock, eds., *Congress Investigates: A Critical and Documentary History*, rev. ed., 2 vols. (Facts on File, 2011) (surveying twenty-nine investigations from 1792 to 2006); Frank J. Smist, *Congress Oversees the United States Intelligence Community*, 2nd ed. (University of Tennessee Press, 1994); Stuart Farson and Mark Phythian, eds., *Commissions of Inquiry and National Security: Comparative Approaches* (Praeger, 2010).

13. Walter Lippmann, *Public Opinion* (Harcourt, Brace, 1922), 289.

14. Edward R. Murrow, *In Search of Light: The Broadcasts of Edward R. Murrow, 1938–1961*, ed. Edward Bliss Jr. (Knopf, 1967), 247–48.

15. See generally Smist, *Congress Oversees*; L. Britt Snider, *The Agency and the Hill: CIA's Relationship with Congress, 1946–2004* (Government Printing Office, 2008.)

16. Betty Medsger, *The Burglary: The Discovery of J. Edgar Hoover's Secret FBI* (Alfred A. Knopf, 2014); Jack Anderson, "6 Attempts to Kill Castro Laid to CIA," *WPost*, January 18, 1971, B7; "Castro Stalker Worked for the CIA," *WPost*, February 23, 1971, B11; Seymour M. Hersh, "Underground for the CIA in New York: An Ex-Agent Tells of Spying on Students," *NYT*, December 29, 1974, 1. (Other Hersh articles on CIA activities ran in the *Times* on December 22 through 31.)

17. See S. Res. 21, 121 Cong. Rec. 1431–33 (1975).

18. He had previously become America's first unelected vice president when Nixon chose him to replace Spiro Agnew, who had been forced from office by a bribery scandal.

19. Loch K. Johnson, *A Season of Inquiry: The Senate Intelligence Investigation* (University Press of Kentucky, 1985), 27–48.

20. See *Church Comm Bk. II*, viii.

21. Smist, *Congress Oversees*, 41 (describing Church Committee's "unity and bipartisanship" as key to its success). Among Smist's sources was Howard Liebengood, an aide to Republican senator Howard Baker: "The Senate Watergate Committee was brutally partisan . . . by way of contrast, on the Church Committee, Republicans and Democrats worked hand in hand on projects together." In *Congress Investigates*, David F. Rudgers refers to Senator Church keeping the Committee on "a predominantly bipartisan plane" with a "measured approach," in contrast to the House Committee, which was "wracked with partisan and ideological discord." Rudgers, "Church Committee," 933, 946.

22. S. Res. 21's initial deadline for completion was "no later than September 1, 1975." But the committee obtained extensions and did not finish until the end of May 1976.

23. Johnson, *Season of Inquiry*, 40; author's recollection.

24. *Covert Action: Hearings Before the S. Select Comm. to Study Governmental Operations with Respect to Intelligence Activities*, 94th Cong. 146 (1975); see "Covert Action in Chile, 1963–1973."

25. There were only two leaks. One referred to *Assassinations*' statement that Kennedy had "frequent contact" with a "close friend" who was also a "close friend" of Mafia boss Sam Giancana—who had been hired by the CIA to kill Fidel Castro. The leak revealed the friend was female and more than just a friend. The second involved a staff member who was overheard giving a journalist information about a senator, not on the committee. The staffer was fired.

26. Initially, the CIA requested the committee to delete thirty names. The committee responded by using pseudonyms for eighteen, coupled with their title. For litigation over one name, SEE WEBSITE.

27. See *Church Comm. Assassinations*; 121 Cong. Rec. 37555–698, 37705, 37782 (1975): Loch K. Johnson, *Strategic Intelligence* (Greenwood Publishing, 2007), 35–36; and see Author's Note, 237–38. See also 121 Cong. Rec. 37673–75 (1975) (Senator Church on releasing CIA names).

28. For the substance of SHAMROCK, see Chapter 6, 117–19; *Church Comm. Bk. II*, 104, 145–46, 169; *Church Comm. Bk. III*, 733, 765–76; L. Britt Snider, "Recollections from the Church Committee's Investigation of NSA: Unlucky SHAMROCK," *Studies in Intelligence* (Winter 1999/2000), available at web.archive.org /web/20131019220002/https://www.cia.gov/library/center-for-the-study-of-intelligence/csi-publications/csi-studies/studies/winter99-00/art4.html.

29. See Snider, "Unlucky SHAMROCK." Snider was the committee's staff member focusing on the NSA. His memo on Shamrock recommended the companies not be named. He recounts meeting with "Fritz," who disagreed for the reasons quoted in the text. So the names stayed in Snider's report to the committee, which, after discussion and a close vote, kept the names in. This was "the first time in the history of executive-legislative relations that a committee of the Congress, with the putative support of its parent body, asserted the right to release a report a president contended was classified." Snider, *The Agency and the Hill*, 276. When written, Snider was the CIA's inspector general. For Snider's comments on how NSA reacted to the Church Committee disclosures, SEE WEBSITE.

30. See *Church Comm. Bk. I* [Note IV], and Additional Views of senators Walter F. Mondale, Gary Hart, and Philip Hart, 567–69. For three explanations for the last-minute reduction in Ford administration cooperation on foreign issues, SEE WEBSITE.

31. For more details on the authorization questions, see *Church Comm. Assassinations*, 108–180 (Castro), and 51–70 (Lumumba). See also *Unchecked and Unbalanced*, 37–43.

32. But see *Church Comm. Assassinations*, 304 (Additional Views of Howard Baker).

33. For the Church Committee's public hearings, see *Unauthorized Storage of Toxic*

Agents, vol. 1 (September 16, 17, and 18, 1975); *Huston Plan*, vol. 2 (September 23, 24, and 25, 1975); *Internal Revenue Service*, vol. 3 (October 2, 1975); *Mail Opening*, vol. 4 (October 21, 22, and 24, 1975); *The National Security Agency and Fourth Amendment Rights*, vol. 5 (October 29 and November 6, 1975); *Federal Bureau of Investigation*, vol. 6 (November 18 and 19 and December 2, 3, 9, 10, and 11, 1975); *Covert Action*, vol. 7 (December 4 and 5, 1975) of *Hearings Before the S. Select Comm. to Study Governmental Operations with Respect to Intelligence Activities*, 94th Cong. 45 (1975).

34. Johnson, *Season of Inquiry*, 57 (quoting Sen. Barry Goldwater).

35. See *Church Comm. Assassinations*, 6–7, 148–61, 260–67.

36. See *Church Comm. Bk. I*, 11.

37. See *Church Comm. Bk. II*, 137.

38. Ibid., 139, 265.

39. *Church Comm. Bk. II*, 333–35; *Church Comm. Bk. I*, 457–61. See Inspector General Act of 1978, Pub. L. No. 95-452, 92 Stat. 1101 (1978) (codified as amended at 5 U.S.C. App. 3).

40. See *Church Comm. Bk. II*, 289–343.

41. See *Church Comm. Bk. II*, 296–332 (recommendations); *FBI Statutory Charter, Hearings Before the S. Comm. on the Judiciary*, 95th Congress 18–26 (1978) (reproducing Levi Guidelines); Emily Berman, *Domestic Intelligence: New Powers, New Risks* (Brennan Center for Justice, 2011), 7–20 (analyzing subsequent changes to the guidelines).

42. *Church Comm. Bk. II*, viii.

43. Although this was part of the Epilogue to the committee's first report, the importance of the people "hear[ing] the story and learn[ing] from it" underlay all the Committee's work. *Church Comm. Assassinations*, 285.

44. See generally Bruce Tap, *Over Lincoln's Shoulder: The Committee on the Conduct of the War* (University Press of Kansas, 1998). Some of the investigations harmed the war effort. "[C]ommittee members, largely ignorant of military science, attempted constantly to direct and influence military decisions. The result of their interference spawned distrust and jealousies among the top Union military commanders, helped undermine bipartisan support for the war, increased popular misconceptions about the nature of warfare, and contributed to the politicization of military appointments." Ibid., 8.

45. See David McCullough, *Truman* (Simon & Schuster, 1992), 258.

46. See West Coast Hotel v. Parris, 300 U.S. 379 (1937). By upholding the minimum-wage law, the decision took the steam out of FDR's troubled "court-packing" plan to counter earlier Supreme Court anti–New Deal decisions by adding additional Justices to the Court.

47. See *Attack upon Pearl Harbor: Report of the Commission Appointed by the President of the United States to Investigate and Report the Facts Relating to the Attack Made by Japanese Armed Forces upon Pearl Harbor in the Territory of Hawaii on*

December 7, 1941 (1942), S. Doc. No. 77-159. The Senate Watergate Committee was, on the other hand, an example of a successful investigation of current events.

48. See John D. Macoll, "The Clapp Committee on Campaign Finance Corruption, 1912–13," in Bruns, Hostetter, and Smock, *Congress Investigates*, vol. 1, 395.

49. "Government Contracts, The Frauds of the Contractors, Full and Authentic Digest of the Report of the Van Wyck Investigating Committee," *NYT*, February 6, 1862, 2. See David Herbert Donald, *Lincoln* (Simon & Schuster, 1995), 325–26; Doris Kearns Goodwin, *Team of Rivals: The Political Genius of Abraham Lincoln* (Simon & Schuster, 2005), 413.

50. Wesley McCune and John R. Beal, "The Job That Made Truman President," *Harper's Magazine*, June 1945, 621; McCullough, *Truman*, 271.

51. See Commission on Wartime Contracting in Iraq and Afghanistan, *Transforming Wartime Contracting: Controlling Costs, Reducing Risks. Final Report to Congress* (2011).

52. See Financial Crisis Inquiry Commission, *The Financial Crisis Inquiry Report: Final Report of the National Commission on the Causes of the Financial and Economic Crisis in the United States* (Government Printing Office, 2011). For an example of criticism of the Commission and its report, see Joe Nocera, "Inquiry Is Missing the Bottom Line," *NYT*, January 29, 2011, B1.

53. See Smist, *Congress Oversees*, 135, 140 (chap. 4, "The Nedzi and Pike House Committees, 1975–76"). Nedzi was replaced by Congressman Otis Pike, who knew something about intelligence from work on the Armed Services Committee, but who had not been among the few who "oversaw" the intelligence agencies. In 1967, Pike had revealed hidden waste by the Defense Department, such as paying $32.13 for switches priced by the manufacturer at $1.30. See *Review of Defense Procurement Policies, Procedures, and Practices, Part II—Small Purchases: Hearings Before the Subcomm. for Special Investigations of the H. Comm. on Armed Services*, 90th Cong. 127 (1967).

54. See Richard W. Stevenson, "President Names Kissinger to Lead 9/11 Commission," *NYT*, November 28, 2002, A1; Dan Eggen, "Kissinger Quits Post As Head of 9/11 Panel; Withdrawal a Setback for White House," *WPost*, December 14, 2002, A1; Scot J. Paltrow, "Full Disclosure: White House Hurdles Delay 9/11 Commission Investigation," *WSJ*, July 8, 2003, A1; "Step Down, Mr. Kissinger," editorial, *Los Angeles Times*, December 13, 2002, 18.

55. Senators William S. Cohen and George J. Mitchell, *Men of Zeal: A Candid Inside Story of the Iran-Contra Hearings* (Penguin, 1989), 148–50. For examples of North's counterattacks and appeals to patriotism, see *Iran-Contra Investigation: Joint Hearings Before the S. Select Comm. on Secret Military Assistance to Iran and the Nicaraguan Opposition and the H. Select Comm. to Investigate Covert Arms Transactions with Iran*, 100th Cong. 9: (July 7–10, 1987): for full citations, SEE WEBSITE.

56. Cohen and Mitchell, *Men of Zeal*, 164.

57. Walter Pincus, "North Says He and His Superiors Lied About Contra Aid," *WPost*, July 9, 1987, A1.

58. "That Smile, That Scowl—That Face," *WPost*, July 9, 1987, C1.

59. "The Witness, Headlong and Heart on the Sleeve," *WPost*, July 9, 1987, C1.

60. Cohen and Mitchell, *Men of Zeal*, 154.

61. See *WPost*, July 9, 1987, which covered North's second-day testimony in great detail. For further discussion of the *Post*'s July 9 issue, see Cohen and Mitchell, *Men of Zeal*, 157.

62. Cohen and Mitchell, *Men of Zeal*, 165, 154.

63. Ibid., 24, 53, 74–75.

64. Ibid., 75, 164 (commenting on Nields's appearance).

65. See generally Ferdinand Pecora, *Wall Street Under Oath: The Story of Our Modern Money Changers* (Simon & Schuster, 1939); Michael Perino, *The Hellhound of Wall Street: How Ferdinand Pecora's Investigation of the Great Crash Forever Changed American Finance* (Penguin, 2010); Joel Seligman, *The Transformation of Wall Street: A History of the Securities and Exchange Commission and Modern Corporate Finance*, 3rd ed. (Aspen, 2003); Ron Chernow, "Where Is Our Ferdinand Pecora?," op-ed, *NYT*, January 6, 2009, A25: "Damnation of Mitchell," *Time*, March 6, 1933, 47.

66. Black, "Inside a Senate Investigation," 278, 280.

67. Ibid., 278 ("preceded"); author's experience. See McCullough, *Truman*, 260 ("no substitute"); McCune and Beal, "Job That Made Truman President," 618, 621.

68. See *Attack upon Pearl Harbor*, 20.

69. See *Pearl Harbor Attack: Hearings Before the Joint Comm. on the Investigation of the Pearl Harbor Attack*, pt. 39, 79th Cong. 23–178 (1946) (the Army investigation), 297–329 (the Navy investigation).

70. Harry S. Truman, news conference, August 30, 1945, in *Public Papers of the Presidents of the United States: Harry S. Truman, April 12–December 31, 1945* (Government Printing Office, 1961), 250.

71. Wayne Thompson, "The Pearl Harbor Committee, 1945–46," in Bruns, Hostetter, and Smock, *Congress Investigates*, vol. 2, 675–89.

72. Thompson, "Pearl Harbor Committee," 690.

73. Investigation of the Pearl Harbor Attack, S. Doc. No. 79-244 (1946), 154.

74. See, e.g., Smist, *Congress Oversees*, 175–77, 188–90, 211–13; Snider, *The Agency and the Hill*, 37–39.

75. Smist, *Congress Oversees*, 170–71.

76. Abraham Lincoln, "In Response to a Serenade," November 10, 1864, in *Collected Works of Abraham Lincoln*, vol. 8, 99–102. See Scott Shane, "To Investigate or Not: Four Ways to Look Back at Bush," *NYT*, February 22, 2009, WK3.

77. See Barack Obama, "Statement on the Release of Department of Justice Office of Legal Counsel memos Concerning Interrogation Techniques," April 16, 2009, in Daily Comp. Pres. Docs. 2009 DCPD No. 00263 (statement on the release of OLC memos). See also "The Missing Memos," ProPublica, April 16, 2009, web.

archive.org/web/20140525160353/http://www.propublica.org/special/missing-memos (listing released and still-secret memos); *Unchecked and Unbalanced*, 77–96.

78. Barack Obama, "The President's News Conference," February 9, 2009, in Daily Comp. Pres. Docs. 2009 DCPD No. 00073, 13.

79. Leahy quoted in Ariane de Vogue, "Leahy Seeks Bush Admin. 'Truth Commission,'" ABC News, February 9, 2009, web.archive.org/web/20090214233401 /http://abcnews.go.com/TheLaw/LawPolitics/story?id=6840437. For my previous calls for an investigation, SEE WEBSITE.

80. Paul Light's *Government by Investigation* has a useful distinction between oversight and investigations at 16–17. The best studies of congressional oversight of intelligence are: Snider, *The Agency and the Hill*, Smist, *Congress Oversees*; David M. Barrett, *The CIA and Congress: The Untold Story from Truman to Kennedy* (University Press of Kansas, 2005); and many pieces by the prodigious Professor Loch K. Johnson, including *Strategic Intelligence*; "Congressional Supervision of America's Secret Agencies: The Experience and Legacy of the Church Committee," *Public Administration Review* 64 (January 2004): 3–14; "Accountability and America's Secret Foreign Policy: Keeping a Legislative Eye on the Central Intelligence Agency, *Foreign Policy Analysis* 1 (March 2005): 99–120; "Ostriches, Cheerleaders, Skeptics, and Guardians: Role Selection by Congressional Intelligence Overseers," *SAIS Review of International Affairs* 18 (Spring 2008): 93–108; *Strategic Intelligence*, ed. Loch K. Johnson, vol. 4, *Intelligence and Accountability* (Praeger Security International, 2007).

81. Snider, *The Agency and the Hill*, 75. See also Smist, *Congress Oversees*, 82–85.

82. Snider, *The Agency and the Hill*, 310.

83. Hoekstra's letter, dated May 18, 2006, was first reported in Eric Lichtblau and Scott Shane, "Ally Told Bush Project Secrecy Might Be Illegal," *NYT*, July 9, 2006, A1. See also Ted Gup, *Nation of Secrets: The Threat to Democracy and the American Way of Life* (Doubleday, 2007), 53.

84. Barry Goldwater to Director of Central Intelligence William Casey, April 9, 1984, reproduced in "Text of Goldwater's Letter to the Head of C.I.A.," *NYT*, April 11, 1984, A9; "Goldwater Writes CIA Director Scorching Letter," *WPost*, April 11, 1984, A17; Snider, *The Agency and the Hill*, 291.

85. The statutory provision for Gang of Eight intelligence notifications is in 50 U.S.C. §§ 413–413b (2012). Gang of Four intelligence notifications have no basis in statute but "have constituted a practice generally accepted by the leadership of the intelligence committees" for highly sensitive non-covert action intelligence activities. Marshall Curtis Erwin, "Gang of Four Congressional Intelligence Notifications," *Congressional Research Service*, 2013.

86. Marshall Curtis Erwin, "Sensitive Covert Action Notifications: Oversight Options for Congress," *Congressional Research Service*, 2013. See Erwin, "Gang of Four Congressional Intelligence Notifications," (describing Gang of Four notification process).

87. See generally Denis McDonough, Mara Rudman, and Peter Rundlet, *No Mere*

Oversight: Congressional Oversight of Intelligence Is Broken (Center for American Progress, 2006).

88. As Nicholas Katzenbach predicted some forty years ago, such "consultation" with Congress may "easily result in recriminations about the nature and quality of the information provided." Nicholas deB. Katzenbach, "Foreign Policy, Public Opinion and Secrecy," *Foreign Affairs* (October 1973). 1, 15. It has.

89. Barack Obama, "The President's News Conference," August 9, 2013, in Daily Comp. Pres. Docs., 2013 DCPD No. 00562, 5.

90. Charlie Savage, "Senators Say Patriot Act Is Being Misinterpreted." *NYT*, May 27, 2011, 17. [Two senators claimed on Thursday that the Justice Department had secretly interpreted the so-called Patriot Act in a twisted way. "I want to deliver a warning this afternoon: When the American people find out how their government has secretly interpreted the Patriot Act, they will be stunned and they will be angry," Mr. Wyden said.] See Ryan Lizza, "State of Deception: Why Won't the President Rein in the Intelligence Community?," *New Yorker*, December 16, 2013, 48–61 (more on Wyden's efforts).

91. Matt Sledge and Michael McAuliff, "CIA Torture Report Approved by Senate Intelligence Committee," *Huffington Post*, October 13, 2012, web.archive.org/web/20140310180202/http://www.huffingtonpost.com/2012/12/13/cia-torture-report_n_2295083.html.

92. Mark Mazzetti, "C.I.A. Inquiry Is Set in Clash on Detentions," *NYT*, March 5, 2014, A1.

93. Senator Dianne Feinstein, speaking on *CIA Detention and Interrogation Report*, 160 Cong. Rec. S1487 (March 11, 2014); Mark Mazzetti and Jonathan Weisman, "Conflict Erupts in Public Rebuke on C.I.A. Inquiry," *NYT*, March 12, 2014, A1.

94. Greg Miller and Adam Goldman, "Public Blowup Had a Long, Slow Fuse," *WPost*, March 13, 2014, A1. Mark Mazzetti and Carl Hulse, "Inquiry by C.I.A. Affirms It Spied on Senate Panel," *NYT*, August 1, 2014, A1.

95. Greg Miller and Adam Goldman, "Senate Panel Votes to Release CIA Interrogation Report," *WPost*, April 4, 2014, A5; David S. Joachim, "Panel Votes to Reveal How C.I.A. Interrogated," *NYT*, April 4, 2014, A6.

96. Bradley Klapper, "Leaked Findings Paint Pattern of CIA Deception," Associated Press, April 11, 2014, Mark Mazzetti, "Redactions of Report on C.I.A. Stoke Ire," *NYT*, August 6, 2014, A14. The challenged redactions included some issues where the administration seems to be taking unreasonable positions and one where the committee could bend. Information that was obtained by intelligence-gathering methods other than the brutal interrogations was redacted even though this is necessary to make the committee's point that the interrogations were not fruitful. On the other hand, the committee would lose nothing by using pseudonyms for the agents who did the interrogations that are different from the pseudonyms previously given them by the CIA. web.archive.org/web/20140513222548/http://bigstory.ap.org

/article/leaked-findings-paint-pattern-cia-deception; Burgess Everett, "Senate Dems Antsy over W.H. Release of CIA Report," *Politico*, May 4, 2014, web.archive.org /web/20140513223503/http://www.politico.com/story/2014/05/senate-dems-antsy-over-wh-release-of-cia-report-106334.html.

97. Everett, "Senate Dems Antsy."

98. Dianne Feinstein to Barack Obama, April 7, 2014, available at web.archive .org/web/20140527130906/http://www.fas.org/irp/news/2014/04/feinstein-040714 .pdf.

99. S. Res. 400 §8, 94th Cong. (1976).

100. *See 9/11 Comm'n Report*, 421. The commission recommended "Members should serve indefinitely on the intelligence committees, without set terms, thereby letting them accumulate expertise." Ibid. 598.

10: Congress II: The Freedom of Information Act

1. Department of Defense Directive: Clearance of Department of Defense Public Information, March 29, 1955, reproduced at 101 Cong. Rec. 12958 (1955). See Herbert N. Foerstel, *Freedom of Information and the Right to Know* (Greenwood Press, 1999), 21; Michael R. Lemov, *People's Warrior: John Moss and the Fight for Freedom of Information and Consumer Rights* (Fairleigh Dickinson University Press, 2011), 50.

2. Clarifying and Protecting the Right of the Public to Information and for Other Purposes, S. Rep. No. 88-1219 (1964), 4, 8, 10. The act was used "more as an excuse for withholding than as a disclosure statute." FOIA was designed to eliminate "such phrases," to "establish a general philosophy of full agency disclosure" unless clearly "excepted," and to provide a court remedy for wrongful withholding. Ibid.

3. See David E. Pozen, "Deep Secrecy," *Stanford Law Review* 62, no. 2 (2010): 257, 314. The article describes FOIA (and FISA) as "the closest thing we have to a constitutional amendment on state secrecy," where the "proponents made their case in explicit constitutional terms."

4. See Lemov, *People's Warrior*, 41–72. For coordination between the House and the Senate, SEE WEBSITE.

5. Harrison Wellford, "Rights of People: The Freedom of Information Act," in *None of Your Business: Government Secrecy in America*, ed. Norman Dorsen and Stephen Gillers (Viking Press, 1974), 209 (quoting a government lawyer).

6. *Freedom of Information: Executive Privilege: Secrecy in Government: Hearings Before the Subcomm. on Administrative Practice and Procedure and Separation of Powers of the S. Comm. on the Judiciary and the Subcomm. on Intergovernmental Relations of the S. Comm. on Government Operations*, vol. 2, 93rd Cong. 105 (1973) (testimony of Harrison Wellford, Center for Study of Responsive Law).

7. *Availability of Information from Federal Departments and Agencies: Hearings Before the Special Subcomm. on Government Information of the H. Comm. on Government* Operations, pt. 9, sec. 4, 85th Cong. 2286 (1957) (questioning of Robert Dechert,

Department of Defense General Counsel by John Moss). See Bruce Ladd, *Crisis in Credibility* (New American Library, 1968), 192. The Special Subcommittee on Government Information is hereinafter referred to as the "Moss Committee," for its chairman, John E. Moss.

8. See Lemov, *People's Warrior*, 49–50. Moss had met with Harold Cross, author of *The People's Right to Know: Legal Access to Public Records and Proceedings* (Columbia University Press 1953).

9. See Lemov, *People's Warrior*, 50–51; Ladd, *Crisis in Credibility*, 190.

10. Lemov, *People's Warrior*, 50–54, 56–58, 60, 63; Ladd, *Crisis in Credibility*, 190–203. For selected news items on the committee, see "Behind the Paper Curtain," editorial, *Los Angeles Times*, September 16, 1963, A4; Richard L. Lyons, "Moss Renamed to Head House Anti-Secrecy Unit," *WPost* February 1, 1959, A2; Tom Nelson, "Moss Raps Ike's Stand on Secrets," *WPost*, November 15, 1958, A13; "A Crack in the Wall of Government Secrecy," editorial, *Hartford Courant*, January 19, 1957, 8; "The Paper Curtain," editorial, *WPost*, August 5, 1956, E4. For congressional reports, see Moss Committee, *Replies from Federal Agencies to Questionnaire*, 84th Cong. (1955); *Availability of Information from Federal Departments and Agencies; Hearings Before the [Moss Committee]*, 17 parts, 86th Cong. (1957–59); Moss Committee, *Federal Statutes on the Availability of Information* (committee print), 86th Cong. (1960); Clarifying and Protecting the Right of the Public to Information, H.R. Rep. No. 89-1497 (1966). For an extended list, including hearings, see "Library Pages," John E. Moss Foundation Library, web.archive.org/web/20131011024134/http://johne mossfoundation.org/library0.htm.

11. Availability of Information from Federal Departments and Agencies: Twenty-Fifth Intermediate Report, H.R. Rep. No. 84-2947 (1956), 38.

12. Moss Committee, *Replies*, passim (asking agencies, at question 3, "What terms do you use to describe restrictions placed on imparting information?").

13. Availability of Information from Federal Departments and Agencies (Department of Defense), H.R. Rep. No. 85-1884 (1958), 72.

14. *Availability of Information from Federal Departments and Agencies* (Progress of Study September 1961–December 1962), H.R. Rep. No. 87-1257 (1961), 81; See also Lemov, *People's Warrior*, 56–60 (providing additional examples).

15. Lemov, *People's Warrior*, 55–56; Ladd, *Crisis in Credibility*, 208–9. For the negative testimony of Johnson administration officials, SEE WEBSITE.

16. *Clarifying and Protecting the Right of the Public to Information*, H.R. Rep. No. 89-149, 12.

17. 112 Cong. Rec. 13641–42 (1966).

18. Ibid., 13653. For Rumsfeld's post-9/11 comments about FOIA, SEE WEBSITE.

19. 112 Cong. Rec. 13641 (1966).

20. Ibid., 13654.

21. Administration of the Freedom of Information Act, H.R. Rep. No. 92-1419 (1972), 8–12. The subcommittee found "entrenched bureaucracy is stubbornly

resisting the efforts of the public to find and pry open the hidden doors which conceal the Government's business from its citizens." Ibid. 38. The report was issued after forty-one days of hearings. See also Wellford, "Rights of People," 195–214. For the Supreme Court, see text of n31 infra.

22. *Amending the Freedom of Information Act*, S. Rep. No. 93-854 (1974), 3.

23. 120 Cong. Rec. 17016 (1974) (remarks by Sen. Ted Kennedy).

24. For examples, SEE WEBSITE.

25. 120 Cong. Rec. 17016 (1974).

26. 119 Cong. Rec. 33133 (1973).

27. 120 Cong. Rec. 6815 (1974).

28. *Executive Privilege: Secrecy in Government: Freedom of Information: Hearings Before the Subcomm. on Administrative Practice and Procedures and Separation of Powers of the S. Comm. on the Judiciary and the Subcomm. on Intergovernmental Relations of the S. Comm. on Government* Operations, vol. 1, 93rd Cong. 175 (1973).

29. Ibid., 176, 218.

30. See 120 Cong. Rec. 17016–17 (1974) (remarks by Sen. Ted Kennedy on changes to FOIA).

31. Environmental Protection Agency v. Mink, 410 U.S. 73 (1973).

32. 120 Cong. Rec. 17019 (1974).

33. See *EPA v. Mink*, 410 U.S. at 80 (White), 94–95 (Stewart), 97 (Brennan and Marshall), 108–9 (Douglas).

34. *Amending the Freedom of Information Act*, 13–17. See also 120 Cong. Rec. 17021 (1974) (remarks by Sen. Roman Hruska summarizing the committee report).

35. 120 Cong. Rec. 17023 (1974).

36. Ibid., 17028.

37. Ibid., 16390-91 (1974) (proposed Amendment No. 1356 to FOIA).

38. *Conference Report, Freedom of Information Act Amendments*, H.R. Rep. No. 93-1380 (1974), 9.

39. Ibid., 12.

40. Message from the President of the United States Vetoing H.R. 1247, H.R. Doc. No. 93-383 (1974).

41. The House of Representatives voted 371 to 31 to override President Ford's veto on November 20, and the Senate followed the next day, 65 to 27.

42. *Freedom of Information Act and Amendments of 1974 Source Book*, 475. For other congressional statements about misuse of secrecy, SEE WEBSITE.

43. Electronic Freedom of Information Act Amendments of 1996, No. 104-231, 110 Stat. 3048 (1996) (codified as amended at 5 U.S.C. § 552 note). See Electronic Freedom of Information Amendments of 1996, H.R. Rep. No. 104-795 (1996); Electronic Freedom of Information Improvement Act of 1995, S. Rep. No. 104-272 (1996). See also David C. Vladeck, "Information Access—Surveying the Current Legal Landscape of Federal Right-to-Know Laws," *Texas Law Review* 86 (2008): 1787.

44. See Martin E. Halstuk, "Speed Bumps on the Information Superhighway: A

Study of Federal Agency Compliance with the Electronic Freedom of Information Act of 1996," *Communication Law and Policy* 5, no. 4 (2000): 423; David C. Vladeck, "Information Access." See also Openness Promotes Effectiveness in our National Government Act of 2007, 110 Pub. L. No. 175, 121 Stat. 2524 (2007) (codified at 5 U.S.C. § 552 note); Exec. Order No. 13526 (December 29, 2009), 75 Fed. Reg. 707 (allowing information to be classified or reclassified after being requested through FOIA).

45. Department of Justice, *Office of Information Policy: Summary of Annual FOIA Reports for Fiscal Year 2012* (2013).

46. See Seth F. Kreimer, "Rays of Sunlight in a Shadow 'War': FOIA, The Abuses of Anti-Terrorism and the Strategy of Transparency," *Lewis and Clark Law Review* 11 (2007): 1141–220; Nicholas Riccardi, "FBI Keeps Watch on Activists," *Los Angeles Times*, March 27, 2006, 1; Jameel Jaffer and Amrit Singh, *Administration of Torture: A Documentary Record from Washington to Abu Ghraib and Beyond* (Columbia University Press, 2007).

47. David T. Barstow, "The Freedom of Information Act and the Press: Obstruction or Transparency," *Social Research* 77, no. 3 (2010): 805 (article based on a presentation at "Limiting Knowledge in a Democracy," New School Social Research Conference, February 24, 2010). For more on Barstow's experience with FOIA, SEE WEBSITE.

48. Eric Umansky, "FOIA Eyes Only," *Slate*, December 31, 2004, web.archive.org/web/20120211093844/http://www.slate.com/articles/news_and_politics/hey_waitaminute/2004/12/foiaeyesonly.html (characterizing *WSJ* reporter Jess Bravin).

49. Barstow, "Freedom of Information Act and the Press," 807.

50. Openness Promotes Effectiveness in our National Government Act of 2007, 110 Pub. L. No. 175, 121 Stat. 2524 (codified as amended at 5 U.S.C. § 552 note).

51. Antonin Scalia, "The Freedom of Information Act Has No Clothes," *Regulation: AEI Journal on Government and Society*, (March–April 1982), 14–15.

52. Ibid. See also Martin Arnold, "Congress, the Press and Federal Agencies Are Taking Sides for Battle over Government's Right to Secrecy," *NYT*, November 15, 1974, 15.

53. Scalia, "The Freedom of Information Act Has No Clothes," 16. Scalia's comparison of relative use remains generally true. But there is substantial use of FOIA by public-interest groups, and it is likely that corporate use of FOIA adds to political support for the law.

54. See also Seth F. Kreimer, "Rays of Sunlight," 1169–85.

55. Seth Rosenfeld, *Subversives: The FBI's War on Student Radicals, and Reagan's Rise to Power* (Farrar, Straus and Giroux, 2012), ix, 4–5, 505–12. See Rosenfeld v. U.S. Department of Justice, 761 F. Supp. 1440 (N.D. Cal. 1991), *aff'd in part, rev'd in part*, 57 F.3d 803 (9th Cir., 1995).

56. Rosenfeld, *Subversives*, 505–12.

11: The Courts and Secrecy

1. Courts also approve settlements conditioned on a court order that the settlement be kept secret. A number of sealed settlements involve public safety. For concerns expressed about such settlements, SEE WEBSITE.

2. 418 U.S. 684 (1974).

3. For discussion of the tilt by academics, see, e.g., David E. Pozen, "The Mosaic Theory, National Security and the Freedom of Information Act," *Yale Law Journal* 115 (2005): 628, 634, 637–38 ["government almost always wins in FOIA national security litigations"]; Meredith Fuchs, "Judging Secrets: The Role Courts Should Play in Preventing Unnecessary Secrecy," *Administration Law Review* 58 (2006): 131, 132 ["Case after case demonstrates the growth of judicial deference to government secrecy claims"]; "Keeping Secrets: Congress, the Courts and National Security Information," *Harvard Law Review* 103 (1990): 609 [courts have "consistently deferred to executive branch [FOIA] classification decisions"]; Robert M. Chesney, "State Secrets and the Limits of National Security Litigation," *George Washington Law Review* 75 (2007): 1249, 1314 [state secrets privilege is "tilted sharply in favor of security"]; David Rudenstine, "The Irony of a Faustian Bargain: A Reconsideration of the Supreme Court's 1953 *United States v. Reynolds* Decision," *Cardozo Law Review* 34 (2013): 1283, 1391, 1389 [courts' legal doctrines "insulate the executive branch from any meaningful judicial review in cases implicating national security," including "a de facto absolute state secrets privilege"]; Seth F. Kreimer, "The Freedom of Information Act and the Ecology of Transparency," *Journal of Constitutional Law* 10, no. 5 (2008): 1011, 1054 [in "global war on terror" FOIA cases, courts have manifested "deference bordering on abject abdication"].

For judges' discussion of the tilt, see Patricia Wald (Chief Judge of the DC Circuit), "Two Unsolved Constitutional Problems," *University of Pittsburgh Law Review* 49 (1988): 753, 760 [*de novo* review specifically required by FOIA in national security cases often seems to be done in a "perfunctory way"]; Josh Gerstein, "Judge: Courts too deferential on classified information," *On the Courts* (blog), *Politico*, May 13, 2013, www.politico.com/blogs/under-the-radar/2013/05/judge-courts-too-defer ential-on-classified-information-163826.html (quoting Royce Lamberth, a judge in the District of Columbia, speaking to federal employees who process FOIA requests). Lamberth, a former judge of the Foreign Intelligence Surveillance Court, said "most judges give almost blind deference" to FOIA national security claims, adding that his views were informed by "horrible examples" of intelligence agency misconduct that would have been exposed and addressed if courts had a more "robust" interpretation of FOIA rights.

4. Environmental Protection Agency v. Mink, 410 U.S. 73, 95 (1973) (Stewart J., concurring).

5. For derivation of the term "Brandeis brief," SEE WEBSITE.

6. See Korematsu v. United States, 323 U.S. 214 (1944).

7. See Korematsu v. United States, 584 F. Supp. 1406 (N.D. Cal. 1984); Peter Irons, *Justice at War: The Story of the Japanese American Internment Cases* (Univ. of California Press, 1983), 286–91. See also Brief of Amicus Curiae Fred Korematsu in Support of Petitioners, January 14, 2014, filed in Rasul v. Bush, 2004 U.S. S. Ct. Briefs LEXIS 38.

8. See Hirabayashi v. United States, 828 F.2d 591 (9th Cir. 1987).

9. Acting Solicitor General Neal Katyal, "Confession of Error: The Solicitor General's Mistakes During the Japanese-American Internment Cases," *Justice Blog* (blog), U.S. Department of Justice, May 20, 2011, web.archive.org/web/20140207172918/http://blogs.justice.gov/main/archives/1346.

10. United States v. Reynolds, 345 U.S.1 (1953). See Rudenstine, "Irony of a Faustian Bargain"; see also Louis Fisher, "The State Secrets Privilege: Relying on *Reynolds*," *Political Science Quarterly* 122, no. 3 (2007): 385–408.

11. Reynolds v. United States, 192 F.2d 987, 990 (3d Cir. 1951). See Rudenstine, "Irony of a Faustian Bargain," 1317, 1345 (how government officials and lawyers evaded the truth).

12. See *Reynolds*, 192 F.2d 987 (3d Cir. 1951).

13. Ibid., at 995–97.

14. See *Reynolds*, 345 U.S. at 10.

15. Ibid. at 11.

16. Ibid., at 12.

17. John W. Persons, *Report of Special Investigation of Aircraft Accident Involving TB-29-100XX No. 45-21866*, United States Air Force (1950), reprinted in Petition for a Writ of Error *Coram Nobis* to Remedy Fraud upon This Court, *In re* Herring, 539 U.S. 940 (2003) (denying writ), available at web.archive.org/web/20130821043906/http://www.fas.org/sgp/jud/reynoldspet.pdf. See generally Rudenstine, "Irony of a Faustian Bargain" Chesney, "State Secrets"; and Louis Fisher, *In The Name of National Security: Unchecked Presidential Power and the Reynolds Case* (University Press of Kansas, 2006); Barry Siegel, *Claim of Privilege: A Mysterious Plane Crash, a Landmark Supreme Court Case, and the Rise of State Secrets* (HarperCollins, 2008). For more on the report, SEE WEBSITE.

18. Siegel, *Claim of Privilege*, 133, 297–98.

19. But see Barrington D. Parker's dissent in Arar v. Ashcroft, 585 F.3d 559, 614–15 (2d Cir. 2009).

20. New York Times v. United States, 403 U.S. 713 (1971).

21. Erwin N. Griswold, "Secrets Not Worth Keeping: The Courts and Classified Information," op ed, *WPost*, February 15, 1989, A25. In the Supreme Court, Griswold had expressed doubt about the breadth of the government's secrecy claims, but without using the categorical language of his retrospective view. And see Floyd Abrams, *Speaking Freely: Trials of the First Amendment* (Penguin Books, 2006), 51–52; Floyd Abrams, *Friend of the Court: On the Front Lines with the First Amend-*

ment (Yale University Press, 2013), 152–53 (additional examples of government admissions after the Supreme Court decision).

22. Clapper v. Amnesty International USA, 133 S. Ct. 1138 (2013).

23. Ibid. at 1141, 1148.

24. Ibid. at 1155–65.

25. *Clapper*, 133 S. Ct. 1138 Brief for Petitioners at 18, 53 (Westlaw; 2012 WL 3090949).

26. *Current and Projected National Security Threats to the United States: Hearing Before the S. Select Comm. on Intelligence*, 113th Cong. 66 (2013) (testimony of Director of National Intelligence James Clapper); James Clapper, interview by Andrea Mitchell, NBC News, June 9, 2013. See also James Bamford, "They Know Much More Than You Think," *New York Review of Books*, August 15, 2013, 4.

27. See Scott Shane, "NSA Violated Rules on Use of Phone Logs, Intelligence Court Found in 2009," *NYT*, September 11, 2013, A14; Judge John D. Bates, Foreign Intelligence Surveillance Court, Memorandum Opinion (October 3, 2011) ["The Court is troubled that the government's revelations regarding NSA's acquisition of Internet transactions mark the third instance in less than three years in which the government has disclosed a substantial misrepresentation regarding the scope of a major collection program."], available at web.archive.org/web/20131026003333/http://www.fas.org/irp/agency/doj/fisa/fisc100311.pdf; Judge Reggie B. Walton, Foreign Intelligence Surveillance Court, In Re Production of Tangible Things from [redacted] (March 5, 2009) ["The government has compounded its non-compliance with the Court's orders by repeatedly submitting inaccurate descriptions. . . ."], available at web.archive.org/web/20140523235210/https://www.fas.org/irp/agency/doj/fisa/fisc030209.pdf.

28. See *Unchecked and Unbalanced*, 187–92 (discussing obligations of government lawyers generally); Lincoln Caplan, *The Tenth Justice: The Solicitor General and the Rule of Law* (Random House, 1987) (exploring the special responsibilities of the Solicitor General).

29. *Reynolds*, 192 F.2d at [995], quoting Edward Livingston.

30. James Madison, *Federalist Papers No. 51*, 322 (emphasis added).

31. See also David E. Pozen, "Deep Secrecy," *Stanford Law Review* 62, no. 2 (2010): 257, 314.

32. Exec. Order No. 13526 (December 29, 2009), 75 Fed. Reg. 707 §§ 1.2 (1)(2). For citations for the executive orders on classification, SEE WEBSITE.

33. Also, since 1953, preambles to executive orders on classification have referred to the importance of "citizens of the United States be[ing] informed" (Exec. Order No. 10501), or "our democratic principles require that the American people be informed of the activities of their Government" (Exec. Order No. 13526). Courts do not reference these provisions.

34. In addition, the preamble of the Obama order adds: "Protecting information

critical to our Nation's security and demonstrating our commitment to open Government through accurate and accountable application of classification standards and routine, secure, and effective declassification are equally important priorities." (Exec. Order 13526, first para.)

35. United States v. Nixon, 418 U.S. 683 (1974).

36. For Nixon's response to the Church Committee, see "Appendix: Select Committee Interrogatories for Former President Richard M. Nixon," in *Bk. IV: Supplementary Detailed Staff Reports on Foreign and Military Intelligence*, S. Rep. No. 94-755 (1976) 157-58. Nixon's remarks to Frost are in "Excerpts from Interview with Nixon About Domestic Effects of Indochina War," *NYT*, May 20, 1977, A16.

37. *Nixon*, 418 U.S. at 705, citing Marbury v. Madison, 5 U.S. 137, 177 (1803).

38. Ibid.

39. Ibid.

40. Ibid. at 708. The Court also noted the president's need for "complete candor and objectivity," 706.

41. See also Eric Lane, Frederick A.O. Schwarz Jr., and Emily Berman, "Too Big a Canon in the President's Arsenal: Another Look at *United States v. Nixon*," *George Mason Law Review* 17 (2010): 737–88.

42. *Nixon*, 418 U.S. at 708. For differences between confidentiality for judicial and executive branch deliberations, SEE WEBSITE.

43. Ibid., at 706, 707.

44. See Chapter 10, 198–201, discussing the 1974 FOIA amendments. For Judge David Tatel's dissent from dismissal of a FOIA case that captures key points about judicial deference, SEE WEBSITE.

45. See, e.g., *Unchecked and Unbalanced*, 67–72.

46. See ibid., 97–123 (describing rendition and extraordinary rendition).

47. El-Masri v. United States, 479 F.3d 296 (4th Cir. 2007). On the questionable invocation of the state secrets doctrine, an ACLU human rights adviser wrote of the wide public discussion of CIA rendition—including El-Masri's—by U.S. officials, international human-rights groups, the media, etc. Declaration of Steven Macpherson Watt filed in El-Masri v. Tenet, 437 F. Supp. 2d 530 (E.D. Va. 2006).

48. See Comm. on Legal Affairs and Human Rights of the Council of Europe, "Alleged Secret Detentions and Unlawful Inter-State Transfers of Detainees Involving Council of Europe Member States," Doc. No. 10957 (June 2006), available at web.archive.org/web/20121002224434/http://assembly.coe.int/Documents/WorkingDocs/doc06/edoc10957.pdf; Comm. on Legal Affairs and Human Rights of the Council of Europe, "Secret Detentions and Illegal Transfers of Detainees Involving Council of Europe Member States: Second Report," Doc. No. 11302 rev. (June 2007), available at web.archive.org/web/20140407182350/http://assembly.coe.int/committeeDocs/2007/Emarty_20070608_noEmbargo.pdf referring to El-Masri's "degrading and inhumane treatment" in Afghanistan. Temporary Comm. of the Euro-

pean Parliament, "Interim Report on the Alleged Use of European Countries by the CIA for the Transportation and Illegal Detention of Prisoners," Doc. A6-0213/2006 (June 2006), 9, 11; "Report on the alleged use of European countries by the CIA for the Transportation and Illegal Detention of Prisoners," Doc. A6-0020/2007 (January 2007), 22. See also Judgment, El-Masri v. Former Yugoslav Republic of Macedonia, Application No. 39630/09 (December 13, 2012). An inquiry launched by the German parliament also concluded that "convincing evidence" supported El-Masri's account (Judgment 17-18).

49. Mohamed v. Jeppesen Dataplan, Inc., 614 F.3d 1070 (9th Cir. 2010) (en banc). See Mohamed v. Secretary of State for Foreign and Commonwealth Affairs, (2001) 1 QB 218 (decision of the United Kingdom Court of Appeal [Civil Division]).

50. Mohammed v. Obama, 689 F. Supp. 2d 38, 64 (D.D.C. 2009).

51. Mohamed v. Jeppesen Dataplan, 614 F.3d 1070, 1094 (9th Cir. 2010).

52. See Arar v. Ashcroft, 585 F.3d 559 (2d Cir., en banc, 2009) (7–4 ruling).

53. *Unchecked and Unbalanced*, 98–99, 104, 113, 116, 117.

54. Commission of Inquiry into the Actions of Canadian Officials in Relation to Maher Arar, *Report of the Events Relating to Maher Arar: Analysis and Recommendations*, (2006), 9, 13, 14, 20–25, 30, 32–36, 45.

55. Office of the Prime Minister, "Prime Minister Releases Letter of Apology to Maher Arar and His Family and Announces Completion of Mediation Process," news release, January 26, 2007, available at web.archive.org/web/20140329044113/http://pm.gc.ca/eng/news/2007/01/26/prime-minister-releases-letter-apology-maher-arar-and-his-family-and-announces.

56. *Arar*, 585 F. 3d at 610, 611 (Parker, dissenting).

57. See Judge Guido Calabresi's dissent in *Arar*, 585 F.3d at 630: "[W]hen the history of this distinguished court is written, today's majority decision will be viewed with dismay."

58. Stephen J. Schulhofer, "Oversight of National Security Secrecy in the United States," in *Secrecy, National Security and the Vindication of Constitutional Law*, ed. David Cole, Federico Fabbrini, and Arianna Vedaschi (Edward Elgar Publishing, 2013) 39.

59. See Washington Post v. Department of Defense, 766 F. Supp. 1, 3–4 (D.D.C. 1991). See also In Re Department of Defense, 848 F.2d 232, 239 (D.C. Cir. 1988) (upholding appointment of special master).

60. See Fuchs, "Judging Secrets," 131, 174.

61. See 18 U.S.C. §App. 3; Serrin Turner and Stephen J. Schulhofer, *The Secrecy Problem in Terrorism Trials* (Brennan Center for Justice, 2005), 17–25, discussing CIPA and contending there are many ways to manage secrecy in trying terrorism cases in federal courts.

62. See Stephen J. Schulhofer, "Checks and Balances in Wartime: American, British and Israeli Experiences," *Michigan Law Review* 102 (2004): 1923–31; Sudha Setty, "Judicial Formalism and the State Secrets Privilege," *William Mitchell Law Review*

38 (2012): 1629–54; "Litigating Secrets: Comparative Perspectives on the State Secrets Privilege," *Brooklyn Law Review* 75 (2009): 201–60.

63. Setty, "Judicial Formalism," 19–20, quoting opinion by Justice Ayala Procaccia.

64. Rosenfeld v. U.S. Department of Justice, 761 F. Supp. 1440 (N.D. Cal. 1991); *aff'd in part, rev'd in part*, 57 F.3d 803 (9th. Cir. 1995); Korematsu v United States, 584 F. Supp. 1406 (N.D. Cal. 1984).

65. Roger A. Burns, Daniel L. Hosteller, and Raymond W. Smock, eds., *Congress Investigates: A Critical and Documentary History*, rev. ed., vol. 2 (Facts on File, 2011), 678, 679.

66. Douglas Jehl, "Clinton Revamps Policy on Secrecy of U.S. Documents," *NYT*, April 18, 1995, A1.

67. Exec. Order No. 13526 (December 29, 2009), 75 Fed. Reg. 707 § 5.3.

68. See the annual reports of the (Information Security Oversight Office) (ISOO) reporting on results of mandatory declassification review. (E.g., National Archives and Records Administration, *Information Security Oversight Office 2012 Annual Report to the President 2013*).

69. Robert Barnes, "Where Transparency Is No Match for Tradition," *WPost*, October 28, 2013, 17: Adam Liptak, "Bucking a Trend, Supreme Court Justices Reject Video Coverage," *NYT*, February 19, 2013, 15.

70. For a comparison of TV coverage of Congress and the Court, SEE WEBSITE.

71. Linda Greenhouse, "2 Justices Indicate Supreme Court Is Unlikely to Televise Sessions," *NYT*, April 5, 2006, A16. In a 2007 hearing, Justice Kennedy testified he "hope[d] that the Senate would defer to us, as a separate branch of the government," on the issue of televised hearings, *Judicial Security and Independence: Hearing Before the S. Comm. on the Judiciary*, 110th Cong. 13 (2007).

72. See Adam Liptak, "Seeking Justice? Try the Courtroom, Not the Line Outside," *NYT*, April 16, 2013, A13.

73. United States v. Marchetti, 466 F.2d 1309, 1316 (4th Cir. 1972) (Judge Haynsworth, quoting Louis Henkin, "The Right to Know and the Duty to Withhold: The Case of the Pentagon Papers," *University of Pennsylvania Law Review* 120 [1971]: 273–74).

74. Similar justifications apply to jury deliberations, although a jury verdict does not explain jurors' reasoning. For thoughts about why publishing information about jury deliberations might undermine confidence in juries, see Kenji Yoshino, *A Thousand Times More Fair: What Shakespeare's Plays Teach Us About Justice* (HarperCollins, 2011), chap. 4.

75. See Michael I. Sovern, *An Improbable Life: My Sixty Years at Columbia and Other Adventures* (Columbia University, 2014), 136.

76. See Bob Woodward and Scott Armstrong, *The Brethren: Inside the Supreme Court* (Simon & Schuster, 1979). For contentions that *The Brethren* affected a Supreme Court decision, SEE WEBSITE.

77. Many Supreme Court Justices of the past hundred years left collections of papers in repositories; however, Justice Owen Roberts and Chief Justice Edward Douglas White destroyed their papers; 23 of 103 justices left no papers at all; 22 more left only small collections. Alexandra Wigdor, *The Personal Papers of Supreme Court Justices: A Descriptive Guide* (Garland, 1986), 31–34. See Dean Acheson, *Morning and Noon: A Memoir* (Houghton Mifflin, 1965), 82–83, describing commencement of saving Justice Brandeis's judicial papers.

78. *Final Report of the National Study Commission on Records and Documents of Federal Officials* (Government Printing Office, 1977), 3.

79. Herbert Brownell, "Who Really Owns the Papers of Departing Federal Officials?," *New York State Bar Journal* 50 (1978): 234.

80. Barack Obama, *The Audacity of Hope: Thoughts on Reclaiming the American Dream* (Three Rivers Press, 2006), 83.

81. Learned Hand, "The Spirit of Liberty," speech in New York City on May 21, 1944, reprinted in Learned Hand, *The Spirit of Liberty: Papers and Addresses of Learned Hand* (Alfred A. Knopf, 1952), 143–44.

82. James Bradley Thayer, *John Marshall* (Houghton Mifflin, 1901), 107.

83. There are a few exceptions: rights like individuals possessing guns and the ability to spend huge amounts on elections, including by corporations and labor unions.

Part IV: Conclusion

1. Abraham Lincoln, "First Inaugural Address," March 4, 1861, in *My Fellow Americans*, 52.

2. Walter Lippmann, *The Phantom Public* (Macmillan, 1924), 13–14.

3. Leslie H. Gelb, "Today's Lessons from the Pentagon Papers," *LIFE*, September 17, 1971, 34–36.

4. For civic literacy, see Michael X. Delli Caprini, *What Americans Know About Politics and Why It Matters* (Yale University Press, 1996); National Center for Education Statistics, *The Nation's Report Card: Civics 2010* (Department of Education, 2010); Eric Lane and Meg Barnette, *A Report Card on New York's Civic Literacy* (Brennan Center for Justice, 2011); Michelle J. Glennon, "National Security and Double Government," *Harvard National Security Journal* (2014): 5. For former Justices Souter and O'Connor on the importance of civic literacy, SEE WEBSITE.

5. See Eleanor Randolph, "Is U.S. Keeping Too Many Secrets?," op.-ed, *Los Angeles Times*, May 17, 1997, A1: "'The government's obsession with secrecy creates a citizens' obsession with conspiracy,'" quoting a First Amendment expert.

6. For Clapper's statement plus his apology, see Chapter 11, 210. See also James Bamford, "They Know Much More Than You Think," *New York Review of Books*, August 15, 2013, 4. For Alexander, see *National Defense Authorization Act for Fiscal Year 2013: Budget Request for Information Technology and Cyber Operations Programs: Hearing Before the Subcomm. on Emerging Threats and Capabilities of the H. Comm.*

on Armed Services, 112th Cong. 5–6, 51–71 (2012). For the FISA court, see Scott Shane, "NSA Violated Rules on Use of Phone Logs, Intelligence Court Found in 2009," *NYT*, September 11, 2013, A14; Judge John D. Bates, Foreign Intelligence Surveillance Court, Memorandum Opinion (October 3, 2011), available at web.archive .org/web/20131026003333/http://www.fas.org/irp/agency/doj/fisa/fisc100311.pdf; Judge Reggie B. Walton, Foreign Intelligence Surveillance Court, In Re Production of Tangible Things from [redacted] (March 5, 2009), available at web.archive.org /web/20140523235315/https://www.fas.org/irp/agency/doj/fisa/fisc-030209.pdf. For Clapper and Snowden, SEE WEBSITE.

7. 100 Cong. Rec. 2986–88 (1954).

8. For a review of "punctuated equilibrium," see Stephen Jay Gould and Niles Eldredge, "Punctuated Equilibrium Comes of Age," *Nature* 336, no. 6452 (1993): 223–27. For use in other fields, SEE WEBSITE.

9. Don Burke, the CIA's "Intellipedia Doyen," referred to punctuated equilibrium at a 2008 conference. Suzanne Spaulding, "No More Secrets: Then What?," *Huffington Post* (blog), June 24, 2010, web.archive.org/web/20110512001204 /http://www .huffingtonpost.com/-suzanne-e-spaulding/no-more-secrets-then-what_b_623997 .html. For more on Burke, SEE WEBSITE.

10. Ron Chernow, *Washington: A Life* (Penguin, 2010), 200. See generally Anthony Cave Brown, *Bodyguard of Lies* (Harper & Row, 1975) (the story of the "intricate deceptions that hid the secrets of D-Day from Hitler and sealed the Allied victory").

11. See Michael Moss, "Pentagon Study Links Fatalities to Body Armor," *NYT*, January 7, 2006, A1: "A secret Pentagon study has found that at least 80 percent of the marines who have been killed in Iraq from wounds to their upper body could have survived if they had extra body armor. That armor has been available since 2003 but until recently the Pentagon has largely declined to supply it to troops despite calls from the field for additional protection, according to military officials." See also Robert M. Gates, *Duty: Memoirs of a Secretary at War* (Alfred A. Knopf, 2014), 119, crediting an April 2007 Pentagon summary of a *USA Today* article for alerting him to lives that could be saved by speeding production of fortified armored vehicles.

12. See Bob Drogin, *Curveball: Spies, Lies, and the Con Man Who Caused a War* (Random House, 2007). Eight years after Colin Powell's UN presentation, which relied heavily on Curveball's allegations, the informant admitted he had lied. See James Risen, "Iraqi Says He Made Up Tale of Biological Weapons Before War," *NYT*, February 16, 2011, A7.

13. Colin Powell, "Remarks to the United Nations Security Council," February 5, 2003.

14. Dwight D. Eisenhower, "Farewell Address," January 17, 1961, in *My Fellow Americans*, 156.

15. As expressed by a veteran political reporter: "Something clearly happens to a newly elected president, regardless of party, the moment he receives his first full-

fledged national security briefing." Walter Shapiro, "Why Does Obama Talk Like Rand Paul but Govern Like Dick Cheney?," Yahoo! News, June 6, 2013, web.archive.org /web/20130606205555/http://news.yahoo.com-why-does-obama-talk-like-rand-paul-but-govern-like-dick-cheney–201343244.html.

16. For Moynihan and Goldwater, see Frank J. Smist Jr., *Congress Oversees the United States Intelligence Community, 1947–1989* (University of Tennessee Press, 1990), 98–99, 122–23.

17. Trent Lott and Ron Wyden, "Hiding the Truth in a Cloud of Black Ink," op-ed, *NYT*, August 26, 2004, A27; "Lott Seeks Oversight of Classified Data" *NYT*, July 11, 2004, A12.

18. 159 Cong. Rec H5028 (2013).

19. Dan Roberts and Spencer Ackerman, "Anger Swells After NSA Phone Records Court Order Revelations," *The Guardian*, June 6, 2013, web.archive.org /web/20140211120342/http://www.theguardian.com/world/2013/jun/06/obama-administration-nsa-verizon-records; Jim Sensenbrenner, "This Abuse of the Patriot Act Must End," *Comment Is Free* (blog), *The Guardian*, June 9, 2013, web.archive. org/web/21040315104659/http://www.guardian.com/commentisfree/2013/jun/09 /abuse-patriot-act-must-end; Jonathan Weisman, "Momentum Builds Against N.S.A. Surveillance," *NYT*, July 29, 2013, A1.

20. Patrick Leahy and Jim Sensenbrenner, "The Case for NSA Reform," *Politico*, op-ed, October 28, 2013.

21. Laurence H. Silberman, "Hoover's Institution," *WSJ*, July 20, 2005, A12.

22. Eric Lichtblau and Scott Shane, "Ally Told Bush Project Secrecy Might Be Illegal," *NYT*, July 9, 2006, A1.

23. New York Times v. United States, 403 U.S. 713, 729 (1971) (Potter Stewart, adding: "[t]he system becomes one to be disregarded by the cynical or the careless, and to be manipulated by those intent on self-protection or self-promotion. I should suppose, in short, that the hallmark of a truly effective internal security system would be the maximum possible disclosure.").

24. *Commission on Government Security: Hearings Before the Subcomm. on Reorganization of the S. Comm. on Government Operations*, 84th Cong. 467 (1955), (McGeorge Bundy testimony, quoting a Harvard physicist).

25. See Alane Kochems, *No More Secrets: National Security Strategies for a Transparent World*, post-workshop report (American Bar Association Standing Committee on Law and National Security, Office of the National Counterintelligence Executive, and National Strategy Forum, 2011), 9.

26. Ibid., 2, 4, 7, 9.

27. Ibid., 2.

28. *America the Vulnerable*, 244–45.

29. Ibid., 80.

30. Dave Turek, "The Case Against Digital Sprawl," *Management Blog* (blog), *Bloomberg Businessweek*, May 2, 2012, web.archive.org/web/20140122045235/http://

www.businessweek. com/articles/2012-05-02/the-case-against-digital-sprawl; Randy Rieland, "Big Data or Too Much Information," *Innovations* (blog), *Smithsonian*, May 7, 2012, web.archive.org/web/20140525212816/http://www.smithsonianmag.com /innovation/big-data-or-too-much-information-82491666/?no-ist. Google executive chairman and then-CEO Eric Schmidt said every two days we create the same amount of information as we did from the dawn of civilization through 2003. "Eric Schmidt at Techonomy," YouTube video, 38:19, from a panel at the Techonomy Conference in Lake Tahoe, California, on August 4, 2010, posted by Google, www.youtube.com /watch?v=UAcCIsrAq70.

31. *America the Vulnerable*, 199.

32. Ibid., 10–11, 83, 209.

33. Ibid., 83, 193, 208.

34. I was working as Assistant Commissioner for Law Revision in the Attorney General's Office of the Government of Northern Nigeria on a precursor of the Peace Corps funded by the Ford Foundation and organized by MIT .

35. Abraham Lincoln taught that "public sentiment is everything. With public sentiment, nothing can fail; without it nothing can succeed. Consequently he who moulds public sentiment goes deeper than he who enacts statutes or pronounces decisions." Abraham Lincoln, "First Debate with Stephen A. Douglas at Ottawa, Illinois," August 21, 1858, in *Collected Works of Abraham Lincoln*, vol. 3, 27.

Author's Note: Personal Encounters with Secrecy

1. "The United States and South Africa: American Investments Support and Profit from Human Degradation," *Christianity and Crisis*, November 28, 1966, 265–69.

2. *Church Comm. Assassinations*, Epilogue, 285.

3. S. Res. No. 94-21(1975).

4. See Walter F. Mondale, *The Good Fight: A Life in Liberal Politics* (Scribner, 2010), 140–41.

5. See *Church Comm. Assassinations, Bk. II* and *Bk. III*.

6. *Church Comm. Assassinations*, Epilogue, 285.

7. *Church Comm. Bk. I*, 458n42 (citing George Bush testimony, 4/8/76, p 41).

8. Ludtke v. Kuhn, 461 F. Supp. 86 (S.D.N.Y. 1979).

9. Doug Brew, "Life at Synanon Is Swinging," *Time*, December 26, 1977, 20.

10. Synanon Foundation, Inc. v. Time, Inc., 5 Med. L. Rptr. 1924 (Ca. Super. Ct., Alameda Cnty., 1979).

11. See, e.g., Frederick A.O. Schwarz Jr., "Lawyers for Government Have Unique Responsibilities and Opportunities to Influence Public Policy," *New York Law School Law Review* 53, no. 3 (2008): 375.

12. See Frederick A.O. Schwarz Jr. and Eric Lane, "The Policy and Politics of Charter Making: The Story of New York City's 1989 Charter," *New York Law School Law Review* 42 (1998): 723–1015.

13. Judith Miller, "He Gave Away $600 Million, and No One Knew," *NYT* January 23, 1997, A1.

14. Frederick A.O. Schwarz Jr., "Memorandum for Fellow Board Members: Thoughts on Changes in Atlantic's Confidentiality and Anonymity Policies," January 2001, 6 (on file with author).

15. *Unchecked and Unbalanced*: A brilliant and energetic young lawyer, Aziz was then co-head of the Brennan Center's project on liberty and national security and is now a professor at the University of Chicago Law School.

16. Frederick A.O. Schwarz Jr., "Abuses of Presidential Power: Where Do We Go from Here, Addressing the Culture of Secrecy," January 31, 2009, reprinted in Bernice K. Leber, "President's Message: A Gold Medal Career, an Agent for Change: Frederick A. O. Schwarz, Jr.," *New York State Bar Association Journal* 81, no. 3 (March–April 2009): 5–9.

Index

About the Author

Frederick A.O. ("Fritz") Schwarz Jr. is chief counsel at the Brennan Center for Justice at NYU School of Law. He was chief counsel for the U.S. Senate's Church Committee, the chief lawyer for New York City, and chair of its campaign finance board and charter revision commission. For many years, he was a litigation partner at Cravath, Swaine & Moore. He co-authored *Unchecked and Unbalanced: Presidential Power in a Time of Terror* (The New Press) with Aziz Z. Huq and lives in New York.

Publishing in the Public Interest

Thank you for reading this book published by The New Press. The New Press is a nonprofit, public interest publisher. New Press books and authors play a crucial role in sparking conversations about the key political and social issues of our day.

We hope you enjoyed this book and that you will stay in touch with The New Press. Here are a few ways to stay up to date with our books, events, and the issues we cover:

- Sign up at www.thenewpress.com/subscribe to receive updates on New Press authors and issues and to be notified about local events
- Like us on Facebook: www.facebook.com/newpressbooks
- Follow us on Twitter: www.twitter.com/thenewpress

Please consider buying New Press books for yourself; for friends and family; or to donate to schools, libraries, community centers, prison libraries, and other organizations involved with the issues our authors write about.

The New Press is a 501(c)(3) nonprofit organization. You can also support our work with a tax-deductible gift by visiting www.thenewpress.com/donate.